Critical Thinking

ISBN 0-13-064760-8

9 780130 647603

90000

FINANCIAL TIMES

Prentice Hall

In an increasingly competitive world, it is quality
of thinking that gives an edge—an idea that opens new
doors, a technique that solves a problem, or an insight
that simply helps make sense of it all.

We work with leading authors in the various arenas
of business and finance to bring cutting-edge thinking
and best learning practice to a global market.

It is our goal to create world-class print publications
and electronic products that give readers
knowledge and understanding which can then be
applied, whether studying or at work.

To find out more about our business
products, you can visit us at www.ft-ph.com

Pearson
Education

Critical Thinking

Tools for Taking Charge of Your Professional and Personal Life

Richard W. Paul • Linda Elder

FINANCIAL TIMES
Prentice Hall

An Imprint of Pearson Education

Upper Saddle River, NJ • New York • London • San Francisco • Toronto
Sydney • Tokyo • Singapore • Hong Kong • Cape Town
Madrid • Paris • Milan • Munich • Amsterdam

www.ft-ph.com

A CIP record for this book can be obtained from the Library of Congress

Production supervisor: *Wil Mara*
Cover design director: *Jerry Votta*
Cover design: *Nina Scuderi*
Manufacturing buyer: *Maura Zaldivar*
Executive editor: *Jim Boyd*
Editorial assistant: *Allyson Kloss*
Marketing manager: *Bryan Gambrel*
Composition: *Scott Suckling/MetroVoice*

 FINANCIAL TIMES
Prentice Hall

©2002 Pearson Education, Inc.
Publishing as Financial Times Prentice Hall
Upper Saddle River, New Jersey 07458

Financial Times Prentice Hall books are widely used by corporations and government
agencies for training, marketing, and resale.

For information regarding corporate and government bulk discounts please contact:
Corporate and Government Sales (800) 382-3419 or corpsales@pearsontechgroup.com

Company and product names mentioned herein are the trademarks or registered
trademarks of their respective owners.

Printed in the United States of America

19 18 17 16 15 14

ISBN 0-13-064760-8

Pearson Education LTD.
Pearson Education Australia PTY, Limited
Pearson Education Singapore, Pte. Ltd.
Pearson Education North Asia Ltd.
Pearson Education Canada, Ltd.
Pearson Educación de Mexico, S.A. de C.V.
Pearson Education—Japan
Pearson Education Malaysia, Pte. Ltd.

FINANCIAL TIMES PRENTICE HALL BOOKS

For more information, please go to www.ft-ph.com

Dr. Judith M. Bardwick
Seeking the Calm in the Storm: Managing Chaos in Your Business Life

Thomas L. Barton, William G. Shenkir, and Paul L. Walker
Making Enterprise Risk Management Pay Off:
How Leading Companies Implement Risk Management

Michael Basch
CustomerCulture: How FedEx and Other Great Companies Put the
Customer First Every Day

J. Stewart Black and Hal B. Gregersen
Leading Strategic Change: Breaking Through the Brain Barrier

Deirdre Breakenridge
Cyberbranding: Brand Building in the Digital Economy

William C. Byham, Audrey B. Smith, and Matthew J. Paese
Grow Your Own Leaders: How to Identify, Develop, and Retain
Leadership Talent

Jonathan Cagan and Craig M. Vogel
Creating Breakthrough Products: Innovation from Product Planning
to Program Approval

Subir Chowdhury
The Talent Era: Achieving a High Return on Talent

Sherry Cooper
Ride the Wave: Taking Control in a Turbulent Financial Age

James W. Cortada
21st Century Business: Managing and Working
in the New Digital Economy

James W. Cortada
Making the Information Society: Experience, Consequences,
and Possibilities

Aswath Damodaran
The Dark Side of Valuation: Valuing Old Tech, New Tech,
and New Economy Companies

Henry A. Davis and William W. Sihler
Financial Turnarounds: Preserving Enterprise Value

Sarv Devaraj and Rajiv Kohli
*The IT Payoff: Measuring the Business Value
of Information Technology Investments*

Nicholas D. Evans
*Business Agility: Strategies for Gaining Competitive Advantage
through Mobile Business Solutions*

Kenneth R. Ferris and Barbara S. Pécherot Petitt
Valuation: Avoiding the Winner's Curse

David Gladstone and Laura Gladstone
*Venture Capital Handbook: An Entrepreneur's Guide
to Raising Venture Capital, Revised and Updated*

David R. Henderson
The Joy of Freedom: An Economist's Odyssey

Philip Jenks and Stephen Eckett, Editors
*The Global-Investor Book of Investing Rules: Invaluable Advice
from 150 Master Investors*

Thomas Kern, Mary Cecelia Lacity, and Leslie P. Willcocks
*Netsourcing: Renting Business Applications and Services
Over a Network*

Al Lieberman, with Patricia Esgate
*The Entertainment Marketing Revolution: Bringing the Moguls, the
Media, and the Magic to the World*

Frederick C. Militello, Jr., and Michael D. Schwalberg
Leverage Competencies: What Financial Executives Need to Lead

D. Quinn Mills
*Buy, Lie, and Sell High: How Investors Lost Out on Enron and the
Internet Bubble*

Dale Neef
E-procurement: From Strategy to Implementation

John R. Nofsinger
*Investment Blunders (of the Rich and Famous)…And What You Can
Learn From Them*

John R. Nofsinger
*Investment Madness: How Psychology Affects Your Investing…
And What to Do About It*

To those willing to work not only toward improving their own lives, but also toward creating a new world, where justice and good sense are the norm rather than the exception, and where power serves reason rather than reason serving power.

CONTENTS

ACKNOWLEDGMENT

We wish to acknowledge our appreciation to Gerald Nosich—a model of good sense, depth of vision, and unfailing friendship. His active commitment to the ideal of critical thinking extends beyond 20 years. He stands as living proof that humans can combine in one life: reason, compassion, and justice.

Preface

Y ou are what you think. Whatever you are doing, whatever you feel, whatever you want—all are determined by the quality of your thinking. If your thinking is unrealistic, your thinking will lead to many disappointments. If your thinking is overly pessimistic, it will deny you due recognition of the many things in which you should properly rejoice.

Test this idea for yourself. Identify some examples of your strongest feelings or emotions. Then identify the thinking that is correlated with those examples. For example, if you *feel* excited about going to work, it is because you *think* that positive things will happen to you while you are at work, or that you will be able to accomplish important tasks. If you dread going to work, it is because you *think* it will be a negative experience.

In a similar way, if the quality of your life is not what you wish it to be, it is probably because it is tied to the way you *think* about your life. If you think about it positively, you will feel positive about it. If you think about it negatively, you will feel negative about it.

For example, suppose you recently accepted a job in a new city. You accepted said job because you had the view that you were ready for a change, that you wanted to experience living in a different place, that you wanted to find a new set of friends—in short, in many ways you wanted to start a new life. And let's suppose that your expectations of what would happen when you took the new job did not come to fruition. If this were the thrust of your thinking, you would now feel disappointed and maybe even frustrated (depending on how negative your experience has been interpreted *by your thinking*).

For most people, most of their thinking is subconscious, that is, never explicitly put into words. For example, most people who think negatively would not say of themselves, "I have chosen to think about myself and my experience in largely negative terms. I prefer to be as unhappy as I can be. "

The problem is that when you are not aware of your thinking you have no chance of "correcting" it. When thinking is subconscious, you are in no position to see any problems in it. And, if you don't see any problems in it, you won't be motivated to change it.

The truth is that since few people realize the powerful role that thinking plays in their lives, few gain significant command of their thinking. And therefore, most people are in many ways "victims" of their own thinking, harmed rather than helped by it. Most people are their own worst enemy. Their thinking is a continual source of problems, preventing them from recognizing opportunities, keeping them from exerting energy where it will do the most good, poisoning relationships, and leading them down blind alleys.

This book will—if you let it—improve the quality of your thinking, and therefore, help you achieve your goals and ambitions, make better decisions, and understand where others are trying to influence your thinking. It will help you take charge of what you do in your professional and personal life, how you relate to others, and even what emotions you feel. It's time for you to discover the power and role of thinking in your life. You are capable of achieving more significant professional goals. You can become a better problem solver. You can use power more wisely. You can become less subject to manipulation. You can live a fuller, a more happy and secure life. The choice is yours. We invite you to read on, and progressively take the steps that create that personal control and power as a day-to-day reality.[1]

---

1. How to read this book: There are two ways to read this book: sequentially and as the spirit moves you. Both are valid. You may be motivated to begin with some of the later chapters. That's fine, since all of the chapters have been written to be (roughly) intelligible on their own. Of course, the chapters also build on one another, so if you proceed sequentially you will be least puzzled by the logic of what is being said. In any case, if you are motivated to begin with a later chapter, we recommend that you familiarize yourself with the content in the first six chapters. We suggest that you skim those chapters so that you have a frame of reference for any of the later chapters with which you might want to begin. And make sure you come back to the early chapters for a deeper reading before you conclude that you understand the power of the book. Each of the chapters helps illuminate the others. And they all converge on, and add depth to, a set of central themes. We highly recommend that you take the time to do the "Test the Idea" activities throughout the book. They provide an important vehicle for internalizing key ideas.

Chapter 1

Thinking in a World of Accelerating Change and Intensifying Danger

The Nature of the Post-Industrial World Order

The world is swiftly changing. With each passing day, the pace of life and change quickens. The pressure to respond intensifies. New global realities are rapidly working their way into the deepest structures of our lives: economic, social, cultural, political, and environmental realities—realities with profound implications for thinking and learning, business and politics, human rights, and human conflicts. These realities are becoming increasingly complex; many represent significant dangers and threats. And they all turn on the powerful dynamic of accelerating change.

A Complex World of Accelerating Change

Can we deal with incessant and accelerating change and complexity without revolutionizing our thinking? Traditionally, our thinking has been designed for routine, for habit, for automation and fixed procedure. We learned how to do our job, and then we used what we learned over and over. But the problems we now face, and will increasingly face, require a radically different form of thinking, thinking that is more complex, more adaptable, and more sensitive to divergent points of view. The world in which we now live requires that we continually relearn, that we routinely rethink our decisions, and that we regularly reevaluate the way we work and live. In short, there is a new world facing us, one in which the power of the mind to command itself, to regularly engage in self-analysis, will increasingly determine the quality of our work, the quality of our lives, and perhaps even, our very survival.

1

Consider a simple feature of daily life: drinking water from the tap. With the increase of pollution, the poisoning of ground water, the indirect and long-term negative consequences of even small amounts of any number of undesirable chemicals, how are we to judge whether or not our drinking water is safe? Increasingly, governments are making decisions about how many lives to risk based on the financial consequence of saving them, about whether, for example, to put less money into the improvement of water quality at increased risks to human health. How are we to know whether the risk the government is willing to take with our lives is in line with our willingness to be at risk? This is just one of hundreds of decisions that require that we think critically about the ever-more changing world we face.

Consider the quiet revolution that is taking place in global communications. From fax machines to E-Mail, from complex electronic marketing systems to systems that track us and penetrate our private lives, we are not only providing positive opportunities for people to be more efficient with their time, but also systems that render us vulnerable and wield power over us. On the one hand, we have networks where goods, services, and ideas are freely exchanged with individuals the world over, and on the other hand, we face worldwide surveillance systems that render privacy an illusion. How are we to respond to these revolutionary changes? What is one to resist and what is one to support? When is a new system cost effective? Who should control it? For what ends should it be used? Who is to monitor its impact on human lives and well being? How are we to preserve our traditional freedoms, at home and abroad? How are we to protect our families and ourselves? How are we to preserve our human rights and have lives of autonomy, security, and integrity? What are we willing to give up in the pursuit of greater convenience and ease of communication?

And while we ponder the many issues related to technological advancement, we must also juggle and judge work and child care, efficiency and clogged transportation systems, expensive cars and inconvenient office space, increased specialization and increasing obsolescence, increased state power and decreased civil freedoms.

A Threatening World

We are caught up not only in an increasing swirl of challenges and decisions, but in an increasingly threatening world as well:

- A world in which we can no longer anticipate the knowledge or data we will need on the job, because we can no longer predict the kinds of jobs we will be doing.

- A world in which powerful technologies are interfaced with simplistic thinking about complex issues: "Get tough on crime!" "Three strikes and you're out!" "Zero tolerance!" "Adult crime, adult time!"

- A world in which national mass media gain more and more power over the minds of people.

- A world in which the incarceration of more and more people for longer and longer periods of time is becoming one of the largest industries, employing hundreds of thousands of professionals with vested interests in maintaining a large prison population: builders, architects, lawyers, police, federal investigators, prosecutors, social workers, counselors, psychologists, prison guards, and others.

- A world in which privacy is increasingly penetrated by multiple invasive technologies: face-recognition software, DNA testing, e-mail review systems, credit card tracking, and auto-tracking systems.

- A world in which global forces—subject to virtually no control—make far-reaching decisions that deeply impact our lives.

- A world in which self-serving ideologies are advanced in expensive media campaigns.

- A world in which increasing numbers of people advocate the use of violence as a response to real or perceived injustice.

- A world in which increasing numbers of people willingly accept significant diminution of individual rights and freedoms in exchange for increasing police and governmental powers of surveillance and detention.

- A world in which increasing numbers of civilians find themselves trapped in the crossfire of warring groups and ideologies.

- A world in which both freedom and safety are increasingly diminished for greater and greater numbers of people.

Change, Danger, and Complexity: Interwoven

Accelerating change, danger, and complexity do not function alone. They are deeply intermeshed, interactive, and transforming.

Consider the problem of solid waste management. This problem involves every level of government, every department: from energy to water quality, to planning, to revenues, to public health. Without a cooperative venture, without bridging territorial domains, without overcoming the implicit adversarial process within which we currently operate, the responsible parties at each tier of government cannot even *begin* to solve these problems. When they do communicate, they often speak from a position of vested interest, less concerned with public good than in furthering a self-serving agenda.

Consider the issues of depletion of the ozone layer, world hunger, over-population, and AIDS. Without the intellectual ability to reason through these complex problems, without being able to analyze the layers within them, without knowing how to identify and pursue the information we need to solve them, we are adrift in a sea of confusion. Without a grasp of the political realities, economic pressures, and scientific data (on the physical environment and its changes)—all of which are simultaneously changing as well—we cannot reverse the trend of deterioration of the quality of life for all who share the earth.

Consider, finally, the problem of terrorism and its link to the problem of ever-diminishing freedom. Predictable and unpredictable "enemies" threaten increasing numbers of innocent people. Though the root causes of terrorism almost always stems from complex issues, terrorism itself is often treated simplistically. People routinely, and uncritically, accept their national media's portrayal of world affairs, though national media in every country typically distort why their nation's "enemies" think and act as they do. Similarly, people readily accept their government's portrayal of world issues. When one's own country, or their allies, attack and kill civilians, such actions are defined by the national governments (and their symbiotic media) as 'defensive' in nature. Unethical practices by one's own government are covered-up, played down, or defended as a last recourse. Similar practices on the part of one's enemy are highlighted and trumpeted, often fomenting national outrage. Mob action, national vendettas, and witch hunts commonly result. The words "good" and "evil" are freely used to justify violence and terror inflicted on enemies—whether "real" or imagined.

But the problem of terrorism is inseparable from the problem of preserving essential human rights and freedoms. In "solving" one problem, we can easily create another. Let us look at a very small part of the evidence. Statewatch (www.statewatch.org/news) a European public interest watchdog group, reports on a letter from President Bush proposing a "lengthy list of more than 40 demands to the European Union for cooperation on anti-terrorism measures," many of which indiscriminately cover "criminal investigations, data surveillance, border controls, and immigration policies." Yet Tony Bunyan, Statewatch editor, comments: "Many of the demands have nothing to do with combating terrorism...." At the same time, the UK parliamentary Joint Committee on Human Rights, comprised of Ministers and Lords, has issued a report that is highly critical of the British government's proposed Anti-Terrorism, Crime and Security Bill. The report claims that the bill violates the European Convention on Human Rights, and questions both the definition of "terrorist activity" and the extension of police powers inherent in the bill.

The fact is that governments world-wide seem prepared to abandon traditional citizen rights and protections to accommodate sweeping extensions of police and government power—in the pursuit of those labeled "terrorists." The *New York Times* reports (Nov. 22, 2001): "As Americans debate how ruthless a war to wage against terrorism, India's leaders have seized on the Sept. 11 attack to push a draconian new anti-terror law that has stirred furious opposition..." The new ordinance allows authorities "to tap telephones, monitor e-mail, detain people without charge for up to six months, conduct secret trials in jails, and keep the identity of witnesses secret." According to the Times, under a similar previous Indian law, "...more than 75,000 people were arrested, but only 1% convicted…[while] many of the accused languished in jail for years" without hope of bail.

It is, of course, not uncommon for governments touting themselves as democratic to abuse freedom and deny basic liberties. Those concerned with human rights remind us that it is restraints on the government that separate a free society from a police state. We stand in need of the best legal thinking to provide for appropriate police and governmental power while yet preserving the restraints that are the bedrock of essential human freedoms.

This is a glimpse (and very partial analysis) of the world our children and we now face.

The Challenge of Becoming Critical Thinkers

The question of how to survive in the world is a question that continually transforms itself. Accelerating change, increasing complexity, and intensifying danger sound the death knell for traditional methods of learning. How can we adapt to reality when reality won't give us the time to master it before it changes, again and again, in ways we can but partially anticipate? Unfortunately, the crucial need for ever-new modes of thought to adapt to new problems and situations in new and humane ways is ignored by most cultures and most schools. Short-term thinking, which leads to quick-fix solutions, is largely the rule of the day. Great power is wielded around the world by little minds. Critical thinking is not a social value in any society. If we are to take up the challenge of becoming critical thinkers, we face a battery of hitherto unanswered questions that define the detailed agenda of this book. This question-centered agenda provides the impetus for reformulating our worldview. Through it, we can appreciate the intellectual work required to change our thinking in foundational ways. Through it, we can grasp the need to regularly re-examine the extent of our ignorance. Through it, we can grasp the need for regular exercise of disciplined thinking. Through it, we can understand the long-term nature of intellectual development, social change, and personal growth and transformation.

Every chapter of this book highlights crucial questions we need to ask about thinking. All deal with essential dimensions of the problems we face in thinking. All challenge our perseverance and courage. In the end, we must face ourselves honestly and forthrightly.

Recommended Reading

Heilbroner, Robert, *Twenty-First Century Capitalism* (House of Anansi Press, Limited: Concord, Ontario, 1992).

Reich, Robert, *The Work of Nations* (Vintage Books: New York, NY, 1992).

Chapter 2

Becoming a Critic of Your Thinking

The mind is its own place and in itself can make a hell of heaven or a heaven of hell.

—John Milton, *Paradise Lost*

How Skilled is Your Thinking (Right Now)?

There is nothing more practical than sound thinking. No matter what your circumstance or goals, no matter where you are, or what problems you face, you are better off if your thinking is skilled. As a professional—shopper, employee, citizen, lover, friend, parent—in every realm and situation of your life, good thinking pays off. Poor thinking, in turn, inevitably causes problems, wastes time and energy, engenders frustration and pain.

Critical thinking is the disciplined art of ensuring that you use the best thinking you are capable of in any set of circumstances. The general goal of thinking is to "figure out the lay of the land." We all have multiple choices to make. We need the best information to make the best choices.

What is really going on in this or that situation? Are they trying to take advantage of me? Does so-and-so really care about me? Am I deceiving myself when I believe that…? What are the likely consequences of failing to…? If I want to do…, what is the best way to prepare for it? How can I be more successful in doing…? Is this my biggest problem, or do I need to focus my attention on something else? Responding to such questions successfully is the daily work of thinking. That's why we are THINKERS.

7

Nothing you can do, of course, guarantees that you will discover the complete truth about anything, but there is a way to get better at it. Excellence of thought and skill in thinking are real possibilities. However, to maximize the quality of your thinking, you must learn how to become an effective "critic" of your thinking. And to become an effective critic of your thinking, you have to make *learning about thinking* a priority.

Ask yourself these—rather unusual—questions: What have you learned about how you think? Did you ever *study* your thinking? What information do you have, for example, about how the intellectual processes that occur as your mind thinks? More to the point, perhaps, what do you really know about how to analyze, evaluate, or reconstruct your thinking? Where does your thinking come from? How much of it is of "good" quality? How much of it is of "poor" quality? How much of your thinking is vague, muddled, inconsistent, inaccurate, illogical, or superficial? Are you, in any real sense, in control of your thinking? Do you know how to test it? Do you have any conscious standards for determining when you are thinking well and when you are thinking poorly? Have you ever discovered a significant problem in your thinking and then changed it by a conscious act of will? If anyone asked you to teach them what you have learned, thus far in your life, about thinking, would you really have any idea what that was or how you learned it?

If you are like most, the only honest answers to these questions run along the lines of: "Well, I suppose I really don't know much about my thinking or about thinking in general. I suppose in my life I have more or less taken my thinking for granted. I don't really know how it works. I have never really studied it. I don't know how I test it, or even if I do test it. It just happens in my mind automatically." In other words, serious study of thinking, serious thinking about thinking, is rare. It is not a subject in most schools. It is not a subject taught at home. But if you focus your attention for a moment on the role that thinking is playing in your life, you may come to recognize that, in fact, everything you do, want, or feel is influenced by your thinking. And if you become persuaded of that, you will be surprised that humans show so little interest in thinking. We are like monkeys uninterested in what goes on when we "monkey around." What is more, if you start, then, to pay attention to thinking in a manner analogous to the way a botanist observes plants, you will be on your way to becoming a truly exceptional person. You will begin to notice what few others notice. You will be the rare monkey who knows what monkeying around is all about. You will be the rare monkey who knows how and why he is monkeying around, the rare monkey skilled in assessing and improving his monkeying. Here are some things you will eventually discover: that all of us have, somewhere along the way, picked up bad habits of thinking. All of us, for example, make generalizations when we don't have the evidence to back them up, allow stereotypes to influence our thinking, form some false beliefs, tend to look at the world from one fixed point of view, ignore or attack points of view that conflict with our own, fabricate illusions and myths that we subconsciously confuse with what is true and real, and think deceptively about many aspects of our experience. As you discover these problems, we hope you will begin to ask yourself some key questions: "Is it possible for me to learn to avoid bad habits of thought? Is it possible for me to develop good habits of thought? Is it possible for me to think at a high, or at least, *higher*, level?" These are problems and questions that few discover or ask. Nevertheless, every major insight you gain into good or bad thinking can significantly enhance your life. You can begin to make higher quality decisions. You can gain power, very important power, you presently lack. You can open up new doors for yourself, see new options, minimize significant mistakes, and maximize potential understandings.

Test the Idea: Beginning to Think about your Thinking

To begin to think about your thinking, make a list of any problems you believe currently exist with your thinking. Try to be as explicit as possible. The more problems you can identify the better. For each problem you identify, complete the following statements:

1) One problem with my thinking is...

2) This is a problem because...

Good Thinking Is as Easy as Bad Thinking
(But It Requires Hard Work to Develop It)

It is important to realize that thinking itself is not difficult. Humans naturally think without having to exert much energy or engage in any real intellectual work. We can easily see thinking manifest, for example, in very young children who have few or no skills of mind. It is clear that children are thinking when they are trying to figure out their "world" and how it operates, when they are determining what they can get away with and what they can't, when they are distinguishing between people who like them and people who don't, when they are asserting what they want and what they don't want. In a similar way adults are continually thinking about their world, figuring things out, making decisions, making choices. Thus, thinking *per se* is natural to humans; it comes easy to us. What does not come easy is consistent high quality thinking across the dimensions of one's life. That is, it is not easy to discover our bad habits and do something about them.

To make significant gains in the quality of your thinking, you will have to engage in a kind of work that most humans find unpleasant, if not painful—intellectual work. Yet once this thinking is done and we move our thinking to a higher level of quality, it is not hard to keep our thinking at that level. Still there is a price you have to pay to step up to the next level. One doesn't become a skillful critic of thinking over night, any more than one becomes a skillful basketball player or dancer over night. To become better at thinking, you must be willing to put the work into thinking that skilled improvement always requires. We say "No pain, no gain!" when thinking of what physical conditioning requires. In this case, it would be more precise to say:

"No *intellectual* pain, no *intellectual* gain!" This means you must be willing to practice special "acts" of thinking that are initially at least uncomfortable, and sometimes
challenging and difficult. You have to learn to do with your mind "moves" analogous
to what accomplished athletes learn to do (through practice and feedback) with their
bodies. Improvement in thinking, in other words, is similar to improvement in other
domains of performance, where progress is a product of sound theory, commitment,
hard work, and practice. This book will point the way to what you need to practice
to become a skilled thinker, yet it cannot, of course, provide you with the internal
motivation to do the required work. This must come from you (See Figure 2.1).

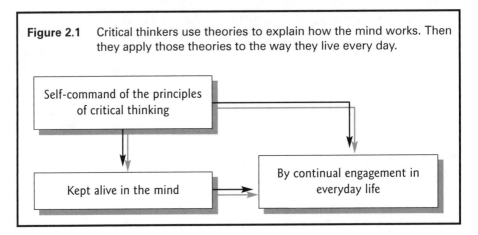

Figure 2.1   Critical thinkers use theories to explain how the mind works. Then
they apply those theories to the way they live every day.

Let's now develop the analogy between physical and intellectual development. This
analogy, we believe, goes a very long way, and provides us with just the right prototype
to keep before our minds. If you play tennis, and you want to play better, there is
nothing more advantageous than to look at some films of excellent players in action
and then painstakingly compare how they address the ball in comparison to you. You
study their performance. You note what you need to do more of, what you need to do
less of, and you practice, practice, practice. You go through many cycles of practice/
feedback/practice. Your practice heightens your awareness of the IN's and OUT's of
the art. You develop a vocabulary for talking about your "performance." Perhaps you
get a coach. And slowly, progressively, you improve. Similar points could be made for
ballet, distance running, piano playing, chess, reading, writing, shopping, parenting,
teaching, performing complex tasks on the job, etc.

One major problem, however, is that all the activities of skill development with which
we are typically familiar are visible. We could watch a film of the skill-in-action. But
imagine a film of a person sitting in a chair THINKING. It would look like the person was doing nothing. Yet, increasingly, workers are being paid precisely for the
thinking they are able to do, not for their physical strength or physical activity. Therefore, though most of our thinking is *invisible*, it represents one of the most important

things about us. Its quality will in all likelihood determine whether we will become rich or poor, powerful or weak. Yet we typically think without explicitly noticing how we are doing it. We take our thinking for granted. You might compare the way we learn how to think with the way we learned how to speak our native language. We learned, for example, the grammar of our language without explicitly knowing how to talk about that grammar, without knowing its principles, rules, and exceptions. But if I said, "Where the up cow is down?" you would recognize immediately that, grammatically speaking, that arrangement of words does not make sense. You know it violates grammatical rules without, perhaps, being able to state what rules were violated.

Of course, in addition to learning the grammar of our native language, we also learned a wide variety of "concepts," ways of organizing and interpreting our experience. Our grammatical mistakes were easily noted by anyone proficient in the grammar of the language, but our misuse of the concepts of the language often go unnoticed—especially when the misuse is common among our associates. We could say that the logic of grammar is much better known than the logic of concepts.

Grammatical mistakes are easier to recognize than "conceptual" ones. For example, one who says, "I love you," when they ought to have said, "I feel physically attracted to you," is very unlikely to say later: "I misused the concept of love, leading you to come to the conclusion that I was committed to your welfare when in fact I am not. Actually, I was just interested in having sex with you." Often people will remain married to others whose behavior toward them clearly implies that they do not love them. The inconsistency in behavior is hidden perhaps by periodic verbalizations ("I love you dearest") on birthdays or special events. Important concepts, like the concept of love, friendship, integrity, freedom, democracy, and ethics are often twisted and distorted in common life and thought. Our subconscious interest is often in getting what we want, not in describing ourselves (or the world) in a true and honest fashion.

That being said, most of our concepts are "invisible" to us, though implicit in our talk and behavior. So is much of our thinking! We would be amazed, and sometimes shocked, if we saw all of our thinking displayed for us on a large screen.

But to develop as a thinker you must begin to think of your thinking as involving an implicit set of structures, "concepts," for example, being one important set, whose use can be improved only when you begin to take the tools of thinking seriously. You develop as a thinker when you explicitly notice the thinking you are doing and when you become committed to recognizing both strengths and weaknesses in that thinking. You develop as a thinker as you build your own "large screen" on which to view your thinking.

Critical thinking, then, provides the tools of mind you need to think well through any and everything that requires thought—at work and in all parts of life (Figure 2.2 & 2.3). As your box of intellectual skills develops, you gain instruments that you can deliberately and mindfully use in order to reason better through the "thinking" tasks implicit in your short and long-range goals. There are better and worse ways to pursue whatever you are after. Good thinking enables you to maximize the one and minimize the other.

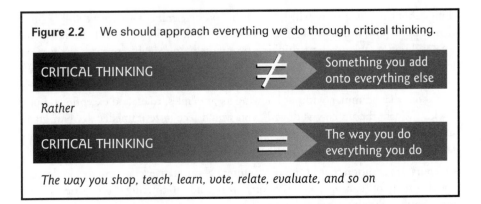

Figure 2.2   We should approach everything we do through critical thinking.

CRITICAL THINKING ≠ Something you add onto everything else

Rather

CRITICAL THINKING = The way you do everything you do

The way you shop, teach, learn, vote, relate, evaluate, and so on

---

Test the Idea: Understanding the Importance of Concepts

See if you can think of a time in which you "misused" an important concept. Hint: Think of an idea that you commonly use in your thinking such as friendship, trust, truthfulness, or respect. Has there ever been a time when you implied you were someone's friend but acted against that person (like gossiping behind that person's back or lying to them). Write out your answer.

It is only through applying the fundamentals of critical thinking to a wide range of human problems that one begins to appreciate their power and usefulness. Think of it this way. If we were coaching you in tennis, we would remind you again and again to keep your eye on the ball. Could you imagine telling your coach, "Why do I have to keep my eye on the ball? I already did that once." The same logic applies to the principles of skilled thinking. If you want to be proficient, you have to re-direct your eyes to the fundamentals, again and again and again.

The Hard Cruel World

What help can you expect from the world about you in becoming a critical thinker? In the ordinary case, very little. Family, schools, acquaintances, employers—each have agendas that are not focused on the value of critical thinking in our lives. Most people—family members, teachers, acquaintances, business associates—have multiple problems in their own thinking: prejudices, biases, misconceptions, ideological rigidity. Few can help us directly and effectively to improve ours. Whether in a personal or public world, whether in a private or a business world, action agendas, only partially understood by those maintaining them, are the order of the day. If we are "in the way," if we act out of keeping with what is expected of us, we are likely to be introduced to the "school of hard knocks." Like it or not, we need to learn how to analyze the logic of the circumstances and persons with which we must deal and act realistically. For example, if you find yourself working in an organization, you must be prepared to take into account the actual structure of power within it, along with group definitions of reality, bureaucratic thinking, and other variables that may diminish the quality of day-to-day thinking. Nevertheless, it would be folly to speak candidly without thinking of the likely consequences of that speech. Critical thinking helps us to see with new eyes. It does not require us to endanger ourselves or act against our best interest. We must integrate three dimensions of thought. We must be idealistic (and thus capable of imagining a better world). We must be realistic (and thus see things as they are). And we must be pragmatic (and thus adopt effective measures for moving toward our ideals).

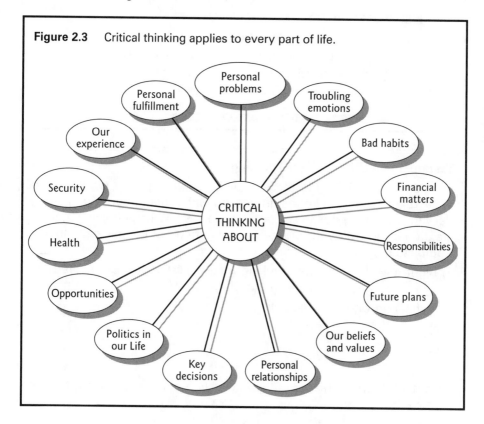

Figure 2.3   Critical thinking applies to every part of life.

Become a Critic of Your Own Thinking

One of the most important things you can do for yourself is to begin the process of becoming a "critic" of your thinking. You do this not to negate or "dump on" yourself, but to improve yourself, to begin to practice the art of skilled thinking and lifelong learning. To do this you must "discover" your thinking, see its structure, observe its implications, and recognize its basis and vantage point. You must come to recognize that,

Figure 2.4   Critical thinking adds a second level of thinking to ordinary thinking. The second level analyzes and assesses our ordinary thinking.

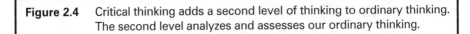

SECOND-ORDER THINKING
is first-order thinking raised to the
level of conscious realization (analyzed,
assessed, and reconstructed).

FIRST-ORDER THINKING
is spontaneous and nonreflective. It contains
insight, prejudice, truth and error, good and
bad reasoning, indiscriminately combined.

Test the Idea: Critique Your Thinking

Consider your thinking in these domains of your life: at work, in personal relationships, in sports, in dealing with others of your gender, in dealing with the opposite sex, as a reader, as a writer, in planning your life, in dealing with your emotions, in figuring out complex situations. Complete these statements:

1) Right now, I believe my thinking across all domains of my life is of _____ quality. I based this judgment on _____.

2) In the following areas, I think very well:

   a)

   b)

   c)

3) In the following areas, my thinking is OK, not great, but not terrible either:

   a)

   b)

   c)

4) In the following areas, my thinking is probably pretty poor:

   a)

   b)

   c)

through commitment and daily practice, you can make foundational changes in your thinking. You need to learn about your "bad" habits of thought and about what you are striving for (habits of thought that routinely improve your thinking). At whatever level you think, you need to recognize that you can learn to think better (Figure 2.4)

Conclusion

Critical thinking works (Table 2.1). It is practical. It enables you to be more successful, to save time and energy, and experience more positive and fulfilling emotions. It is in your interest to become a better critic of your thinking: as an employee, professional, manager, scholar, parent, consumer, citizen, etc.… If you are not progressively improving the quality of your life, you have not yet discovered the true power of critical thinking.

Table 2.1 Why critical thinking?	
The Problem	**A Definition**
Everyone thinks. It is our nature to do so. But much of our thinking, left to itself, is biased, distorted, partial, uninformed, or downright prejudiced. Yet the quality of our life and that of what we produce, make, or build depends precisely on the quality of our thought. Shoddy thinking is costly, both in money and in quality of life. Excellence in thought, however, must be systematically cultivated.	Critical thinking is that mode of thinking—about any subject, content, or problem—in which the thinker improves the quality of his or her thinking by skillfully taking charge of the structures inherent in thinking and imposing intellectual standards upon them.

The Result

A well-cultivated critical thinker:
- raises vital questions and problems, formulating them clearly and precisely;
- gathers and assesses relevant information, and effectively interprets it;
- comes to well-reasoned conclusions and solutions, testing them against relevant criteria and standards;
- thinks openmindedly within alternative systems of thought, recognizing and assessing, as need be, their assumptions, implications, and practical consequences; and
- communicates effectively with others in figuring out solutions to complex problems.

Critical thinking is, in short, self-directed, self-disciplined, self-monitored, and self-corrective thinking. It presupposes assent to rigorous standards of excellence and mindful command of their use. It entails effective communication and problem-solving abilities.

Chapter 3

Becoming a
Fair-Minded Thinker

Weak versus Strong Critical Thinking

Critical thinking involves basic intellectual skills, but these skills can be used to serve two incompatible ends: self-centeredness or fair-mindedness. As we develop the basic intellectual skills that critical thinking entails, we can begin to use those skills in a selfish or in a fair-minded way. In other words, we can develop in such a way that we learn to see mistakes in our own thinking, as well as the thinking of others. Or we can merely develop some proficiency in making our opponent's thinking look bad.

Typically, people see mistakes in other's thinking without being able to credit the strengths in those opposing views. Liberals see mistakes in the arguments of conservatives; conservatives see mistakes in the arguments of liberals. Believers see mistakes in the thinking of nonbelievers; nonbelievers see mistakes in the thinking of believers. Those who oppose abortion readily see mistakes in the arguments for abortion; those who favor abortion readily see mistakes in the arguments against it.

We call these thinkers weak-sense critical thinkers. We call the thinking "weak" because, though it is working well for the thinker in some respects, it is missing certain important higher-level skills and values of critical thinking. Most significantly, it fails to consider, in good faith, viewpoints that contradict its own viewpoint. It lacks fair-mindedness.

Another traditional name for the weak-sense thinker is found in the word sophist. Sophistry is the art of winning arguments regardless of whether there are obvious problems in the thinking being used. There is a set of lower-level skills of rhetoric, or argumentation, by which one can make bad thinking look good and good thinking look bad. We see this often in unethical lawyers and politicians who are merely concerned with winning. They use emotionalism and trickery in an intellectually skilled way.

Sophistic thinkers succeed only if they do not come up against what we call strong-sense critical thinkers. Strong-sense critical thinkers are not easily tricked by slick argumentation. As William Graham Sumner (1906) said almost a century ago, they

> *cannot be stampeded ... are slow to believe ... can hold things as possible or probable in all degrees, without certainty and without pain ... can wait for evidence and weigh evidence ... can resist appeals to their dearest prejudices....*

Perhaps even more important, strong-sense critical thinkers strive to be fair-minded. They use thinking in an ethically responsible manner. They work to understand and appreciate the viewpoints of others. They are willing to listen to arguments they do not necessarily hold. They change their views when faced with better reasoning. Rather than using their thinking to manipulate others and to hide from the truth (in a weak-sense way), they use thinking in an ethical, reasonable manner.

We believe that the world already has too many skilled selfish thinkers, too many sophists and intellectual con artists, too many unscrupulous lawyers and politicians who specialize in twisting information and evidence to support their selfish interests and the vested interests of those who pay them. We hope that you, the reader, will develop as a highly skilled, fair-minded thinker, one capable of exposing those who are masters at playing intellectual games at the expense of the well-being of innocent people. We hope as well that you develop the intellectual courage to argue publicly against what is unethical in human thinking. We write this book with the assumption that you will take seriously the fair-mindedness implied by strong-sense critical thinking.

To think critically in the strong sense requires that we develop fair-mindedness at the same time that we learn basic critical thinking skills, and thus begin to "practice" fair-mindedness in our thinking. If we do, we avoid using our skills to gain unfair advantage over others. We avoid using our thinking to get what we want at the expense of the rights and needs of others. We treat all thinking by the same high standards. We expect good reasoning from those who support us as well as those who oppose us. We subject our own reasoning to the same criteria we apply to reasoning to which we are unsympathetic. We question our own purposes, evidence, conclusions, implications, and points of view with the same vigor that we question those of others.

Developing fair-minded thinkers try to see the actual strengths and weaknesses of any reasoning they assess. This is the kind of thinker we hope this book will help you become. So, right from the beginning, we are going to explore the characteristics that are required for the strongest, most fair-minded thinking. As you read through the rest of the book, we hope you will notice how we are attempting to foster "strong-sense" critical thinking. Indeed, unless we indicate otherwise, every time we now use the words "critical thinking," from this point onward, we will mean critical thinking in the strong sense.

In the remainder of this chapter, we will explore the various intellectual "virtues" that fair-minded thinking requires (Figure 3.1). There is much more to fair-mindedness than most people realize. Fair-mindedness requires a family of interrelated and interdependent states of mind.

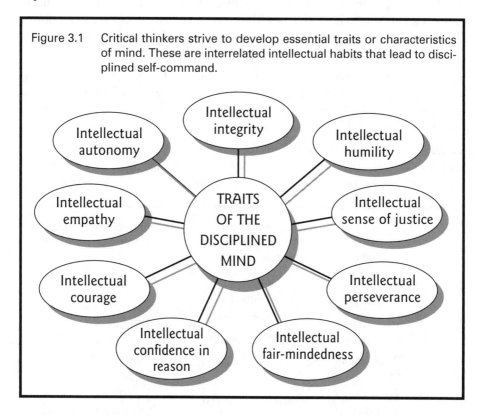

Figure 3.1   Critical thinkers strive to develop essential traits or characteristics of mind. These are interrelated intellectual habits that lead to disciplined self-command.

In addition to fair-mindedness, strong-sense critical thinking implies higher-order thinking. As you develop as a thinker and internalize the traits of mind that we shall soon discuss, you will develop a variety of skills and insights that are absent in the weak-sense critical thinker.

As we examine how the various traits of mind are conducive to fair-mindedness, we will also look at the manner in which the traits contribute to quality of thought (in general). In addition to the fairness that strong-sense critical thinking implies, depth of thinking and high quality of thinking are also implied. Weak-sense critical thinkers develop a range of intellectual skills (for example, skills of argumentation) and may achieve some success in getting what they want, but they do not develop any of the traits highlighted in this chapter.

It is important to note that many people considered successful in business or in their profession are, in fact, selfish thinkers. In self-indulgent and materialistic cultures, the idea "if it is good for me it is good for everyone" is tacitly assumed when not overtly stated. The pursuit of money, often at the expense of the rights and needs of others, is considered not only acceptable, but also commendable. Nevertheless when the pursuit of wealth and power is unbridled, injustice often results. The human mind is readily able to justify its own selfishness and lack of consideration for others. The powerful find many reasons to ignore the interests of the weak (Figure 3.2).

True critical thinkers, in the strong sense, realize the ease with which the mind can ignore the rights and needs of others. They recognize that to be reasonable and just is not to comply with nature but to defy it. They recognize the difficulty of entering into points of view different from our own. They are willing to do the work that is required to go beyond selfish thinking.

Let us turn to the component traits of the strong-sense critical thinker. After we take up each individual trait as it stands in relation to fair-mindedness, we will highlight its significance as a contributor to the general development of high levels of thinking.

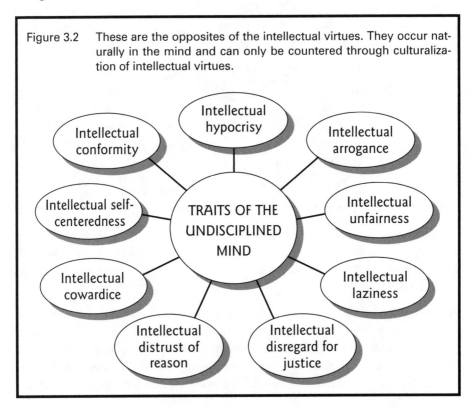

Figure 3.2   These are the opposites of the intellectual virtues. They occur naturally in the mind and can only be countered through culturalization of intellectual virtues.

What Does Fair-Mindedness Require?

First, the basic concept:

> *Fair-mindedness entails a consciousness of the need to treat all viewpoints alike, without reference to one's own feelings or selfish interests, or the feelings or selfish interests of one's friends, company, community, or nation. It implies adherence to intellectual standards (such as accuracy and sound logic), uninfluenced by one's own advantage or the advantage of one's group.*

To be fair-minded is to strive to treat every viewpoint relevant to a situation in an unbiased, unprejudiced way. It entails a consciousness of the fact that we, by nature, tend to prejudge the views of others, placing them into "favorable" (agrees with us) and "unfavorable" (disagrees with us) categories. We tend to give less weight to contrary views than to our own. This is especially true when we have selfish reasons for opposing views. For example, the manufacturers of asbestos advocated its use in homes and schools, and made large profits on its use, even though they knew for many years that the product was carcinogenic. They ignored the viewpoint and welfare of the innocent users of their product. If we can ignore the potentially harmful effects of a product we manufacture, we can reap the benefits that come with large profits without experiencing pangs of conscience. Thus, fair-mindedness is especially important when the situation calls on us to consider the point of view of those who welfare is in conflict with our short-term vested interest.

The opposite of fair-mindedness is intellectual self-centeredness. It is demonstrated by the failure of thinkers to treat points of view that differ significantly from their own by the same standards that they treat their own.

Achieving a truly fair-minded state of mind is challenging. It requires us to simultaneously become intellectually humble, intellectually courageous, intellectually empathetic, intellectually honest, intellectually perseverant, confident in reason (as a tool of discovery and learning), and intellectually autonomous.

Without this family of traits in an integrated constellation, there is no true fair-mindedness. But these traits, singly and in combination, are not commonly discussed in everyday life, and are rarely taught. They are not discussed on television. Your friends and colleagues will not ask you questions about them.

In truth, because they are largely unrecognized, these traits are not commonly valued. Yet each of them is essential to fair-mindedness and the development of critical thinking. Let us see how and why this is so.

Intellectual Humility: Having Knowledge of Ignorance

We will begin with the fair-minded trait of intellectual humility:

> *Intellectual humility may be defined as having a consciousness of the limits of one's knowledge, including a sensitivity to circumstances in which one's native egocentrism is likely to function self-deceptively. This entails being aware of one's biases, one's prejudices, the limitations of one's viewpoint, and the extent of one's ignorance. Intellectual humility depends on recognizing that one should not claim more than one actually knows. It does not imply spinelessness or submissiveness. It implies the lack of intellectual pretentiousness, boastfulness, or conceit, combined with insight into the logical foundations, or lack of such foundations, of one's beliefs.*

The opposite of intellectual humility is intellectual arrogance, a lack of consciousness of the limits of one's knowledge, with little or no insight into self-deception or the limitations of one's point of view. Intellectually arrogant people often fall prey to their own bias and prejudice, and frequently claim to know more than they actually know.

When we think of intellectual arrogance, we are not necessarily implying a person who is outwardly smug, haughty, insolent, or pompous. Outwardly, the person may appear humble. For example, a person who uncritically believes in a cult leader may be outwardly self-effacing ("I am nothing. You are everything"), but intellectually he or she is making a sweeping generalization that is not well founded, and has complete faith in that generalization.

Unfortunately, in human life people of the full range of personality types are capable of believing they know what they don't know. Our own false beliefs, misconceptions, prejudices, illusions, myths, propaganda, and ignorance appear to us as the plain, unvarnished truth. What is more, when challenged, we often resist admitting that our thinking is "defective." We then are intellectually arrogant, even though we might feel humble. Rather than recognizing the limits of our knowledge, we ignore and obscure those limits. From such arrogance, much suffering and waste result.

It is not uncommon for the police, for example, to assume a man is guilty of a crime because of his appearance, because he is black for example, or because he wears an earring, or because he has a disheveled and unkempt look about him. Owing to the prejudices driving their thinking, the police are often incapable of intellectual humility. In a similar way, prosecutors have been known to withhold exculpatory evidence against a defendant in order to "prove" their case. Intellectually righteous in their views, they feel confident that the defendant is guilty. Why, therefore, shouldn't they suppress evidence that will help this "guilty" person go free?

Intellectual arrogance is incompatible with fair-mindedness because we cannot judge fairly when we are in a state of ignorance about the object of our judgment. If we are ignorant about a religion (say, Buddhism), we cannot be fair in judging it. And if we have misconceptions, prejudices, or illusions about it, we will distort it (unfairly) in our judgment. We will misrepresent it and make it appear to be other than it is. Our false knowledge, misconceptions, prejudices, and illusions stand in the way of the possibility of our being fair. Or if we are intellectually arrogant, we will be inclined to judge too quickly and be overly confident in our judgment. Clearly, these tendencies are incompatible with being fair (to that which we are judging).

Why is intellectual humility essential to higher-level thinking? In addition to helping us become fair-minded thinkers, knowledge of our ignorance can improve our thinking in a variety of ways. It can enable us to recognize the prejudices, false beliefs, and habits of mind that lead to flawed learning. Consider, for example, our tendency to accept superficial learning. Much human learning is superficial. We learn a little and think we know a lot. We get limited information and generalize hastily from it. We confuse cutesy phrases with deep insights. We uncritically accept much that we hear and read—especially when what we hear or read agrees with our intensely held beliefs or the beliefs of groups to which we belong.

The discussion in the chapters that follow encourages intellectual humility and will help to raise your awareness of intellectual arrogance. See if you, from this moment, can begin to develop in yourself a growing awareness of the limitations of your knowledge and an increasing sensitivity to instances of your inadvertent intellectual arrogance. When you do, celebrate that sensitivity. Reward yourself for finding weaknesses in your thinking. Consider recognition of weakness an important strength, not a weakness. As a starter, answer the following questions:

- Can you construct a list of your most significant prejudices? (Think of what you believe about your country, your religion, your company, your friends, your family, simply because others—colleagues, parents, friends, peer group, media—conveyed these to you.)

- Do you ever argue for or against views when you have little evidence upon which to base your judgment?

- Do you ever assume that your group (your company, your family, your religion, your nation, your friends) is correct (when it is in conflict with others) even though you have not looked at the situation from the point of view of the others with which you disagree?

Test the Idea: Intellectual Humility

Name a person you think you know fairly well. Make two lists. In the first list include everything you know for sure about the person. In the second list include everything you know you don't know about him/her. For example: "I know for sure that my spouse likes to garden, but I'm also sure that I have never really understood what her fears and personal desires were. I know many superficial things about her, but about her inner self I know little." Support what you claim by writing out an explanation of your thinking.

Intellectual Courage: Being Willing to Challenge Beliefs

Now let's consider intellectual courage:

> *Intellectual courage may be defined as having a consciousness of the need to face and fairly address ideas, beliefs, or viewpoints toward which one has strong negative emotions and to which one has not given a serious hearing. Intellectual courage is connected to the recognition that ideas that society considers dangerous or absurd are sometimes rationally justified (in whole or in part). Conclusions and beliefs inculcated in people are sometimes false or misleading. To determine for oneself what makes sense, one must not passively and uncritically accept what one has learned. Intellectual courage comes into play here because there is some truth in some ideas considered dangerous and absurd, and distortion or falsity in some ideas strongly held by social groups to which we belong. People need courage to be fair-minded thinkers in these circumstances. The penalties for nonconformity can be severe.*

The opposite of intellectual courage, *intellectual cowardice*, is the fear of ideas that do not conform to one's own. If we lack intellectual courage, we are afraid of giving serious consideration to ideas, beliefs, or viewpoints that we perceive as dangerous. We feel personally threatened by some ideas when they conflict significantly with our personal identity—when we feel that an attack on the ideas is an attack on us as a person.

All of the following ideas are "sacred" in the minds of some people: being a conservative, being a liberal; believing in God, disbelieving in God; believing in capitalism, believing in socialism; believing in abortion, disbelieving in abortion; believing in capital punishment, disbelieving in capital punishment. No matter what side we are on, we often say of ourselves: "I am a (an) [insert sacred belief here; for example, I am a Christian. I am a conservative. I am a socialist. I am an atheist]."

Once we define who we are in relation to an emotional commitment to a belief, we are likely to experience inner fear when that idea or belief is questioned. Questioning the belief seems to be questioning us. The intensely personal fear that we feel operates as a barrier in our minds to being fair (to the opposing belief). When we do seem to consider the opposing idea, we subconsciously undermine it, presenting it in its weakest form, in order to reject it. This is one form of intellectual cowardice. Sometimes, then, we need intellectual courage to overcome our self-created inner fear—the fear we ourselves have created by linking our identity to a specific set of beliefs.

Intellectual courage is just as important in our professional as in our personal lives. If, for example, we are unable to analyze the work-related beliefs we hold, then we are essentially trapped by those beliefs. We do not have the courage to question what we have always taken for granted. We are unable to question the beliefs collectively held by our co-workers. We are unable to question, for example, the ethics of our decisions and our behavior at work. But fair-minded managers, employers, and employees do not hesitate to question what has always been considered "sacred" or what is taken for granted by others in their group. It is not uncommon, for example, for employees to think within a sort of "mob mentality" against management, which often includes routinely gossiping to one another about management practices, especially those practices that impact them. Those with intellectual courage, rather than participating in such gossip in a mindless way, will begin to question the source of the gossip. They will question whether there is good reason for the group to be disgruntled, or whether the group is irrational in its expectations of management.

Another important reason to acquire intellectual courage is to overcome the fear of rejection by others because they hold certain beliefs and are likely to reject us if we challenge those beliefs. This is where we invest the group with the power to intimidate us, and such power is destructive. Many people live their lives in the eyes of others and cannot approve of themselves unless others approve of them. Fear of rejection is often lurking in the back of their minds. Few people challenge the ideologies or belief systems of the groups to which they belong. This is the second form of intellectual cowardice. Both make it impossible to be fair to the ideas that are contrary to our, or our group's, identity.

You might note in passing an alternative way to form your personal identity. This is not in terms of the content of any given idea (what you actually believe) but, instead, in terms of the process by which you came to it. This is what it means to take on the identity of a critical thinker. Consider the following resolution:

> *I will not identify with the content of any belief. I will identify only with the way I come to my beliefs. I am a critical thinker and, as such, am ready to abandon any belief that cannot be supported by evidence and rational considerations. I am ready to follow evidence and reason wherever they lead. My true identity is that of being a critical thinker, a lifelong learner, and a person always looking to improve my thinking by becoming more reasonable in my beliefs.*

With such an identity, intellectual courage becomes more meaningful to us, and fair-mindedness more essential. We are no longer afraid to consider beliefs that are contrary to our present beliefs. We are not afraid of being proven wrong. We freely admit to having made mistakes in the past. We are happy to correct any mistakes we are still making: Tell me what you believe and why you believe it, and maybe I can learn from your thinking. I have cast off many early beliefs. I am ready to abandon as many of the present beliefs as are not consistent with the way things are.

Test the Idea*:*
Intellectual Courage I

Select one group to which you belong. Complete the following statements:

1. One main belief common to members of this group that might be questioned is ... (here you want to identify at least one belief that may lead group members to behave irrationally).
2. This belief might be questioned because...
3. I would or would not be able to stand up to my group, pointing out the problems with this belief, because...

Intellectual Courage II

Try to think of a circumstance in which either you or someone you knew defended a view that was unpopular in a group to which you belonged. Describe the circumstances, and especially how the group responded. If you can't think of an example, what is the significance of that realization?

Intellectual Empathy: Entertaining Opposing Views

Next let's consider intellectual empathy, another trait of mind necessary to fair-mindedness:

> *Intellectual empathy is an awareness of the need to imaginatively put oneself in the place of others so as to genuinely understand them. To have intellectual empathy is to be able to accurately reconstruct the viewpoints and reasoning of others and to reason from premises, assumptions, and ideas other than one's own. This trait also correlates with the willingness to remember occasions when one was wrong in the past despite an intense conviction of being right, and with the ability to imagine being similarly deceived in a case at hand.*

The opposite of intellectual empathy is *intellectual self-centeredness*. It is thinking centered on self. When we think from a self-centered perspective, we are unable to understand others' thoughts, feelings, and emotions. From this natural perspective, we are the recipients of most of our attention. Our pain, our desires, and our hopes are most pressing. The needs of others pale into insignificance before the domination of our own needs and desires. We are unable to consider issues, problems, and questions from a viewpoint that differs from our own and that, when considered, would force us to change our perspective.

How can we be fair to the thinking of others if we have not learned to put ourselves in their intellectual shoes? Fair-minded judgment requires a good-faith effort to acquire accurate knowledge. Human thinking emerges from the conditions of human life, from very different contexts and situations. If we do not learn how to take on the perspectives of others and to accurately think as they think, we will not be able to fairly judge their ideas and beliefs. Actually trying to think within the viewpoint of others is not easy, though. It is one of the most difficult skills to acquire. The extent to which you have intellectual empathy has direct implications for the quality of your life. If you cannot think within the viewpoint of your supervisor, for example, you will have difficulty functioning successfully in your job and you may often feel frustrated. If you cannot think within the viewpoints of your subordinates, you will have difficulty understanding why they behave as they do. If you cannot think within the viewpoint of your spouse, the quality of your marriage will be adversely affected. If you cannot think within the viewpoints of your children, they will feel misunderstood and alienated from you.

Test the Idea:
Intellectual Empathy I

Try to reconstruct the last argument you had with someone (a supervisor, colleague, friend, or intimate other). Reconstruct the argument from your perspective and that of the other person. Complete the statements below. As you do, watch that you do not distort the other's viewpoint. Try to enter it in good faith, even if it means you have to admit you were wrong. (Remember that critical thinkers want to see the truth in the situation.) After you have completed this activity, show it to the person you argued with to see if you have accurately represented that person's view.

1. My perspective was as follows (state and elaborate your view):

2. The other person's view was as follows (state and elaborate the other person's view):

Intellectual Integrity: Holding Ourselves to the Same Standards to Which We Hold Others

Let us now consider intellectual integrity:

> Intellectual integrity is defined as recognition of the need to be true to one's own thinking and to hold oneself to the same standards one expects others to meet. It means to hold oneself to the same rigorous standards of evidence and proof to which one holds one's antagonists—to practice what one advocates for others. It also means to honestly admit discrepancies and inconsistencies in one's own thought and action, and to be able to identify inconsistencies in one's own thinking.

The opposite of intellectual integrity is intellectual hypocrisy, a state of mind unconcerned with genuine integrity. It is often marked by deep-seated contradictions and inconsistencies. The appearance of integrity means a lot because it affects our image with others. Therefore, hypocrisy is often implicit in the thinking and action behind human behavior as a function of natural egocentric thinking. Our hypocrisy is hidden from us. Though we expect others to adhere to standards to which we refuse to adhere, we see ourselves as fair. Though we profess certain beliefs, we often fail to behave in accordance with those beliefs.

To the extent that we have intellectual integrity, our beliefs and actions are consistent. We practice what we preach, so to speak. We don't say one thing and do another.

Suppose I were to say to you that our relationship is really important to me, but you find out that I have lied to you about something important to you. My behavior lacks integrity. I have acted hypocritically.

Clearly, we cannot be fair to others if we are justified in thinking and acting in contradictory ways. Hypocrisy by its very nature is a form of injustice. In addition, if we are not sensitive to contradictions and inconsistencies in our own thinking and behavior, we cannot think well about ethical questions involving ourselves.

Consider this political example. From time to time the U.S. media discloses highly questionable practices by the CIA. These practices run anywhere from documentation of attempted assassinations of foreign political leaders (say, attempts to assassinate President Castro of Cuba) to the practice of teaching police or military representatives in other countries (say, Central America or South America) how to torture prisoners to get them to disclose information about their associates. To appreciate how such disclosures reveal a lack of intellectual integrity, we only have to imagine how the U.S. government and citizenry would respond if another nation were to attempt to assassinate the president of the U.S or trained U.S. police or military in methods of torture. Once we imagine this, we recognize a basic inconsistency common in human behavior and a lack of intellectual integrity on the part of those who plan, engage in, or approve of, such activities.

All humans sometimes fail to act with intellectual integrity. When we do, we reveal a lack of fair-mindedness on our part, and a failure to think well enough as to grasp the internal contradictions in our thought or life.

Test the Idea:
Intellectual Integrity

Write about a dimension of your life that you suspect holds some inconsistencies or contradictions (where you probably are not holding yourself to the same standard to which you hold those whom you dislike or disagree with). Think of a situation where your behavior contradicts what you say you believe. This might be in your relationship with an employee, or a spouse, for example. Explain what inconsistencies may be present in your behavior.

Intellectual Perseverance:
Working Through Complexity and Frustration

Let us now consider intellectual perseverance:

> *Intellectual perseverance can be defined as the disposition to work one's way through intellectual complexities despite the frustration inherent in the task. Some intellectual problems are complex and cannot be easily solved. One has intellectual perseverance when one does not give up in the face of intellectual complexity or frustration. The intellectually perseverant person displays firm adherence to rational principles despite the irrational opposition of others, and has a realistic sense of the need to struggle with confusion and unsettled questions over an extended time to achieve understanding or insight.*

The opposite of intellectual perseverance is *intellectual laziness*, demonstrated in the tendency to give up quickly when faced with an intellectually challenging task. The intellectually indolent, or lazy, person has a low tolerance for intellectual pain or frustration.

How does a lack of intellectual perseverance impede fair-mindedness? Understanding the views of others requires that we do the intellectual work to achieve that understanding. That takes intellectual perseverance-insofar as those views are very different from ours or are complex in nature. For example, suppose you are a Christian wanting to be fair to the views of an atheist. Unless you read and understand the reasoning of intelligent and insightful atheists, you are not being fair to those views. Some intelligent and insightful atheists have written books to explain how and why they think as they do. Some of their reasoning is complicated or deals with issues of some complexity. It follows that only those Christians who have the intellectual perseverance to read and/or understand atheists can be fair to atheist views. Of course, a parallel case could be developed with respect to atheists' understanding the views of intelligent and insightful Christians.

Finally, it should be clear how intellectual perseverance is essential to all areas of higher-level thinking. Virtually all higher-level thinking requires some intellectual perseverance to overcome. It takes intellectual perseverance to reason well through complex questions on the job, to work through complex problems in intimate relationships, to solve problems in parenting. Many give up during early stages of working through a problem. Lacking intellectual perseverance, they cut themselves off from all the insights that thinking through an issue at a deep level provides. They avoid intellectual frustration, no doubt, but they end up with the everyday frustrations of not being able to solve complex problems.

Test the Idea:
Intellectual Perseverance

Most people have more physical perseverance than intellectual perseverance. Most are ready to admit, "No pain, no gain!" when talking about the body. Most give up quickly, on the other hand, when faced with a frustrating intellectual problem. Thinking of your own responses, in your work or your personal life, how would you evaluate your own intellectual perseverance (on a scale of 0–10)? Write out what you are basing your score on.

Confidence in Reason:
Recognizing that Good Reasoning Has Proven Its Worth

Let us now consider the trait of confidence in reason:

> *Confidence in reason is based on the belief that one's own higher interests and those of humankind will be best served by giving the freest play to reason. Reason encourages people to come to their own conclusions by developing their own rational faculties. It is the faith that, with proper encouragement and cultivation, people can learn to think for themselves. As such, they can form insightful viewpoints, draw reasonable conclusions, and develop clear, accurate, relevant, and logical thought processes., In turn, they can persuade each other by appealing to good reason and sound evidence, and become reasonable persons, despite the deep-seated obstacles in human nature and social life. When one has confidence in reason, one is "moved" by reason in appropriate ways. The very idea of reasonability becomes one of the most important values and a focal point in one's life. In short, to have confidence in reason is to use good reasoning as the fundamental criterion by which to judge whether to accept or reject any belief or position.*

The opposite of confidence in reason is *intellectual distrust of reason*, given by the threat that reasoning and rational analysis pose to the undisciplined thinker. Being prone toward emotional reactions that validate present thinking, egocentric thinkers often express little confidence in reason. They do not understand what it means to have faith in reason. Instead, they have confidence in the truth of their own belief systems, however flawed their beliefs might be.

In many ways we live in an irrational world surrounded by many forms of irrational beliefs and behaviors. For example, despite the success of science in providing plausible explanations based on careful study of evidence gathered through disciplined observations, many people still believe in unsubstantiated systems such as astrology. Many people, when faced with a problem, follow their "gut" impulses. Many follow leaders whose only claim to credibility is that they are skilled in manipulating a crowd and whipping up enthusiasm. Few people seem to recognize the power of sound thinking in helping us to solves our problems and live a fulfilling life. Few people, in short, have genuine confidence in reason. In the place of faith in reason, people tend to have uncritical or "blind" faith in one or more of the following (often as a result of irrational drives and emotions):

1. Faith in charismatic national leaders (think of leaders such as Hitler, able to excite millions of people and manipulate them into supporting genocide of an entire religious group).
2. Faith in charismatic cult leaders.
3. Faith in the father as the traditional head of the family (as defined by religious or social tradition).
4. Faith in institutional authorities (employers, "the company," police, social workers, judges, priests, evangelical preachers, and so forth).
5. Faith in spiritual powers (such as a "holy spirit," as defined by various religious belief systems).
6. Faith in some social group, official or unofficial (faith in a gang, in the business community, in a church, in a political party, and so on).
7. Faith in a political ideology (such as communism, capitalism, Fascism).
8. Faith in intuition.
9. Faith in one's unanalyzed emotions.
10. Faith in one's gut impulses.
11. Faith in fate (some unnamed force that supposedly guides the destiny of us all).
12. Faith in social institutions (the courts, schools, charities, business communities, governments).
13. Faith in the folkways or mores of a social group or culture.
14. Faith in one's own unanalyzed experience.
15. Faith in people who have social status or position (the rich, the famous, the powerful).

Some of the above are compatible, under some conditions, with faith in reason. The key factor is the extent to which some form of faith is based on sound reasoning and evidence. The acid test, then, is: Are there good grounds for having that faith? For example, it makes sense to have faith in a friend if that friend has consistently acted as a friend over an extended time. On the other hand, it does not make sense to have faith in a new acquaintance, even if one finds oneself emotionally attracted to that individual and that person professes his or her friendship.

As you examine and evaluate your own thinking on the nature of different kinds of faith, and the extent to which you have appropriate confidence in reason and evidence, ask yourself to what extent you can be moved by well-reasoned appeals. Suppose you meet someone who shows so much of an interest in your significant other that you feel intensely jealous and negative toward that person. Would you shift your view if you receive evidence by a dependable friend that the person you are negative about is actually exceptionally kind, thoughtful, and generous? Do you think you could shift your view, even when, deep down, you want your significant other to reject this person in favor of you? Have you ever given up a belief you held dear because, through your reading, experience, and reflection, you became persuaded that it was not reasonable to believe as you did? Are you ready and willing to admit that some of your most passionate beliefs (for example, your religious or political beliefs) may in fact be "wrong?"

Test the Idea: Faith in Reason

Think of a recent situation in which you felt yourself being defensive and you now realize that you were not able to listen to an argument that you did not agree with, though the argument had merit. In this situation, you apparently could not be moved by good reasons. Briefly write what happened in the situation. Then write the reasonable arguments against your position that you were not willing to listen to. Why weren't you able to give credit to the other person's argument? In answering this question, see if you can use the list of sources of faith that people usually rely on.

Intellectual Autonomy: Being an Independent Thinker

The final intellectual trait we will consider here is intellectual autonomy:

Intellectual autonomy may be defined as internal motivation based on the ideal of thinking for oneself; having rational self-authorship of one's beliefs, values, and way of thinking; not being dependent on others for the direction and control of one's thinking.

Autonomous persons are persons in charge of their lives. They are not irrationally dependent on others and not controlled by infantile emotions. They have self-control. They are competent. They complete what they begin. In forming beliefs, critical thinkers do not passively accept the beliefs of others. Rather, they think through situations and issues for themselves and reject unjustified authorities while recognizing the contributions of reasonable authority. They mindfully form principles of thought and action and do not mindlessly accept those presented to them. They are not limited by the accepted way of doing things. They evaluate the traditions and practices that others often accept unquestioningly. Independent thinkers strive to incorporate knowledge and insight into their thinking, independent of the social status of the source. They are not willful, stubborn, or unresponsive to the reasonable suggestions of others. They are self-monitoring thinkers who strive to amend their own mistakes. They function from values they themselves have freely chosen.

Of course, intellectual autonomy must be understood not as a thing-in-itself. Instead, we must recognize it as a dimension of our minds working in conjunction with, and tempered by, the other intellectual virtues.

The opposite of intellectual autonomy is *intellectual conformity*, or intellectual or emotional dependence. Intellectual autonomy is difficult to develop because social institutions, as they now stand, depend heavily on passive acceptance of the status quo, whether intellectual, political, or economic. Thinking for oneself almost certainly leads to unpopular conclusions not sanctioned by dominant groups. There are always many rewards for those who simply conform in thought and action to social pressure.

Consequently, the large masses of people are unknowing conformists in thought and deed. They are like mirrors reflecting the belief systems and values of those who surround them. They lack the intellectual skills and the incentive to think for themselves. They are intellectually conforming thinkers (Figure 3.3).

Even those who spend years getting a Ph.D. may be intellectually dependent, both academically and personally. They may uncritically accept faulty practices in the discipline as it stands, uncritically defending the discipline against legitimate critics. The result often is unwarranted human harm and suffering.

One cannot be fair-minded and lack intellectual autonomy, for independent thinking is a prerequisite to thinking within multiple perspectives. When we intellectually conform, we are only able to think within "accepted" viewpoints. But to be fair-minded is to refuse to uncritically accept beliefs without thinking through the merits (and demerits) of those beliefs for oneself.

Test the Idea: Intellectual Autonomy

Briefly review some of the variety of influences to which you have been exposed in your life (influence of culture, company, family, religion, peer groups, media, personal relationships). See if you can discriminate between those dimensions of your thought and behavior in which you have done the least thinking for yourself and those in which you have done the most. What makes this activity difficult is that we often perceive ourselves as thinking for ourselves when we are actually conforming to others. What you should look for, therefore, are instances of your actively questioning beliefs, values, or practices to which others in your "group" were, or are, conforming.

Recognizing the Interdependence of Intellectual Virtues

The traits of mind essential for critical thinking are interdependent. Consider intellectual humility. To become aware of the limits of our knowledge, we need the intellectual courage to face our own prejudices and ignorance. To discover our own prejudices, in turn, we often must intellectually empathize with and reason within points of view with which we fundamentally disagree. To achieve this end, we typically must engage in intellectual perseverance, as learning to empathically enter a point of view against which we are biased takes time and significant effort. That effort will not seem justified unless we have the necessary confidence in reason to believe we will not be tainted or "taken in" by whatever is false or misleading in the opposing viewpoint.

Furthermore, merely believing we won't be harmed considering "alien" viewpoints is not enough to motivate most of us to consider them seriously. We also must be motivated by an intellectual sense of justice. We must recognize an intellectual responsibility to be fair to views we oppose. We must feel obliged to hear them in their strongest form to ensure that we are not condemning them out of ignorance or bias on our part. At this point, we come full circle to where we began: the need for intellectual humility.

To begin at another point, consider intellectual integrity or good faith. Intellectual integrity is clearly a difficult trait to develop. We are often motivated—generally without admitting to or being aware of this motivation—to set up inconsistent standards in thinking. Our egocentric or sociocentric tendencies, for example, make us ready to believe positive information about those that we like and negative information about those that we dislike. We likewise are strongly inclined to believe what serves to justify our selfish interests or validate our strongest desires. Hence, all humans have some innate mental tendencies to operate with double standards, which is typical of intellectual bad faith. These modes of thinking sometimes correlate well with getting ahead in the world, maximizing our power or advantage, and getting more of what we selfishly want.

Nevertheless, it is difficult to operate explicitly or overtly with a double standard. We therefore need to avoid looking at the evidence too closely. We need to avoid scrutinizing our own inferences and interpretations too carefully. At this point, a certain amount of intellectual arrogance is quite useful. I may assume, for example, that I know just what you're going to say (before you say it), precisely what you are really after (before the evidence demonstrates it), and what actually is going on (before I have studied the situation carefully). My intellectual arrogance makes it easier for me to avoid noticing the unjustifiable discrepancy between the standards I apply to you and the standards I apply to myself. Not having to empathize with you makes it easier to avoid seeing my self-deception. I also am better positioned if I lack a need to be fair to your point of view. A little background fear of what I might discover if I seriously consider the inconsistency of my own judgments can be quite useful as well. In this case, my lack of intellectual integrity is supported by my lack of intellectual humility, empathy, and fair-mindedness.

Going in the other direction, it will be difficult to use a double standard if I feel a responsibility to be fair to your point of view. This responsibility requires me to empathetically view things from your perspective, and to do so with some humility, recognizing that I could be wrong, and that you could be right. The more I dislike you personally, or feel wronged in the past by you or by others who share your way of thinking, the more pronounced in my character the trait of intellectual integrity and good faith must be to compel me to be fair.

We can begin to analyze the extent to which we have developed these interdependent traits of mind by focusing on our reactions to situations in the workplace. Imagine, for example, that your company decides to reorganize your division and some people lose their jobs. To what extent are you able to *intellectually empathize*, not only with your colleagues who lost their jobs, but also with the managers who made the decision? To what extent do you see *intellectual humility* operating in your thinking, so that you recognize what you do know and what you do not know about the situation? To what extent are you able to *think autonomously* so that you are not trapped in the group's reaction to the situation? To what extent is your thinking driven by an *intellectual sense of justice* to all parties involved? To what extent are you able to *think with integrity* so that you apply the same standards to all parties involved in the situation?

Conclusion

True excellence in thinking is not simply the result of isolated intellectual skills. There are inevitable problems in the thinking of persons who, without knowing it, lack intellectual virtues. Instead, they frequently display the traits of the undisciplined mind. To the extent one is unconsciously motivated to believe what one wants to believe, what is most comfortable to believe, what puts one in a good light, what serves one's selfish interest, one is unable to function as a rational person. As you work through this book, we hope you find yourself internalizing the essential traits. We hope you will resist the influence of both the conformist thinkers around you and the egocentric thinker within you. We hope you will recognize that skilled thinking can be used for good or for ill. We hope you will see that it is the intellectual virtues that guide thinking toward fair-mindedness. Such virtues enable us to enter, in good faith, all viewpoints relevant to a complex issue before coming to final conclusions, to seek out weaknesses in our thinking, to be moved by reasoning that is superior to our own. When possible we have the advantage in seeing all sides and are able to work with them, supporting in each what we see as sound and respectfully disagreeing with that which we see as flawed.

Natural versus Critical Thinking

- As humans we think; as critical thinkers we analyze our thinking.

- As humans we think egocentrically; as critical thinkers we expose the egocentric roots of our thinking to close scrutiny.

- As humans we are drawn to standards of thinking unworthy of belief; as critical thinkers we expose inappropriate standards and replace them with sound ones.

- As humans we live in systems of meanings that typically entrap us; as critical thinkers we learn how to raise our thinking to conscious examination, enabling us to free ourselves from many of the traps of undisciplined, instinctive thought.

- As humans we use logical systems whose root structures are not apparent to us; as critical thinkers we develop tools for explicating and assessing our participation in the logical systems in which we live.

- As humans we live with the illusion of intellectual and emotion freedom; as critical thinkers we take explicit intellectual and emotional command of who we are, what we are, and the ends to which our lives are tending.

- As human thinkers we are governed by our thoughts; as critical thinkers we learn how to govern the thoughts that govern us.

Chapter 4

Self-Understanding

T he preceding chapters emphasized that:

- Critical thinking requires the development of basic intellectual skills, abilities, and insights;
- Becoming a skilled thinker is like becoming skilled in basketball, ballet, or saxophone playing;
- These skills can be used to serve two incompatible ends: self-centeredness or fair-mindedness;
- The skills of critical thinking can be learned in a "weak" sense (selfish thinking);
- We are focused on the development of critical thinking in a "strong" sense (i.e., serving fair-minded thinking);
- Fair-mindedness requires that we develop a network of interrelated traits of mind;
- Developing as a thinker is challenging, requiring internal motivation.

Our goal in this chapter is to lay a foundation for understanding better how the human mind works. We will begin by taking a further look at human egocentrism and the obstacle it represents. We then will take a look at some of the most basic distinctions we can use to achieve greater self-command.

Our latent egocentrism asserts itself through each of the basic functions of the mind. We must understand those functions, as they work in relationship to each other.

Only through our practical insight into how our mind operates can we hope to understand, and transform, ourselves.

Monitoring the Egocentrism in Your Thought and Life

One of the fundamental challenges most humans face in developing is that our life is dominated by a tendency to think and feel egocentrically. Our life is deeply situated in our own immediate desires, pains, thoughts, and feelings. We seek immediate gratification or long-term gratification based on an essentially selfish perspective. We are not typically or fundamentally concerned with whether our perceptions or meanings are accurate, though we may think we are. We are not significantly concerned with personal growth, self-insight, or ultimate integrity, though we think we are. We are not deeply motivated to discover our own weaknesses, prejudices, or self-deception. Rather, we seek to get what we want, avoid the disapproval of others, and justify ourselves in our own mind.

The tendency for humans to think in an egocentric fashion means that, typically, we have little or no real insight into the nature of our own thinking and emotions. For example, many of us unconsciously believe that it is possible to acquire knowledge without much thought, that it is possible to read without exerting intellectual energy, and that good writing is a talent one is born with—not a product of practice and hard work. As a result, we tend to evade responsibility for our own development. We do not seek to learn new ways of looking at things. Much of our thinking is stereotypical and simplistic, yet our egocentrism prevents us from recognizing this. We create the inner chains that enslave us.

These inner chains can have a negative effect on our relationships, success, growth, and happiness. It is not possible to get beyond the egocentrism that you and I inherit as human beings by ignoring our ego or pretending that we are decent people. We can restrain our egocentrism only by developing explicit habits that enable us to do so. We get beyond egocentric emotional responses not by denying that we ever respond in such a way but, rather, by owning these responses when they occur and restructuring the thinking that is feeding those emotions.

For example, each of us wants to see ourselves as an ethical person. Yet, through our egocentrism we often behave in ways that are blatantly unethical. Industries, for example, often engage in systematic practices that result in large amounts of pollutants in the environment. Yet if asked to explain their behavior, they will instead justify it through rationalization. They will make comments such as "We meet and exceed all of the federal regulations for pollution control, and in fact we do more than most companies to ensure that we don't pollute." Yet these companies are often hiding behind the concept of "federal regulations." They are not essentially concerned with the ethical or unethical nature of their behavior. Rather they are concerned simply with *following the regulations.* In cases such as these, industry leaders are unconcerned with whether they are actually polluting. They may not even know whether they are causing damage to the environment. And very often they do not want to know. Through their egocentrism they are able to avoid self-scrutiny. They are able to go on engaging in practices that will yield the highest monetary gain, without reference to the impact of the behavior on the environment.

We will return to the problem of dealing with egocentrism later. But you should begin to think about what egocentrism is and to monitor your thinking for evidence of it.

Test the Idea: Beginning to Understand Egocentrism

Think of the most self-centered person you know. This may be someone who is fundamentally selfish or arrogant. Describe the person's behavior in detail. Based on the person's behavior, how would you describe his/ her thinking? What types of feelings does he/she seem to display? What is the person motivated to do? To what extent does the person use other people to get what he/she wants? To what extent does the person exhibit sincere concern for the thoughts and feelings of others?

Making a Commitment to Fair-Mindedness

Though no one defines himself or herself as an egocentric person, each of us should recognize that being egocentric is an important part of what we have to understand in dealing with the structure of our mind. One of the ways to begin to confront our own egocentrism is by exploring the extent to which we have allowed our identity to be egocentrically shaped. For example, as we previously emphasized, we are all born into a culture, a nation, and a family. Our parents inculcate into us particular beliefs (about the family, personal relationships, marriage, childhood, obedience, religion, politics, schooling, and so on). We form associations with people who have certain beliefs (which they have encouraged, or expected, us to accept). We are, in the first instance, a product of these influences. Only through self-understanding can we begin to be more than a product of influences.

If we uncritically believe what we were taught to believe, these beliefs are likely to become part of our egocentric identity. When they do, it affects the manner in which we believe. For example, we are all egocentric to the extent that an examination of our attitudes reveals that we unconsciously use egocentric standards to justify our beliefs:

1. "It's true because I believe it." People don't say this aloud, but we often find ourselves assuming that others are correct when they agree with us and incorrect when they do not. The way we respond to people indicates that we egocentrically assume we have a unique insight into the truth.

2. "It's true because we believe it." Our behavior indicates that we egocentrically assume that the groups to which we belong have a unique insight into the truth. Our religion, our company, our country, our friends are special—and better.

3. "It's true because I want to believe it." Our behavior indicates that we more readily believe what coincides with what we egocentrically want to believe, even to the point of absurdity.

4. "It's true because I have always believed it." Our behavior indicates that we more readily believe what coincides with beliefs we have long held. We egocentrically assume the rightness of our early beliefs.

5. "It's true because it is in my selfish interest to believe it." Our behavior indicates that we more readily believe what coincides with beliefs that, when held, serve to advance our wealth, power, or position, even if they conflict with the ethical principles that we insist we hold.

If we consciously recognize these tendencies in ourselves and deliberately and systematically seek to overcome them by thinking fair-mindedly, our definition of ourselves can aid our development as thinkers. We then begin to divide our thoughts into two categories: 1) thoughts that serve to advance the agenda of our egocentric nature, and 2) thoughts that serve to develop our rational fair-mindedness. To effectively do this, we need to develop a special relationship to our mind; we must become a student of our mind's operations, especially of its pathology.

Recognizing the Mind's Three Distinctive Functions

The mind has three basic functions—thinking, feeling, and wanting (Figures 4.1 & 4.2).

1. The function of *thinking* is to create meaning. Thinking makes sense of the events of our lives; it sorts events into named categories and finds patterns for us. It continually tells us: This is what is going on. This is what is happening. Notice this and that. This is how it makes sense to understand the situation. It is the part of the mind that figures things out.

2. The function of *feeling* is to monitor or evaluate the meanings created by the thinking function—evaluating how positive and negative the events of our life are, given the meaning we are ascribing to them. It continually tells us: This is how you should feel about what is happening in your life. You're doing really well. Or, alternatively, watch out—you are getting into trouble!

3. The function of *wanting* allocates energy to action, in keeping with our definitions of what is desirable and possible. It continually tells us: This is what is worth getting. Go for it! Or, conversely, it tells: This is not worth getting. Don't bother.

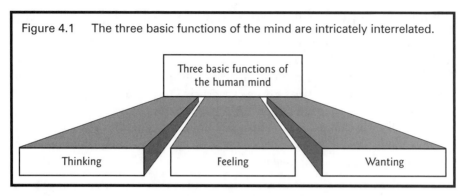

Figure 4.1   The three basic functions of the mind are intricately interrelated.

Looked at this way, our mind is continually communicating three kinds of things to us: 1) what is going on in our life; 2) feelings (positive or negative) about those events; and 3) things to pursue, where to put our energy (in the light of 1 and 2).

What is more, there is an intimate, dynamic interrelation between thinking, feeling, and wanting (Figure 4.3). Each is continually influencing the other two. When, for example, we think we are being threatened, we feel fear, and we inevitably want to flee from or attack whatever we think is threatening us. When we think that attending a meeting will be a waste of time, we will want to avoid attending it and will feel bored if compelled to attend.

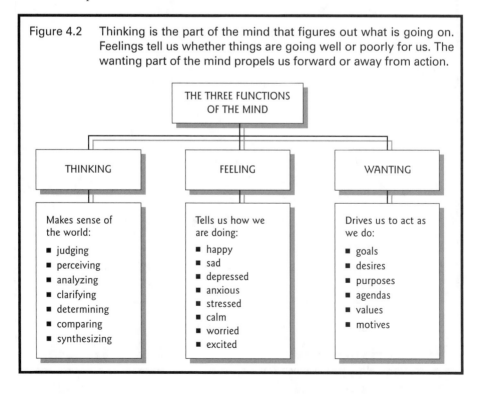

Figure 4.2   Thinking is the part of the mind that figures out what is going on. Feelings tell us whether things are going well or poorly for us. The wanting part of the mind propels us forward or away from action.

Understanding That You Have a Special Relationship to Your Mind

It should now be clear that everyone lives in a special and intimate relationship to his or her mind—at least unconsciously. The trick is to make that unconscious relationship conscious and deliberate. All of our activity is a product of inward ideas of who and what we are, ideas of what we are experiencing (from moment to moment), of where we are going (our future), of where we have come from (our past). And, in addition, all of these ideas are in a state of continual interplay with our emotions and feelings about them. Emotions and feelings function as ongoing evaluators of the quality of our lives and circumstances.

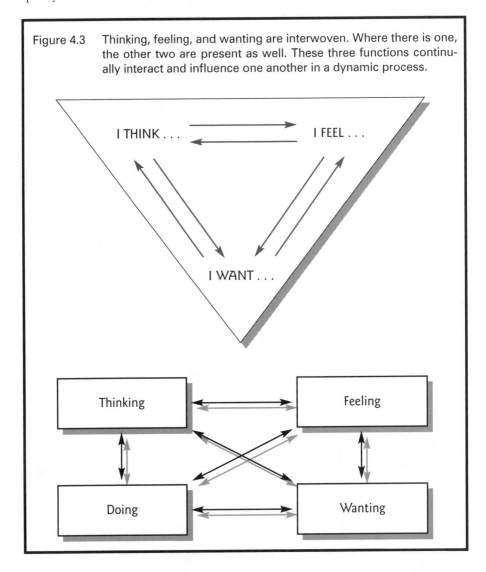

Figure 4.3 Thinking, feeling, and wanting are interwoven. Where there is one, the other two are present as well. These three functions continually interact and influence one another in a dynamic process.

For every positive thought the mind "believes," the mind naturally tends to generate a positive emotion to fit it. Conversely, for every negative thought, the mind tends to generate a negative emotion. If we explicitly recognize the continual interrelationships among these three functions of our mind, we will gain a central insight that we can begin to use to our advantage. Then we can begin to exercise command over our own mind's functions. Let's look into this idea more closely.

We experience joy, happiness, frustration, pain, confusion, desire, passion, and indifference because we give a meaning to every situation we experience, because we think about it in a particular fashion, and because we connect it to feelings we experienced in what we perceived as similar or related circumstances. The meaning we create can be grounded in insight, objective reality, a fantasy, or even a dysfunctional interpretation of reality. For example, two people in the same situation may react completely differently, with one person experiencing pain and frustration while the other experiences curiosity and excitement.

Consider two employees faced with the task of improving office procedures in order to improve productivity. The first experiences resentment at being required to change what appears to be "working just fine." This person gives a negative meaning to the task of improvement, considering it unnecessary and time consuming (when so many other things are more important). Given the negative thinking this person is engaging in, s/he will feel negative emotions about the task.

In the same situation, another person might welcome the opportunity for improvement. Defining the situation as a chance to be creative and to think independently about ways to improve procedures, she/he looks forward to the task. Positive, rather than negative, emotions result from such a definition.

The actual task at hand is precisely the same. Nevertheless, the difficulty or ease with which a person handles the challenge, the decision to take up the challenge or avoid it altogether, ultimate success or failure, is determined fundamentally by the manner in which the situation is interpreted through one's thinking (Figure 4.4). Different emotions follow from these differences in thought and action.

When we understand the interrelated roles of thoughts, feelings, and motivation, when we can see that for every feeling state we experience, a related thought process exists that motivates us to some action, we can begin to analyze thoughts underlying our emotions and desires. If I am frustrated in a meeting, I can ask myself: What is the thinking in my mind that is leading to this feeling of frustration? What exactly am I frustrated with? What is the thinking that leads me to be frustrated (Figure 4.5 & 4.6)?

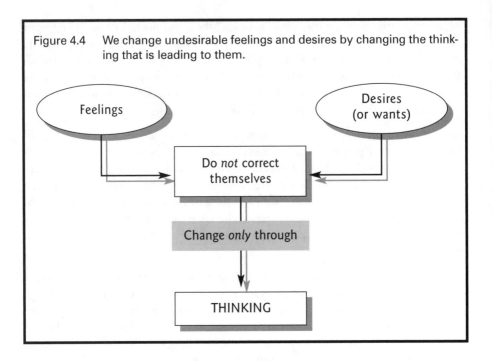

Figure 4.4   We change undesirable feelings and desires by changing the think-
              ing that is leading to them.

**Test the Idea: Understanding the Relationship Between the
Three Functions of the Mind**

Think of a situation you were in recently where you experienced a
negative emotion such as anger, frustration, depression, insecurity, or
fear:

1. Write out in detail what was going on in the situation and how you
   felt in the situation.

2. Now try to figure out the thinking you were doing in the circumstance
   that led to the negative feeling. Write out the thinking in detail.

3. Then write how your thinking and feeling impacted your behavior. (In
   other words, given the thinking and feeling, what were you motivated to do?)

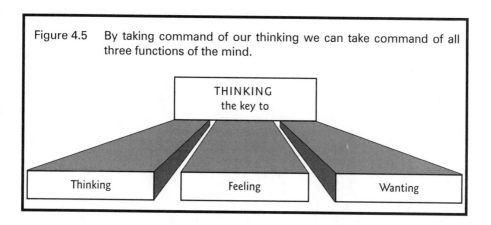

Figure 4.5   By taking command of our thinking we can take command of all three functions of the mind.

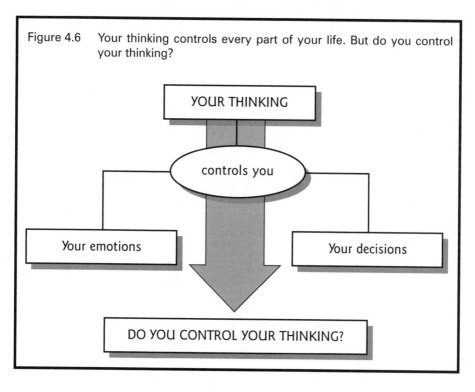

Figure 4.6   Your thinking controls every part of your life. But do you control your thinking?

Chapter 5

The First Four Stages of Development: What Level Thinker Are You?

M ost of us are not what we could be. We are less. We have great capacity, but most of it is dormant and undeveloped. Improvement in thinking is like improvement in basketball, ballet, or playing the saxophone. It is unlikely to take place in the absence of a conscious commitment to learn. As long as we take our thinking for granted, we don't do the work required for improvement.

Development in thinking is a gradual process requiring plateaus of learning and just plain hard work. It is not possible to become an excellent thinker by simply taking a beginning course. Changing one's habits of thought is a long-range project, happening over years, not weeks or months. The essential traits of a critical thinker, which we examined briefly in Chapter 3, require an extended period of development.

Here are the stages we go through if we aspire to develop as thinkers (Figure 5.1):

Stage 1   The Unreflective Thinker (we are unaware of significant problems in our thinking)

Stage 2   The Challenged Thinker (we become aware of problems in our thinking)

Stage 3   The Beginning Thinker (we try to improve, but without regular practice)

Stage 4   The Practicing Thinker (we recognize the necessity of regular practice)

Stage 5   The Advanced Thinker (we advance in accordance with our practice)

Stage 6   The Master Thinker (skilled and insightful thinking becomes second nature)

In this chapter, we will explain the first four stages with the hope that understanding these stages, even at a provisional level, will help you begin to grasp what is necessary in order to develop as a thinker. Only through years of advanced practice can one become an "advanced" or "master" thinker.

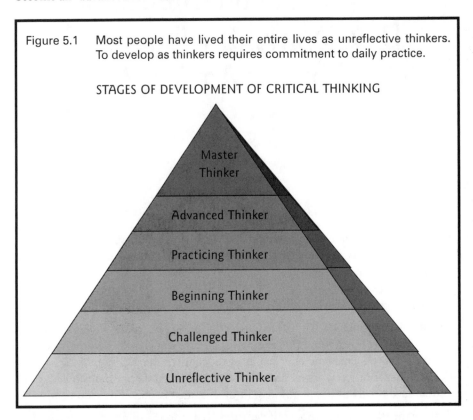

Figure 5.1   Most people have lived their entire lives as unreflective thinkers. To develop as thinkers requires commitment to daily practice.

STAGES OF DEVELOPMENT OF CRITICAL THINKING

Master Thinker

Advanced Thinker

Practicing Thinker

Beginning Thinker

Challenged Thinker

Unreflective Thinker

Stage One: The Unreflective Thinker— Are You an Unreflective Thinker?

We all are born as unreflective thinkers, fundamentally unaware of the role that thinking is playing in our lives. Most of us also die this way. At this unreflective stage, we have no useful conception of what thinking entails. For example, as unreflective thinkers we don't notice that we are continually making assumptions, forming concepts, drawing inferences, and thinking within points of view. At this stage, we don't know how to analyze and assess our thinking. We don't know how to determine whether our purposes are clearly formulated, our assumptions justified, or our conclusions logically drawn. We are unaware of intellectual traits and so are not striving to embody them.

At this stage poor thinking causes many problems in our lives, but we are unaware of this. We think of our beliefs as truth. We think of our decisions as sound. We lack intellectual standards and have no idea what such standards might be. We lack intellectual traits, but are not aware that we lack them. We unconsciously deceive ourselves in many ways. We create and maintain pleasant illusions. Our beliefs feel reasonable to us, and so we believe them with confidence. We walk about the world with confidence that things really are the way they appear to us. We judge some people to be "good" and some to be "bad." We approve of some actions. We disapprove of others. We make decisions, react to people, go our way in life, and do not seriously question the thinking we do or its implications.

At this stage, our egocentric tendencies play a dominant role in our thinking, yet we do not recognize this. We lack the skills and the motivation to notice how self-centered and prejudiced we are, how often we stereotype others, how frequently we irrationally dismiss ideas because we don't want to change our behavior or our comfortable way of looking at things.

Test the Idea
Reflecting on Your Knowledge of Thinking

Are you at the unreflective stage of development? Test yourself by writing your answers to the following:

1. Can you describe the role that thinking is playing in your life? (Be as clear and as detailed as you can.)
2. What was a recent assumption you made (that you should not have made)?
3. What is a recent concept you formed (that you previously lacked)?
4. List five inferences you made in the last hour.
5. Name and explain a point of view that you sometimes use to guide your thinking.
6. Briefly describe how you analyze and assess thinking.
7. Name some intellectual standards you use. Explain how you apply them.
8. Explain the role of egocentric thinking in your life.
9. Take one or two intellectual traits and explain what you are doing to try to embody them.

If you have trouble answering these questions, you may well be at the unreflective stage in your development as a thinker. If you are, you do not need to apologize for it or feel badly about it. Most people are at this stage and don't know it. Traditional schooling and the way people are typically reared do not help them become skilled thinkers. Often, parents and teachers themselves are unreflective thinkers. This is the product of a vicious circle. Unreflective persons raise unreflective persons. Once you recognize explicitly that you are at this stage, however, you are ready to move to the next stage. And when you move to the next stage, you may be close to breaking out of the vicious circle of unreflectiveness. This requires that we become honestly reflective—that we begin to notice some problems in our thinking, that we begin to recognize that our thinking is often egocentric and irrational, that changes in our own thinking are essential.

Honest reflectiveness leads to a healthy motivation to change. It is functional and productive. You must not only see problems in your thinking but also have some sense of how those problems might be addressed. You must become reasonably articulate about what you have to do to improve. Motivation is crucial. Without a drive to change, nothing of much significance will happen.

Stage Two: The Challenged Thinker—Are You Ready to Accept the Challenge?

We cannot solve a problem we do not own. We cannot deal with a condition we deny. Without knowledge of our ignorance, we cannot seek the knowledge we lack. Without knowledge of the skills we need to develop, we will not develop those skills.

As we begin to become aware that "normal" thinkers often think poorly, we move into the second stage of critical thinking development. We begin to notice that we often:

- Make questionable assumptions;
- Use false, incomplete, or misleading information;
- Make inferences that do not follow from the evidence we have;
- Fail to recognize important implications in our thought;
- Fail to recognize problems we have;
- Form faulty concepts;
- Reason within prejudiced points of view; and
- Think egocentrically and irrationally.

We move to the "challenged" stage when we become aware of the way our thinking is shaping our lives, including the recognition that problems in our thinking are causing problems in our lives. We are beginning to recognize that poor thinking can be life-threatening, that it can lead literally to death or permanent injury, that it can hurt others as well as ourselves. For example, we might reflect upon the thinking of:

- The person who is a perpetual procrastinator;
- The irrational manager who can't understand why his employees "don't get it;"
- The person who is angry at the world in general;

- The teenager who thinks that smoking is cool;
- The woman who thinks that Pap smears are not important;
- The motorcyclist who reasons that helmets obstruct vision and, therefore, it is safer to ride without one;
- The person who thinks he can drive safely while drunk;
- The person who decides to marry a self-centered person with the thought that he or she will "change" after marriage.

We also recognize the difficulty involved in "improving" our thinking. If you are at this stage in your own thinking, you recognize that the problem of changing your habits of thought is an important challenge requiring extensive and difficult changes in your normal routines.

Some signs of emerging reflectiveness are that:

- You find yourself striving to analyze and assess your thinking;
- You find yourself working with the structures of mind that create, or make possible, thinking (for example: concepts, assumptions, inferences, implications, points of view);
- You find yourself thinking about the qualities that make thinking sound—clarity, accuracy, precision, relevance, logicalness—though you may have only an initial grasp of how these qualities can be achieved;
- You find yourself becoming interested in the role of self-deception in thinking, though your understanding is relatively "abstract" and you may not be able to give many examples from your own life.

At this point in your development, there is a distinct danger of self-deception. Many resist accepting the true nature of the challenge—that their own thinking is a real and significant problem in their life. If you do as many do, you will revert to the unreflective stage. Your experience of thinking about your thinking will fade. Your usual habits of thought will remain as they are. For example, you may find yourself rationalizing in the following way:

> My thinking is not that bad. Actually I've been thinking well for quite a while. I question a lot of things. I'm not prejudiced. Besides that, I'm very critical. And I'm not near as self-deceived as lots of people I know.

If you reason in this way, you will not be alone. You will join the majority. The view—"if everyone were to think like me, this would be a fine world"—is the dominant view. Those who share this view range from the poorly schooled to the highly schooled. There is no evidence to suggest that schooling correlates with human reflectiveness. Indeed, many college graduates are intellectually arrogant as a result of their schooling. There are unreflective thinkers who did not go beyond elementary school, but there are also ones who have done post-graduate work and now have advanced degrees; unreflective people are found in the upper, middle, and lower class. They include psychologists, sociologists, philosophers, mathematicians, doctors, senators, judges, governors, district attorneys, lawyers, and indeed people of all professions.

In short, absence of intellectual humility is common among all classes of people, in all walks of life and at all ages. It follows that active or passive resistance to the challenge of critical thinking is the common, not the rare case. Whether in the form of a careless shrug or outright hostility, most people reject the challenge of critical thinking. That is why some soul-searching is important at this point in the process.

Test the Idea
Begin to Challenge Your Thinking
Make a list of areas of your life where you clearly recognize that your thinking is problematic. Be as detailed as possible. By doing so you are beginning to challenge your thinking. Beware of the native egocentric tendency to convince one's self that there are no problems with one's thinking. Think of it this way, the more problems in your thinking you can discover, the more likely you will be to take up the challenge to improve your thinking.

Stage Three: The Beginning Thinker—
Are You Willing to Begin?

When a person actively decides to take up the challenge to grow and develop as a thinker, that person enters the stage we call "beginning thinker." This is the stage of thinking in which one begins to take thinking seriously. This is a preparatory stage before one gains explicit command of thinking. It is a stage of dawning realizations. It is a stage of developing willpower. It is not a stage of self-condemnation but, rather, of emerging consciousness. It is analogous to the stage in which an alcoholic person recognizes and fully accepts the fact that he or she is an alcoholic. Imagine an alcoholic saying, "I am an alcoholic, and only I can do something about it." Now imagine yourself saying, "I am a weak, undisciplined thinker, and only I can do something about it."

Once people recognize that they are "addicted" to poor thinking, they must begin to recognize the depth and nature of the problem. As beginning thinkers, we should recognize that our thinking is sometimes egocentric. For example, we may notice how little we consider the needs of others and how much we focus on getting what we personally want. We may notice how little we enter the point of view of others and how much we assume the "correctness" of our own. We may even sometimes catch ourselves trying to dominate others to get what we want, or alternatively, acting out the role of submitting to others (for the gains that submissive behavior brings). We may begin to notice the extent to which we are conformists in our thinking.

As thinkers thinking about thinking, we are merely beginning to:

- Analyze the logic of situations and problems;

- Express clear and precise questions;

- Check information for accuracy and relevance;

- Distinguish between raw information and someone's interpretation of it;

- Recognize assumptions guiding inferences;

- Identify prejudicial and biased beliefs, unjustifiable conclusions, misused words, and missed implications;

- Notice when our selfish interests bias our viewpoint.

Thus, as beginning thinkers we are becoming aware of how to deal with the structures at work in thinking (purposes, questions, information, interpretations, etc.). We are beginning to appreciate the value of thinking about our thinking in terms of its clarity, accuracy, relevance, precision, logicalness, justifiability, breadth, and depth. But we are still at a low level of proficiency in these activities. They feel awkward to us. We have to force ourselves to think in disciplined ways. We are like a beginner in ballet. We feel foolish adopting the basic positions. We don't feel graceful. We stumble and make mistakes. No one would pay money to watch us perform. We ourselves don't like what we see in the mirror of our minds.

To reach this beginning stage in thinking, our values must begin to shift. We must begin to explore the foundation of our thinking and discover how we have come to think and believe as we do. Let us consider this goal in a little more detail. Reflect now on some of the major influences that shaped your thinking (and ours):

- You were born into a culture (European, American, African, Asian).

- You were born at some point in time (in some century in some year).

- You were born in some place (in the country, in the city, in the North or South, East or West).

- You were raised by parents with particular beliefs (about the family, about personal relationships, about marriage, about childhood, about obedience, about religion, about politics, about schooling).

- You formed various associations (largely based on who was around you— associations with people with a viewpoint, values, and taboos).

If you were to change any one of these influences, your belief system would be different. Suppose you had been born in the Middle Ages as a serf in the fields in France. Can you see that if you had, virtually all of your beliefs would be altered? See if you can perform similar reflective experiments of your own. For example, imagine other changes in these influences and then imaginatively compare some of the beliefs you likely would have with the beliefs you actually do have. You will begin to appreciate how much you, and every other human, are a product of influences over which you, and they, had little or no control. Neither you nor we directed these influences upon us. Their effects, clearly, were both good and bad.

If, for example, we assume that many of these influences engendered false beliefs in us, it follows that in our minds right now there are false beliefs and we are acting on them. Yet, notice that the mind has no mechanism for screening out false beliefs. We all carry around in our minds prejudices from our culture, prejudices from where we were born and raised, prejudices from our parents, and prejudices from our friends and associates. Finding ways to locate those flawed beliefs and replace them with more reasonable ones is part of the agenda of critical thinking.

Another way to look at the forces, rational and irrational that shaped our minds is in terms of "modes of influence."

For example, we think within a variety of domains: sociological, philosophical, ethical, intellectual, anthropological, ideological, political, economical, historical, biological, theological, and psychological. We ended up with our particular beliefs because we were influenced to do so in the following ways:

- Vocational: our minds are influenced by our work environment;
- Sociological: our minds are influenced by the social groups to which we belong;
- Philosophical: our minds are influenced by our personal philosophy;
- Ethical: our minds are influenced by the extent to which we behave in accordance with our obligations and the way we define our obligations;
- Intellectual: our minds are influenced by the ideas we hold, by the manner in which we reason and deal with abstractions and abstract systems;
- Anthropological: our minds are influenced by cultural practices, mores, and taboos;
- Ideological and political: our minds are influenced by the structure of power and its use by interest groups around us;
- Economic: our minds are influenced by the economic conditions under which we live;
- Historical: our minds are influenced by our history and by the way we tell our history;
- Biological: our minds are influenced by our biology and neurology;

- Theological: our minds are influenced by our religious beliefs and attitudes;

- Psychological: our minds are influenced by our personality and personal psychology;

- Physiological: our minds are influenced by our physical condition, stature, and weight.

Reflections such as these should awaken in us a sense of how little we really know about our own minds. Our minds are largely unexplored worlds, inner worlds that have been taking shape for the whole of our lives. This inner world is the most important fact about us, for it is where we live. It determines our joy and frustration. It limits what we can see and imagine. It highlights what we do see. It can drive us crazy. It can provide us with solace, peace, and tranquility. If we can appreciate these facts about us, we will find the motivation to take charge of our thinking, to be something more than clay in the hands of others, to become, in fact, the ruling force in our own lives.

Test the Idea
Move to the Beginning Thinker Stage

Try to figure out the extent to which, and in what ways, your thinking has been influenced by the following factors:

1. Your culture
2. Your family
3. Your personal history
4. Your colleagues
5. Your supervisors

As you do so, try to imagine how your thinking might be different if you had been born in a different culture with different influences than those you have had in your life. Obviously you cannot know precisely how you would differ, but the idea is to step outside yourself and imagine that if the above factors were different for you, your thinking would differ accordingly.

Let's now consider two lurking traps that can derail the beginning thinker:

Trap #1, the temptation of dogmatic absolutism—believing that truth is acquired not through reasoning and inquiry but, rather, through some predetermined nonintellectual faith.

Trap #2, the temptation of subjective relativism—believing that there are no intellectual standards by which to judge anything as true or false.

Both traps promise easy answers. To advance as a beginning thinker and not fall into one or the other of these traps requires developing confidence in reason as a way of acquiring sound knowledge and insight. These two pathologies are mirror images of each other. If we become either a subjective relativist or a dogmatic absolutist, we will lose our motivation to develop as a critical thinker. As a subjective relativist, we will come to believe that everyone automatically acquires "their own truth" in some inexplicable subjective way. As a dogmatic absolutist, we end up following wherever our "faith" leads us. In both cases, there is no real place for the intellectual work and discipline of critical thinking. Both render it superfluous. Both free us from any intellectual responsibility.

If we avoid these traps, if we recognize how we have been shaped by forces beyond our control, if we discover that there are skills that can help us begin to take charge of our minds, if we develop some initial confidence in reason, if we develop some intellectual humility and perseverance, we are ready to begin creating a genuine foundation on which we can rebuild our identity and character as thinkers and persons of integrity.

The key question is how? How exactly can we do this? We shall focus on this question to the end of this chapter. In a sense, it is the most vital goal of the whole book.

Stage Four: The Practicing Thinker—
Good Thinking Can Be Practiced Like Basketball, Tennis, or Ballet

Are you committed to regular practice? When people explicitly recognize that improvement in thinking requires regular practice, and adopt some regimen of practice, then, and only then, have they become what we call "practicing thinkers."

There is no one way to go about this process of designing a regimen of practice. There are many potential ways, some better, and some worse for you. For example, you might thumb through some of the other chapters of this book. Each provides some suggestions for improving your thinking. You can use any of these suggestions as a starting point.

You might review the "Test the Idea" activities. You might study the elements of thought, the standards for thought, and the traits of mind. You might analyze Chapter 9, on making intelligent decisions, and Chapters 15 and 16, on strategic thinking. Think of it this way: Everything you read in this book represents a resource for you to use in devising a systematic plan for improving your thinking. It's a good idea to read it with this orientation.

If you are like most people, you can discover some practical starting points. The problem will be in following through on any that you find. This is the problem in most areas of skill development: People do not usually follow through. They do not establish habits of regular practice. They are discouraged by the strain and awkwardness of early attempts to perform well.

You need to make decisions regarding a plan you think is do-able for you. This means a plan you can live with, one that will not burn you out or overwhelm you. Ultimately, success comes to those who are persistent and who figure out strategies for themselves.

Still, at this stage you probably don't know for sure what will work for you, only what seems like it might. You have to field-test your ideas. To be realistic, you should expect to experiment with a variety of plans before you find one that works well for you.

What you should guard against is discouragement. You can best avoid discouragement by recognizing from the outset that you are engaged in the field-testing of plans. You should prepare yourself for temporary failure. Success is to be understood as the willingness to work your way through a variety of relative failures. The logic is analogous to trying on clothes. Many that you try may not fit or look good on you, but you plod on anyway with the confidence that eventually you will find something that fits and looks good on you.

Consider another analogy. If you want to become skilled at tennis, you improve not by expecting yourself to begin as an expert player. You improve not by expecting to win every game you play or by mastering new strokes with little practice. Rather, you improve when you develop a plan that you can modify as you see what improves your "game." Today you may decide to work on keeping your eye on the ball. Tomorrow you may coordinate watching the ball with following through as you swing. Every day you rethink your strategies for improvement. Development of the human mind is quite parallel to the development of the human body. Good theory, good practice, and good feedback are essential.

A "Game Plan" for Improvement

As you begin to take your thinking seriously, you need to think about what you can do consistently every day to improve your thinking. Because excellence in thinking requires a variety of independent skills and traits that work together, you can choose to work on a range of critical thinking skills at any given point in time. The key is in focusing on fundamentals and on making sure that you don't try to do too much. Choose your point of attack, but limit it. If you overdo it, you will probably give up entirely. But if you don't focus on fundamentals, you will never have them as a foundation in your thought.

Start slowly, and emphasize fundamentals. The race is to the tortoise, not the hare. Be a good and wise tortoise. The solid, steady steps you take every day are what determine where you ultimately end up.

A Game Plan for Devising a Game Plan

There is nothing magical about the ideas we have put together to stimulate your thought about a game plan. No one of them is essential. Nevertheless, each represents a plausible point of attack, one way to begin to do something plausible to improve thinking in a regular way. Though you probably can't do all of these at the same time, we recommend an approach in which you experiment with all of these. You can add any others you find in this book or come up with yourself. We will explain how this works after you familiarize yourself with some of the options.

1. Use "wasted" time. All humans waste some time. We all fail to use all of our time productively or even pleasurably. Sometimes we jump from one diversion to another without enjoying any of them. Sometimes we make ourselves irritated about matters beyond our control. Sometimes we fail to plan well, causing us negative consequences that we easily could have avoided (for example, we spend time unnecessarily trapped in traffic—though we could have left a half hour earlier and avoided the rush). Sometimes we worry unproductively. Sometimes we spend time regretting what is past. Sometimes we just stare off blankly into space.

   The key is that the time is "spent," and if we had thought about it and considered our options, we would not have deliberately spent our time in that way. So our idea is this: Why not take advantage of the time you normally waste, by practicing good thinking during that time. For example, instead of sitting in front of the TV at the end of the day flicking from channel to channel in a vain search for a program worth watching, you could spend that time, or at least part of it, thinking back over your day and evaluating your strengths and weaknesses. You might ask yourself questions like these:

   - When did I do my worst thinking today?
   - When did I do my best thinking?
   - What did I actually think about today?
   - Did I figure out anything?
   - Did I allow any negative thinking to frustrate me unnecessarily?
   - If I had to repeat today, what would I do differently? Why?
   - Did I do anything today to further my long-term goals?
   - Did I do what I set out to do? Why or why not?
   - Did I act in accordance with my own expressed values?
   - If I were to spend every day this way for 10 years, would I, at the end, have accomplished something worthy of that time?

   It is important to take a little time with each question. It also would be useful (perhaps in a daily journal) to record your observations so you are forced to spell out details and be explicit in what you recognize. As time passes, you also will be able to look back and search for patterns in your daily thinking and in your observations and assessments of that thinking.

2. Handle a problem a day. At the beginning of each day (perhaps driving to work), choose a problem to work on when you have free moments. Figure out the logic of the problem by identifying its elements. Systematically think through the

questions: What exactly is the problem? How can I put it into the form of a question?

3. Internalize intellectual standards. Each week, develop a heightened awareness of one of the universal intellectual standards presented in Chapter 7. Focus one week on clarity, the next on accuracy, and so on. For example, if you are focusing on clarity for the week, try to notice when you are being unclear in communicating with others. Notice when others are unclear in what they are saying. When you are reading, notice whether you are clear about what you are reading. When you write a memo, ask yourself whether you are clear about what you are trying to say and in conveying your thoughts in writing. In doing this, you will practice four techniques of clarification: 1) stating what you are saying with some consideration given to your choice of words; 2) elaborating on your meaning in other words; 3) giving examples of what you mean from experiences you have had; and 4) using analogies, metaphors, pictures, or diagrams to illustrate what you mean. You will state, elaborate, illustrate, and exemplify your points, and you will regularly ask others to do the same.

4. Keep an intellectual journal. Each week, write out a certain number of journal entries. The steps are to:
   - Describe only situations that are emotionally significant to you (situations you care deeply about);
   - Describe only one situation at a time;
   - Describe (and keep this separate) what you did in response to that situation (being specific and exact);
   - Analyze, in the light of what you have written, what precisely was going on in the situation; dig beneath the surface;
   - Assess the implications of your analysis. (What did you learn about yourself? What would you do differently if you could relive the situation?)

5. Practice intellectual strategies. Choose a strategy from Chapter 16, on strategic thinking. While using that strategy, record your observations in a journal, including what you are learning about yourself and how you can use the strategy to improve your thinking.

6. Reshape your character. Choose one intellectual trait to strive for each month, focusing on how you can develop that trait in yourself. For example, concentrating on intellectual humility, begin to notice when you admit you are wrong. Notice when you refuse to admit you are wrong, even in the face of glaring evidence that you are in fact wrong. Notice when you become defensive when another person tries to point out a deficiency in your work or your thinking. Notice when your arrogance keeps you from learning, when you say to yourself, for example, "I already know everything I need to know about this subject" or, "I know as much as he does. Who does he think he is, forcing his opinions onto me?"

7. Deal with your ego. Daily, begin to observe your egocentric thinking in action by contemplating questions like these: As I reflect upon my behavior today, did I ever become irritable over small things? Did I do or say anything irrational to get my way? Did I try to impose my will upon others? Did I ever fail to speak my mind when I felt strongly about something, and then later feel resentment?

Once you identify egocentric thinking in operation, you can work to replace it with more rational thought through systematic self-reflection. What would a rational person feel in this or that situation? What would a rational person do? How does that compare with what you did? (Hint: If you find that you continually conclude that a rational person would behave just as you behaved, you are probably engaging in self-deception.) (See Chapter 10 for more ways to identify egocentric thinking.)

8. Redefine the way you see things. We live in a world, both personal and social, in which every situation is defined; it is given a fundamental meaning. How a situation is defined determines not only how we feel about it, but also how we act in it and what implications it has for us. Virtually every situation, however, can be defined in more than one way. This fact carries with it tremendous opportunities for all of us to make our life more of what we want it to be. In principle, it lies within your power to make your life much happier and more fulfilling than it is.

Many of the negative definitions that we give to situations in our lives could in principle be transformed into positive definitions. As a result, we can gain when otherwise we would have lost. We can be happy when otherwise we would have been sad. We can be fulfilled when otherwise we would have been frustrated. In this game plan, we practice redefining the way we see things, turning negatives into positives, dead-ends into new beginnings, mistakes into opportunities to learn. To make this game plan practical, we should create some specific guidelines for ourselves. For example, we might make ourselves a list of five to ten recurrent negative situations in which we feel frustrated, angry, unhappy, or worried. We then could identify the definition in each case that is at the root of the negative emotion. Next, we would choose a plausible alternative definition for each and then plan for our new responses as well as our new emotions.

Suppose, for example, you are not a "morning person," that is, you do not like to get up early in the morning, preferring instead to sleep late. But let's say that your job requires you to get up early. You do not have a choice about whether to get up early. But you do have a choice about how you define the situation. You can either, on a daily basis, resent having to get up early, or you can redefine how you see your circumstance. You can remind yourself, for example, that you are able to get more done if you get an early start. You can focus your mental energy on being more productive (rather than being grumpy). Perhaps you have to get up early enough to see the sunrise, something you would never be able to see with a habitual pattern of sleeping late. If so, you can find daily pleasure in waking up with the sunrise.

Or let's say that you are in a job that is eliminated by the company for which you have worked for many years. As a result you are angry, dwelling on the injustice of the situation. But you have a choice. You can wallow in your resentment, or you can redefine the situation. You can see your unemployment as an opportunity to do something new; something interesting, something you would never have done had you not lost your job. Perhaps you decide to go back to college. Perhaps you decide to enter a new field of employment. The point is that you can choose not to be trapped by your thinking. Rather, you can take every opportunity you find to make lemonade out of lemons.

Or let's imagine that you feel constantly swamped at work. It seems that everyday is another day of too much work and not enough time. When you use your thinking to sort through your priorities and become creative about how to get your work done, you can begin to take control of the situation rather than being controlled by it. Instead of feeling frustration and anxiety, you can refuse to be a victim in the situation. In other words, you can define the situation differently in your mind. Instead of focusing on what you aren't getting done, you can focus on what you are accomplishing. Instead of doing all the work yourself, you might be able to delegate it or outsource it. In other words, through your thinking, you can redefine the situation, thereby redefining the way you experience it. (We are not assuming that doing this will be EASY. You may want to practice doing this in small ways first.)

9. Get in touch with your emotions. Whenever you feel some negative emotion, systematically ask yourself: "What, exactly, is the thinking that leads to this emotion? How might this thinking be flawed? What am I assuming? Should I be making these assumptions? What information is my thinking based on? Is that information reliable?" and so on. (See Chapter 6.)

10. Analyze group influences on your life. Closely analyze the behavior that is encouraged and discouraged in the groups to which you belong. For a given group, what are you required or expected to believe? What are you "forbidden" from doing? If you conclude that your group does not require you to believe anything, or has no taboos, you can conclude that you have not deeply analyzed the practices and thinking of that group. To gain insight into the process of socialization and group membership, you might review an introductory text in sociology. (See Chapter 11.)

When designing strategies, the key point is that you are engaged in an experiment. You are testing strategies in your professional and personal life. You are integrating them, and building on them, in light of your actual experience. All strategies have advantages and disadvantages. One plausible way to do this is to work with all of the strategies on the list below in any order of your choosing:

1. Use "wasted" time.
2. Handle a problem a day.
3. Internalize intellectual standards.
4. Keep an intellectual journal.
5. Practice intellectual strategies.
6. Reshape your character.
7. Deal with your ego.
8. Redefine the way you see things.
9. Get in touch with your emotions.
10. Analyze group influences on your life.

Suppose you find the strategy, "Redefine the way you see things" to be intuitive to you, so you use it to begin. Soon you find yourself noticing many situations in your life in which social definitions become obvious. You recognize how your behavior is shaped and controlled by the definitions these situations imply:

1. "I'm giving a party."
2. "We're going to have a meeting."
3. "Why don't you run for election?"
4. "The funeral is Tuesday."
5. "Jack is an acquaintance, not really a friend."

You begin to see how important and pervasive social definitions are. You begin to redefine situations in ways that run contrary to some commonly accepted definitions. You notice then how redefining situations and relationships enables you to "get in touch with your emotions." You recognize that the way you think (that is, you define things) generates the emotions you feel. When you think you are threatened (you define a situation as "threatening"), you feel fear. If you define a situation as a "failure," you may feel depressed. On the other hand, if you define that same situation as a "lesson or opportunity to learn," you feel empowered to learn. When you recognize this control that you are capable of exercising, the two strategies begin to work together and reinforce each other.

Next consider how you could integrate strategy #10 ("Analyze group influences on your life") into your practice. One of the main things that groups do is to control us by controlling the definitions we are allowed to use. When a group defines some things as "cool" and some as "dumb," members of the group try to appear "cool" and not appear "dumb." When the boss of a business says, "That makes a lot of sense," his subordinates know they are not to say, "No, it is ridiculous." They know this because defining someone as the "boss" gives him or her special privileges to define situations and relationships.

You now have three strategies interwoven: You "redefine the way you see things," "get in touch with your emotions," and "analyze group influences on your life." The three strategies are integrated into one. You now can experiment with any of those below, looking for opportunities to integrate them into your thinking and your life:

- Use wasted time.
- Handle a problem a day.
- Internalize intellectual standards.
- Keep an intellectual journal.
- Practice intellectual strategies.
- Reshape your character.
- Deal with your ego.

If you follow through on a plan, you are going beyond being a beginning thinker; you are becoming a "practicing" thinker. Good luck in your pursuit of a plan for yourself.

Chapter 6

The Parts of Thinking

O ne of the most important sets of skills in thinking develops through one's understanding of the parts of thinking. In other words, we are better able to find problems in our thinking when we are able to take our thinking apart. In this chapter, we focus on these parts. In the next chapter, we focus on intellectual standards, the key to the assessment of thinking.

Thus, as you work through this chapter and the next, you will begin to understand some of the most fundamental concepts critical thinkers use on a daily basis, for it is through the analysis and assessment of thinking that critical thinking occurs. To analyze thinking we must be able to take thinking apart and scrutinize how we are using each part. Once we have done so, we apply the standards for thinking to those parts (standards such as clarity, accuracy, relevance, logicalness, fairness, etc.). Once we have a clear understanding of the parts of thinking (or elements of reasoning) and the intellectual standards, and once we begin to use them in our thinking on a daily basis, we begin to see the quality of our lives significantly improve.

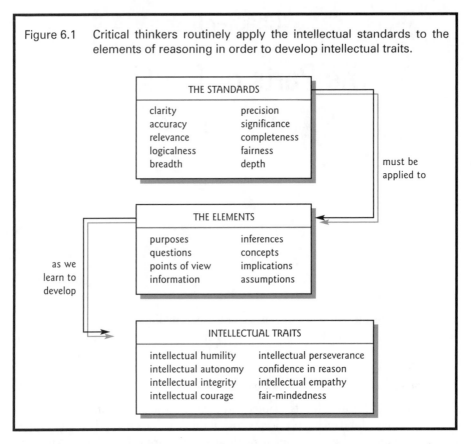

Figure 6.1 Critical thinkers routinely apply the intellectual standards to the elements of reasoning in order to develop intellectual traits.

THE STANDARDS

clarity	precision
accuracy	significance
relevance	completeness
logicalness	fairness
breadth	depth

must be applied to

THE ELEMENTS

purposes	inferences
questions	concepts
points of view	implications
information	assumptions

as we learn to develop

INTELLECTUAL TRAITS

intellectual humility	intellectual perseverance
intellectual autonomy	confidence in reason
intellectual integrity	intellectual empathy
intellectual courage	fair-mindedness

Here we begin with a brief discussion of reasoning, the mental process the mind uses to make sense of whatever we seek to understand.

Reasoning Is Everywhere in Human Life

The words *thinking* and *reasoning* are used in everyday life as virtual synonyms. Reasoning, however, has a more formal flavor. This is because it highlights the intellectual dimension of thinking.

Reasoning occurs whenever the mind draws conclusions on the basis of reasons. We draw conclusions whenever we make sense of things. The result is that whenever we think, we reason. Usually we are not aware of the full scope of reasoning in our lives.

We begin to reason from the moment we wake up in the morning. We reason when we figure out what to eat for breakfast, what to wear, whether to stop at the store on the way to school, whether to go with this or that friend to lunch. We reason as we interpret the oncoming flow of traffic, when we react to the decisions of other drivers, when we speed up or slow down. We reason when we figure out solutions to problems. We reason when we formulate problems. We reason when we argue.

One can draw conclusions, then, about everyday events or, really, about anything at all: about strategic planning, newspaper articles, poems, microbes, people, numbers, historical events, social settings, psychological states, character traits, the past, the present, or the future.

To reason well, we must scrutinize the process we are using. What are we trying to figure out? What information do we need? Do we have that information? How could we check it for accuracy? The less conscious we are of how we are thinking, the easier it is to make some mistake or error.

Test the Idea
Becoming More Aware of the Role of Reasoning in Your Life

Make a list of all the things you did today. Then, for each act, figure out the thinking that led you to do, or guided you while doing, the act. (Remember that most of your thinking is unconscious.) For example, when you left your house this morning, you may have stopped at the store for food. This act makes no sense unless you somehow had come to the conclusion that you needed some food. Then, while at the store, you bought a certain number of items. This action resulted from the tacit conclusion you came to that you needed some items and not others.

Realize that every time you make a decision, that decision represents a view or conclusion you reasoned to. For each action you identify, answer these two questions: 1) What exactly did I do? and 2) What thinking is presupposed in my behavior?

Does Reasoning Have Parts?

The parts of thinking can also be called the elements of reasoning or the fundamental structures of thought. We will use these expressions interchangeably. The elements or parts of reasoning are those essential dimensions of reasoning that are present whenever and wherever reasoning occurs—independent of whether we are reasoning well or poorly (Figure 6.2). Working together, these elements shape reasoning and provide a general logic to the use of thought.

When we become adept at identifying the elements of our reasoning (Figure 6.3), we are in a much better position to recognize flaws in our thinking, by locating problems in this or that part. We are in a much better position, in other words, to analyze the mistakes in our thinking (or mistakes in the thinking of others).

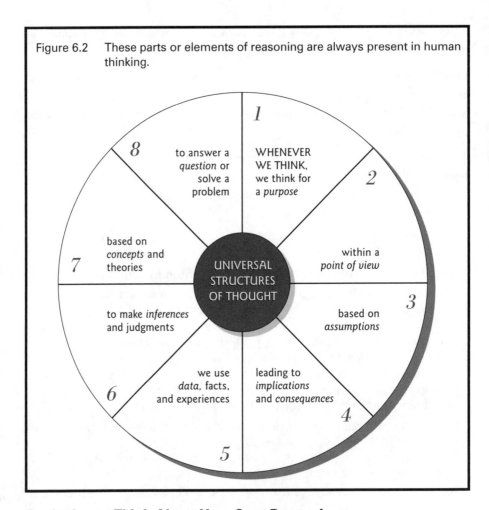

Figure 6.2   These parts or elements of reasoning are always present in human thinking.

Beginning to Think About Your Own Reasoning

Reasoning is a process whereby one draws conclusions on the basis of reasons. On the surface, reasoning seems somewhat simple, as if it has no component structures. Looked at more closely, however, it implies the ability to engage in a set of interrelated intellectual processes.

It is useful to practice making conscious what is subconscious in your thinking. Then you can better understand what's going on beneath the surface of your thought. In this chapter, we introduce you to important ideas you can use for this task.

Figure 6.3   Critical thinkers understand the importance of taking thinking apart in order to analyze it for flaws.

Critical thinkers routinely   take their thinking apart

The Elements of Thought: A First Look

Let us begin by looking at the parts of thinking as they stand in an interrelated set. It is possible to name them in just one, somewhat complex, sentence:

Whenever you reason, you do so in some circumstances,
making some inferences (that have some implications and consequences)
based on some reasons or information (and assumptions)
using some concepts,
in trying to settle some question (or solve some problem)
for some purpose
within a point of view.

If you like, you can put it in two sentences (also see Figure 6.4):

Whenever you are reasoning,
you are trying to accomplish some purpose,
within a point of view,
using concepts or ideas.
You are focused on some issue or question, issue, or problem,
using information
to come to conclusions,
based on assumptions,
all of which have implications.

Let us now examine, at least provisionally, each of these crucial concepts. We will be using them throughout this book. It is essential that they become a comfortable part of your vocabulary. As you read these explanations, see if you can write out your understanding of them, with an example drawn from your own experience.

By reasoning, we mean making sense of something by giving it some meaning in one's mind. Virtually all thinking is part of our sense-making activities. We hear scratching at the door and think, "It's the dog." We see dark clouds in the sky and think, "It looks like rain." Some of this activity operates at a subconscious level. For example, all of the sights and sounds about me have meaning for me without my explicitly noticing that they do. Most of our reasoning is unspectacular. Our reasoning tends to become explicit to us only when someone challenges it and we

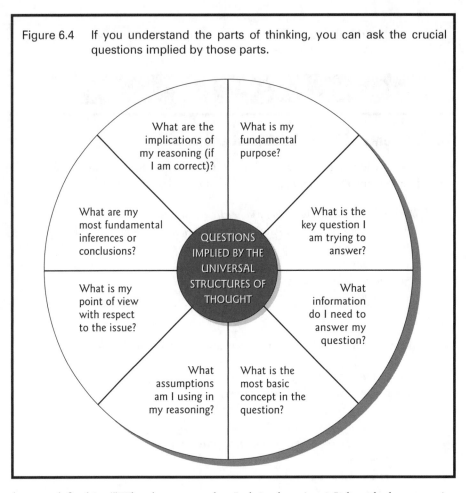

Figure 6.4   If you understand the parts of thinking, you can ask the crucial questions implied by those parts.

have to defend it. ("Why do you say that Jack is obnoxious? I thought he was quite pleasant."). Throughout life, we begin with a goal or purpose and then figure out what to do to achieve our goal. Reasoning is what enables us to come to these decisions using ideas and meanings.

By reasoning having a purpose, we mean that when humans think about the world, we do not do so randomly but, rather, in line with our goals, desires, needs, and values. Our thinking is an integral part of a patterned way of acting in the world, and we act, even in simple matters, with some set of ends in view. To understand someone's thinking—including one's own—we must understand the functions it serves, what it is about, the direction it is moving, and the ends that make sense of it. Most of what we are after in our thinking is not obvious to us, though. Raising human goals and desires to the level of conscious realization is an important part of critical thinking.

By reasoning within a point of view, we mean that our thinking has some comprehensive focus or orientation. Our thinking is focused on something from some angle. We can change either what we focus on or the angle of our focus. We often give names to the angle from which we are thinking about something. For example, we could look at something politically or scientifically, poetically or philosophically. We might look at something conservatively or liberally, religiously or secularly. We might look at something from a cultural or a financial perspective, or both. Once we understand how people are approaching a question or topic (what their comprehensive perspective is), we are usually much more able to understand the whole of their thinking.

By using concepts in reasoning, we mean the general categories or ideas by which we interpret, classify, or group the information we use in our thinking. For example, in this book the concepts of critical thinking and uncritical thinking are important. Everything written in this book can be classified as an attempt to explain one or the other of these two important ideas. Each of these ideas is explained, in turn, by means of other ideas. Thus, the concept of thinking critically is explained by reference to yet other concepts such as "intellectual standards for thought." Each profession or discipline (business, psychology, science, geology, literature, history) develops its own set of concepts or technical vocabulary to facilitate its thinking. All sports require a vocabulary of concepts that enables those who are trying to understand or master the game to make sense of it. Try to explain baseball to someone without using these ideas: strike, ball, shortstop, inning, at bat, hit, run, safe, out, balk. To play the game, we must interpret everything we do in it by means of concepts such as these. The rules would not make sense without them. The game would be incomprehensible.

By reasoning upon some question, issue, or problem, we mean that when we think about the world in line with our goals, desires, needs, and values, we often face questions we need to answer, problems we need to solve, and issues we need to resolve. Therefore, when we find ourselves confronting a difficulty, it makes sense to say, "What is the question we need to answer?" or, "What is the problem we need to solve?" or, "What is the issue we need to resolve?" To improve our ability to think well, it is important to learn how to put the questions, problems, and issues we need to deal with in a clear and distinct way. If we change the question, we change the criteria we have to meet to settle it. If we modify the problem, we need to modify how we are going to solve the problem. If we shift the issue, new considerations become relevant to its resolution.

By using information in our reasoning, we mean using some set of facts, data, or experiences to support our conclusions. Whenever someone is reasoning, it makes sense to ask, "Upon what facts or information are you basing your reasoning?" The factual basis for reasoning can be important. For example, in a newspaper ad, the following pieces of information were used in support of an argument against capital punishment:

> *"Since the death penalty was reinstated by the Supreme court in 1976, for every 7 prisoners who were executed, one prisoner awaiting execution was found to be innocent and released."*

> *"At least 381 homicide convictions have been overturned since 1963 because prosecutors concealed evidence of innocence or presented evidence they knew to be false."*

> *"A study by the U.S. General Accounting Office found racial prejudice in death sentencing...: killers of whites were proportionally more likely to be executed than were killers of blacks."*

> *"Since 1984, 34 mentally retarded people have been executed (New York Times, November 22, 1999)."*

Can you see how information such as this—if true—gives strength to the reasoning? The opposing position would, of course, advance information of its own to try to challenge or counter this information. Two important critical thinking axioms are: check your facts and check your data!

By coming to conclusions we mean taking something (which we believe we know) and figuring out something else on the basis of it. When we do this, we make inferences. For example, if my boss walks right by me without saying hello, I might come to the conclusion (make the inference) that he or she is angry with me. If the market goes up for six straight months, I might infer that it will go up again in the next month. If my business was successful with a strategy last year, I might infer that it will work again next year. In everyday life, we are continually making inferences (coming to conclusions) about the people, things, places, and events of our lives.

By reasoning based on assumptions we mean whatever we take for granted as true in order to figure something else out. Thus, if you infer that since a candidate is a Republican, he or she will support a balanced budget, you assume that all Republicans support a balanced budget. If you infer that foreign leaders presented in the news as "enemies" or "friends" of the U.S. are in fact enemies or friends, you assume that the news in the U.S. is always accurate in its presentation of the character of foreign leaders. If you infer that someone who invites you to their apartment after a party "to continue this interesting conversation" is really interested in you romantically or sexually, you assume that the only reason for going to someone's apartment late at night after a party is to pursue a romantic or sexual relationship. All reasoning has some basis in the assumptions we make (but usually do not openly express).

By the implications of reasoning, we mean that which follows from our thinking. It means that to which our thinking is leading us. If you say to someone that you "love" him, you imply that you are concerned with his welfare. If you make a promise, you imply that you intend to keep it. If you call a country a "democracy," you imply that the political power is in the hands of the people at large (as against in the hands of a powerful minority). If you call yourself a "feminist," you imply that you are in favor of the political, social, and economic equality of the sexes. We often test the credibility of people by seeing if they are true to the implications of their own words. "Say what you mean and mean what you say" is a sound principle of critical thinking (and of personal integrity, for that matter).

An Everyday Example: Jack and Jill

Let's now look at, and then analyze, a disagreement that might arise in everyday life—in this case, between lovers who come to different conclusions about a situation they both experienced.

Suppose Jack and Jill, who are in a romantic relationship, go to a party, during which Jack spends most of the evening talking with Susan. On their way back, Jack, sensing that Jill is upset, asks, "What's wrong?"

After some hesitation, Jill says, "I didn't appreciate your spending the whole night flirting with Susan!"

Jack: Flirting ... flirting, I was not flirting!

Jill: What would you call it?

Jack: Being friendly. I was being friendly.

Jill: When a man spends the whole evening focused on one woman, sits very close to her, looks at her in a romantic way, periodically touches her in supposedly casual ways, he is engaged in what can only be called flirting.

Jack: And when a woman spends her whole evening watching everything her boyfriend does, collecting evidence as if preparing for a trial, a boyfriend who has always been faithful to her, she is engaged in what can only be called paranoia.

Jill: Paranoid? How dare you call me that!

Jack: Well, how else can I describe your behavior? You're obviously distrustful and insecure. You're accusing me without a good reason for doing so.

Jill: Don't act like this is the only time you flirted. I heard from your friends that you were quite a lady's man before we got together.

Jack: And I heard about your possessiveness and jealousy from your friends. I think you need to deal with your own problems before you cast stones at me. Perhaps you need counseling.

Jill: You're nothing but a typical male. You think that women are to be measured by conquest. You're so focused on getting strokes for that male ego of yours that you can't see or admit what you're doing. If you can't see fit to change your behavior, I must question the wisdom of our having a relationship.

Jack: I agree. I, too, question our relationship, but I question it on the basis of your paranoia. I think I deserve an apology!

Analysis of the Example

Now let's analyze this exchange using the elements of thought:

- Purpose. Both Jack and Jill presumably seek a successful romantic relationship. That is their implied shared goal.

- Problem. They see a problem or issue standing in the way, a problem they conceptualize differently. To Jack, the problem is, "When is Jill going to deal with her paranoia?" To Jill, the problem is, "When is Jack going to take responsibility for his flirtatious behavior?"

- Conclusions. Both Jacks and Jill's inferences (conclusions) about the situation derive from the same behavior in the same circumstance, but they clearly see the behavior differently. To Jack, his behavior is to be understood as merely "friendly." To Jill, Jack's behavior can be understood only as "flirtation."

- Facts. The raw facts of the situation include everything Jack actually said and did at the party. Other relevant facts include Jack's behavior toward other women in his past. Additional facts include Jill's behavior toward former boyfriends and any other facts that bear on whether she is acting out of insecurity or "paranoia."

- Assumptions. Jack is assuming that he is not self-deceived in his motivation with respect to Susan and other women. Jack also is assuming that he is competent to identify paranoia in another person's behavior. Further, he is assuming that a woman could not behave in the way that Jill did without being paranoid. Jill is assuming that Jack's behavior is not compatible with ordinary friendliness. Both of them assume that what they have heard about the other from friends is accurate. Both assume themselves to be justified in their behavior in the situation.

- Concepts. There are four key concepts in the reasoning: flirtation, friendliness, paranoia, and male ego.

- Implications. Both Jack and Jill imply by their reasoning that the other person is entirely to blame for any differences between them regarding Jack's behavior at the party. Both seem to imply that the relationship is hopeless.

- Point of view. Both Jack and Jill may be seeing the other through the bias of a gender-based point of view.

Both see themselves as a victim of the other. Both see themselves as blameless.

Given what we know about the dispute, it is not possible to assess who is correct and to what extent. To decide whose interpretation of the situation is most plausible, we would need more facts. There is a variety of subtle but observable behaviors that—if we could verify them in the behavior of Jack toward Susan—might lead us to conclude that Jill is correct and that Jack was behaving flirtatiously. Or, if we heard the conversation firsthand, we might decide that Jill's response is unjustified.

The Elements of Thought in Relationship

The trick in learning the elements of thought is to express these ideas in a number of different ways until their nonlinear interrelationships begin to become intuitive to you. For example, you might think of the parts of reasoning as analogous to the essential parts of the human body. They are all present whether we are healthy or not. Like the parts of the body, the parts of thought function in an interdependent fashion. One way to express those interrelationships is that:

- Our purpose affects the manner in which we ask questions;

- The manner in which we ask questions affects the information we gather;

- The information we gather affects the way we interpret it;

- The way we interpret information affects the way we conceptualize it;

- The way we conceptualize information affects the assumptions we make;

- The assumptions we make affect the implications that follow from our thinking;

- The implications that follow from our thinking affect the way we see things, our point of view.

Test the Idea
Thinking Through the Elements of Your Reasoning

Select an important conclusion that you have reasoned to—for example, a decision to purchase a house or car or take a new job, or even to get married. Identify the circumstances in which you made that decision, some of the inferences you made in the process (about the likely advantages and disadvantages). State the likely implications of your decision, the consequences it has had, and will have, in your life, the information you took into account in making this decision, the way you expressed the question to yourself, the way you looked at your life and your future (while reasoning through the question). See if you can grasp the interrelationship of all of these elements in your thinking. Don't be surprised if you find this to be a difficult task.

In the remainder of this chapter, we will give a more detailed account of concepts, assumptions, inferences, implications, and point of view. We will direct special attention to the distinction between inferences and assumptions, as we find that people often have difficulty distinguishing these two. But once you become comfortable differentiating these two elements, the others tend to fall into place much more readily. Light is shed on all the elements throughout this book. Periodically put down the book and see if you can elaborate on the elements of thought in your own words using your own examples. Success in these acts of active elaboration are what will make the concepts yours. You must talk ideas, write ideas, think ideas into your system.

The Relationship Between the Elements

Because the elements do not exist in isolation but in relation to each other, it is important not to think of the distinctions between them as absolute. The distinctions are always a relative matter. For example, if our purpose is to figure out how to spend less money, the question we have to figure out is, "What can I do to ensure that I spend less money?" The question is a virtual reformulation of the purpose. What is more, the point of view might be expressed as "viewing my spending habits to determine how to decrease my expenditures." This seems a virtual reformulation of purpose and question. The point is that it is important to recognize an intimate overlap among all of the elements by virtue of their interrelationship. At times, formulating some of the elements explicitly may seem to be a redundancy. Don't give way to this feeling. With practice, you will come to recognize the analytic power of making the distinctions explicit.

Thinking to Some Purpose

A British scholar by the name of Susan Stebbing wrote a book (1939) on the importance of purpose in thinking. In it, she said: "To think logically is to think relevantly to the purpose that initiated the thinking: all effective thinking is directed to an end." We agree. All thinking pursues a purpose. We do not think without having something we are trying to accomplish, without having some aim in view, something we want. When humans think about the world, we do not do so randomly but, rather, in line with our goals, desires, needs, and values. Our thinking is an integral part of a patterned way of acting in the world, and we act, even in simple matters, with some set of ends in view. To understand someone's thinking—including one's own—we must understand the functions it serves, what it is about, the direction it is moving, and the ends that make sense of it.

Much of what we are after in our thinking is not obvious to us. Raising human goals and desires to the level of conscious realization is an important part of critical thinking. Though we always have a purpose in thinking, we are not always fully aware of that purpose. We may have some vague idea of it. Perhaps we have not clearly come to terms with our purpose. For example, you might call a meeting to discuss an important issue with your staff, but you may not know exactly what you are trying to accomplish in the meeting. As a result, the thinking during the meeting may diverge in many unhelpful directions. Without a clear sense of what you are about, the thinking you do may be very unproductive.

One problem with human thinking is that we sometimes pursue contradictory ends. We might want to become educated and also want to avoid doing any intellectual work. We might want others to love us, but not behave in loving ways toward them. We might want people to trust us, but behave in ways that undermine trust. The purpose we might explicitly state may be simply what we would like to believe of ourselves. Our real purpose, however, might be one that we would be ashamed to admit. We might think we want to pursue a medical career to help and care for people when our actual purpose may be to make a lot of money, gain prestige and status, and be admired by others. We must be careful, therefore, not to assume that our purposes are consistent with one another or that our announced purposes are our actual purposes.

Also, the purposes we pursue influence and are influenced by our point of view, as well as by the way we see the world. Our purposes shape how we see things, and how we see things shapes what we seek. Each person formulates his or her purpose from a given point of view, determined by the context of his or her own experience. To understand our goals and objectives, then, we should consider the perspectives from which we see the world or some situation in it.

A hairdresser, for example, because of her perspective, might be more concerned than most janitors with personal appearance. Looking good and helping others to look good are more intimately connected with her view of herself and the world. An orthodontist would naturally think much more about teeth and their appearance than

---

Test the Idea
Identifying Your Purposes: Understanding Your Thinking

To begin to see how intimately interconnected thinking is to purpose, we suggest the following activity. First, make a list of five fundamental goals you have. Then comment on how your thinking is shaped by those goals. Fill in the blanks: "One of my purposes is _____. I can achieve this purpose best by _____."

Second, identify five things that you think about a lot. Then comment on how those things are tied to your fundamental purposes. For example, if you spend a considerable amount of time thinking about how to improve your performance at work in order to make more money, one of your purposes is probably to make as much money as you can. Or if you spend a lot of time thinking about how to improve your intimate relationship, one of your purposes is probably to have a more meaningful intimate relationship.

most other people would. Having straight teeth would naturally seem more significant to her than it might to, say, most professional football players. The orthodontist's purpose in fostering straight teeth arises out of her perspective or point of view

Thinking with Concepts

Concepts are like the air we breathe. They are everywhere. They are essential to our life, but we rarely notice them. Yet only when we have conceptualized a thing in some way can we think about it. Nature does not give us instruction in how things are to be conceptualized. We must create that conceptualization, alone or with others. Once it is conceptualized, we integrate a thing into a network of ideas (as no concept stands alone).

Humans approach virtually everything in our experience as something that can be "decoded." Things are given meaning by the power of our mind to create a conceptualization and to make inferences on the basis of it—hence, we create further conceptualizations. We do this so routinely and automatically that we don't typically recognize ourselves as engaged in these processes. In our everyday life, we don't first experience the world in "concept-less" form and then deliberately place what we experience into categories so as to make sense of things. Rather, it is as if things are given to us with their name inherent in them. So we see trees, clouds, grass, roads, people, children, sunsets, and so on. We apply these concepts intuitively, as if the names belong to the things by nature, as if we had not created these concepts in our own minds.

If you want to develop as a thinker, you must come to terms with this human power of mind—to create concepts through which we see and experience the world—for it is precisely this capacity of which you must take charge in taking command of your thinking. You must become the master of your own conceptualizations. You must develop the ability to mentally "remove" this or that concept from the things named by the concept, and try out alternative ideas. As general semanticists often say: "The word is not the thing! The word is not the thing!" If you are trapped in one set of concepts (ideas, words), you can think of things in only one way. Word and thing become one and the same in your mind.

To figure out the proper use of words, the proper way to conceptualize things, events, situations, emotions, abstract ideas, it is important to first achieve a true command of the uses of words. For example, if you are proficient in the use of the English language, you recognize a significant difference in the language between needing and wanting, between having judgment and being judgmental, between having information and gaining knowledge, between being humble and being servile, between stubbornness and having the courage of your convictions. Command of distinctions such as these, and many others, in the language has a significant influence upon the way you interpret your experience. People who do not have this command confuse these important discriminations and distort the important realities they help us distinguish.

Test the Idea
Testing Your Understanding of Basic Concepts

To the extent that you have a sound command of the English language, you should be able to state the essential differences between related but distinguishably different realities that are marked by words or expressions in our language. To the extent that you can, you are conceptualizing the ideas labeled with these words in keeping with educated use.

In this activity, you will test your ability to do this. What follows is a set of related words, each pair illustrating an important distinction marked by our language. For each set, write down your understanding of the essential difference between each word pair.

After you have done this for each set of words, look up the words in the dictionary, and see how close your ideas of the essential difference of the word pair were to the actual distinctions the dictionary entries state or imply. (We recommend the Webster's New World Dictionary.)

1. clever/cunning
2. selfish/self-motivated
3. power/control
4. friend/acquaintance
5. love/romance
6. anger/rage
7. believe/know
8. jealousy/envy
9. socialize/educate

In learning to speak our native language, we learn thousands of concepts. When properly used, these concepts enable us to make legitimate inferences about the objects of our experience. Unfortunately, nothing in the way we ordinarily learn to speak a language forces us to use concepts carefully or prevents us from making unjustifiable inferences in using them.

Often we misuse or confuse ideas because of our indoctrination into a social system, resulting in a distortion of our experience. As developing thinkers, we must continually distinguish the concepts and ideas implicit in our social conditioning from the concepts and ideas implicit in the natural language we speak. For example, people from many different countries and cultures speak the same natural language. The peoples of

Canada, Ireland, Scotland, England, Australia, Canada, and the United States all speak English. By and large, they implicitly share (to the extent to which they are proficient in the language) the same set of concepts (codified in the 23 volumes of the Oxford English Dictionary). Nevertheless, the people in these countries are not socially conditioned in the same way.

What is more, a person from China or Tibet could learn to speak the English language fluently without in any sense sharing in the same social conditioning. Because of this, natural languages (French, German, English, Swahili, or Hindi are examples) are repositories of concepts that, by and large, are not to be equated with the concepts implicit in the social indoctrination of any social or cultural group speaking the language. This is a difficult insight to gain, but it is a powerful and essential one.

In the United States, for example, most people are socially conditioned to believe that capitalism is superior to any other economic system (it is called "free enterprise"). Americans assume that no country can be truly democratic unless it has a capitalistic economic system. Furthermore, Americans assume that the major opposing systems, socialism or communism, are either wrong, enslaving, or evil (the "Evil Empire"). People in the U.S. are encouraged to think of the world in these ways by movies, the news, schooling, political speeches, and many other social rituals. Raised in the United States, Americans internalize different concepts, beliefs, and assumptions about themselves and the world than they would have had they grown up in China or Iran, for example.

Nevertheless, in a decent dictionary of the English language, lexicographers would not confuse these socially implied meanings and psychological associations with the foundational meanings of the words. The term communism would not be defined as "an economic system that enslaves the people." The word capitalism would not have the definition, "an economic system essential to a democratic society."

Nevertheless, because we are socialized to believe that we, as a people, are free, reasonable, just, and caring, we assume that our behavior matches what these words imply. Words often substitute, in human life, for the realities named by them. Fundamental contradictions or inconsistencies in our lives, then, go unquestioned. This is part of the self-deceptive tendencies to which the human mind is prone.

Critical thinkers learn how to strip off surface language and consider alternative ways to talk and think about things. For example, when thinking sociocentrically, we become trapped in the view of our peer group and society with little or no conscious awareness of what it would be to rationally decide upon alternative ways to conceptualize situations, persons, and events. Most people are awed by social ritual, in particular the trappings of social authority, status, and prestige. They live their life, as it were, in surface structures. Critical thinkers learn how to think sociologically. They therefore come to recognize when their ideas are controlled by social rituals, social expectations, and taboos.

Thinking with Information

It is impossible to reason without using some set of facts, data, or experiences as a constituent part of one's thinking. Finding trustworthy sources of information and refining one's own experience critically are important goals of critical thinkers. We must be vigilant about the sources of information we use. We must be analytically critical of the use we make of our own experience. Experience may be the best teacher, but biased experience supports bias, distorted experience supports distortion, and self-deluded experience supports self-delusion. We, therefore, must not think of our experience as sacred in any way but, instead, as one important dimension of thought that must, like all others, be critically analyzed and assessed.

Numerous problems exist in human life because people fail to understand the important role that information plays in everything we do. People often, for example, fail to see that they are excluding important information from their thinking when reasoning through a complex problem. People often operate on automatic pilot when it comes to their use of information. But when they are explicitly aware of the importance of information, they are much more careful in the conclusions they come to. They seek information when others would ignore the need to do so. They question the information they have, as well as the information that others are using. They realize that their thinking can only be as good as the information they use to come to conclusions.

Distinguishing Between Inert Information, Activated Ignorance, and Activated Knowledge

The mind can take in information in three distinctive ways: 1) by internalizing inert information; 2) by forming activated ignorance; and 3) by achieving activated knowledge.

Inert Information

By inert information, we mean taking into the mind information that, though memorized, we do not understand—despite the fact that we think we do. For example, many people have taken in, during their schooling, a lot of information about democracy that leads them to believe they understand the concept. Often, a good part of the information they have internalized consists of empty verbal rituals. For example, many children learn in school that "democracy is government of the people, by the people, for the people." This catchy phrase often sticks in their mind. It leads them to think they understand what it means, though most of them do not translate it into any practical criteria for assessing the extent to which democracy does or does not exist in any given country. Most people, to be explicit, could not intelligibly answer any of the following questions:

1. What is the difference between a government of the people and a government for the people?

2. What is the difference between a government for the people and a government by the people?

3. What is the difference between a government by the people and a government of the people?

4. What exactly is meant by "the people?"

Thus, people often do not sufficiently think about information they memorized in school to transform it into something truly meaningful in their mind. Much human information is, in the mind of the humans who possess it, merely empty words (inert or dead in the mind). Critical thinkers try to clear the mind of inert information by recognizing it as such and transforming it, through analysis, into something meaningful.

Test the Idea
In Search of Inert Information
Review information you were taught in school or at home. Look for what you may have repeated often on command, to see if it qualifies for what we are calling inert information. Review, for example, the Pledge of Allegiance to the flag, slogans within subject fields, memorized bits and pieces of content, and sayings you have often heard, but probably have not made sense of. See how many candidates you can locate for inert information. Test each one with this criterion: If you cannot explain it or effectively use it, it is likely to be inert information in your mind. If, by chance, you do not find this sort of information, don't assume that you are free of inert information.

Activated Ignorance

By activated ignorance, we mean taking into the mind, and actively using, information that is false, though we mistakenly think it to be true. The philosopher Rene Descartes came to confidently believe that animals have no actual feelings, but are simply robotic machines. Based on this activated ignorance, he performed painful experiments on animals and interpreted their cries of pain as mere noises.

Some people believe, through activated ignorance, that they understand things, events, people, and situations that they do not. They act upon their false ideas, illusions, and misconceptions, often leading to needless waste, pain, and suffering. Sometimes activated ignorance is the basis for massive actions involving millions of people (think of the consequences of the Nazi idea that Germans were the master race and Jews an inferior race). Sometimes it is an individual misconception that is acted on only by one person in a limited number of settings. Wherever activated ignorance exists, it is dangerous.

It is essential, therefore, that we question our beliefs, especially when acting upon them has significant potential implications for the harm, injury, or suffering of others. It is reasonable to suppose that everyone has some beliefs that are, in fact, a form of activated ignorance. Eliminating as many such beliefs as we can is a responsibility we all have. Consider automobile drivers who are confident they can drive safely while they are intoxicated. Consider the belief that smoking does not have any significant negative health effects.

It is not always easy to identify what is and is not activated ignorance. The concept of activated ignorance is important regardless of whether we determine information we come across is false or misleading. What we need to keep in mind are clear-cut cases of activated ignorance so we have a clear idea of it, and personal vigilance with respect to the information we come across that is potentially false. Most people who have acted harmfully as a result of their activated ignorance have probably not realized that they hurt others. Ignorance treated as the truth is no trivial matter.

Test the Idea
In Search of Activated Ignorance
Review what you were taught in school, college, at work, or at home. Seek what you used to believe to be true but now have found to be false and harmful. For example, you probably picked up some activated ignorance from your peer group as you were growing up. Think of things you learned "the hard way." See how many candidates you can locate for activated ignorance. Test each one with this criterion: At one time I thought this was true. Now I know it is false. If, by chance, you do not find any, don't assume that you are free of activated ignorance. Pursue why you are having trouble finding it.

Activated Knowledge

By activated knowledge, we mean taking into the mind, and actively using, information that is not only true but that, when insightfully understood, leads us by implication to more and more knowledge.

Scientists have activated knowledge of the scientific method. They use this method (of hypothesis, prediction, controlled experiment, observation, and provisional conclusions) to acquire more and more knowledge. The method is powerful, enforces discipline on human thinking, and provides safeguards against misuse.

The basic principles of mathematics represented activated knowledge about numbers, shapes, space, and motion that enable the careful thinker to develop precise conclusions based on precise information.

The basic principles of critical thinking represent activated knowledge of the parts of thinking, standards by which thinking can be assessed, and ways in which thinking can be improved. These principles can be applied again and again with the consequence that we discover further knowledge on the basis of our present knowledge and disciplined thought about new information.

Some Key Questions to Ask When Pursuing Information

One of the most important skills in critical thinking is that of evaluating information. This skill begins with the important recognition that information and fact, information and verification, are not the same thing. It requires also the important recognition that everything presented as fact or as true is not. A third important recognition is that the prestige or setting in which information is asserted, as well as the prestige of the person or group asserting it, are no guarantee of accuracy or reliability. Consider the following, very helpful, maxim: An educated person is one who has learned that information almost always turns out to be at best incomplete and very often false, misleading, fictitious, and mendacious—that is, information is often just dead wrong.

Careful professionals use a wide variety of safeguards in the disciplines in which they work. It is not possible to learn these safeguards separately from an actual study of the disciplines. However, it is possible to develop a healthy skepticism about information in general, especially about information presented in support of a belief that serves the vested interests of a person or group. This skepticism is given in the regular asking of key questions about information presented to us:

• To what extent could I test the truth of this claim by direct experience?

• To what extent is believing this consistent with what I know to be true or have justified confidence in?

• How does the person who advances this claim support it?

• Is there a definite system or procedure for assessing claims of this sort?

• Does the acceptance of this information advance the vested interest of the person or group asserting it?

• Is the person asserting this information made uncomfortable by having it questioned?

These questions, both singly and as a group, are no panacea. Everything depends on how we follow up on them. Used with good judgment, they help us to lower the number of mistakes we make in assessing information. They do not prevent us from making such mistakes. In later chapters, we will follow up on these concerns in a deeper way. You should begin now, however, to practice asking the above questions when information is presented to you as true and important.

Test the Idea
Assessing Information

Assess the following claims by figuring out whether you think they are true or false. Explain your reasoning:

1. You hear a male colleague say that women are not as good as men in supervisory roles because they are too "soft" on employees and too emotional in crises.

2. A friend of yours claims that astrology is accurate because he has used it to figure out why people he knew were behaving as they were. He also claims that you can use it to predict people's most likely behavior, including deciding whom it would make sense to marry (or not to marry).

3. You hear someone say, "Science should use statements from the Bible to help assess scientific findings because anything that contradicts the Bible (the word of God) must be false."

4. You read about a person who is reported to have returned from the dead as the result of resuscitation after a heart attack. The person says there is definitely a spirit world because he met a spirit while he was dead.

5. A friend of yours claims that the universe is run on spiritual principles, citing the fact that once, when he was alone in the desert, the universe gave him a mantra (a chant).

6. You hear a woman say that it is clear that no man can truly understand a woman because there is no way, as a man, he can have the experience of a woman.

Distinguishing Between Inferences and Assumptions

As we have said, the elements of reasoning interrelate. They are continually influencing and being influenced by one another. We now will focus at length on the crucial relationship between two of the elements: inference and assumption. Learning to distinguish inferences from assumptions is an important skill in critical thinking. Many confuse the two elements. Let us begin with a review of the basic meanings:

1. Inference: An inference is a step of the mind, an intellectual act by which one concludes that something is true in light of something else's being true, or seeming to be true. If you come at me with a knife in your hand, I probably would infer

that you mean to do me harm. Inferences can be accurate or inaccurate, logical or illogical, justified or unjustified.

2. Assumption: An assumption is something we take for granted or presuppose. Usually it is something we previously learned and do not question. It is part of our system of beliefs. We assume our beliefs to be true and use them to interpret the world about us. If you believe that it is dangerous to walk late at night in big cities and you are staying in Chicago, you will infer that it is dangerous to go for a walk late at night. You take for granted your belief that it is dangerous to walk late at night in big cities. If your belief is a sound one, your assumption is sound. If your belief is not sound, your assumption is not sound. Beliefs, and hence assumptions, can be unjustified or justified, depending upon whether we do or do not have good reasons for them. Consider this example: "I heard a scratch at the door. I got up to let the cat in." My inference was based on the assumption (my prior belief) that only the cat makes that noise, and that she makes it only when she wants to be let in.

We humans naturally and regularly use our beliefs as assumptions and make inferences based on those assumptions. We must do so to make sense of where we are, what we are about, and what is happening. Assumptions and inferences permeate our lives precisely because we cannot act without them. We make judgments, form interpretations, and come to conclusions based on the beliefs we have formed (see Figure 6.5).

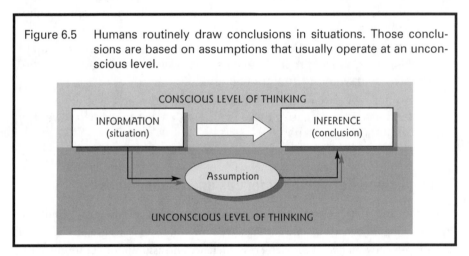

Figure 6.5 Humans routinely draw conclusions in situations. Those conclusions are based on assumptions that usually operate at an unconscious level.

If you put humans in any situation, they start to give it some meaning or other. People automatically make inferences to gain a basis for understanding and action. So quickly and automatically do we make inferences that we do not, without training, notice them as such. We see dark clouds and infer rain. We hear the door slam and infer that someone has arrived. We see a frowning face and infer that the person is angry. If our friend is late, we infer that she is being inconsiderate. We meet a tall guy and infer that he is good at basketball, an Asian and infer that she will be good at math. We meet a well-dressed person and infer he or she is successful. We think of the business we would like to start and infer it will be successful—because we ourselves desire what it will sell.

As we write, we make inferences as to what readers will make of what we are writing. We make inferences as to the clarity of what we are saying, what requires further explanation, what has to be exemplified or illustrated, and what does not. Many of our inferences are justified and reasonable, but some are not.

As always, an important part of critical thinking is the art of bringing what is subconscious in our thought to the level of conscious realization. This includes the skill of identifying and reconstructing the inferences we make so the various ways in which we shape our experiences through our inferences become more and more apparent to us. This skill enables us to separate our experiences into two categories. We learn to distinguish the raw data of our experience from our interpretations of those data, from the inferences we are making about them. Eventually we need to realize that the inferences we make are heavily influenced by our point of view and the assumptions we have made about people and situations. This puts us in the position of being able to broaden the scope of our outlook, to see situations from more than one point of view, and hence to become more open-minded.

Often different people make different inferences because they bring to situations different points of view. They see the data differently. To put it another way, they have different assumptions about what they see. For example, if two people see a man lying in a gutter, one might infer, "There's a drunken bum." The other might infer, "There's a man in need of help." These inferences are based on different assumptions about the conditions under which people end up in gutters, and these assumptions are connected to the point of view about people that each has formed. The first person assumes, "Only drunks are to be found in gutters." The second person assumes, "People lying in the gutter are in need of help."

The first person may have developed the point of view that people are fundamentally responsible for what happens to them and ought to be able to take care of themselves. The second may have developed the point of view that the problems people have are often caused by forces and events beyond their control. The reasoning of these two people, in terms of their inferences and assumptions, could be characterized in the following way:

Person One	**Person Two**
Situation: A man is lying in the gutter.	Situation: A man is lying in the gutter.
Inference: That man's a bum.	Inference: That man is in need of help.
Assumption: Only bums lie in gutters.	Assumption: Anyone lying in the gutter is in need of help.

As persons concerned with developing our thinking, we want to begin to notice the inferences we are making, the assumptions we are basing those inferences on, and the point of view about the world we are developing. To do this, we need lots of practice in noticing our inferences and then figuring the assumptions that lead to them.

Test the Idea
Distinguishing Between Information, Inferences, and Assumptions

As thinkers, it is important that we be able to distinguish among information, inferences, and assumptions. Whenever we are in a situation, we naturally make inferences. We come to conclusions about the situation or give it meaning through our interpretations. And these inferences result from the assumptions we made or are making.

For example:

- If it were 12:00 noon, what might you infer? (It's time for lunch.)
- If there are black clouds in the sky? (It's probably going to rain.)
- If Jack comes to work with a black eye? (He was probably in a fight and hit by someone.)
- If there are webs in the corners of the ceiling? (Spiders made them.)
- If there is heavy traffic on the freeway? (I will probably be late for work).

Then:

- If it were 12:00 noon and you inferred that it was time for lunch, what did you assume? (That whenever it is 12 noon, it is time for lunch.)
- If there are black clouds in the sky and you infer that it's probably going to rain, what did you assume? (That it usually rains when there are black clouds in the sky.)
- If Jack comes to work with a black eye and you infer that he must have been hit by someone, what did you assume? (That the only time you develop a black eye is when you have been hit by someone.)

In the following activity, we will provide you with situations (information). We want you to figure out what someone might infer (rightly or wrongly) in the situation. Usually there is a range of possible inferences that different people might make, depending on their various beliefs.

Then, having stated what you think someone might infer, figure out the assumption that would lead someone to make that inference. As a suggestion, first figure out a likely inference (whether rational or irrational), then, and only then, try to figure out the assumption. The assumption will be a generalization that led the person to make the inference. We have provided two examples to help you begin.

Information	Possible Inference which one might make	Assumption Leading to the Inference
1. You see a woman in a wheelchair.	She must have a sad life.	All people in wheelchairs have a sad life.
2. A police officer trails your car closely for several blocks.	He is going to pull me over.	Whenever a police officer trails people he is going to pull them over.
3. You see a child crying next to her mother in the grocery story.		
4. You do not get an increase in salary while others in your department do.		
5. You meet a beautiful woman with blond hair.		
6. You notice a man in the bookstore reading a book by Karl Marx.		
7. While in a restaurant, your friend orders a steak cooked very rare.		
8. A colleague tells you she is pregnant and is going to have an abortion.		
9. Your teenage son comes home late from a late-night date.		
10. Your spouse is talking to an attractive member of the opposite sex at a late night party.		
11. The telephone rings in the middle of the night.		
12. Your significant other does not call you when promised.		

Our goal of becoming aware of the inferences we make and the assumptions that underlie our thinking enables us to begin to gain command over our thinking. Because all human thinking is inferential in nature, command of our thinking depends on command of the inferences embedded in it and thus of the assumptions that underlie it. Consider the way in which we plan and think our way through everyday events. We think of ourselves as preparing for breakfast, eating our breakfast, getting ready for work, arriving on time, attending meetings, completing necessary tasks, making plans for lunch, paying bills, engaging in small talk, and so on. Another way to put this is to say that we are continually interpreting our actions, giving them meanings, and making inferences about what is going on in our lives.

That is, we must choose among a variety of possible meanings. For example, am I "relaxing" or "wasting time"? Am I being "determined" or "stubborn"? Am I "joining" a conversation or "butting in"? Is someone "laughing with me" or "laughing at me"? Am I "helping a friend" or "being taken advantage of?" Every time we interpret our actions, every time we give them a meaning, we are making one or more inferences on the basis of one or more assumptions.

As humans, we continually make assumptions about ourselves, our jobs, our mates, our teachers, our parents, and the world in general. We take some things for granted simply because we can't question everything. Sometimes we take the wrong things for granted. For example, I run off to the store (assuming that I have enough money with me) and arrive to find that I have left my money at home. I assume that I have enough gas in the car only to find that I have run out of gas. I assume that an item marked down in price is a good buy only to find that it was marked up before it was marked down. I assume that it will not, or that it will, rain. I assume that my car will start when I turn the key and press the gas pedal. I assume that I mean well in my dealings with others.

We make hundreds of assumptions without knowing it—without thinking about it. Most of them are sound and justifiable. Some, however, are not. The question then becomes: "How can we begin to recognize the inferences we are making, the assumptions we are basing those inferences on, and the point of view, the perspective on the world that we are forming?"

As we become skilled in identifying our inferences and assumptions, we are in a good position to question the extent to which any one of our assumptions is justified. For example, are we justified in assuming that everyone eats lunch at 12:00 noon? Are we justified in assuming that it usually rains when there are black clouds in the sky? Are we justified in assuming that black eyes are only caused by someone hitting another person? The point is that we all make many assumptions as we go about our daily life and we ought to be able to recognize and question them. As you develop these critical intuitions, you should increasingly notice your inferences and those of others. You should increasingly notice what you and others are taking for granted. You should increasingly notice how your point of view shapes your experiences.

Test the Idea
Getting More Practice in Differentiating Inferences and Assumptions

Using the same format as we used in the previous activity, come up with 10 "episodes" of thinking for yourself, which include a situation, a possible inference in the situation, and the assumption leading to the inference.

Information	Possible Inference one might make	Assumption Leading to the Inference
1.		
2.		
3.		
4.		
5.		
6.		
7.		
8.		
9.		
10.		

Understanding Implications

Among the most important skills of critical thinking is the ability to distinguish between what a statement or situation actually implies and what people may merely (and wrongly) infer from it. An inference, again, is a step of the mind that results in a conclusion. For example, if the sun rises, we can infer that it is morning. Critical thinkers try to monitor their thinking so they infer only that which is implied in a situation—no more, no less. If I feel ill and go to the doctor for a diagnosis, I want the doctor to infer exactly what my symptoms imply. For example, I do not want her to infer that I simply have a cold requiring no medication when in fact I have a bacterial infection requiring antibiotics. My symptoms imply that I have a certain illness, which in turn implies a certain course of treatment. I want the doctor to accurately infer what my illness is, then accurately infer the proper treatment for it.

It is often the case that, in thinking, people fail to think successfully through the implications of a situation. They fail to think through the implications of a problem or decision. As a result, negative consequences often follow.

In any situation, three kinds of implications may be involved: possible ones, probable ones, and necessary ones. For example, every time you drive your car, one possible implication is that you may have an accident. If you drink heavily and drive very fast on a crowded roadway in the rain, one probable implication is that you will have an accident. If you are driving fast on a major highway and all the brake fluid drains out of your brake cylinders and another car immediately in front of you comes to a quick stop, one inescapable implication is that you will have an accident.

We reserve the word "consequences" for what actually happens in a given case. In short, a consequence is what in fact occurs in some situation. If we are good at identifying (making sound inferences about) possible, probable, and inevitable implications, we can take steps to maximize positive consequences and minimize negative ones. On the one hand, we do not want possible or probable negative implications to become real consequences. On the other hand, we do want to realize potential positive implications. We want to understand and take advantage of the real possibilities inherent in a situation.

We study the logic of things to become skilled in recognizing implications and acting accordingly. The art of doing this well is the art of making sound inferences about the implications of a situation by understanding exactly the logic of what is going on. As thinkers, then, we want to think through all of the implications (possible, probable, and inevitable) of a potential decision before we make a decision and act on it.

In addition to implications that follow from concrete situations are implications that follow from the words we use. These follow from meanings inherent in natural languages. There are always implications of the words we use in communicating with people. If, for example, I tell my daughter that she cannot go to a friend's house because she failed to clean up her room, I am implying that she knew she had a responsibility to clean up her room if she wanted to go to a friend's house. My statement to my daughter and my view that she should have consequences for failing to clean her room are reasonable if:

1. I have previously communicated to her my desire for her to keep her room clean, and

2. I have adequately explained my reasoning and the consequences that will follow if she fails to comply with my request.

As thinkers, then, we want to be aware of what precisely we are implying when we say things. We also want to take into account the reasonability of what we are implying. If we do, we say what we mean and mean what we say—an important principle of integrity.

Just as there are implications of the language we use in communicating, there are implications of the way we say things. For example, the statement "Why didn't you clean the kitchen?" asked calmly has different implications from the same statement shouted aggressively. In the first instance, I perhaps am implying only that I think you should have cleaned the kitchen, and nothing more. In the second, I am implying that your failure to do so is a serious matter, warranting a severe reprimand.

What is more, as we may fail to notice the implications of a situation or of what we say, we also may fail to notice the implications of what others say to us. People often fail to infer precisely what others are, and are not, implying in their use of language. People often read things into what is being said, inferring more than what is being implied. If, for example, your spouse says he wishes you had consulted him before making a large purchase and means to imply nothing more, you do not want to infer that he thinks you are not a wise decision-maker. Nor does it imply that he doesn't want you to ever make important decisions on your own, or that he thinks he is better at making decisions than are you.

In sum, as developing thinkers, we want to realize the important role of implications in human life. When we are thinking through a problem, issue, or question, we want to think through all the significant implications of the decisions we might make. We want to infer only what is being implied in specific situations. When we use language, we want to be aware of what we are implying. When others are speaking to us, either verbally or in writing, we want to figure out what they are logically implying. In every case, we want to interpret precisely the logic of what is actually going on and infer only what is truly implied, no more, no less.

Test the Idea
Thinking Through the Implications of Your Potential Decisions

As we have said, the ability to think through the implications of a decision you are faced with or a problem you are trying to solve is an important critical-thinking skill. In this activity we want you to think of a problem you need to find a solution to or a decision you need to make. Complete these statements:

1. The problem or decision I am facing is…
2. Some potential solutions to the problem, or decisions I might make, are…
3. For each of these solutions or decisions, some implications that might logically follow from my acting upon the solution or decision are…

Thinking Within and Across Points of View

Point of view is one of the most challenging elements to master. On the one hand, it is highly intuitive to most people that when we think, we think with a point of view. On the other hand, when we ask people, in the midst of reasoning something through, to identify or explain their point of view, they are likely to begin expressing anything and everything they are thinking about. Clearly, most people do not have a clear sense of how to identify someone's point of view, including their own.

Let us begin by recognizing that there are many potential sources for our point of view: time, culture, religion, gender, discipline, profession, peer group, economic interest, emotional state, social role, or age group—to name a few. For example, we can look at the world from:

- A point in time (16th, 17th, 18th, 19th century)
- A culture (Western, Eastern, South American, Japanese, Turkish, French)
- A religion (Buddhist, Christian, Muslin, Jewish)
- A gender (male, female)
- Sexual orientation (homosexual, heterosexual)
- A professional (lawyer, manager, psychologist, teacher)
- A discipline (biological, chemical, geological, astronomical, historical, sociological, philosophical, anthropological, literary, artistic, musical, dance, poetic, medical, nursing, sport)
- A social group
- A professional group
- An economical interest
- An emotional state
- An age group
- A company philosophy

Our dominant point of view as individuals reflects some combination of these dimensions. Unfortunately, most of us are little aware of the extent to which these factors shape our point of view. Typically, people do not say, "This is how I see it from the point of view of...." Typically, people say something that implies, "This is the way things are." Our minds tend to absolutize our experience. We easily lose a sense of the partiality of how we look at things.

This is not an argument for intellectual relativity (the self-refuting view that everything is relative and therefore nothing can be proved). Looking at things from some point of view does not negate our ability to distinguish accurate from inaccurate statements. Doctors look at patients from the point of view of medical health, and that does not make their diagnoses relative or arbitrary.

Using Critical Thinking to Take Charge of How We See Things

As in the case of all the elements, one takes charge of their point of view by practicing bringing it out into the open. The more we recognize point of view at work in our thinking and in the thinking of others, the more points of view we learn to think within, the more effectively will we use point of view in our thinking.

Test the Idea
Practice in Making Explicit Our Point of View

What follows is a list of possible objects of our thinking. Choose from this list seven possible ones to think about. Then identify how you would look at each, from your point of view. For example, you might decide, "When I look at people, I see a struggle to find happiness" or, "When I look at the future, I see myself as a lawyer taking cases that protect the environment" or, "When I look at the health care system, I see a system that does not provide adequately for the poor." Once you write your sentence, see if you can further characterize how what you said explains your point of view.

life	my future	lifelong learning
men	the problems we face as a nation	the future
women	the problems we face as a species	welfare
human conflict	mass transportation	welfare recipients
learning	the environment	drug use
the past	people without health insurance	science
politics	our health care system	human values
power	modern lifestyle	abortions
art	the modern American city	the police
television	New Age ideas	elections
computers	human sexuality	vegetarians
the news	marriage	liberals
my economic future	life in America	conservatives
education in the future	religion	radicals
	income tax	

Complete the following, given the seven objects you have chosen to look at:

1. When I look at _____, I see (from my point of view)

2. When I look at _____, I see (from my point of view)

3. When I look at _____, I see (from my point of view)

4. When I look at _____, I see (from my point of view)

5. When I look at _____, I see (from my point of view)

6. When I look at _____, I see (from my point of view)

7. When I look at _____, I see (from my point of view)

The Point of View of the Critical Thinker

Critical thinkers share a common core of purposes with other critical thinkers, in keeping with the values of critical thinking. This fact has a variety of implications, one of the most important of which is that critical thinkers perceive explicit command of the thinking process as the key to command of behavior. Applied to the learning process, this entails that they see reading, writing, speaking, and listening as modes of skilled thinking.

When they read, they see the text as a verbal representation of the thinking of the author. They strive to enter the writer's point of view. They strive to reconstruct the author's thinking in their own mind. When they write, they think explicitly about the point of view of their intended audience. They use their insight into the thinking of the likely audience to present their thinking in the most accessible way. Their speaking reflects a parallel emphasis. They use the dialogue to find out specifically the point of view and concerns of those with whom they are talking. They do not try to force their ideas on others. They recognize that people must think their own way to ideas and beliefs. They, therefore, share experiences and information more than final conclusions. They listen attentively to the thinking of others. They ask more questions than they make assertions.

Critical thinkers have a distinctive point of view concerning themselves. They see themselves as competent learners. They have a "can do" vision of their own learning. They do not see opposing points of view as a threat to their own beliefs. They see all beliefs as subject to change in the face of new evidence or better reasoning. They see themselves as lifelong learners.

Conclusion

Just as the first step in learning basketball, tennis, soccer, or indeed any sport is to learn the most fundamental elements of the sport, the first step to learning critical thinking is to learn the most basic elements of thinking. These are the bread and butter of disciplined thinking, for if we cannot accurately analyze the parts of someone's thinking, we are in a poor position to assess it.

Analysis of the elements of thought is a necessary, but not a sufficient, condition of evaluation. To evaluate requires knowledge of the intellectual standards that highlight the qualities signaling strengths and weaknesses in thinking. For example, it is a strength in reasoning to be clear, a weakness to be unclear; a strength to be accurate, a weakness to be inaccurate. We shall focus on standards such as these in the next chapter, explaining and illustrating how they apply to the elements of thought.

Chapter 7

The Standards for Thinking

O ne of the fundamentals of critical thinking is the ability to assess one's own reasoning. To be good at assessment requires that we consistently take apart our
thinking and examine the parts with respect to standards of quality. We do this using
criteria based on clarity, accuracy, precision, relevance, depth, breadth, logicalness,
and significance. Critical thinkers recognize that, whenever they are reasoning, they
reason to some purpose (element of reasoning). Implicit goals are built into their
thought processes. But their reasoning is improved when they are clear (intellectual
standard) about that purpose or goal. Similarly, to reason well, they need to know
that, consciously or unconsciously, they are using information (element of reasoning)
in thinking. But their reasoning improves if and when they make sure that the information they are using is accurate (intellectual standard).

Put another way, when we assess our reasoning, we want to know how well we are
reasoning. We do not identify the elements of reasoning for the fun of it. Rather, we
assess our reasoning using intellectual standards because we realize the negative
consequences of failing to do so. In assessing our reasoning, then, we recommend
these intellectual standards as minimal:

- Clarity
- Relevance
- Logicalness
- Accuracy
- Depth

- Significance
- Precision
- Breadth
- Fairness

These are not the only intellectual standards a person might use. They are simply among those that are most fundamental. In this respect, the elements of thought are more basic, because the eight elements we have identified are universal—present in all reasoning of all subjects in all cultures. On the one hand, one cannot reason with no information about no question from no point of view with no assumptions. On the other hand, there are a wide variety of intellectual standards from which to choose—such as credibility, predictability, feasibility, and completeness—that we don't use routinely in assessing reasoning.

As critical thinkers, then, we think about our thinking with these kinds of questions in mind: Am I being clear? Accurate? Precise? Relevant? Am I thinking logically? Am I dealing with a matter of significance? Is my thinking justifiable in context? Typically, we apply these standards to one or more elements.

Test the Idea
Beginning to Think About Intellectual Standards
Consider the list of intellectual standards below. Then try to identify times in your work when you have explicitly focused on them. For example, can you think of a time in a meeting where you focused on clarifying what someone was saying? Can you think of a time when you questioned the relevance of what someone was saying (e.g., "How is this relevant to the issue we are discussing?") Can you think of a time when you questioned the fairness of a potential decision?

Here are the standards to consider:
- Clarity
- Relevance
- Logicalness
- Accuracy
- Depth
- Significance
- Precision
- Breadth
- Fairness

Taking a Deeper Look at Universal Intellectual Standards

Thinking critically requires command of fundamental intellectual standards. Critical thinkers routinely ask questions that apply intellectual standards to thinking. The ultimate goal is for these questions to become so spontaneous in thinking that they form a natural part of our inner voice, guiding us to better and better reasoning. In this section, we focus on the standards and questions that apply across the various facets of your life.

Clarity

Questions that focus on clarity include:

- Could you elaborate on that point?

- Could you express that point in another way?

- Could you give me an illustration?

- Could you give me an example?

- Let me state in my own words what I think you just said. Tell me if I am clear about your meaning.

Clarity is a gateway standard. If a statement is unclear, we cannot determine whether it is accurate or relevant. In fact, we cannot tell anything about it because we don't yet know what is being said. For example, the question "What can be done about the education system in America?" is unclear. To adequately address the question, we would need a clearer understanding of what the person asking the question is considering the "problem" to be. A clearer question might be, "What can educators do to ensure that students learn the skills and abilities that help them function successfully on the job and in their daily decision-making?" This question, because of its increased clarity, provides a better guide to thinking. It lays out in a more definitive way the intellectual task at hand.

Test the Idea
Converting Unclear Thoughts to Clear Thoughts

Can you convert an unclear thought to one that is clear? Suppose you are engaged in a discussion about welfare and one person says, "Let's face it—welfare is corrupt!" What does this mean? What could it mean?

It could mean some very different things. It could mean, "The very idea of giving people goods and services they have not personally earned is equivalent to stealing money from those who have earned it" (a moral claim). Or it could mean, "The welfare laws have so many loopholes that people are receiving money and services that were not envisioned when the laws were initially formulated" (a legal claim). Or it could mean, "The people who receive welfare so often lie and cheat to falsify the documents they submit that they should be thrown in jail" (a claim about the ethical character of the recipients).

Now, take this statement: "She is a good employee." This statement is unclear. Because we don't know the context within which this statement is being made, we aren't sure in what way "she" is "good." Formulate three possible meanings of this statement.

Now take the statement, "He is a jerk." Again, formulate three possible different meanings of this statement.

When you become skilled in differentiating what is clear and what is unclear, you will find that much of the time we are unclear both about what we are thinking and about what we are saying.

Clarifying a Problem You Face at Work

Now take a problem you are currently facing at work. Write down the problem as clearly as possible. Then see if you can reformulate the problem so that it is even clearer. Reformulate the problem until you are very clear about the issue you are facing.

Accuracy

Questions focusing on making thinking more accurate include:

- Is that really true?
- How could we check to see if that is accurate?
- How could we find out if that is true?

A statement may be clear but not accurate, as in, "Most dogs weigh more than 300 pounds." To be accurate is to represent something in accordance with the way it actually is. People often present or describe things or events in a way that is not in accordance with the way things actually are. People frequently misrepresent or falsely describe things, especially when they have a vested interest in the description. Advertisers often do this to keep a buyer from seeing the weaknesses in a product. If an advertisement states, "Our water is 100% pure" when, in fact, the water contains trace amounts of chemicals such as chlorine and lead, it is inaccurate. If an advertisement says, "this bread contains 100% whole wheat" when the whole wheat has been bleached and enriched and the bread contains many additives, the advertisement is inaccurate.

Good thinkers listen carefully to statements and, when there is reason for skepticism, question whether what they hear is true and accurate. In the same way, they question the extent to which what they read is correct, when asserted as fact.

Critical thinking, then, implies a healthy skepticism about public descriptions as to what is and is not fact.

At the same time, because we tend to think from a narrow, self-serving perspective, assessing ideas for accuracy can be difficult. We naturally tend to believe that our thoughts are automatically accurate just because they are ours, and therefore that the thoughts of those who disagree with us are inaccurate. We also fail to question statements that others make that conform to what we already believe, while we tend to question statements that conflict with our views. But as critical thinkers, we force ourselves to accurately assess our own views as well as those of others. We do this even if it means facing deficiencies in our thinking.

Test the Idea
Recognizing Inaccurate Statements

Can you identify a statement that you heard recently that was clear but inaccurate? You will find an abundance of examples in everyday statements that people often make in praise or criticism. People in general have a tendency to make two kinds of inaccurate statements: false positives about the people they personally like (these would be untrue positive statements about people they like) and false negatives about the people they personally dislike (untrue negative things about people they don't like). Politically motivated statements tend to follow a similar pattern. See if you can think of an example of an inaccurate statement from your recent experience. Write out your answer.

In Search of the Facts

One of the most important critical thinking skills is the skill of assessing the accuracy of "factual" claims (someone's assertion that such-and-so is a fact).

In an ad in the *New York Times* (Nov. 29, 1999, p. A15), a coalition of 60 nonprofit organizations accused the World Trade Organization (a coalition of 134 nation states) of operating in secret, undermining democratic institutions and the environment. In the process of doing this, the nonprofit coalition argued that the working class and the poor have not significantly benefited as a result of the last 20 years of rapid expansion of global trade. They alleged, among other things, the following facts:

1. "American CEOs are now paid, on average, 419 times more than line workers, and the ratio is increasing."
2. "Median hourly wages for workers are down by 10% in the last 10 years."
3. "The top 20% of the U.S. population owns 84.6% of the country's wealth."
4. "The wealth of the world's 475 billionaires now equals the annual incomes of more than 50% of the world population combined."

Using whatever sources you can find (including the Website of the Turning Point Project, the nonprofit coalition, www.turnpoint.org), discuss the probable accuracy of the factual claims. For example, visit the Web site of the World Trade Organization (www.wto.org). They might challenge some of the facts alleged or advance facts of their own that put the charges of the nonprofit coalition into a different perspective.

Precision

Questions focusing on making thinking more precise include:

• Could you give me more details?

• Could you be more specific?

A statement can be both clear and accurate but not precise, as in "Jack is overweight." (We don't know how overweight Jack is—1 pound or 500 pounds.) To be precise is to give the details needed for someone to understand exactly what is meant. Some situations don't call for detail. If you ask, "Is there any milk in the refrigerator?" and I answer "Yes," both the question and the answer are probably precise enough for the circumstance (though it might be relevant to specify how much milk is there). Or imagine that you are ill and go to the doctor. He wouldn't say, "Take 1.4876946 antibiotic pills twice per day." This level of specificity, or precision, would be beyond that which is useful in the situation.

In many situations, however, specifics are essential to good thinking. Let's say that your friend is having financial problems and asks you, "What should I do about my situation?" In this case, you want to probe her thinking for specifics. Without the full specifics, you could not help her. You might ask questions such as, "What precisely is the problem? What exactly are the variables that bear on the problem? What are some possible solutions to the problem-in detail?

Test the Idea
Recognizing when Precision is Needed

Can you think of a recent situation at work or at home in which you needed more details to figure something out, a circumstance in which, because you didn't have the details, you experienced some negative consequences? For example, have you ever been given directions to someone's house, directions that seemed precise enough at the time? Yet when you tried to find the person's house, you got lost because of lack of details in the directions?

First identify a situation in which the details and specifics were important (for example, in buying a house, a computer, or a car). Then identify the negative consequences that resulted because you didn't get the details you needed to think well in the situation.

Relevance

Questions focusing on relevance include:

- How is this idea connected to the question?

- How does that bear on the issue?

- How does this idea relate to this other idea?

- How does your question relate to the issue we are dealing with?

A statement can be clear, accurate, and precise, but not relevant to the question at issue. For example, students often think the amount of effort they put into a course should contribute to raising their grade in the course. Often, however, effort does not measure the quality of student learning and therefore is irrelevant to the grade. Something is relevant when it is directly connected with and bears upon the issue at hand. Something is also relevant when it is pertinent or applicable to a problem we are trying to solve. Irrelevant thinking encourages us to consider what we should set aside. Thinking that is relevant stays on track. People are often irrelevant in their thinking because they lack discipline in thinking. They don't know how to analyze an issue for what truly bears on it. Therefore, they aren't able to effectively think their way through the problems and issues they face.

Test the Idea
Recognizing Irrelevant Statements

Can you identify a statement you heard recently that was clear, accurate, and sufficiently precise, but irrelevant to the circumstance, problem, or issue? Though we all sometimes stray from a question or task, we need to be sensitive to when failure to stay on task may have a significant negative implication.

Identify, first, circumstances in which people tend to introduce irrelevant considerations into a discussion (for example, in meetings, in response to questions in class, in everyday dialogue when they have a hidden agenda—or simply want to get control of the conversation for some reason).

Depth

Questions focusing on depth of thought include:

- How does your answer address the complexities in the question?

- How are you taking into account the problems in the question?

- How are you dealing with the most significant factors in the problem?

We think deeply when we get beneath the surface of an issue or problem, identify the complexities inherent in it, and then deal with those complexities in an intellectually responsible way. Even when we think deeply and deal well with the complexities in a question, we may find the question difficult to address. Still, our thinking will work better for us when we can recognize complicated questions and address each area of complexity in it.

A statement can be clear, accurate, precise, and relevant, but superficial—lacking in depth. Let's say you are asked what should be done about the problem of drug use in America and you answer by saying, "Just say no." This slogan, which was for several years used to discourage children and teens from using drugs, is clear, accurate, precise, and relevant. Nevertheless, it lacks depth because it treats an extremely complex issue superficially—i.e. it hardly addresses the pervasive problem of drug use among people in our culture. It does not address the history of the problem, the politics of the problem, the economics of the problem, the psychology of addiction, and so on.

Test the Idea
Recognizing Superficial Approaches
Identify a problem you have experienced at work where the solutions presented to the problem were superficial in nature. If decisions were made based on this surface thinking, what were the consequences that followed from the decision? If final decisions have not yet been made on this issue, try to think of some implications (or potential consequences) of following the superficial thinking that has been presented to deal with the problem.

Breadth

Questions focusing on making thinking broader include:

- Do we need to consider another point of view?
- Is there another way to look at this question?
- What would this look like from a conservative standpoint?
- What would this look like from the point of view of...?

A line of reasoning may be clear, accurate, precise, relevant, and deep, but lack breadth. Examples are arguments from either the conservative or the liberal standpoint that get deeply into an issue but show insight into only one side of the question.

When we consider the issue at hand from every relevant viewpoint, we think in a broad way. When multiple points of view are pertinent to the issue, yet we fail to give due consideration to those perspectives, we think myopically, or narrow-mindedly. We do not try to understand alternative, or opposing, viewpoints.

Humans are frequently guilty of narrow-mindedness for many reasons: limited education, innate socio-centrism, natural selfishness, self-deception, and intellectual arrogance. Points of view that significantly disagree with our own often threaten us. It's much easier to ignore perspectives with which we disagree than to consider them, when we know at some level that to consider them would mean to be forced to reconsider our views.

Let's say, for example, that you like to watch/listen to TV in the bedroom as a way of falling to sleep. But let's say that your spouse has difficulty falling to sleep while the TV is on. The question at issue, then, is "Should you have the TV on in the bedroom while you and your spouse are falling asleep?" It is easy enough to rationalize your "need" to have the TV on every night while falling asleep, by saying such things to your spouse as "It is impossible for me to fall asleep without the TV on. And, after all, I really don't ask that much of you. Besides, you don't seem to have any real problem falling to sleep with the TV on." Yet both your viewpoint and your spouse's are relevant to the question at issue. When you recognize your spouse's viewpoint as relevant, and then intellectually empathize with it—when you enter her/his way of thinking so as to *actually understand* it—you will be thinking broadly about the issue. You will realize common consideration would require you to come to an agreement that fully takes into account both ways of looking at the situation. But if you don't force yourself to enter her/his viewpoint, you do not have to change your self-serving behavior. One of the primary mechanisms the mind uses to avoid giving up what it wants is unconsciously to refuse to enter viewpoints that differ from its own.

Test the Idea
Thinking Broadly About an Issue
Take the question, "Is abortion morally justified?" Some argue that abortion is not morally justifiable, and others argue that it is. Try to state and elaborate on each of these points of view in detail. Articulate each point of view objectively, regardless of your personal views. Present each point of view in such a way that a person who actually takes that position would assess it as accurate. Each line of reasoning should be clear, accurate, precise, relevant, and deep. Try not to take a position on the issue yourself.

Logicalness

Questions that focus on making thinking more logical include:

- Does all of this fit together logically?

- Does this really make sense?

- Does that follow from what you said?

- How does that follow from the evidence?
- Before, you implied this, and now you are saying that. I don't see how both can be true.

When we think, we bring together a variety of thoughts in some order. When the combined thoughts are mutually supporting and make sense in combination, the thinking is logical. When the combination is not mutually supporting, is contradictory in some sense, or does not make sense, the combination is not logical. Because humans often maintain conflicting beliefs without being aware that we are doing so, it is not unusual to find inconsistencies in human life and thought.

Let's say we know, by looking at standardized tests of students in schools and the actual work they are able to produce, that for the most part students are deficient in basic academic skills such as reading, writing, speaking, and the core disciplines such as math, science, and history. Despite this evidence, teachers often conclude that there is nothing they can do to change their instruction to improve student learning (and in fact that there is nothing fundamentally wrong with the way they teach). Given the evidence, this conclusion seems illogical. The conclusion doesn't seem to follow from the facts.

Let's take another example. Say that you know a person who has had a heart attack, and her doctors have told her she must be careful what she eats. Yet she concludes that what she eats really doesn't matter. Given the evidence, her conclusion is illogical. It doesn't make sense.

Test the Idea
Recognizing Illogical Thinking
Identify a situation at work where decisions made seemed to be based on illogical thinking—thinking that didn't make sense to you.
1. What was the situation?
2. What was the thinking in the situation that you consider to be illogical? Why do you think it was illogical?
3. What were some consequences that followed from the illogical thinking?

Significance

Questions that focus on making thinking more significant include:

- What is the most significant information we need to address this issue?
- How is that fact important in context?
- Which of these questions is the most significant?
- Which of these ideas or concepts is the most important?

When we reason through issues, we want to concentrate on the most important information (relevant to the issue) in our reasoning and take into account the most important ideas or concepts. Too often we fail in our thinking because we do not recognize that, though many ideas may be relevant to an issue, it does not follow that all are equally important. In a similar way, we often fail to ask the most important questions and are trapped by thinking only in terms of superficial questions, questions of little weight. In college, for example, few students focus on important questions such as, "What does it mean to be an educated person? What do I need to do to become educated?" Instead, students tend to ask questions such as, "What do I need to do to get an "A" in this course? How many pages does this paper have to be? What do I have to do to satisfy this professor?"

In our work, we too often focus on that which is pressing, at the expense of focusing on that which is significant. In our personal lives, we also often focus on the trivial mundane details, rather than the important bigger picture of our lives. Very few people, for example, have seriously thought about questions such as:

- What is the most important thing I could do in my life?

- What are the most important things I should try to accomplish this week, this month, this year?

- How can I help my children become kind, caring, contributing members of society?

- How can I best relate to my spouse so that she understands the deep love I feel for her?

- How can I keep my mind focused on the things that matter most to me (rather than the unimportant trivial details)?

Test the Idea
Focusing on Significance in Thinking

Think about your life, about the way you spend your time, in terms of the amount of time you spend on significant versus trivial things. As you do so, write the answers to these questions:

1. What is the most important goal or purpose you should focus on at this point in your life? Why is this purpose important? How much time do you spend focused on it?

2. What are the most trivial or superficial things you spend time focused on (things such as your appearance, impressing your friends or colleagues, spending money on things you don't need, chatting about insignificant things at parties, and the like)?

3. What can you do to reduce the amount of time you spend on the trivial, and increase the amount of time you spend on the significant?

Fairness

Questions that focus on ensuring that thinking is fair include:

- Is my thinking justified given the evidence?
- Am I taking into account the weight of the evidence that others might advance in the situation?
- Are these assumptions justified?
- Is my purpose fair given the implications of my behavior?
- Is the manner in which I am addressing the problem fair—or is my vested interest keeping me from considering the problem from alternative viewpoints?
- Am I using concepts justifiably, or am I using them unfairly in other to manipulate someone (and selfishly get what I want)?

When we think through problems, we want to make sure that our thinking is justified. To be justified is to think fairly in context. In other words, it is to think in accord with reason. If you are vigilant in using the other intellectual standards covered thus far in the chapter you will (by implication) satisfy the standard of fairness. We include fairness in its own section because of the powerful nature of self-deception in human thinking. For example, we often deceive ourselves into thinking that we are being fair and justified in our thinking when in fact we are refusing to consider significant relevant information that would cause us to change our view (and therefore not pursue our selfish interest). We often pursue unfair purposes in order to get what we want even if we have to hurt others to get it. We often use concepts in an unjustified way in order to manipulate people. And we often make unjustified assumptions, unsupported by facts, which then lead to faulty inferences.

Let's focus on an example where the problem is unjustified thinking owing to ignoring relevant facts. Let's say, for instance, that Kristi and Abbey share the same office. Kristi is cold natured and Abbey is warm-natured. During the winter, Abbey likes to have the window in the office open while Kristi likes to keep it closed. But Abbey insists that it's "extremely uncomfortable" with the window closed. The information she is using in her reasoning all centers around her own point of view—that she is hot, that she can't work effectively if she's hot, that if Kristi is cold she can wear a sweater. But the fact is that Abbey is not justified in her thinking. She refuses to enter Kristi's point of view, to consider information supporting Kristi's perspective, because to do so would mean that she would have to give something up. She would have to adopt a more reasonable, or fair, point of view.

When we reason to conclusions, we want to check to make sure that the assumptions we are using to come to those conclusions are justifiable given the facts of the situation. For example, all of our prejudices and stereotypes function as assumptions in thinking. And no prejudices and stereotypes are justifiable given their very nature. For example, we often make broad sweeping generalizations such as:

- Liberals are soft on crime
- Elderly people aren't interested in sex
- Young men are only interested in sex
- Jocks are cool
- Blondes are dumb
- Cheerleaders are airheads
- Intellectuals are nerds

The problem with assumptions like these is that they cause us to make basic—and often serious—mistakes in thinking. Because they aren't justifiable, they cause us to prejudge situations and people and draw faulty inferences—or conclusions—about them. For example, if we believe that all intellectuals are nerds, whenever we meet an intellectual we will infer that he or she is a nerd (and act unfairly toward the person).

In sum, justifiability, or fairness, is an important standard in thinking because it forces us to see how we are distorting our thinking in order to achieve our self-serving ends (or to see how others are distorting their thinking to achieve selfish ends).

Test the Idea
Are You Always Fair?

All of us want to see ourselves as imminently fair. Yet because we are by nature self-serving, we are not always able to consider the rights and needs of others in equivalent terms as we do our own. Indeed, one of the most difficult things for people to do is identify times when they are unfair. Yet highly skilled thinkers, aware of this human tendency, routinely search for problems in their thinking.

In the spirit of this idea, try to think of several times in the past few weeks where you were not fair. You are looking for situations where your behavior was selfish or self-serving and as a result, you negated another person's desires or rights. You placed your desires first. Remember that the more examples you can think of, the better. Also remember that, because of our native egocentrism, we are highly motivated to hide our unfair thoughts and behavior. Try not to fall into this trap.

Bringing Together the Elements of Reasoning and the Intellectual Standards

We have considered the elements of reasoning and the importance of being able to take them apart, to analyze them so we can begin to recognize flaws in our thinking. We also have introduced the intellectual standards as tools for assessment. Now let us look at how the intellectual standards are used to assess the elements of reason (Table 7.1 & Figure 7.1).

Table 7.1   Powerful questions are implied by the intellectual standards. Critical thinkers routinely ask them.

Clarity

Could you elaborate?
Could you illustrate what you mean?
Could you give me an example?

Accuracy

How could we check on that?
How could we find out if that is true?
How could we verify or test that?

Precision

Could you be more specific?
Could you give me more details?
Could you be more exact?

Depth

What factors make this a difficult problem?
What are some of the complexities of this question?
What are some of the difficulties we need to deal with?

Relevance

How does that relate to the problem?
How does that bear on the question?
How does that help us with the issue?

Logicalness

Does all of this make sense together?
Does your first paragraph fit in with your last?
Does what you say follow from the evidence?

Significance

Is this the most important problem to consider?
Is this the central idea to focus on?
Which of these facts are the most important?

Breadth

Do we need to look at this from another perspective?
Do we need to consider another point of view?
Do we need to look at this in other ways?

Table 7.1 Powerful questions are implied by the intellectual standards. Critical thinkers routinely ask them. *(continued)*

Fairness

Is my thinking justifiable in context?
Are my assumptions supported by evidence?
Is my purpose fair given the situation?
Am I using my concepts in keeping with educated usage or am I distorting them to get what I want?

Figure 7.1 Critical thinkers routinely apply the intellectual standards to the elements of reasoning.

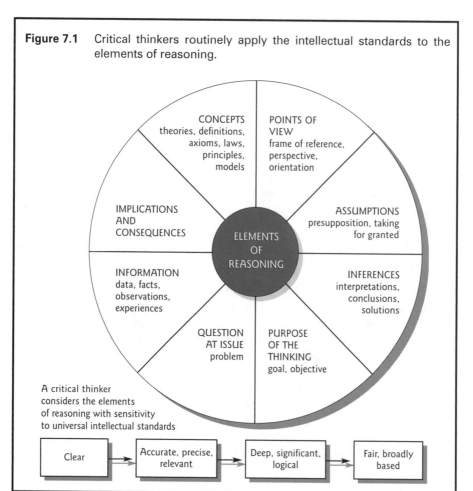

Purpose, Goal, or End in View

Whenever we reason, we do so to some end, to achieve an objective, to satisfy some desire or fulfill a need. One source of problems in human reasoning is traceable to defects at the level of goal, purpose, or end. If the goal is unrealistic, for example, or contradictory to other goals we have, if it is confused or muddled, the reasoning used to achieve it will suffer as a result.

As a developing critical thinker, then, you should get in the habit of explicitly stating the purposes you are trying to accomplish. You should strive to be clear about your purpose in every situation. If you fail to stick to your purpose, you are unlikely to achieve it. Let's say that your purpose in parenting is to help your children develop as life-long learners and contributing members of society. If you keep this purpose clearly in mind and consistently work to achieve it, you are more likely to be successful. But it is easy to lose sight of such an important purpose in the daily life of dealing with children. It is all too easy to get pulled into daily battles over whether a child's room is kept clean, whether they wear clothes considered "appropriate," whether they can get their nose pierced or their stomach tattooed. To achieve your purpose, you must revisit again and again what it is you are trying to accomplish. You must ask yourself on a daily basis questions like, "What have I done today to help my child develop as a rational, caring person?"

As an employee, you can begin to ask questions that improve your ability to focus on purpose in your work. For example: Am I clear as to my purpose—in this meeting, in this project, in dealing with this issue, in this discussion? Can I specify my purpose precisely? Is my purpose a significant one? Realistic? Achievable? Justifiable? Do I have contradictory purposes?

Test the Idea
Bringing Intellectual Standards to Bear Upon Your Purpose

Think of an important problem in your life. This can be a problem in a personal relationship, at your place of work, etc. Now state your purpose in the situation clearly and precisely. What exactly are you trying to accomplish? Is your purpose fair, or justifiable? Is it realistic?

Question at Issue or Problem to Be Solved

Whenever you attempt to reason something through, there is at least one question to answer—one question that emerges from the problem to be solved or issue to resolve. An area of concern in assessing reasoning, therefore, revolves around the very question at issue.

An important part of being able to think well is assessing your ability to formulate a problem in a clear and relevant way. It requires determining whether the question you are addressing is an important one, whether it is answerable, whether you understand the requirements for settling the question, for solving the problem.

As an employee, you can begin to ask yourself questions that improve your ability to focus on the important questions in your work. You begin to ask: What is the most fundamental question at issue (in this meeting, in this project, in this discussion)? What is the question, precisely? Is the question simple or complex? If it is complex, what makes it complex? Am I sticking to the question (in this discussion, in this project I am working on)? Is there more than one important question to be considered here (in this meeting, etc.)?

Test the Idea
Bringing Intellectual Standards to Bear Upon the Question at Issue
Go back to the important problem in the previous activity. Now state the problem you are trying to address. Then state the question that emerges from that problem. State your question clearly and precisely. What complexities, if any, are inherent in the problem? Is there more than one question that you need to address to effectively reason through the problem?

Point of View, or Frame of Reference

Whenever we reason, we must reason within some point of view or frame of reference. Any "defect" in that point of view or frame of reference is a possible source of problems in the reasoning.

A point of view may be too narrow, may be based on false or misleading information, may contain contradictions, and may be narrow or unfair. Critical thinkers strive to adopt a point of view that is fair to others, even to opposing points of view. They want their point of view to be broad, flexible, and justifiable, to be clearly stated and consistently adhered to. Good thinkers, then, consider alternative points of view as they reason through an issue.

As an employee, you begin to ask yourself questions that improve your ability to focus on point of view in your work. These questions might be: From what point of view am I looking at this issue? Am I so locked into my point of view that I am unable to see the issue from other points of view? Must I consider multiple points of view to reason well through the issue at hand? What is the point of view of my colleague? How is she seeing things differently than I? Which of these perspectives seems more reasonable given the situation?

Test the Idea
Bringing Intellectual Standards to Bear Upon Points of View
Continue with the problem from the last two activities. Now state the point or points of view that are relevant to the issue at hand. State each point of view clearly and precisely. Make sure you are considering all relevant points of view (that you are thinking broadly), and that you are representing each point of view accurately (even if it means sympathetically expressing a view that you do not personally hold).

Information, Data, Experiences

Whenever we reason, there is some "stuff," some phenomena about which we are reasoning. Any "defect," then, in the experiences, data, evidence, or raw material upon which a person's reasoning is based is a possible source of problems.

Those who reason should be assessed on their ability to give evidence that is gathered and reported clearly, fairly, and accurately. Therefore, as a developing thinker, you should assess the information you use to come to conclusions, whether you are reasoning through issues at work or reasoning through a problem in your personal life. You should assess whether the information you are using in reasoning is relevant to the issue at hand and adequate for achieving your purpose. You should assess whether you are taking the information into account consistently or distorting it to fit your own (often self-serving) point of view.

At work, you can begin to ask yourself questions that improve your ability to focus on information in your work. These questions might be: What is the most important information I need to reason well through this issue? Are there alternate information sources I need to consider? How can I check to see if the information I am using is accurate? Am I sure that all of the information I am using is relevant to the issue at hand?

Test the Idea
Bringing Intellectual Standards to Bear Upon the Information You are Using in Your Reasoning
Continue with the problem you have been working on. Now state the information you are using in your thinking. This could be data, facts, or experiences that, in conjunction with your assumptions, lead you to conclusions. It could come from your experience, word of mouth, research, the media, or other sources. State the information clearly. How could you determine whether the information is accurate and relevant to the question at issue?

Concepts, Theories, Ideas

All reasoning uses some ideas or concepts and not others. These concepts include the theories, principles, axioms, and rules implicit in our reasoning. Any defect in the concepts or ideas of the reasoning is a possible source of problems in our reasoning.

As an aspiring critical thinker, you begin to focus more deeply on the concepts you use. You begin to assess the extent to which you are clear about those concepts, whether they are relevant to the issue at hand, and whether your principles are inappropriately slanted by your point of view. You begin to direct your attention to how you use concepts, what concepts are most important, and how concepts are intertwined in networks.

As a person interested in developing your mind, you begin to ask questions that improve your ability to focus on the importance of concepts in your life. These questions may include: What is the most fundamental concept I am focused on in this situation? How does this concept connect with other key concepts I need to consider? What are the most important theories I need to consider? Am I clear about the important concepts in this meeting? What questions do I need to ask to get clear about the concepts we are discussing?

Test the Idea
Bringing Intellectual Standards to Bear upon the Concepts You Use

Continue with the problem you have been working on. Now state the most important concepts you are using to guide your reasoning. For example, if you are concerned with how you can keep in physical shape while also dedicating enough time to family and work, your key concepts might be physical fitness, good family relationships, and productive work life. (You usually can find the key concepts you are using in your reasoning by looking at your question and purpose.) Elaborate on each of these concepts so you understand exactly how you are using them. State your concepts clearly and precisely.

Assumptions

All reasoning must begin somewhere. It must take some things for granted. Any defect in the assumptions or presuppositions with which reasoning begins is a possible source of problems in the reasoning.

Assessing skills of reasoning involves assessing our ability to recognize and articulate assumptions, again according to relevant standards. Our assumptions may be clear or unclear, justifiable or unjustifiable, consistent or contradictory.

As a person interested in developing your mind, you begin to ask questions that improve your ability to analyze the assumptions you and others are using. These questions could include: What am I taking for granted? Am I justified in taking this for granted? What are others taking for granted? What is being assumed in this meeting? What is being assumed in this relationship? What is being assumed in this discussion? Are these assumptions justifiable, or should I question them?

Test the Idea
Bringing Intellectual Standards to Bear Upon Your Assumptions

Continue with the problem you have been working on. Now state the most important assumptions you are making in your reasoning. What are you taking for granted that might be questioned? Using the previous example of how to keep in physical shape while also dedicating enough time to your family and your work, your main assumptions might be:

1. High-quality family relationships are more important than work productivity.
2. I know enough about physical fitness to do appropriate exercises.
3. I must spend a considerable amount of time at work in order to support my family.
4. I have enough time to do all of the above well.

State your assumptions clearly and precisely. Make sure they are justifiable in the context of the issue.

Implications and Consequences

Whenever we reason, implications follow from our reasoning. When we make decisions, consequences result from those decisions. As critical thinkers, we want to understand implications whenever and wherever they occur. We want to be able to trace logical consequences. We want to see what our actions are leading to. We want to anticipate possible problems before they arise.

No matter where we stop tracing implications, there always will be further implications. No matter what consequences we do see, there always will be other and further consequences. Any defect in our ability to follow the implications or consequences of our reasoning is a potential source of problems in our thinking. Our ability to reason well, then, is measured in part by our ability to understand and enunciate the implications and consequences of reasoning.

In your work and personal life, you begin to ask yourself questions that improve your ability to focus on the important implications in your thinking and the thinking of others. These questions could include, for example: What are the most important implications of this decision? What are the implications of my doing this versus my doing that? Have we thought through the implications decision in this meeting? Have I thought through the implications of my parenting behavior? Have I thought through the implications of the way I treat my spouse?

Test the Idea
Thinking Through the Implications of Your Reasoning

Continue with the problem you have been working on. Now state the most important implication of potential decisions you might make. Fill in these blanks: If I decide to do _____, then _____ is likely to follow. If I decide to act differently by doing _____, then _____ is likely to follow.

In this activity, you are emphasizing the logical implications and potential consequences of each potential decision. Make sure you emphasize important implications of each decision. For further practice, what would be the most likely implications of (1) getting married, (2) staying in your hometown for the whole of your life, (3) staying in the same job for the whole of your life, (4) deciding to get a divorce (if you are married)?

Inferences

All reasoning proceeds by steps in which we reason as follows: "Because this is so, that also is so (or is probably so)" or, "Because this, therefore that." The mind perceives a situation or a set of facts and comes to a conclusion based on those facts. When this step of the mind occurs, an inference is made. Any defect in our ability to make logical inferences is a possible problem in our reasoning. For example, if you see a person sitting on the street corner wearing tattered clothing, a worn bed roll beside him and a bottle wrapped in a brown paper bag in his hand, you might infer that he is a bum. This inference is based on the facts you perceive in the situation and of what you assume about them. The inference, however, may or may not be logical in this situation.

Critical thinkers want to become adept at making sound inferences. First, you want to learn to identify when you or someone else has made an inference. What are the key inferences made in this discussion? Upon what are the inferences based? Are they justified? What is the key inference (or conclusion) I made in this meeting? Was it justified? What is the key inference in this way of proceeding, in solving this problem in this way? Is this inference logical? Is this conclusion significant? Is this interpretation justified? These are the kinds of questions you begin to ask.

As a person interested in developing your mind, you should ask questions that improve your ability to spot important inferences wherever they occur. Given the facts of this case, is there more than one logical inference (conclusion, interpretation) one could come to? What are some other logical conclusions that should be considered? From this point on, develop an inference detector, the skill of recognizing the inferences you are making in order to analyze them.

Test the Idea
Bringing Intellectual Standards to Bear Upon Your Inferences

Continue with the problem you have been working on. Now state the inferences, or conclusions, you might come to (about the information you have) in solving your problem. You may have already stated these in the activities above. Once you have thought through the potential conclusions you might come to in reasoning through the question at issue, state a possible final conclusion. Be clear and precise in stating each potential conclusion. Make sure your inferences make good sense, based on the information and concepts you are using.

Using Intellectual Standards to Assess Your Thinking: Brief Guidelines

As we have emphasized, all reasoning involves eight elements, each of which has a range of possible mistakes. Here we summarize some of the main "checkpoints" you should use in reasoning (See also Tables 7.2–7.9).

1. **All reasoning has a purpose.**
   - Take time to state your purpose clearly.
   - Choose significant and realistic purposes.
   - Distinguish your purpose from related purposes.
   - Make sure your purpose is fair in context (that it doesn't involve violating the rights of others).
   - Check periodically to be sure you are still focused on your purpose and haven't wandered from your target.

2. **All reasoning is an attempt to figure out something, to settle some question, solve some problem.**
   - Take time to clearly and precisely state the question at issue.
   - Express the question in several ways to clarify its meaning and scope.
   - Break the question into sub-questions (when you can).
   - Identify the type of question you are dealing with (historical, economic, biological, etc.) and whether the question has one right answer, is a matter of mere opinion, or requires reasoning from more than one point of view.
   - Think through the complexities of the question (think deeply through the question).

3. **All reasoning is based on assumptions.**
   - Clearly identify your assumptions and determine whether they are justifiable.
   - Consider how your assumptions are shaping your point of view.

4. **All reasoning is done from some point of view.**
   - Clearly identify your point of view.
   - Seek other relevant points of view and identify their strengths as well as weaknesses.
   - Strive to be fair-minded in evaluating all points of view.
5. **All reasoning is based on data, information, and evidence.**
   - Restrict your claims to those supported by the data you have.
   - Search for information that opposes your position as well as information that supports it.
   - Make sure that all information used is clear, accurate, and relevant to the question at issue.
   - Make sure you have gathered sufficient information.
   - Make sure, especially, that you have considered all significant information relevant to the issue.
6. **All reasoning is expressed through, and shaped by, concepts and ideas.**
   - Clearly identify key concepts.
   - Consider alternative concepts or alternative definitions for concepts.
   - Make sure you are using concepts with care and precision.
   - Use concepts justifiably (not distorting their established meanings).
7. **All reasoning contains inferences or interpretations by which we draw conclusions and give meaning to data.**
   - Infer only what the evidence implies.
   - Check inferences for their consistency with each other.
   - Identify assumptions that lead you to your inferences.
   - Make sure your inferences logically follow from the information.
8. **All reasoning leads somewhere or has implications and consequences.**
   - Trace the logical implications and consequences that follow from your reasoning.
   - Search for negative as well as positive implications.
   - Consider all possible significant consequences.

Test the Idea
Checkpoints in Thinking

For all of the eight categories outlined, transform each checkpoint into a question or a set of questions; figure out one or more questions that the checkpoint implies. When you have completed your list and you are actively using the questions you formulated, you will have powerful tools for thinking.

Under the first category, All reasoning has a purpose, for example, the first checkpoint is, "Take time to state your purpose clearly" Two questions implied by this checkpoint are: "What exactly is my purpose?" and "Am I clear about my purpose?"

Table 7.2   This chart focuses on *purpose in thinking*. It is useful in understanding the intellectual standards to be applied to purpose and in differentiating between the use of purpose in thinking by skilled and unskilled reasoners.

PURPOSE
(All reasoning has a purpose)

Primary standards: (1) clarity, (2) significance, (3) achievability, (4) consistency, (5) justifiability

Common problems: (1) unclear, (2) trivial, (3) unrealistic, (4) contradictory, (5) unfair

Principle: To reason well, you must clearly understand your purpose, and your purpose must be fair-minded.

Skilled Reasoners	Unskilled Reasoners	Critical Reflections
take the time to state their purpose clearly.	are often unclear about their central purpose.	Have I made the purpose of my reasoning clear? What exactly am I trying to achieve? Have I stated the purpose in several ways to clarify it?
distinguish it from related purposes.	oscillate between different, sometimes contradictory, purposes.	What different purposes do I have in mind? How do I see them as related? Am I going off in somewhat different directions? How can I reconcile these contradictory purposes?
periodically remind themselves of their purpose to determine whether they are straying from it.	lose track of their fundamental object or goal.	In writing this proposal, do I seem to be wandering from my purpose? How do my third and fourth paragraphs relate to my central goal?
adopt realistic purposes and goals.	adopt unrealistic purposes and set unrealistic goals.	Am I trying to accomplish too much in this project?
choose significant purposes and goals.	adopt trivial purposes and goals as if they were significant.	What is the significance of pursuing this particular purpose? Is there a more significant purpose I should be focused on?
choose goals and purposes that are consistent with other goals and purposes they have chosen	inadvertently negate their own purposes. do not monitor their thinking for inconsistent goals.	Does one part of my proposal seem to undermine what I am trying to accomplish in another part?
adjust their thinking regularly to their purpose.	do not adjust their thinking regularly to their purpose.	Does my argument stick to the issue? Am I acting consistently within my purpose?
choose purposes that are fair-minded, considering the desires and rights of others equally with their own desires and rights.	choose purposes that are self-serving at the expense of others' needs and desires.	Is my purpose self-serving or concerned only with my own desires? Does it take into account the rights and needs of other people?

Table 7.3 This chart focuses on *questions in thinking*. It is useful in understanding the intellectual standards to be applied to questions and in differentiating between the use of questions in thinking by skilled and unskilled reasoners.

QUESTION AT ISSUE OR CENTRAL PROBLEM

(All reasoning is an attempt to figure something out, to settle some question, solve some problem.)

Primary standards: (1) clarity and precision, (2) significance, (3) answerability, (4) relevance

Common problems: (1) unclear and unprecise, (2) insignificant, (3) not answerable, (4) irrelevant

Principle: To settle a question, it must be answerable, and you must be clear about it and understand what is needed to adequately answer it.

Skilled Reasoners	Unskilled Reasoners	Critical Reflections
are clear about the question they are trying to settle.	are often unclear about the question they are asking.	Am I clear about the main question at issue? Am I able to state it precisely?
can re-express a question in a variety of ways.	express questions vaguely and find questions difficult to reformulate for clarity.	Am I able to reformulate my question in several ways to recognize the complexity of it?
can break a question into sub-questions.	are unable to break down the questions they are asking.	Have I broken down the main question into sub-questions? What are the sub-questions embedded in the main question?
routinely distinguish questions of different types.	confuse questions of different types and thus often respond inappropriately to the question they ask.	Am I confused about the type of question I am asking? For example: Am I confusing a legal question with an ethical one? Am I confusing a question of preference with a question requiring judgment?
distinguish significant from trivial questions.	confuse trivial questions with significant ones.	Am I focusing on trivial questions while other significant questions have been addresses?
distinguish relevant questions from irrelevant ones.	confuse irrelevant questions with relevant ones.	Are the questions I'm raising in this discussion relevant to the main question at issue?
are sensitive to the assumptions built into the questions they ask.	often ask loaded questions.	Is the way I'm putting the question loaded? Am I taking for granted from the outset the correctness of my own position?
distinguish questions they can answer from questions they can't.	try to answer questions they are not in a position to answer.	Am I in a position to answer the question? What information would I need to have before I could answer the question?

Table 7.4	This chart focuses on *point of view in thinking*. It is useful in understanding the intellectual standards to be applied to point of view and in differentiating between the use of point of view in thinking by skilled and unskilled reasoners.

POINT OF VIEW

(All reasoning is done from some point of view.)

Primary standards: (1) flexibility, (2) fairness, (3) clarity, (4) breadth, (5) relevance

Common problems: (1) restricted, (2) biased, (3) unclear, (4) narrow, (5) irrelevant

Principle: To reason well, you must identify those points of view relevant to the issue and enter these viewpoints empathetically.

Skilled Reasoners	Unskilled Reasoners	Critical Reflections
keep in mind that people have different points of view, especially on controversial issues.	do not credit alternative reasonable viewpoints.	Have I articulated the point of view from which I am approaching this issue? Have I considered opposing points of view regarding this issue?
consistently articulate other points of view and reason from within those points of view to adequately understand other points of view.	cannot see issues from points of view that are significantly different from their own; cannot reason with empathy from alien points of view.	I may have characterized my own point of view, but have I considered the most significant aspects of the problem from the point of view of others?
seek other viewpoints, especially when the issue is one they believe in passionately.	can sometimes give other points of view when the issue is not emotionally charged but cannot do so for issues they feel strongly about.	Am I presenting X's point of view in an unfair manner? Am I having difficulty appreciating X's viewpoint because I am emotional about this issue?
confine their monological reasoning to problems that are clearly monological.*	confuse multilogical with monological issues; insist that there is only one frame of reference within which a given multilogical question must be decided.	Is the question here monological or multilogical? How can I tell? Am I reasoning as if only one point of view is relevant to this issue when in reality other viewpoints are relevant?
recognize when they are most likely to be prejudiced.	are unaware of their own prejudices.	Is this prejudiced or reasoned judgement? If prejudiced, where does it come from?
approach problems and issues with a richness of vision and an appropriately broad point of view.	reason from within inappropriately narrow or superficial points of view.	Is my approach to this question too narrow? Am I considering other viewpoints so I can adequately address the problem?

* Monological problems are ones for which there are definite correct and incorrect answers and definite procedures for getting those answers. In multilogical problems, there are competing schools of thought to be considered.

Table 7.5 This chart focuses on *information in thinking*. It is useful in understanding the intellectual standards to be applied to information and in differentiating between the use of information in thinking by skilled and unskilled reasoners.

INFORMATION

(All reasoning is based on data, information, evidence, experience, research.)

Primary standards: (1) clear, (2) relevant, (3) fairly gathered and reported, (4) accurate, (5) adequate, (6) consistently applied

Common problems: (1) unclear, (2) irrelevant, (3) biased, (4) inaccurate, (5) insufficient, (6) inconsistently applied

Principle: Reasoning can be only as sound as the information it is based on.

Skilled Reasoners	Unskilled Reasoners	Critical Reflections
assert a claim only when they have sufficient evidence to back it up.	assert claims without considering all relevant information.	Is my assertion supported by evidence?
can articulate and evaluate the information behind their claims.	don't articulate the information they are using in their reasoning and so do not subject it to rational scrutiny.	Do I have evidence to support my claim that I haven't articulated? Have I evaluated for accuracy and relevance the information I am using?
actively search for information *against* (not just *for*) their own position.	gather information only when it supports their own point of view.	Where is a good place to look for evidence on the opposite side? Have I looked there? Have I honestly considered information that doesn't support my position?
focus on relevant information and disregard what is irrelevant to the question at issue.	do not carefully distinguish between relevant information and irrelevant information.	Are my data relevant to the claim I'm making? Have I failed to consider relevant information?
draw conclusions only to the extent that they are supported by the data and sound reasoning.	make inferences that go beyond what the data support.	Does my claim go beyond the evidence I've cited?
state the evidence clearly and fairly.	distort the data or state it inaccurately.	Is my presentation of the pertinent information clear and coherent? Have I distorted information to support my position?

Table 7.6 This chart focuses on *concepts in thinking*. It is useful in understanding the intellectual standards to be applied to concepts and in differentiating between the use of concepts in thinking by skilled and unskilled reasoners.

CONCEPTS AND IDEAS
(All reasoning is expressed through, and shaped by, concepts and ideas.)
Primary standards: (1) clarity, (2) relevance, (3) depth, (4) accuracy
Common problems: (1) unclear, (2) irrelevant, (3) superficial, (4) inaccurate
Principle: Reasoning can only be as clear, relevant, realistic, and deep as the concepts that shape it.

Skilled Reasoners	Unskilled Reasoners	Critical Reflections
are aware of the key concepts and ideas they and others use.	are unaware of the key concepts and ideas they and others use.	What is the main concept I am using in my thinking? What are the main concepts others are using?
are able to explain the basic implications of the key words and phrases they use.	cannot accurately explain basic implications of their key words and phrases.	Am I clear about the implications of key concepts? For example: Does the word *cunning* have negative implications that the word *clever* does not?
are able to distinguish special, nonstandard uses of words from standard uses.	are not able to recognize when their use of a word or phrase departs from educated usage.	Where did I get my definition of this central concept? For example: Where did I get my definition of the concept of… Have I put my unwarranted conclusions into the definition?
are aware of irrelevant concepts and ideas and use concepts and ideas in ways relevant to their functions.	use concepts in ways inappropriate to the subject or issue.	Am I using the concept of "love" appropriately? For example: Do I unknowingly act as if loving a person implies a right to treat them discourteously?
think deeply about the concepts they use.	fail to think deeply about the concepts they use.	Am I thinking deeply enough about this concept? For example: The concept of health care, as I describe it, does not take into account the patient's rights and privileges. Do I need to consider the idea of health care more deeply?

Table 7.7 This chart focuses on *assumptions in thinking*. It is useful in understanding the intellectual standards to be applied to assumptions and in differentiating between the use of assumptions in thinking by skilled and unskilled reasoners.

ASSUMPTIONS

(All reasoning is based on assumptions—beliefs we take for granted.)

Primary standards: (1) clarity, (2) justifiability, (3) consistency

Common problems: (1) unclear, (2) unjustified, (3) contradictory

Principle: Reasoning can be only as sound as the assumptions it is based on.

Skilled Reasoners	Unskilled Reasoners	Critical Reflections
are clear about the assumptions they are making.	are often unclear about the assumptions they make.	Are my assumptions clear to me? Do I clearly understand what my assumptions are based upon?
make assumptions that are reasonable and justifiable given the situation and evidence.	often make unjustified or unreasonable assumptions.	Do I make assumptions about the future based on just one experience from the past? Can I fully justify what I am taking for granted? Are my assumptions justifiable given the evidence I am using to support them?
make assumptions that are consistent with each other.	often make assumptions that are contradictory.	Do the assumptions I made in the first part of my argument contradict the assumptions I am making now?
constantly seek to figure out what their assumptions are.	ignore their assumptions.	What assumptions am I making in this situation? Are they justifiable? Where did I get these assumptions?

Table 7.8   This chart focuses on *implications in thinking*. It is useful in understanding the intellectual standards to be applied to implications
and in differentiating between how skilled and unskilled reasoners
think about implications.

IMPLICATIONS AND CONSEQUENCES

(All reasoning leads somewhere. It has implications and,
when acted upon, has consequences.)

Primary standards: (1) significance, (2) logicalness, (3) clarity, (4) precision, (5) completeness

Common problems: (1) unimportant, (2) unrealistic, (3) unclear, (4) imprecise, (5)
incomplete

Principle: To reason well through an issue, you might think through the implications that
follow from your reasoning. You must think through the consequences likely to follow from the decisions you make.

Skilled Reasoners	Unskilled Reasoners	Critical Reflections
trace out a number of significant potential implications and consequences of their reasoning.	trace out few or none of the implications and consequences of holding a position or making a decision.	Did I spell out all the significant consequences of the action I am advocating? If I were to take this course of action, what other consequences might follow that I haven't considered?
clearly and precisely articulate the possible implications and consequences clearly and precisely.	are unclear and imprecise in the possible consequences they articulate.	Have I delineated clearly and precisely the consequences likely to follow from my chosen action?
search for potentially negative as well as potentially positive consequences.	trace out only the consequences they had in mind at the beginning, either positive or negative, but usually not both.	I may have done a good job of spelling out some positive implications of the decision I am about to make, but what are some of the possible negative implications or consequences?
anticipate the likelihood of unexpected negative and positive implications.	are surprised when their decisions have unexpected consequences.	If I make this decision, what are some possible unexpected implications? What are some variables out of my control that might lead to negative consequences?

Table 7.9 This chart focuses on *inferences in thinking*. It is useful in understanding the intellectual standards to be applied to inferences and in differentiating between the use of inferences in thinking by skilled and unskilled reasoners.

INFERENCE AND INTERPRETATION

(All reasoning contains inferences from which we draw conclusions and give meaning to data and situations.)

Primary standards: (1) clarity, (2) logicalness, (3) justifiability, (4) profundity, (5) reasonability, (6) consistency

Common problems: (1) unclear, (2) illogical, (3) unjustified, (4) superficial, (5) unreasonable, (6) contradictory

Principle: Reasoning can be only as sound as the inferences it makes (or the conclusions it comes to).

Skilled Reasoners	Unskilled Reasoners	Critical Reflections
are clear about the inferences they are making clearly articulate their inferences.	are often unclear about the inferences they are making do not clearly articulate their inferences.	Am I clear about the inferences I am making? Have I clearly articulated my conclusions?
usually make inferences that follow from the evidence or reasons presented.	often make inferences that do not follow from the evidence or reasons presented.	Do my conclusions logically follow from the evidence and reasons presented?
often make inferences that are deep rather than superficial.	often make inferences that are superficial.	Are my conclusions superficial, given the problem?
often make inferences or come to conclusions that are reasonable.	often make inferences or come to conclusions that are unreasonable.	Are my conclusions reasonable?
make inferences or come to conclusions that are consistent with each other.	often make inferences or come to conclusions that are contradictory.	Do the conclusions I come to in the first part of my analysis seem to contradict the conclusions that I come to at the end?
understand the assumptions that lead to inferences.	do not seek to figure out the assumptions that lead to inferences.	Is my inference based on a faulty assumption? How would my inference be changed if I were to base it on a different, more justifiable assumption?

Chapter 8

Design Your Life

"The development of general ability for independent thinking and judgment should always be placed foremost, not the acquisition of specialized knowledge."

—Albert Einstein

Fate or Freedom: Which Do You Choose?

Many people talk about their lives as if the events in them were pre-determined, as if some force in the universe had issued a timeless decree by which the order of all things (including their lives) was prescribed and all events controlled by inevitable necessity. If you think about your life as a pre-determined product of forces over which you have no control, then you lose any chance of controlling your life.

The Very Idea of Freedom

The idea of designing one's life is a product of two insights: 1) there is a significant difference between life as it is typically lived and life as it might be lived; and 2) by deliberately changing our thinking, we can live in a manner closer to our ideal than if we uncritically allow our thinking to be shaped by the forces acting on us.

Lifelong learners are skilled thinkers who recognize the different roles that learning can play in life. There is a large difference between being passive as a learner and being active. In a passive learner's life, the only end is that of establishing habits that "work," that enable the individual to "get by." Passive learning tends toward "stagnation," for once I find something that enables me to get by, I then, as a passive learner, lack the motivation to change. What I seek in my learning is confirmation in

129

my present beliefs, in my present judgments, and in my present behavior patterns. I seek a way of defending my status quo.

Test the Idea
To What Extent Are You a Passive Learner?

Think back upon the learning experiences you have had in your life, as well as the opportunities for learning you have had. Answer the following questions: To what extent would you say you have been a passive learner? To what extent have you actively sought out opportunities for learning? To what extent have you taken responsibility for your own learning? To what extent do you see learning as something that happens to you rather than something you make happen? To what extent do you see value in learning?

In the life of a critical thinker, active learning is a tool for continually bridging the gap between what is and what could be. We then recognize the role that learning plays in our lives: establishing habits of continual improvement, of always reaching for the next level of skill, ability, and insight. Critical thinkers are lifelong learners and take charge of their experience, their learning, and the patterned behavior that defines their lives. They, in essence, "design" how they think and feel, and hence lay the foundation for how they live. They recognize that their thinking will shape their emotions and that their emotions impact their thinking. They use this recognition as a tool in self-deliberation (Figure 8.1).

Lifelong learners design their lives by becoming clear as to what their goals, problems, and options are. They think through their decisions. They give careful consideration to their options. They give explicit priorities to goals. They do not simply react to immediate imperatives, the predictable and unpredictable distractions that occur in all of our lives. They create their own imperatives by bringing their foremost goals into the center of their thoughts and actions, and create their own calendar of actions.

Though our choices are always limited, we all have a much larger range of choices than we generally recognize to be so.

Figure 8.1 Thinking is the key to all knowledge.

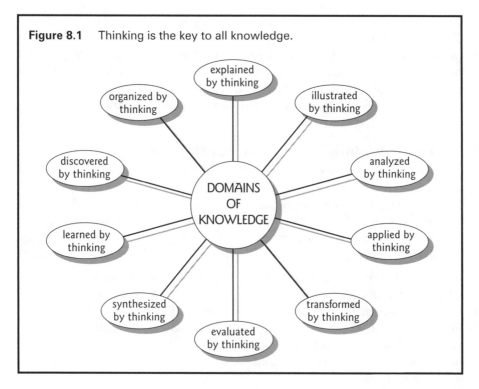

Recognizing the Dual Logic of Experience

For most people, experience is understood as something that "happens to them," not something they create for themselves. But experience is something over which we can all, in principle, exercise significant control. Consider the nature of experience. Experience is a reciprocal relationship between two factors: an objective factor and a subjective one.

The objective dimension of experience is that part of it that we did not generate. It consists in what happens outside our skin, so to speak, in the world about us. Many things happen in the physical and social world over which we have no control. Some we "experience." We have no direct control over what others think, feel, and do. We cannot enter into the minds of people and change them directly. We cannot directly modify the physical or social environment in which we live and act. There are many factors that limit our choices.

But all of the objective factors in our experience must nevertheless be given a meaning, an interpretation. They must become part of our inner life. It is only through this act on our part that a happening or event becomes an "experience." For example, there is much that happens around us that we do not notice and, hence, never becomes part of our experience. Our mind acts as a screen that records and gives a meaning to only a part of what happens around us. The mind ignores the rest. Furthermore, part of the meaning we give an experience is determined by what we decide is important and what is not important. These are crucial decisions of the mind. They exercise immense influence upon our well being. For example, it is our minds that decide what is in our interest or against it, what we should rejoice in and what we should fear, what will help and what hurt us. Unfortunately, our minds often fail us in these matters.

Self-Deception, Insight, and Analyzed Experiences

The human mind, whatever its conscious good will, is subject to powerful, self-deceptive, unconscious egocentricity of mind. A major obstacle to developing intellectual virtues is the presence in the human egocentric mind of what Freud has called "defense mechanisms." Each represents a way to falsify, distort, misconceive, twist, or deny reality. In the distinction between a critically analyzed experience and an unanalyzed one, we can see the opposition between *insight* and *self-deception.*

As suggested above, we rarely subject our experience to critical analysis. We seldom take our experiences apart to judge their truth value. We rarely sort the "lived" integrated experience into its component parts, *raw data versus our inner processing of* the data, or ask ourselves how the interests, goals, and desires we brought to those data shaped and structured that interpretation. Similarly, we rarely consider the possibility that our interpretation (and, hence, our experience) might be selective, biased, or misleading.

This is not to say that our unanalyzed experiences lack meaning or significance. Quite the contrary, in some sense we assess *all that we* experience. We routinely catalogue experiences in accord with our egocentric fears, desires, prejudices, stereotypes, caricatures, hopes, dreams, and assorted irrational drives. We shouldn't assume *a priori* that our rational side controls the shaping of our experience. Our unanalyzed experiences are some combination of rational and irrational thoughts and actions. Only through critical analysis can we hope to isolate and reduce the irrational dimensions of our experience. The ability to do so grows as we analyze more and more of our experience.

Facing Contradictions and Inconsistencies

Of course, more important than the sheer *number* of analyzed experiences is their *quality* and *significance.* This quality and significance depends on how much our analyses enable us to face our own inconsistencies and contradictions. What links the experiences, as analyzed products of the mind, is *insight.* Every critically analyzed experience to some extent produces some insight into who we are. To become more rational, it is not enough to give meaning to our experience. Many experiences are more or less charged with *irrational* meanings. Stereotypes, prejudices, narrow-mindedness, delusions, and illusions of various kinds are sometimes rampant in our thinking.

The process of developing insights is part and parcel of separating experiences into their rational and irrational dimensions, those forming meta-experiences, i.e., higher-order experiences. These meta-experiences become important benchmarks and guides for future thought. They make possible modes of thinking and maneuvers in thinking closed to the irrational mind. Through them we learn to talk insightfully about our experience. Our first-order experiences are no longer sacred. They are materials of the mind that the mind evaluates.

I can reason well in domains in which I am prejudiced—hence, eventually, reason my way out of prejudices—only if I develop benchmarks for such reasoning. Of course, when I am prejudiced it will seem to me that I am not, and similarly, it will seem to me that those who are not prejudiced (as I am) are prejudiced. (To a prejudiced person, an unprejudiced person seems prejudiced.)

I will come to this insight only insofar as I have analyzed experiences in which I was intensely convinced I was correct only to find, after a series of challenges, re-considerations, and new reasoning, that my previous conviction was, in fact, prejudiced. I must take this experience apart in my mind, understand its elements and how they fit together (how I became prejudiced; how I inwardly experienced that prejudice; how intensely that prejudice seemed true and insightful; how I progressively broke that prejudice down through serious consideration of opposing lines of reasoning; how I slowly came to new assumptions, new information, and ultimately new conceptualizations).

Only when one gains analyzed experiences of working and reasoning one's way out of prejudice can one gain the insight essential to self-honesty. Generally, to develop essential insights, we must create a collection of analyzed experiences that represent to us intuitive models, not only of the pitfalls of our own previous thinking and experiencing, but also processes for reasoning our way out of or around them. These model experiences must be charged with meaning for us. We cannot be *indifferent* to them. We must sustain them in our minds by our sense of their importance as they sustain and guide us in our thinking.

In analyzing experiences we should ask at least three questions:

1. What are the raw facts? What is the most neutral description of the situation?
2. What interests, attitudes, desires, or concerns do I bring to the situation?
3. How am I conceptualizing or interpreting the situation in light of my point of view? How else might it be interpreted?

We must also explore the interrelationships of these parts: How did my point of view, values, desires, etc, affect what I noticed about the situation? How did they prevent me from noticing other things? How would I have interpreted the situation had I noticed those other things? How did my point of view, desires, etc, affect my interpretation? How *should* I interpret the situation?

> **Test the Idea**
> **Asking Important Questions in Context**
> Think back upon a recent experience you had. This could have been a meeting you attended or headed. It could have been a discussion you had with your spouse, child, or parent. Answer these questions as you revisit that experience in your mind:
> 1. What were the raw facts in the situation? What is the most neutral description of the situation?
> 2. What interests, attitudes, desires, or concerns did you bring to the situation?
> 3. How did you conceptualize or interpret the situation in light of your point of view? How else might it have been interpreted?

Of course, not all experiences are direct and firsthand. Many come to us vicariously, through the mass media. Such experiences, such influences, are crucial to understanding the uncriticalness of much of our thinking.

Social Forces, the Mass Media, and Our Experience

There are powerful social forces that act through the mass media to influence the "meanings" we give to things. The news media, for one, exert significant influence on how we conceptualize the world. They affect the meanings we give to events across the globe—in Europe, Asia, Africa, South America, etc. They affect the meanings we give to events close to us. They shape our world view. They tell us, in effect, who to trust and who to fear, what gives us security and what threatens us, who to admire and who to scorn, what is significant in our lives and what is insignificant. They create friend and enemy, tell us what our problems are and, typically, tell us how to solve our problems. They imply what is criminal behavior and what is not. They influence what we think about capital punishment, the police, prisons, prisoners, punishments, social workers, poverty, welfare, the medical system, schools, etc. They influence what we consider normal and healthy sexuality and what we consider perverted. They imply when violence is necessary and praise-worthy and when it is inappropriate and to be condemned. Much of this mass media influence upon us is one-sided, superficial, and misleading—when not out-and-out false.

Billions are spent to create, shape, and influence this process. The consequences for the well being of people are enormous. We cannot be critical thinkers and accept the influence that the mass media continually fosters. Whether our viewpoint is conservative or liberal; right, middle, or left; Christian, Jewish, Muslim, Hindu, Agnostic, or atheist—we need to resist mass media influence in our lives. We must decide for ourselves what we think, feel, and want. We cannot do this while under the thrall of the mass media. We must "experience" the world in terms that we ourselves create. We must seek out alternative views. We must find sources that go beyond our national media. We must read widely. We must think broadly.

Of course, it is not enough to know this in the abstract. One must know actively how to correct for it. We must learn how not to be drawn into media-engineered experiences, how to see through them, how to avoid the manner in which they insinuate images into our minds, how they seek to use us where we are most vulnerable, to foster internal confirmation of what is propaganda.

Success in life is best fostered through life-long learning, but an uncritical use of the media in the learning process engenders in us a great deal of activated ignorance, prejudice, misconception, half-truth, and over-simplification. It feeds upon our infantile egocentrism and or uncritical socio-centrism.

To counteract the influence of the mainstream media over our lives, we should seek information from news sources outside of the mainstream, sources such *as The Nation*, and *Counterpoint*.

Test the Idea
Thinking About the Influence of the Media on Our Thinking
Try to locate articles in the newspaper where it appears that the news media is attempting to influence your views as a reader and is using a distorted view to do so. You might do this by looking for an article depicting as ethically wrong a practice that is merely a social convention. Then try to locate articles or books from sources outside of the mainstream that would shed light on how it makes best sense to view the situation.

Reading Backwards

One of the most powerful ways to open our minds to alternative experiences, and thus to counteract the influence of social conditioning and the mass media, is to read "backward." That is, to read books printed in the past: 10 years ago, 20 years ago, 50 years ago, 100 years ago, 200 years ago, 300 years ago, 400 years ago, 500 years ago, 700 years ago, 800 years ago, even 2000 years ago, and more. This provides us with a unique perspective and the ability to step outside of the presuppositions and ideologies of the present day. When we read only in the present, no matter how widely, we are apt to absorb widely shared misconceptions taught and believed today as the truth.

Below is a sampling of the authors of books that we believe enable us to re-think the present. Each has insights that deepen and widen the thinking of the critical reader:

1. **(over 2000 years ago)** The writings of Plato, Aristotle, Aeschylus, and Aristophanes
2. **1200s (over 800 years ago)** The writings of Thomas Aquinas and Dante
3. **1300s (over 700 years ago)** The writings of Boccaccio and Chaucer
4. **1400s (over 500 years ago)** The writings of Eramus and Francis Bacon
5. **1500s (over 400 years ago)** The writings of Machiavelli, Cellini, Cervantes, and Montaigne
6. **1600s (over 300 years ago)** The writings of John Milton, Pascal, John Dryden, John Locke, and Joseph Addison
7. **1700s (over 200 years ago)** The writings of Thomas Paine, Thomas Jefferson, Adam Smith, Benjamin Franklin, Alexander Pope, Edmund Burke, Edward Gibbon, Samuel Johnson, Daniel Defoe, Goethe, Rousseau, and William Blake
8. **1800s (over 100 years ago)** The writings of Jane Austen, Charles Dickens, Emile Zola, Balzac, Dostoevsky, Sigmund Freud, Karl Marx, Charles Darwin, John Henry Newman, Leo Tolstoy, The Brontes, Frank Norris, Thomas Hardy, Emile Durkheim, Edmond Rostand, and Oscar Wilde
9. **1900s (the last 100 years)** The writings of Ambrose Bierce, Gustavus Myers, H.L. Mencken, William Graham Sumner, W.H. Auden, Bertolt Brecht, Joseph Conrad, Max Weber, Aldous Huxley, Franz Kafka, Sinclair Lewis, Henry James, Bernard Shaw, Jean-Paul Sartre, Virginia Woolf, William Appleman Williams, Arnold Toynbee, C. Wright Mills, Albert Camus, Willa Cather, Bertrand Russell, Karl Mannheim, Thomas Mann, Albert Einstein, Simone De Beauvoir, Winston Churchill, William J. Lederer, Vance Packard, Eric Hoffer, Erving Goffman, Philip Agee, John Steinbeck, Ludwig Wittgenstein, William Faulkner, Talcott Parsons, Jean Piaget, Lester Thurow, Robert Reich, Robert Heilbroner, Noam Chomsky, Jacques Barzun, Ralph Nader, Margaret Mead, Bronislaw Malinowski, Karl Popper, Robert Merton, Peter Berger, Milton Friedman, and J. Bronowski

If we learn to read backward, we will begin to recognize some of the stereotypes and misconceptions of the present. We will develop a better sense of what is universal and what is relative; what is essential and what is arbitrary. We will also recognize how arbitrary many of our social values are, as well as how likely we are to have misconceptions that are not apparent to us—just as those in the past had misconceptions that were not apparent to them.

For example, reading widely in the past creates multiple perspectives in the mind that enable one to better understand the complexities of the present. Critical reading creates a lens through which we come to better understand the role in history in our lives, even the role in history of critical thinking itself.

For example, thinking historically we discover that though the idea of critical thinking is old, there has apparently never been a society that taught critical thinking as a basic social value. To the present, critical thinking is being taught only to a minority of citizens, and even then usually in a one-sided way. Critical thinking tends to be taken no further than the skill of attacking and defending ideas, or more usually, the skill of attacking ideas inconsistent with the status quo and defending it in turn. Very often, critical thinking has been indistinguishable from "sophistry," the ability to manipulate people into thinking that the reigning ideology was always "correct and complete." Typically, only a small minority learns and uses critical thinking to question a ruling ideology. We can see this if we scan the history of critical thought.

One of the first thinkers in the history of critical thought is that of Socrates, a Greek teacher from some 2400 years ago. Socrates discovered a method of questioning that, when applied to the leaders of his day, convinced him that most of them could not rationally justify their claims to knowledge. They arrogantly answered his initial questions, but could not intelligibly justify what they thought they knew. For this public exposure of the superficial thinking of authorities, Socrates was rewarded with execution.

Socrates concluded, like Plato and Aristotle after him, that humans typically have no more than a superficial understanding of themselves and their surroundings. This view was expressed by many thinkers over the next 2400 years—including Francis Bacon, Descartes, Pascal, John Stuart Mill, Sigmund Freud, and William Graham Sumner.

It was not until some 1400 years after Socrates that the notion of questioning beliefs became acceptable—albeit only at the university and only under the direction of authorities therein. Of course, in the Renaissance (15th and 16th Centuries), a number of scholars in Europe began to think critically about religion, art, society, human nature, law, and freedom. They proceeded with the assumption that most of the domains of human life were in need of searching analysis and critique. Among these scholars were Colet, Erasmus, and More in England. They followed up on the insight of the ancient Greek thinkers.

Francis Bacon (England) explicitly analyzed the way the human mind, in its normal state, is entrapped by ignorance, prejudice, self-deception, and vested interest. He recognized explicitly that the mind should not be left to its natural tendencies. In his book *The Advancement of Learning*, he argued for the importance of studying the world empirically. He laid the foundation for modern science with his emphasis on the information-gathering processes. He also called attention to the fact that most people, if left to their own devices, develop bad habits of thought (which he called "idols") that lead them to believe what is unworthy of belief. He called attention to "Idols of the Tribe" (the ways our mind naturally tends to trick itself), "Idols of the Cave" (our tendency to see things from our own individual, and often distorted, perspective), "Idols of the Market-Place" (the ways we misuse concepts in our associations with others), and "Idols of the Theater" (our tendency to become trapped in conventional and dogmatic systems of thought). His book could be considered one of the earliest texts in critical thinking, for his agenda was very much the traditional agenda of critical thinking.

Some fifty years later in France, Descartes wrote what might be called the second text in critical thinking, *Rules for the Direction of the Mind*. In it, Descartes argued for the need for a special systematic disciplining of the mind to guide it in thinking. He articulated and defended the need in thinking for clarity and precision. He developed a method of critical thought based on the principle of systematic doubt. He emphasized the need to base thinking on well reasoned foundational assumptions. Every part of thinking, he argued, should be questioned, doubted, and tested.

In the same time period, Sir Thomas More developed a model of a new social order, *Utopia*, in which every domain of the present world was subject to critique. His implicit thesis was that established social systems are in need of radical analysis and critique. The critical thinking of these Renaissance and post-Renaissance scholars opened the way for the emergence of science and for the development of democracy, human rights, and freedom for thought.

In the Italian Renaissance, Hobbes and Locke displayed the same confidence in the critical mind of the thinker that we find in Machiavelli. Neither accepted the traditional picture of things dominant in the thinking of their day. Neither accepted as necessarily rational that which was considered "normal" in their culture. Both looked to the critical mind to open up new vistas of learning. Hobbes adopted a naturalistic view of the world in which everything was to be explained by evidence and reasoning. Locke defended a common sense analysis of everyday life and thought. He laid the theoretical foundation for critical thinking about basic human rights and the responsibilities of all governments to submit to the reasoned criticism of thoughtful citizens.

It was in this spirit of intellectual freedom and critical thought that people such as Robert Boyle (in the 17th Century) and Sir Isaac Newton (in the 17th and 18th Century) did their work. In his *Sceptical Chymist*, Boyle severely criticized the chemical theory that had preceded him. Newton, in turn, developed a far-reaching framework of thought that roundly criticized the traditionally accepted view of the world. He extended the critical thought of such minds as Copernicus, Galileo, and Kepler. After Boyle and Newton, it was recognized by those who reflected seriously on the natural world that egocentric views must be abandoned in favor of views based entirely on carefully gathered evidence and sound reasoning.

Another significant contribution to critical thinking was made by the thinkers of the French Enlightenment: Bayle, Montesquieu, Voltaire, and Diderot. They all began with the premise that the human mind, when disciplined by reason, is better able to figure out the nature of the social and political world. What is more, for these thinkers, reason must turn inward upon itself, in order to determine weaknesses and strengths of thought. They valued disciplined intellectual exchange, in which all views had to be submitted to serious analysis and critique. They believed that all authority must submit in one way or another to the scrutiny of reasonable critical questioning.

Eighteenth Century thinkers extended our conception of critical thought even further, developing our sense of the power of critical thought and of its tools. Applied to the problem of economics, it produced Adam Smith's *Wealth of Nations*. In the same year, applied to the traditional concept of loyalty to the king, it produced the *Declaration of Independence*. Applied to reason itself, it produced Kant's *Critique of Pure Reason*.

In the 19th Century, critical thought was extended even further into the domain of human social life by Comte, Spencer, and Max Weber. Applied to the problems of capitalism, it produced the searching social and economic critique of Karl Marx. Applied to social decision-making and power, it produced a deep analysis of bureaucratic thinking and its tendency to dominate large organizations in such a way as to undermine their original purposes (Max Weber). Applied to the history of human culture and the basis of biological life, it led to Darwin's *Descent of Man*. Applied to the unconscious mind, it is reflected in the works of Sigmund Freud. Applied to cultures, it led to the establishment of the field of Anthropological studies. Applied to language, it led to the field of Linguistics and to many profound analyses of the functions of symbols and language in human life.

In the 20th Century, our understanding of the power and nature of critical thinking has emerged in increasingly more explicit formulations. In 1906, William Graham Sumner published a ground-breaking study of the foundations of sociology and anthropology, *Folkways* (Sumner, reprint, 1940), in which he documented the tendency of the human mind to think sociocentrically and the parallel tendency for schools to serve the (uncritical) function of social indoctrination:

> *"Schools make persons all on one pattern, orthodoxy. School education, unless it is regulated by the best knowledge and good sense, will produce men and women who are all of one pattern, as if turned in a lathe... An orthodoxy is produced in regard to all the great doctrines of life. It consists of the most worn and commonplace opinions which are common in the masses. The popular opinions always contain broad fallacies, half-truths, and glib generalizations (p. 630)."*

At the same time, Sumner recognized the deep need for critical thinking in life and in education:

> *"Criticism is the examination and test of propositions of any kind which are offered for acceptance, in order to find out whether they correspond to reality or not. The critical faculty is a product of education and training. It is a mental habit and power. It is a prime condition of human welfare that men and women should be trained in it. It is our only guarantee against delusion, deception,*

superstition, and misapprehension of ourselves and our earthly circumstances. Education is good just so far as it produces well-developed critical faculty....A teacher of any subject who insists on accuracy and a rational control of all processes and methods, and who holds everything open to unlimited verification and revision is cultivating that method as a habit in the pupils. Men educated in it cannot be stampeded...They are slow to believe. They can hold things as possible or probable in all degrees, without certainty and without pain. They can wait for evidence and weigh evidence...They can resist appeals to their dearest prejudices...Education in the critical faculty is the only education of which it can be truly said that it makes good citizens (pp. 632, 633)."

John Dewey agreed. From his work, we have increased our sense of the pragmatic basis of human thought (its instrumental nature), and especially *its grounding in actual human purposes, goals, and objectives.* From the work of Ludwig Wittgenstein, we have increased our awareness not only of the importance of *concepts* in human thought, but also of the need to analyze concepts and assess their power and limitations within particular contexts and expressed first in "natural" (rather than "technical") languages. From the work of Piaget, we have increased our awareness of the *egocentric and sociocentric tendencies of human thought* and of the special need to develop critical thought that is able to *reason within multiple standpoints,* and to be raised to the level of "conscious realization."

From the work of such scholars as C. Wright Mills, we have increased awareness of the manner in which democratic institutions are undermined and social exploitation takes place in mass societies. From the contribution of depth-psychology and other researchers, we have learned how easily the human mind is self-deceived, how easily it unconsciously constructs illusions and delusions, how easily it rationalizes and stereotypes, projects, and scapegoats. From the work of Irving Goffman and others, we have an increased awareness of how "social definitions" can dominate the mental life of individuals in a society. From the work of many sociologists, we have increased awareness of how the "normal" socialization process serves to perpetuate the existing society—its ideology, roles, norms, and values—however inconsistent these might be with a society's announced picture of itself. From the work of economists like Robert Heilbronner, we have increased awareness of how unbridled economic forces influenced by vested interest groups may act so as to undermine or negate economic, political, and ethical values as well as human rights.

From the massive contribution of all the physical and natural sciences, we have learned *the power of information* and the *importance of gathering information with great care and precision,* and with sensitivity to its potential inaccuracy, distortion, or misuse.

To conclude, a scanning of the history of critical thought heightens our awareness of the power and necessity of critical thinking as well as of its rarity in human experience. Nowhere is there, as far as we can see, a developed community of critical thinkers. No society systematically teaches it to its young. Every society teaches its view of the world as the TRUTH, and invests a good deal of effort into justifying itself to itself. The only community of critical thinkers, to date, exists across cultures and disciplines, across ethnic groups and orientations, across belief systems and life-style agendas.

Test the Idea
Committing Yourself to Reading Backward

Try to commit yourself to reading one book per month that is on our "reading backward" author list, or books by other highly reputable authors from different periods in history. Choose books that represent differing perspectives, differing ways of looking at the world. Should you make such a commitment, as time passes you will experience considerable development in your ability to see things from multiple perspectives and your worldview will significantly broaden.

Implications for the Design of Your Life

If we become committed to designing our own lives, and recognize that, in doing so, we are resisting social forces, and, to greater or lessor extent, acting outside of the expected behavior patterns of the social groups of which we are a member, we also learn to keep some of our thinking private. We learn that others must undergo their own evolution, their own development as critical thinkers and that we cannot give to others the products of our thinking, when it is unorthodox, without their going through a process similar to the one we experienced.

Chapter 9

The Art of Making Intelligent Decisions

To live is to act. To act is to decide. Everyday life is an endless sequence of decisions. Some of the decisions are small and inconsequential, and some are large and life determining. When the pattern of decision-making is rational, we live a rational life. When the pattern is irrational, we live an irrational life. Rational decisions maximize the quality of one's life without violating the rights, or harming the well being, of others. Rational decisions maximize our chances of happiness, successful living, and fulfillment. Critical thinking, when applied to decision-making, enhances the rationality of decisions made by raising the pattern of decision-making to the level of conscious and deliberate choice. No one deliberately chooses to live an irrational life. Many, however, subconsciously choose to live an irrational or unethical life. In doing so, they maximize their chances of unhappiness and frustration, or do harm to others in seeking their own advantage.

There are as many domains of decision-making as there are of thinking. Indeed, the most important decision we can make is how and what to think about things, for how and what we think determines how we feel and how we act. We decide what to think, feel, and do when we act as a parent. We decide what to think, feel, and do when we make decisions about our professional lives. We decide what to think, feel, and do when we make decisions about the social world in which we have been raised and the groups of which we are a member (family, professional, personal associations, nation, etc.). We decide what to think, feel, and do when we make political decisions about the policies, parties, and candidates that we choose to support. We decide what to think, feel, and do when we make decisions about what we are morally obliged to do (and what we are not so obliged to do). We decide what to think, feel, and do when we make decisions about our life-style, about the nature and value of friendship, about the nature of what is most important in our lives. We decide what to think, feel, and do when we think historically, sociologically, professionally, environmentally, and philosophically. What is more, the thinking we do in one domain of our lives often is influenced by the thinking we do in other domains of our lives. Often the domains are overlapping. As a result, the decisions we make in one domain of our lives often are influenced by the decisions we make in other domains of our lives.

To become a skilled decision-maker, one must become a skilled thinker, and to become either is to learn to think about our lives both as a whole and as a complex of parts. The most intimate part of the world in which we live originates in our thoughts and actions and is maintained by these. To become a critical thinker, we must become an intimate observer of the manner in which we construct our own intimate world. We must understand how we have been socialized and the implications of that process. We must understand how our socialization is reinforced and reflected in the social institutions that continue to exert direct and indirect influence on us. We must know when we are acting out social routines and rituals that we were conditioned to accept. We must be able to think inside and outside our world, using the latter to critique the former.

Thinking Globally About Your Life

Every point we make in this chapter should be interpreted and qualified by every point we have made in the chapters that preceded it, especially the chapter on the design of your life. To become an effective decision-maker requires that you gain insight into your life as a whole, for the most basic patterns of thought and behavior in your life represent the most basic decisions you have made. They have continual implications for the quality of your life. You need to reflect on those patterns, analyze and assess them, if you are to make the most important decisions in your life. For example, if you assume that the most basic patterns of your life are not in need of assessment, then any mistakes implicit in those lived patterns continue to generate negative implications and consequences.

Here is a key global question. "To what extent have I questioned, or failed to question, my social conditioning?"

This question includes the sub-questions, "To what extent have I simply accepted the religion I was raised to believe, the politics I was raised to believe, the philosophy I was raised to believe, the values I was raised to believe, and the lifestyle I was raised to believe?" Of course, it is important to recognize that questioning how we have been influenced does not entail that we uncritically reject those influences. It simply means that we cease to assume that they are universally positive or necessarily represent the best choices we could make.

Evaluating Patterns in Decision-Making

How can we determine the extent to which our decision-making is irrational? In the first place, our irrational decisions often will be those we make without realizing we are making them. So let us begin with an analysis of our subconscious decisions.

If you ask yourself how many decisions you made yesterday, you probably will be puzzled as to how to determine the number. In a sense, the absolute number is unimportant. What is important is to recognize the categories of decisions you made and find a way to begin to identify and evaluate patterns within those categories.

We all have basic human needs. Consequently, we all make choices as to how to satisfy those needs. In addition, we all have chosen values and made choices in relation to those values. We all assume that our basic values support our welfare and contribute to our general well being. No one says, to himself or herself, "I choose to live in accordance with values that undermine my welfare and harm me."

And we all make choices that have implications for the well being of others. When we make decisions that undermine or harm others' well being, we make unethical decisions. When we make decisions or choose values that undermine or harm our well being, we make irrational decisions.

Some common patterns of irrational or unethical decision-making are:

- Deciding to behave in ways that undermine our welfare;
- Deciding not to engage in activities that contribute to our long-term welfare;
- Deciding to behave in ways that undermine another's welfare;
- Deciding to associate with people who encourage us to act against our own welfare or the welfare of others.

These categories sound odd, for why would anyone make self-defeating or self-harming decisions? But there is a general answer to this query: immediate gratification and short-term gain. This becomes more apparent when we look at more specific categories within these categories. For example, under "Deciding to behave in ways that undermine one's welfare" are:

- Deciding to eat foods that are unhealthy (foods that shorten our lives or lead to disease or negative qualities of life);
- Deciding to smoke, drink to excess, or use drugs that are harmful;
- Deciding not to exercise or engage in adequate aerobic activities.

Clearly, we make these decisions with immediate pleasure and our short-term satisfaction uppermost in our minds. Indeed, our mind is "wired" for immediate and short-term gratification. Taking into account the long-term requires reflection. We must raise our behavior to the level, as Piaget put it, of conscious realization. Of course, we can be conscious of a problem without taking the steps to correct it. Putting our long-term insights into action requires self-discipline and will power.

When we identify a pattern of irrational decision-making in our life, we have discovered what sometimes is called a bad habit. When we replace a pattern of irrational decision-making with a rational pattern, we replace a bad habit with a good one. The replacement is at the level of action.

Because habits account for hundreds or thousands of decisions over an extended time, we can improve our decision-making significantly by identifying our bad habits and replacing them with good ones. For example, we can make hundreds of rational decisions over time by making the decision to eat healthy foods and not eat unhealthy foods. Once that decision is manifested in behavior over an extended time, it results in a productive habit.

"Big" Decisions

There are two kinds of big decisions to learn to watch for in one's life:

•   Those that have more or less obvious long-term consequences (basic career choices, choice of mate, choice of values, choice of philosophy, basic parental decisions);

•   Those whose long-term consequences must be "discovered" (such as the implications of our daily habits, including those implicit in our eating and exercise habits).

What is most dangerous in general are "un-thought" decisions, the decisions that creep into our lives unnoticed and unevaluated. Clearly, it is not possible to raise all decisions to the level of conscious realization, for then we would have no habits whatsoever. Rather, we aim to evaluate categories or clusters of decisions, on the one hand (big in their collectivity), and the individual big ones.

The Logic of Decision-Making

It is useful to consider the logic of decision-making. That logic is determined by the goal of decision-making and of the question that follows from that goal:

•   The goal: to decide between some set of alternatives, the one most in keeping with our welfare and the welfare of others;

•   The question: put in terms of completing the following sentence: "At this point in my life, faced with the alternatives (A or B or C or D), which is the one most likely to enhance my welfare and the welfare of others?"

The four keys to sound decision-making are:

1. To recognize that you face an important decision,

2. To accurately identify the alternatives,

3. To logically evaluate the alternatives,

4. To have the self-discipline to act on the best alternative.

Each of these factors presents potential problems to the thinker.

Test the Idea
Thinking Seriously About Your Career

Many of us have not seriously thought through the extent to which we are satisfied in our careers. Yet clearly the decision to pursue a certain career is one of the most significant decisions we will make in our lives. Consider the following question: Should I seek a career change or continue to focus my professional energies on opportunities implicit in my present situation? Once you think through this decision, evaluate your thinking by considering the dimensions of decision-making discussed later in this chapter.

Recognizing the Need for an Important Decision

Much of the worst decision-making is the result of the failure to recognize that a decision is at hand. The result, then, is that many decisions are made subconsciously— and therefore, often, egocentrically or sociocentrically. Many decisions that people make about friends, associates, schoolwork, family, choice of amusement (including alcohol and drug use), and personal satisfaction are a result of "mindless" decisions ("It never occurred to me!" "I just didn't realize!"). These are often the "after-the-fact" explanations when the negative implications of the decisions are realized.

Accurately Recognizing the Alternatives

Recognizing that a decision is at hand is not all there is to it. We also must recognize what our alternatives are. Here, many decisions go awry because of failure to accurately identify the alternatives. This failure comes in two forms: 1) thinking that something is an alternative when it is not (thinking unrealistically), and 2) failing to recognize an alternative (thinking too narrowly).

Among the common decisions in the first category of failure are decisions that follow from the following types of thinking:

- "I know he's got major faults, but he loves me and I can help him change!"

- "I know there are lots of problems in our relationship, but we love each other and that is all that matters!"

- "I know I'm not doing well at my job, but I will eventually be recognized!"

- "I know I need to learn this, but I can learn it by cramming the night before the exam!"

The second category of failure (thinking too narrowly) is difficult to correct, as no one believes he is thinking too narrowly (when he is). Actually, the more narrow the thinker, the more confident the thinker that he is broad-minded. A good rule of thumb is that if you can think of only one or two options when making a decision, you probably are thinking too narrowly.

We have found the following twofold rule to be useful:

RULE ONE: THERE'S ALWAYS A WAY.

RULE TWO: THERE'S ALWAYS ANOTHER WAY.

Let's now look at the process of becoming a more skilled decision-maker, in the light of what we have considered thus far.

Putting More Time into Your Decision-Making

If we don't make time for reflective thought about our decisions, we cannot improve them. A real change of behavior requires some thought about our present behavior. The key here is to recognize that we lose a tremendous amount of time through bad decision-making. It is not unusual, for example, for a couple to spend 5 or 10 years in a bad marriage before recognizing it, leaving it, and seeking a more productive relationship. People often lose years through a poor career choice. Students often lose a great deal of time by their chosen—and inefficient—mode of studying. Putting more time into our decisions, and making better decisions as a result, is going to save us a tremendous amount of time that otherwise would result from the need to correct bad decisions.

Being Systematic

People need to think through their major habits. They need to give time to the decisions they make around major needs and blocks of time: eating habits, exercise habits, free time activities, social interactions, and so forth. People have to think critically about how the habits they develop in every part of life affect the overall quality of life. For example, if you spend many hours a day playing computer games, what are some implications of the decision to do so? What important things do you not have time to do?

Dealing with One Major Decision at a Time

Speed thinking usually does not help us think well through our decisions. The more things we try to do simultaneously, and the faster we try to do them, the more likely we will be to do each of the things poorly. Because we live in a fast-paced world, it is difficult to appreciate the importance of taking our time in reasoning through the decisions we face. After making a bad decision, we sometimes say we didn't have enough time to think through the problem. But the problem usually is that we had the time but didn't *take* the time. In general, the more deliberate our approach to decision-making is—the more time we spend thinking through all the aspects of the problem—the better will be our decisions.

Developing Knowledge of Your Ignorance

We are ignorant about most of our decision-making. The more knowledge we gain of our ignorance (of decisions), the more thoughtful our decisions will become. Being able to recognize and face the things we don't know is instrumental in determining what we will have to figure out. We tend not to know what we need to know to make effective decisions, but the primary problem most of us face is that we think we already know everything relevant to making those decisions. We are intellectually arrogant.

Dimensions of Decision-Making

By using the elements of thought as our guide, we can identify at least nine dimensions of decision-making that represent potential problems for thought. These dimensions do not define a procedure that can be followed mindlessly or mechanically. They presuppose good judgment and sound thinking in every dimension.

To be an effective and rational decision-maker:

1. Figure out, and regularly re-articulate, your most fundamental goals, purposes, and needs. Your decisions should help you to remove obstacles and create opportunities to reach your goals, achieve your purposes, and satisfy your needs.

2. Whenever possible, take problems and decisions one by one. State the situation and formulate the alternatives as clearly and precisely as you can.

3. Study the circumstances surrounding the alternative possible decisions to make clear the kind of decision you are dealing with. Figure out what implications follow from the various possible alternatives before you. Differentiate decisions over which you have some control and decisions that seem forced on you. Concentrate your efforts on the most important decisions and those on which you can have the most impact.

4. Figure out the information you need, and actively seek that information.

5. Carefully analyze and interpret the information you collect, drawing what reasonable inferences you can.

6. Figure out your options for action. What can you do in the short term? In the long term? Recognize explicitly your limitations in money, time, and power.

7. Evaluate your options in the situation, taking into account their advantages and disadvantages.

8. Adopt a strategic approach to the decision, and follow through on that strategy. This may involve direct action or a carefully thought-through wait-and-see strategy.

9. When you act, monitor the implications of your action as they begin to emerge. Be ready to revise your strategy at a moment's notice if the situation requires. Be prepared to shift your strategy or your analysis or statement of the kind of decision, or all three, as more information about the decision becomes available to you.

Here we will elaborate on only the first of these dimensions, to illustrate how they might be thought-through.

Regularly Re-Articulate and Reevaluate Your Goals, Purposes, and Needs

All of us live goal-directed lives. We form goals and purposes, and we seek to satisfy them. We form values and seek to acquire what they imply. We have needs and seek to fulfill them. If we were to automatically achieve our goals and purposes and fulfill our needs, we would have no problems or challenging decisions to make. A keen awareness of our goals, purposes, and needs is what often makes us aware of the importance of making a decision. Uncritical thinkers often "walk right by" an opportunity for a decision, not even recognizing that opportunity. For example, if you are in a poor relationship with a person and do not make the decision either to leave the relationship or to take active steps to improve it, the problem it represents is "un-dealt-with." Your implicit decision is to maintain things as they are.

Skilled critical thinkers regularly revisit their conceptions of what is worth pursuing. Very often, we make poor decisions simply because we are pursuing what we ought not to pursue. For example, if you define your happiness in terms of controlling the lives and decisions of the key persons in your life, you are bound to make poor decisions both for yourself and for those whom you seek to control.

Humans often seek excess—excess of wealth (greed), excess of power (domination), excess of food (an unhealthy body). And humans often make unreasonable demands on others—assuming that everyone believes what they believe, values what they value, and should act as they act. Humans often set up inconsistent standards—expecting others to be satisfied with what they themselves would not be satisfied with, or to be judged by criteria that they would resent were that same criteria applied to themselves.

Test the Idea
Creating Problems through Poor Decision-Making

Consider the following strategies for dealing with, or making, decisions. Each represents poor decision-making. Can you see why? Do you see one or more of these examples as a good way to deal with decisions?

1. Staying in an abusive relationship for the sake of the children.
2. Taking drugs to gain an immediate escape from the pain of facing unpleasant realities in your life.
3. Overeating to deal with depression.
4. Establishing an escalating "get tough" policy on crime, leading to larger and larger prison cultures that create more and more hardened criminals.
5. Smoking to win approval in a group.
6. Establishing an escalating "get tough" policy on terrorists, leading to more and more resentment and hatred in the groups resorting to "terrorism," leading to more violent responses.
7. Getting angry and acting out by hitting things or people, throwing things, and shouting.
8. Feeling self-pity when frustrated.

The Early Decisions

(2–11 Years of Age)

By reviewing some of the major decision-making that has shaped our lives, we can gain insight into the problems inherent in the process. For example, in our early life we are not in a position to exercise significant control over our decision-making. Our parents usually give us some opportunity to make decisions, however, when we are very young, we have limited capacity to take the long view. We are naturally dominated by the immediate, and our view of the world is highly egocentric. What is more, many parents exercise excessive control over their children's decision-making, on the one hand, or insufficient control, on the other.

When humans are very young, they need to be restrained from acting egocentrically and sociocentrically so these negative patterns can be modified as soon as possible and with as little damage to themselves and others in the meantime. Even young children, however, need to exercise power in their lives and begin to learn to accept the consequences of their own decisions. Children cannot learn to be responsible for their behavior if they are given no opportunities to make their own decisions.

One of the problems with the decisions of children is that they are often the result of the "party-line" of the peer groups to which they belong. Youth culture—with its media, movies, music, and heroes—plays a large role in the decision-making of most children. Human insecurity drives children to seek recognition and acceptance from other children. Many of their decisions and their behavior reflect an attempt to be liked by and included in their peer group. The behavior patterns that result from these decisions often become the basis of short- and long-term problems.

One way or another, the decisions made by or for us have an impact on our personality and character. Decisions influence our beliefs and attitudes, our sense of ourselves, and our sense of the world in which we live.

Test the Idea
Evaluating Childhood Decisions

Review in your mind your earliest recollections about your life as a child. See if you can remember or reconstruct some of what proved to be significant decisions either made by you or for you. Ask yourself the following questions. If you cannot answer a question, simply move on to the next:

- To what extent did your parents give you opportunities to make decisions?
- When did you begin, or have you not begun, to take the long view in your decisions?
- To what extent were your early decisions highly egocentric?
- To what extent did your parents exercise excessive control over your decision-making?
- To what extent did they exercise insufficient control?
- To what extent did your parents restrain you from acting egocentrically and sociocentrically?
- To what extent would you say that you still are an egocentric or sociocentric decision-maker?
- To what extent did you exercise power in your life as a child and begin to learn to accept the consequences of your own decisions?
- To what extent do you think you have learned, by having to bear the consequences of your own decisions, to become responsible for your own behavior?

Adolescent Decisions

(12-17 Years of Age)

The adolescent years are important in decision-making in our lives. As adolescents, we tend to seek more independence in decision-making, though sometimes without being willing to take more responsibility for those decisions. Indeed, some adolescents seem to take the view: "I have a right to make my own decisions, but you have the responsibility to help me escape the consequences of those decisions whenever those consequences are negative."

Like the very young, adolescents seem to have limited capacity to take the long view. Their immediate view of what is happening to them is often generalized as if it were a lifelong condition (egocentric immediacy). In their desire to achieve independence, adolescents often engage in power struggles with their parents and other authority figures.

Like young children, the decisions of adolescents are often the result of the "party-line" of the peer groups to which they belong. Adolescent youth culture—again, with its media, movies, music, and heroes—plays a key role in the decision-making of most adolescents. Human insecurity drives adolescents to seek recognition and acceptance from other adolescents. Like young children, many of their decisions and behaviors reflect an attempt to achieve this end. The behavior patterns that result from these decisions often become the basis of short- and long-term problems.

Love, sexuality, and a comprehensive view of the world become important to adolescents, though each of these is often understood superficially. The basis for adolescents' conceptions of these is often drawn from movies, music, and television programs that target the adolescent population. This is a formula tailor-made for poor decision-making and bad habits.

For example, media-created heroes often are presented as successful when they use violence to defeat those who are presented as evil. In this good guys/bad guys world, everything is black or white. The evil doers use bullying and power to hurt and intimidate the weak and the good. The weak and the good are rescued only when someone who is good develops the courage to use violence against the evil doers.

In media-created romantic relationships, love is typically automatic, irrational, and at first sight, and has no real relationship to the character of the person. Adolescent media have virtually no heroes who achieve their heroic status because of rational use of their mind or knowledge.

If the decisions, behavior patterns, and habits developed in adolescence were to simply come and go with the early and adolescent years, one could simply wait them out. But this is not the case. All of us are shaped, often for a lifetime, by decisions and habits formed during these important years. As soon as possible, conscious intervention is needed.

Test the Idea
Evaluating Adolescent Decisions

Review in your mind your recollections about your life as an adolescent. Which of your decisions proved to be most significant? Ask yourself the following questions. If you cannot answer a question, simply move on to the next:

- Can you identify some ways in which you were influenced by the media as an adolescent?

- To what extent did your decisions during adolescence reflect an attempt on your part to gain recognition and acceptance from other adolescents? What decisions can you specify?

- To what extent did any of these decisions become the basis for short- or long-term problems?

- To what extent were your decisions regarding romantic relationships based on influences from youth culture?

- Can you identify one bad habit you formed as a result of poor adolescent decision-making?

- To what extent is your conception of love or friendship a reflection of the manner in which love or friendship is treated in movies or music lyrics?

If you have difficulty answering any of the above questions (for example, because it seems to you that you were independent in your decision-making), does it seem plausible to you that someone lives in a culture and yet is not significantly influenced by it?

Early Adult Decisions

(18-35 Years of Age)

The early adult years are important in decision-making in our lives. As young adults, we exercise more independence in decision-making, though sometimes without being willing to take responsibility for those decisions.

Like adolescents, young adults seem to have limited capacity to take the long view. Their immediate view of what is happening to them is often generalized as if it were a lifelong condition (egocentric immediacy). In their desire to achieve independence, young adults often make hasty decisions about marriage, career, and their future.

Like adolescents, young adults often make decisions that are the result of the "party-line" of the peer groups to which they belong. Young adults tend to look to other young adults for their lead. They are also strongly influenced by the mass media.

Human insecurity drives young adults to seek recognition and acceptance from other young adults. Like adolescents, many of their decisions and behaviors reflect an attempt to achieve this end. The behavior patterns that result from these decisions often become the basis of short- and long-term problems.

Love, sexuality, and a pragmatic view of the world become important to young adults, though each of these is often understood superficially. The basis for young adult conceptions of these is often drawn from movies, music, and television programs that target the young adult. This is a formula tailor-made for poor decision-making and bad habits.

If the decisions, behavior patterns, and habits developed in young adulthood were to simply come and go with the early years, one could simply wait them out. But this is not the case. All of us are shaped, often for a lifetime, by decisions and habits formed during these important years. As soon as possible, conscious intervention is needed.

Conclusion

We all live a life driven by our decisions. What is clear from this chapter is that, though no one fully masters the decisions determining the quality of life, all of us can improve our decision-making by the following two measures:

1. Reflecting critically on the nature and role of decisions in our lives;
2. Systematically adopting strategies that enhance the reasonability of our decision-making, in the light of that nature and role;
3. Frequently comparing our global philosophy (or world view) with the actual facts of our lives, seeking to find our contradictions and inconsistencies and gaining a more comprehensive view of the direction and quality of our lives.

In constructing these strategies, what is in our interest is to think and act so as to maximize our awareness of:

- The patterns that underlie our decision-making;
- The extent to which our decisions presently are based on immediate gratification and short-term goals;
- The "big decisions" we face;
- Our ultimate and most primary goals;
- The alternatives available to us;
- The self-discipline necessary to act on the "best" alternative;
- The need for adequate time for self-reflection in our decision-making;
- The need to be systematic;
- The nine dimensions of decision-making;

- Knowledge of the major decisions of our childhood;
- Knowledge of the major decisions of our adolescence.

Becoming an excellent decision-maker is not separable from becoming a good thinker. Decisions are too deeply embedded into the fabric of our lives to be treated as isolated events that we could "automatically" master. An excellent decision-maker has self-understanding, understands how to use the fundamentals of critical thinking, is well aware of the problem of egocentrism and socio-centrism in thought, and is intellectually humble, perseverant, and fair-minded.

Chapter 10

Taking Charge of Your Irrational Tendencies

H umans often engage in irrational behavior. We fight. We start wars. We kill. We are self-destructive. We are petty and vindictive. We "act out" when we don't get our way. We abuse our spouses. We neglect our children. We rationalize, project, and stereotype. We contradict and deceive ourselves in countless ways. We act inconsistently, ignore relevant evidence, jump to conclusions, and say and believe things that don't make good sense. We are our own worst enemy.

The ultimate motivating force behind human irrationality is best understood, we believe, as human egocentrism, the natural human tendency "to view everything within the world in relationship to oneself, to be self-centered" (*Webster's New World Dictionary*, 1986).

Egocentric Thinking

Egocentric thinking, then, results from the fact that humans do not naturally consider the rights and needs of others, nor do we naturally appreciate the point of view of others or the limitations in our own point of view. Humans become explicitly aware of our egocentric thinking only if specially trained to do so. We do not naturally recognize our egocentric assumptions, the egocentric way we use information, the egocentric way we interpret data, the source of our egocentric concepts and ideas, and the implications of our egocentric thought. We do not naturally recognize our self-serving perspective.

Humans live with the unrealistic but confident sense that we have fundamentally figured out *the way things actually are*, and that we have done this objectively. We naturally *believe* in our intuitive perceptions—however inaccurate they may be. Instead of using intellectual standards in thinking, humans often use self-centered psychological standards to determine what to believe and what to reject. Here are the most commonly used psychological standards in human thinking:

- "It's true because I believe it." *Innate egocentrism*: I assume that what I believe is true even though I have never questioned the basis for many of my beliefs.

- "It's true because we believe it." *Innate socio-centrism*: I assume that the dominant beliefs within the groups to which I belong are true even though I have never questioned the basis for many of these beliefs.

- "It's true because I want to believe it." *Innate wish fulfillment*: I believe in, for example, accounts of behavior that put me (or the groups to which I belong) in a positive rather than a negative light even though I have not seriously considered the evidence for the more negative account. I believe what "feels good," what supports my other beliefs, what does not require me to change my thinking is any significant way, what does not require me to admit I have been wrong.

- "It's true because I have always believed it." *Innate self-validation*: I have a strong desire to maintain beliefs that I have long held, even though I have not seriously considered the extent to which those beliefs are justified, given the evidence.

- "It's true because it is in my selfish interest to believe it." *Innate selfishness*: I hold fast to beliefs that justify my getting more power, money, or personal advantage even though these beliefs are not grounded in sound reasoning or evidence.

Test the Idea
Identifying Some of Your Irrational Tendencies

Using the above categories of irrational beliefs as a guide, identify at least one belief you hold in each of the categories:

1. It's true because I believe it.
2. It's true because my group believes it.
3. It's true because I want to believe it.
4. It's true because I have always believed it.
5. It's true because it is in my selfish interest to believe it.

On a scale of 1–10 (10 equating with "highly irrational" and 1 with "highly rational"), where would you place yourself? Why?

If humans are naturally prone to assess thinking in keeping with the above criteria, it is not surprising that we, as a species, have not developed a significant interest in establishing and fostering legitimate intellectual standards. There are too many domains of our thinking that we, collectively, do not want to have questioned. We have too many prejudices that we do not want to be challenged. We are committed to having our selfish interests served. We are not typically concerned with protecting the rights of others. We are not typically willing to sacrifice our desires to meet someone else's basic needs. We do not want to discover that beliefs we have taken to be obvious and sacred might not be either. We will ignore any number of basic principles if doing so enables us to maintain our power or to gain more power and advantage.

Fortunately, humans are not always guided by egocentric thinking. Within each person are, metaphorically speaking, two potential minds: One emerges from innate egocentric, self-serving tendencies, and the other emerges from cultivated rational, higher-order capacities (if cultivated).

We begin this chapter by focusing on the problem of egocentric tendencies in human life (Figure 10.1). We then contrast this defective mode of thinking with its opposite: rational or reasonable thinking. We explore what it means to use our minds to create rational beliefs, emotions, and values—in contrast to egocentric ones. We then focus on two distinct manifestations of egocentric thinking: dominating and submissive behavior.

Figure 10.1 The logic of egocentrism.

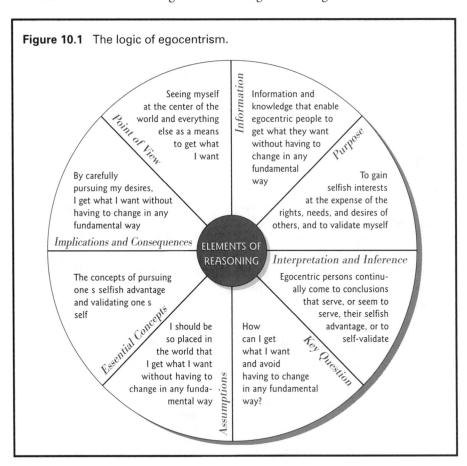

Understanding Egocentric Thinking

Egocentric thinking emerges from our innate human tendency to see the world from a narrow self-serving perspective. We naturally think of the world in terms of how it can serve us. Our instinct is to continually operate within the world, to manipulate situations and people, in accordance with our selfish interests.

At the same time, we naturally assume that our thinking is rational. No matter how irrational or destructive our thinking is, when we are operating from an egocentric perspective, we see our thinking as reasonable. Our thinking seems to us to be right, true, good, and justifiable. Our egocentric nature, therefore, creates perhaps the most formidable barrier to critical thinking.

We inherit from our childhood the sense that we have basically figured out the truth about the world. We naturally believe in our sense of who and what we are. Therefore, if we behave or think irrationally, we are, in a sense, victims of the beliefs and thought processes we have developed through life (because egocentric thinking is commanding us).

As we age, our rational capacities develop to some extent. We come to think more reasonably in some areas of our lives. This can come from explicit instruction or experience. If we are in an environment that models reasonable behavior, we become more reasonable. Yet it is hard to imagine making significant inroads into egocentric thinking unless we become explicitly aware of it and learn how to undermine or

---

Test the Idea
Beginning to Understand Egocentric Thinking

Try to think of a disagreement you were in recently in which you now realize that you were not fair-mindedly listening to the views of someone else. Perhaps you were defensive during the conversation, or were trying to dominate the other person. You were not trying to see the situation from the perspective of the person with whom you were interacting. At the time, however, you believed that you were being reasonable. Now you realize that you were being close-minded. Complete these statements:

1. The situation was as follows…

2. My behavior/thinking in the situation was as follows…

3. I now realize that I was close-minded because…

If you cannot think of an example, think of a situation that you were in recently in which someone else was being close-minded. Also, ask yourself why you cannot think of any examples of close-mindedness on your part.

short-circuit it in some way. The human mind can think irrationally in too many ways while masking itself within a facade of reasonability.

The mere appearance of rationality, of course, is not equivalent to its genuine presence. And, unfortunately, much rational adult behavior is at root, egocentric or sociocentric. This stems, in part, from the fact that people generally do not have a clear understanding of how the human mind functions. Most important, they fail to realize that thinking, if left to itself, is inherently flawed with prejudices, half-truths, biases, vagueness, arrogance, and the like

Understanding Egocentrism as a Mind Within the Mind

Egocentric thinking functions subconsciously, like a mind within us that we deny we have. No one says, "I think I will think egocentrically for a while." Its ultimate goals are gratification and self-validation (Figure 10.2). It does not respect the rights and needs of others—though it may be protective of those with whom it ego-identifies. When we are thinking egocentrically, we see ourselves as right and just. We see those who disagree with us as wrong and unjustified.

Our family, our children, our country, our religion, our beliefs, our feelings, our values are all specially privileged in our egocentric mind. Our validation is crucial to us, and we seek it even if we have been unfair to others or irresponsibly harmed them in a flagrant way. We are interested only in facts we can twist to support us. We dislike or fear people who point out our inconsistencies. If we criticize ourselves, it is not the occasion for significantly changing our behavior but, rather, the means of avoiding such change. For example, if I say, "I know I have a short fuse, but I can't help it. I lose my temper just like my father did!" My criticism justifies my continuing to lose my temper.

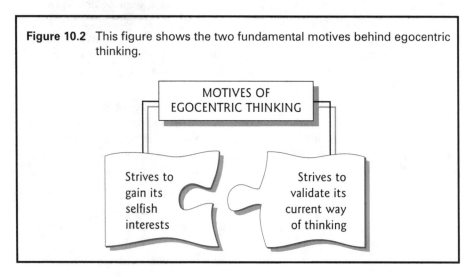

Figure 10.2 This figure shows the two fundamental motives behind egocentric thinking.

MOTIVES OF EGOCENTRIC THINKING

Strives to gain its selfish interests

Strives to validate its current way of thinking

One of the ways we use egocentric thinking, then, is to validate our current belief system. When we feel internally validated, we live comfortably with ourselves even if what we are doing is actually unethical. For example, if I am brought up to believe that people of a certain race are inferior, my egocentric thinking enables me to maintain all of the following beliefs: 1) I am not prejudiced (they simply are inferior); 2) I judge each person I meet on his or her own merits; 3) I am an open-minded person.

With these beliefs operating in my thinking, I do not see myself as jumping to conclusions about members of this race. I do not think of myself as wronging them in any way. I see myself as simply recognizing them for what they are. Though I ignore the evidence that demonstrates the falsity of what I believe, I do not see myself ignoring the evidence. I do not think of myself as a racist, for being a racist is bad, and I am not bad.

Only when we explicitly develop our ability to rationally analyze ourselves can we begin to see these tendencies in ourselves. When we do, it is almost never at the precise moments when our egocentric mind is in control. Once egocentric thinking begins to take control, it spontaneously rationalizes and deceives itself into believing that its position is the only justifiable position. It sees itself as experiencing the truth, no matter how inaccurate a picture of things it is painting. This skilled deceiving of self effectively blocks reasonable thoughts from correcting distorted ones. And the more highly self-deceived we are, the less likely we are to recognize our irrationality, the less likely we are to consider relevant information that our egocentricity is blocking from our view, and the less motivated we are to develop truly rational beliefs and views.

Test the Idea
Discovering Prejudices in Your Beliefs

As egocentric thinkers, we see ourselves as possessing the truth. At the same time, we form many beliefs without the evidence to justify them. We form many prejudices (judgments before the evidence). If this is true, we should be able to begin to unearth some of our prejudices, using our rational capacity. In an attempt to begin this process, complete the following statements:

1. One of the prejudices I have is... (Think of generalizations you tend to make even though you don't have the evidence to justify them. They can be about anything you please: a religion, atheists, men, women, homosexuals, heterosexuals, and so on. Put your prejudice in this form: All x are y, as in all women are ??, or all men are ??.)

2. A more rational belief with which I should replace this faulty belief is...

3. If I use this new belief in my thinking, my behavior would change in the following ways...

"Successful" Egocentrism

Though egocentric thinking is irrational by nature, it can be functional within a dysfunctional logic. For example, it often enables us to selfishly get what we want without having to worry about the rights of the people we deny in getting what we want. This type of thinking—though defective from the points of evidence, sound reasoning, objectivity, and fair play—is often "successful" from the point of view of self-gratification. Hence, though egocentric thinking is inherently flawed, it can be successful in achieving what it is motivated to achieve.

We see this in many persons of power and status in the world—successful politicians, lawyers, businesspeople, and others. They are often skilled in getting what they want and are able to rationalize unethical behavior with great sophistication. The rationalization can be as simple as "This is a hard, cruel world. One has to be realistic. We have to realize we don't live in a perfect world. I wish we did. And, after all, we are doing things the way things have always been done." Conversely, rationalization can be as complex as that masked in a highly developed philosophy, ideology, or party platform.

Hence, though egocentric thinkers may use ethical terms in their rationalizations, they are not responsive to ethical considerations. They do not, in fact, respect ethical principles. They think of ethical principles only when those ethical principles seem to justify their getting what they want for other reasons.

Egocentric thinking, then, is inherently indifferent to ethical principles or genuine conscience. We cannot be exclusively focused at one, and the same time, on getting what we selfishly want and genuinely taking into account the rights and needs of others. The only time egocentric thinking takes others into account is when it is forced to take others into account to get what it wants. Hence, an egocentric politician may take into account the views of a public-interest group only when her re-election depends on their support. She is not focused on the justice of their cause but, rather, on the realization that if she fails to publicly validate those views, that group will refuse to support her re-election. She cares only about what is in her selfish interest. As long as the concern is selfish, by definition, the rights and needs of others are not perceived as relevant.

Corporate executives who ensure that the expected earnings of the company are significantly overstated (to enable them to sell out their stock at a high price) cause innocent people to lose money investing in a company that appears to be (but is not) on the upswing. Most CEOs who manipulate data in this way do not worry about the well being of potential investors. Their justification must be, "Let the buyer beware!" By using this type of justification, they don't have to face the unethical nature of their behavior.

Highly skilled egocentric thought can be generated in every type of human situation, from situations involving the rights and needs of thousands of people to simple, everyday interactions between two people. Imagine that a couple, Max and Maxine, routinely go to the video store to rent movies. Inevitably Max wants to rent an action-packed movie while Maxine wants to rent a love story. Though Maxine is often willing to set aside her choices to go along with Max's desires, Max is never willing to go along with Maxine's choices. Max rationalizes his position to Maxine, telling her that his movie choices are better because they are filled with thrilling action, because love stories are always slow-moving and boring, because his movies are always award-winners, because "no one likes to watch movies that make you cry," because, because, because.... Many reasons are generated. Yet all of them camouflage the real reasons: that Max simply wants to get the types of movies he likes, that he shouldn't have to watch movies that he does not want to watch. In his mind, he should get to do it because he wants to. Period.

Max's egocentrism hides the truth even from himself. He is unable to grasp Maxine's viewpoint. He cannot see how his self-centered thinking adversely affects Maxine. Insofar as his thinking works to achieve his desires, and he is therefore unable to detect any flaws in his reasoning, he is egocentrically successful.

Test the Idea
Recognizing Egocentric Thinking in Action

Think of a situation in which someone you know was trying to selfishly manipulate you into doing something incompatible with your interest. Complete the following statements:

1. The situation was as follows…

2. This person, x, was trying to manipulate me in the following way (by giving me these reasons for going along with him/her)…

3. At the time, these reasons (did/did not) seem rational because…

4. I now believe this person was trying to manipulate me because…

5. I think the real (irrational) reason why he/she wanted me to go along with his/her reasoning is because…

"Unsuccessful" Egocentrism

When egocentric thought is unsuccessful, it creates problems not only for those influenced by the thinker but also for the thinker (Figure 10.3). Let's return to Max and Maxine and the movies for a moment. Imagine that for many months Max and Maxine go through this video-store routine in which, through self-serving argumentation, Max is able to manipulate Maxine into going along with his video choices. But one day Maxine decides that she simply isn't going along with Max's selfish behavior in choosing which movie to rent. She begins to feel resentment toward Max. She begins to think that perhaps Max isn't truly concerned about her. The more she thinks about it, the more she begins to see that Max is selfish in the relationship in a number of ways. Not only is he unwilling to go along with her movie choices, but he also tries to control where they go to lunch every day, when they eat lunch, when they visit with friends, and so on.

Maxine begins to feel manipulated and used by Max, and out of her resentment emerges a defensive attitude toward Max. She rebels. She no longer simply goes along with Max's unilateral decisions. She begins to tell him when she doesn't agree with his choices.

At this point, the table is turned for Max. His egocentric thinking is no longer working for him. He feels anger when he doesn't get his way. Because he lacks insight into his dysfunctional thinking, though, he doesn't realize that he is actually treating Maxine unfairly.

Because Maxine's resentment is now leading to acts of retaliation on her part, Max's life is less successful than it was. Maxine may end up deciding that she is not going to happily agree to Max's movie choices in the future. Her resentment may lead her to seek subtle ways to punish Max for his unfair treatment of her. If she does go along with his movie choices, she might sulk the entire time they are watching the movie. They may both become unhappy as a result of Maxine's rebellion and interrelate in a perpetual state of war, as it were.

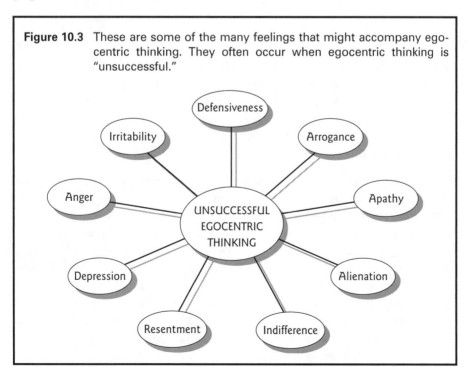

Figure 10.3 These are some of the many feelings that might accompany ego-centric thinking. They often occur when egocentric thinking is "unsuccessful."

This is merely one pattern in a myriad of possible patterns of egocentric thinking leading to personal or social failure. Egocentric thinking and its social equivalent, sociocentric thinking, can lead to social prejudice, social conflict, warfare, genocide, and a variety of forms of dehumanization. Though on occasion some person or group might be "successful" as a result of the ability to wield superior power, quite often the consequences will be highly negative for themselves, as well as their victims. Consider a gang that randomly chooses a person to harass who is wearing the same color sweatshirt that is its group "color." The members begin with verbal assaults, which quickly lead to physical attacks, which in turn result in serious injury to the victim. Consequently, the gang members responsible for the attack are arrested on suspicion, then found guilty of a serious crime, which leads to their imprisonment.

Even if it does not cause direct harm to others, egocentric thinking may lead to chronic self-pity or depression. When problems emerge, it is easy to revert to this type of thinking:

> *I don't know why I should always get the short end of the stick. Just when I think things are going well for me, I have to face another problem. Is there no end? Life seems to be nothing but one problem after another. My boss doesn't think I'm doing a good enough job. My wife is always complaining about something I do. My kids are always getting into trouble at school. And now I've got to figure out how to deal with this car. Life is just a pain in the neck. I don't know why things don't ever go my way.*

Egocentric, self-pitying persons fail to recognize the positives in life. They screen these out in favor of self-pity. They inflict unnecessary suffering on themselves. They say to themselves, "I have a right to feel all the self-pity I want, given the conditions of my life." In situations such as this, because the mind is unable to correct itself, it is its own victim. It chooses to focus on the negative and engage in self-punitive behavior (Figure 10.4).

That is not all. Important moral implications follow from adult egocentrism and socio-centrism. Thinking that ignores the rights and needs of others will necessarily violate those rights and needs. Hence, for example, when humans are under the sway of highly sociocentric thinking, that thinking places the desires and aspirations of the group in a privileged position over other groups. One consequence resulting from such thinking is that the needs and desires of other groups are systematically ignored for the "in group" to justify getting its way. The double standards of the "in group" are camouflaged. To be sure, history is replete with examples of social groups imposing on other groups pain, suffering, and deprivation that they would object to if it were inflicted on them. The inconsistencies characteristic of hypocrisy easily avoid our notice when we are under the sway of socio-centrism.

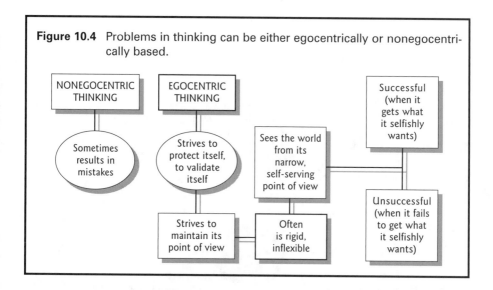

Figure 10.4 Problems in thinking can be either egocentrically or nonegocentrically based.

Test the Idea
Unearthing Dysfunctional Egocentric Thinking
Try to think of a time when your desire to selfishly get what you wanted failed because of your egocentric behavior. Complete these statements:
1. The situation was as follows...
2. When I didn't get what I wanted, I thought ... and behaved...
3. A more rational way to think would have been...
4. A more rational way to act would have been...

Rational Thinking

Although irrationality plays a significant role in human life, human beings are in principle capable of thinking and behaving rationally. Humans can learn to respect evidence even though it does not support their views. We can learn to enter empathically into the viewpoint of others. We can learn to attend to the implications of our own reasoning and behavior. We can become compassionate. We can make sacrifices for others. We can work with others to solve important problems. We can discover our tendency to think egocentrically and begin to correct for that tendency.

Hence, though egocentrism causes us to suffer from illusions of perspective, we can transcend these illusions by practicing the thinking that takes us into the perspective of others. Just as we can assimilate what we hear into our own perspective, so can we learn to role-play the perspectives of others. Just as egocentrism can keep us unaware of the thinking process that guides our behavior, critical thinking can help us learn to

Figure 10.5 The logic of the nonegocentric mind.

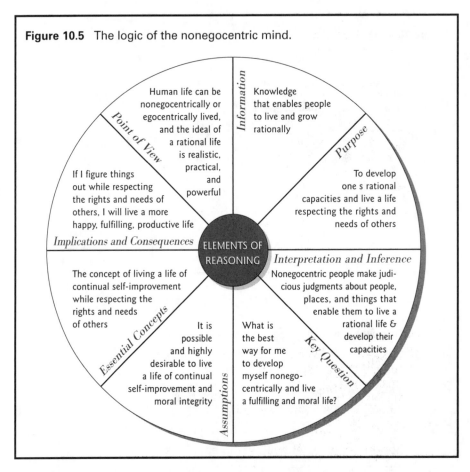

explicitly recognize that thinking process. Just as we can take our own point of view to be absolute, we also can learn to recognize that our point of view is always incomplete and sometimes blatantly self-serving. Just as we can remain completely confident in our ideas even when they are illogical, we can learn to look for lapses of logic in our thinking and recognize those lapses as problematic (Figure 10.5).

We need not continually confuse the world with our own perspective of the world. We can learn to consider and understand others' points of view, to see situations from more than one point of view. We can learn to assess our thinking for soundness. We can strive to become conscious of it as we develop our "second nature."

Each of us has at least the potential for developing a rational mind and using that development to resist or correct for egocentric thought patterns (Table 10.1). This requires a certain level of command over the mind that few people have. It involves disciplined thinking. It means holding oneself accountable. It means developing an inner voice that guides thinking so as to improve it. It means thinking through the implications of thinking before acting. It involves identifying and scrutinizing our purposes and agendas, explicitly checking for egocentric tendencies. It involves identifying irrational thinking and transforming it into reasonable thinking.

Let us imagine the case of Todd and Teresa, who are dating. Todd finds himself feeling jealous when Teresa talks with another man. Then Todd recognizes the feeling of jealousy as irrational. Now he can intervene to prevent his egocentric nature from asserting itself. He can ask himself questions that enable him to begin to distance himself from his "ego." "Why shouldn't she talk to other men? Do I really have any good reason for distrusting her? If not, why is her behavior bothering me?"

Table 10.1 This table compares the tendencies of inherent egocentric thinking with those of cultivated nonegocentric thinking.	
The Egocentric Mind	**The Nonegocentric Mind**
Pursues selfish interests at the expense of the rights, needs, and desires of others while stunting development of the rational mind	Respects the needs and desires of others while pursuing its own needs and desires and is motivated to develop itself, to learn, to grow intellectually
Seeks self-validation	
Can be inflexible (unless it can achieve its selfish interests through flexibility	Is flexible, adaptable
	Strives to be fair-minded
Is selfish	Strives to accurately interpret information
Makes global, sweeping positive or negative generalizations	Strives to gather and consider all relevant information
Distorts information and ignores significant information	Reacts rationally to situations by taking charge of emotions and using emotional energy productively
Reacts with negative, counterproductive emotions when it fails to have desires met	

Through this sort of self-scrutinizing, reasonable persons seek to understand what lies behind their motivation. They come to terms with their own egocentrism. They establish relationships characterized by reasonability and mutual respect. Rational thinking, then, is flexible, disciplined, and fair-minded in its approach. It is able to chart its own course while adhering to ethical demands. It guides itself deliberately away from irrational tendencies in itself.

Thus, just as unconscious, self-deceptive thinking is the vehicle for accomplishing irrational ends, conscious self-perceptive thinking is the vehicle for achieving rational ends (Figure 10.6). An intrinsic dimension of rational thinking, therefore, is raising

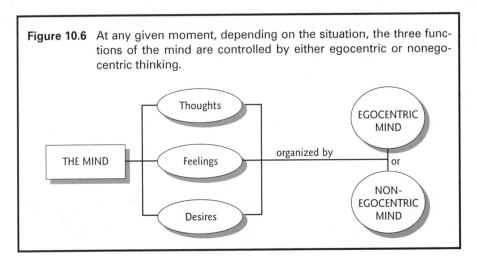

Figure 10.6 At any given moment, depending on the situation, the three functions of the mind are controlled by either egocentric or nonegocentric thinking.

to the conscious level all instinctive irrational thought. We cannot improve by ignoring our bad habits, only by breaking them down. This requires admitting we have bad habits. And it requires an active self-analytic stance.

Following this line of reasoning, a rational act is one that is able to withstand reasonable criticism when brought entirely into the open. All thought that we cannot entirely own up to should be suspect to us. Like a contract with many pages of fine print that the contract writer hopes the reader will not explicitly understand, the egocentric mind operates to hide the truth about what it is actually doing. It hides the truth both from itself and from others, all the while representing itself as reasonable and fair.

Rational thinking, in contrast, is justified by the giving of good reasons. It is not self-deceptive. It is not a cover for a hidden agenda. It is not trapped within one point of view when other points of view are relevant. It strives to gather all relevant information and is committed to self-consistency and integrity. Reasonable people seek to see things as they are, to understand and experience the world richly and fully. Reasonable people are actively engaged in life, willing to admit when they are wrong, and to learn from their mistakes. Indeed, they want to see themselves as wrong when they are wrong.

To develop your rational capacities, then, you have to understand that at any given moment, your thoughts, feelings, and desires can be controlled either by egocentric or by rational thinking. For your rational mind to prevail over your egocentric tendencies, you will function in a way analogous to that of the orchestra leader. The leader controls the process of musical production, maintains discipline within the orchestra, assesses the quality of the sounds, listens for flaws in delivery and points out those flaws for correction, and, through routine scrutiny and continual practice, is finally able to elicit music of high quality.

For you to reach more of your rational potential, you must become a student of the interplay between rational and irrational thought and motivation in your life. You must come to see that, ultimately, your thinking is what is controlling who and what you are, determining the essential quality of your life.

Test the Idea
To What Extent Are You Rational?

Now that you have read an introduction to rationality and irrationality (egocentrism), think about the extent to which you think you are either rational or irrational. Answer these questions:

1. If you were to divide yourself into two parts, one being egocentric and the other rational, to what extent would you say you are either? Would you say you are 100% rational, 50% rational and 50% egocentric, or how would you divide yourself?

2. What reasoning would you give to support your answer to number 1 above? Give examples from your life.

3. To the extent that you are egocentric, what problems does your egocentrism cause?

4. Does your egocentric thinking tend to cause more problems for yourself or for others? Explain.

Two Egocentric Functions

We have introduced you to the distinction between rationality and irrationality. Now we will discuss two distinctively different patterns of egocentric thinking. Both represent general strategies the egocentric mind uses to get what it wants and ways of irrationally acquiring power.

First let's focus on the role that power plays in everyday life. All of us need to feel that we have some power. If we are powerless, we are unable to satisfy our needs. Without power, we are at the mercy of others. Virtually all that we do requires the exercise of some kind of power, whether small or large. Hence, the acquisition of power is essential for human life. But we can pursue power through either rational or irrational means, and we can use the power we get to serve rational or irrational ends.

Two irrational ways to gain and use power are given in two distinct forms of egocentric strategy:

1. The art of dominating others (a direct means to getting what one wants);
2. The art of submitting to others (as an indirect means to getting what one wants).

Insofar as we are thinking egocentrically, we seek to satisfy our egocentric desires either directly, by exercising overt power and control over others, or indirectly, by submitting to those who can act to serve our interest. To put it crudely, the ego either bullies or grovels. It either threatens those weaker or subordinates itself to those more powerful, or both.

Both of these methods for pursuing our interests are irrational, both fundamentally flawed, because both are grounded in unjustified thinking. Both result from the assumption that an egocentric persons' needs and rights are more important than those they exploit for their advantage. We will briefly explore these two patterns of irrational thinking, laying out the basic logic of each.

Before we discuss these patterns, one caveat is in order. As we have mentioned, many situations in life involve using power. However, using power need not imply an inappropriate use. For example, in a business setting, hierarchical protocol requires managers to make decisions with which their employees may not agree. The responsibility inherent in the manager's position calls for that manager to use his or her power to make decisions. Indeed, managers who are unable to use the authority vested in their positions are usually ineffective. They are responsible for ensuring that certain tasks are completed. Therefore, they must use their power to see those tasks to completion. Of course that does not justify their using power unjustifiably to serve selfish ends.

The use of power, then, is and must be part of human life. The fundamental point is that power can be used either rationally or irrationally, depending on the motivation and manner of the person wielding it. Thus, if power is used to serve rational ends, and pursues those ends in a reasonable manner, it is justified. In contrast, if power is used to control and manipulate others for irrational, self-serving ends, that is another matter entirely.

Let us now turn to the two predominant patterns of irrational thinking that all of us use to the extent that we are egocentric. The first we refer to as the dominating ego function: "I can get what I want by fighting my way to the top." The second we term the submissive ego function: "I can get what I want by pleasing others." The egocentric mind chooses one over the other either through habit or through an assessment of the situation (Figure 10.7). For example, it can either forcefully displace those at the top or please those on top and gain its desires thereby. Of course, we must remember that these choices and the thinking that accompanies them function subconsciously.

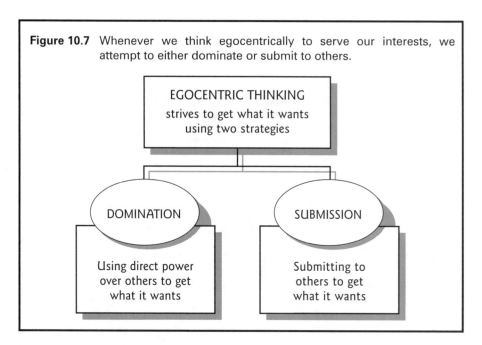

Figure 10.7 Whenever we think egocentrically to serve our interests, we attempt to either dominate or submit to others.

Dominating Egocentrism

Between the two functions of egocentric thinking, perhaps the one more easily understood is the dominating function—or the dominating ego, as we usually will refer to it for the purposes of this chapter. When we are operating within this mode of thinking, we are concerned, first and foremost, to get others to do precisely what we want by means of power over them. Thus, the dominating ego uses physical force, verbal intimidation, coercion, violence, aggression, "authority," and any other form of overt power to achieve its agenda. It is driven by the fundamental belief that to get what we want, we must control others in such a way that were they to resist us, we could force them to do what we want. At times, of course, domination may be quite subtle and indirect, with a quiet voice and what appears to be a mild manner.

For examples of the dominating ego at work, we need only to look to the many people who are verbally or physically abused by their spouses, or the many children similarly abused by their parents. The basic unspoken pattern is, "If others don't do what I want, I force them to do it." Or consider the man in a bar who gets into a fight to force another man away from his girlfriend. His purpose, on the surface, is to protect her. In reality, his purpose may be to ensure that she won't be tempted into a romantic relationship with someone else, or embarrass him in front of his peers.

Domination over others typically generates feelings of power and self-importance (Figure 10.8). Through self-deception, it also commonly entails a high sense of self-righteousness. The dominator is typically arrogant. To the dominator, control over

Figure 10.8 The logic of the dominating ego.

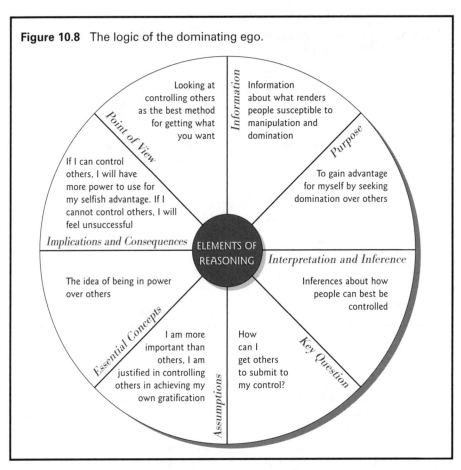

others seems to be right and proper. The dominator uses force and control "for the good" of the person being dominated. The key is that there is self-confirmation and self-gain in using power and forcing others to submit. One key is that others must undergo undeserved inconvenience, pain, suffering, or deprivation as a result.

Given these mutually supporting mental structures, it is difficult for those who successfully dominate others to recognize any problems in their own behavior or reasoning. Why change when, in your mind, you are doing what ought to be done? Hence, as long as the dominating ego is "successful," it experiences positive emotions. To the extent that it is "unsuccessful"—unable to control, dominate, or manipulate others—it experiences negative emotions.

When control is the goal, negative emotions frequently generated from the frustrated failure to control include anger, rage, wrath, rancor, hostility, antagonism, depression, and sadness. Consider the abusive husband who, for many years, is successfully able to control his wife. When she decides to leave him, he may go into a fit of rage and kill her, and perhaps even himself. As long as he thinks he is in control of her, he feels satisfied. But when he no longer can dominate her, his irrational anger may well lead him to the extreme of physical violence.

Examples of the kinds of thinking that dominating persons use in justifying their irrational controlling behavior are:

- "I know more than you do."
- "Since I know more than you, I have an obligation to take charge."
- "If I have to use force to make things right, I should do so because I understand better what needs to be done."
- "If I have more power than you do, it is because I am superior to you in skill and understanding."
- "I have a right to take the lead. I understand the situation best."
- "You are behaving stupidly. I cannot let you hurt yourself."
- "I am an expert. Therefore, there is nothing you can teach me that I don't already know or need to know."

Given these subconscious beliefs and thoughts, it follows that people who operate primarily from the dominating ego would be likely to have difficulties in interpersonal relationships, especially when they come up against another dominating ego or against a strong rational person.

Another benchmark of the dominating ego is its propensity to impose higher standards on others than it imposes on itself. For example, it may require something near perfection in others while ignoring blatant flaws in itself. For a simple, everyday example, we can turn to what often happens in traffic jams. People frequently drive as if their "rights" were sacred ("No one should ever cut me off.") while they frequently cut off others ("I have to get into this lane—too bad if others have to wait."). In short, the dominating ego expects others to adhere to rules and regulations it has the "right" to thrust aside at will.

From an ethical point of view, those who seek control over others frequently violate the rights, and ignore the needs, of others. Selfishness and cruelty are common in these people. It is, of course, difficult to gain any ground by reasoning with people who are under the sway of their dominating ego, for they will use any number of intellectual dodges to avoid taking moral responsibility for their behavior.

Test the Idea
To What Extent are You Egocentrically Dominating?

Think about your typical patterns of interaction with friends, family members, fellow workers, and others. Complete the following statements:

1. I tend to be the most (egocentrically) dominating in the following types of situations...
2. Some examples of my dominating behavior are...
3. I usually am successful/unsuccessful in dominating others. My strategy is...
4. My controlling behavior creates problems because...

In the next section, we lay out the logic of egocentric submissive thinking, thinking that seeks power and security through attachment to those who dominate and wield power. Again we are not assuming that everyone who has power has achieved it by dominating others. They may well have achieved it through rational means. With this caveat in mind, let us begin with a basic outline of the submissive ego.

Submissive Egocentrism

If the hallmark of the dominating ego is control over others, the hallmark of the submissive ego is strategic subservience (Figure 10.9). When in this mode of thinking, people gain power not through the direct struggle for power but, instead, through subservience to those who have power. They submit to the will of others to get those (powerful) others to act in their selfish interest. In this way, people with submissive egos gain indirect power. To be successful, they learn the arts of flattery and personal manipulation. They must become skilled actors and actresses, appearing to be genuinely interested in the well being and interests of the other while in reality pursuing their own interest through the other. At the same time, they must hide this mode of functioning from themselves, as they have to maintain some level of self-respect. If they had to consciously admit to themselves that they were submitting to others to have their own way, they would have trouble feeling justified.

There are countless examples of this mode of functioning in everyday life. The teenage female, for example, who pretends to enjoy fishing (while being inwardly bored by it) so her boyfriend will like her better is engaging in this type of thinking. She submits to his desires and his will only because she wants to gain specific ends (of having a prestigious boyfriend, gaining attention from him, feeling secure in the relationship, and so on). Though she readily agrees to go fishing with him, she probably will end up resenting having done so in the long run—especially once she secures his commitment to her. By virtue of the bad faith implicit in the strategies of

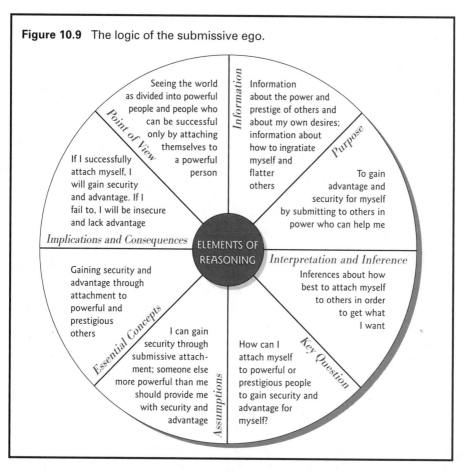

Figure 10.9 The logic of the submissive ego.

the submissive ego, it is common for resentment eventually to develop in the person who functions consistently in this mindset.

If the pattern of thinking of the submissive ego takes root in the young woman we just imagined, she eventually might marry a financially secure man so she can be taken care of, will not have to work, and can enjoy the luxuries of a life without personal sacrifice. Consciously she may deceive herself into believing she loves the man. Yet, because she does not relate to him rationally, the relationship is likely to be dysfunctional.

A similar pattern often occurs in social groups. Within most groups there will be a structure of power, with some playing a dominant and others a submissive role.

Most people will play both roles, depending on the situation. Nazi Germany and the ideology of Fascism provide an excellent example of a system that simultaneously cultivated both dominating and submissive behavior. In this system, nearly everyone had to learn to function within both egocentric types, depending on the context. A hierarchy was established in which everyone was required to give absolute obedience to those above them and to have absolute authority over everyone below them. Only Hitler did not have to use the strategy of submission, as there was no one for him to submit to. Theoretically, no one in such a system has to rationally persuade anyone below him or her in the system. The expectation is clear: Anyone below submits; anyone above dominates.

In the ideology of most human cultures, a greater place is officially given to the use of reason in human life than it was in Fascist society. Much of the official ideology of any society, however, is more window dressing than reality. Suffice it to say that because all societies are stratified and all stratified societies have a hierarchical structure of power, all societies, to date, encourage the thinking of the dominating and submissive ego.

Part of that stratification is found in work-related contexts. In many work situations, men and women alike feel forced to operate in a submissive manner toward their supervisors, allowing themselves to be dominated and manipulated by their superiors so they can stay in favor, keep their jobs, or get promotions.

Thus, the submissive ego operates through artifice and skillful self-delusion to ensure its security, advantage, and gratification. It engages in behavior that is compliant, servile, cowering, acquiescent, to achieve its objectives—though all of these characteristics may be highly disguised. It continually capitulates, defers, caves in, succumbs, and yields to the will of others to gain advantage and maintain its artificial self-esteem.

To avoid the feeling of caving in to superiors, one of the most effective image-saving devices is to adopt the point of view of the superior. In this case, the submission appears as simple agreement: "He didn't pressure me; I agree with him."

As long as the submissive ego achieves "success," it experiences positive emotions—satisfaction, happiness, fulfillment, pleasure, and the like. To the extent that it is not achieving its goals and fails to gain its ends through submission, however, it feels any of a number of negative emotions including bitterness, resentment, animosity, ill will, spitefulness, vindictiveness, enmity, antipathy, and loathing. What is more, depending on the situation, a sense of having failed may lead to insecurity, fear, helplessness, depression, and anxiety.

When unsuccessful, the submissive ego tends to punish itself inwardly, much more than the dominating ego, which, when experiencing pain, tends to respond by inflicting pain on others. Egocentric feelings mirror egocentric thought. Hence, when inflicting pain on itself, the submissive ego sees itself as justified in feeling bad. It experiences a form of sick pleasure in reminding itself that it has every reason to feel negative emotions.

Consider, for example, the woman who believes that her husband should deal with all the unpleasant decisions that have to be made. If he asks her to handle some of those decisions, she goes along with him but is resentful as a result. She may think thoughts such as:

> *Why should I have to deal with these unpleasant decisions? They are his responsibility. I always have to do the things he doesn't want to do. He doesn't really care about me because if he did, he wouldn't ask me to do this.*

She feels justified in thinking these negative thoughts, and in a way she enjoys the feelings of resentment that accompany such thoughts.

The submissive ego often has a "successful" relationship with a person who functions within the dominating-ego mindset. The paradigm case of this phenomenon can be found in marriages in which the male dominates and the female submits. She submits to his will. He may require that she do all the household chores. In return, either implicitly or explicitly, he agrees to take care of her (serve as the primary breadwinner). Although she may at times resent his domination, she understands and, at some level, accepts the bargain. Through rationalization she convinces herself that she probably couldn't do better with any other man, that this one provides the comforts she requires, that in essence she can put up with his domineering behavior because the pay-offs are worth it.

Thus, the submissive ego can experience a form of dysfunctional "success" as long as it feels that it is having its desires met. Take the employee who behaves in a subservient manner to a verbally abusive manager in order to get promotions. As long as the manager takes care of the employee—by looking after his interests, by giving him the promotions he is striving toward—the employee has more positive feelings. When the manager ceases doing this, however, and therefore no longer seems to be concerned with the employee's needs and desires, the employee may feel degraded and resentful of the manager and the subservient role he is forced to play. If given an opportunity, he may turn on his supervisor.

As the submissive ego relates to others, its feelings, behaviors, and thoughts are controlled by beliefs deriving from its own subconscious sense of inferiority. To justify its need to submit to the desires and will of another person, it must perceive itself as inferior to that person. Otherwise it would be unable to rationalize its subservience. It would be forced to recognize its dysfunctional thinking and behavior. Consider the following unconscious beliefs that drive the thinking of the submissive ego:

- "I must go along with this (decision, situation) even though I don't agree with it. Otherwise I won't be accepted."
- "For me to get what I want, I must submit to those who are more powerful than I am."
- "Since I'm not very smart, I must rely on others to think for me."
- "Since I'm not a powerful person, I must use manipulative strategies to get others to get what I want."

As is true for all manifestations of egocentric thinking, none of these beliefs exists in a fully conscious form. They require self-deception. Otherwise the mind would immediately recognize them as irrational, dysfunctional, and absurd. Consequently, what the mind consciously tells itself is very different from the beliefs operating in egocentric functioning. Consider the first belief, "I must go along with this decision even though I don't agree with it. Otherwise I won't be accepted." The conscious thought parallel to this unconscious one is something like: "I don't know enough about the situation to decide for myself. Even though I'm not sure this is the right decision, I'm sure the others are in a better position than I to decide." This is the thought the mind believes it is acting upon, when in reality it is basing its reasoning on the other, unconscious belief. Thinking within this logic, the person is "dishonestly" going along with the decision, in a sense pretending to agree, but all the while doing so only to forward an agenda of acceptance.

In addition to serving as a major barrier to the pursuit of rational relationships, the submissive ego stunts the development of the rational mind, limiting its capacity for insight into self. The submissive ego is enabled to do this through any number of self-protecting beliefs:

- "I'm too stupid to learn this."

- "If I have a question, others might think I'm ignorant."

- "I'm not as smart as others."

- "No matter how hard I try, I can't do any better than I'm already doing."

- "I'll never be able to figure this out."

- "Since I know I'm too dumb to learn this, there's no point in really trying."

Thus, the submissive ego, like the dominating ego, creates significant barriers to development. It routinely turns to others for help when it is capable of performing without that help. The submissive ego experiences frustration, anxiety, and even depression when it fails, or when it anticipates failure, in learning situations. Whereas the dominating ego believes it already knows what it needs to know, the submissive ego often believes it is incapable of learning.

Test the Idea
To What Extent are You Egocentrically Submissive?
Think about your typical patterns of interaction with friends, family members, fellow workers, and others. Complete the following statements:

1. I tend to be the most (egocentrically) submissive in the following types of situations...

2. Some examples of my submissive egocentric behavior are...

3. I am usually successful/unsuccessful when I try to manipulate others through submissiveness. My strategy is…

4. My submissive behavior creates problems because…

To What Extent are You Egocentrically Dominating Versus Submissive?

Think about your typical patterns of interaction with friends, family members, fellow workers, and others. Do you tend to be more dominating or submissive in most situations in which you are egocentric? What about your friends, family members, co-workers? Do they tend to be more dominating or submissive? Given your experience, what problems emerge from people behaving in dominating or submissive ways?

Pathological Tendencies of the Human Mind

We now can put explicitly into words an array of interrelated natural dispositions of the human mind that follow as consequences of the pathology of the natural mind. To significantly develop our thinking, we must overtly identify these tendencies as they operate in our lives, and we must correct them through critical-thinking processes. As you read them, ask yourself whether you recognize these as processes that take place regularly in your own mind (if you conclude, "not me!" think again):

- **Egocentric memory**: the natural tendency to "forget" evidence and information that do not support our thinking and to "remember" evidence and information that do.

- **Egocentric myopia**: the natural tendency to think in an absolutist way within an overly narrow point of view.

- **Egocentric righteousness**: the natural tendency to feel superior in the light of our confidence that we possess the truth when we do not.

- **Egocentric hypocrisy**: the natural tendency to ignore flagrant inconsistencies— for example, between what we profess to believe and the actual beliefs our behavior implies, or between the standards to which we hold ourselves and those to which we expect others to adhere.

- **Egocentric oversimplification**: the natural tendency to ignore real and important complexities in the world in favor of simplistic notions when consideration of those complexities would require us to modify our beliefs or values.

- **Egocentric blindness**: the natural tendency not to notice facts and evidence that contradict our favored beliefs or values.

- **Egocentric immediacy**: the natural tendency to overgeneralize immediate feelings and experiences, so that when one event in our life is highly favorable or unfavorable, all of life seems favorable or unfavorable to us.

- **Egocentric absurdity**: the natural tendency to fail to notice thinking that has "absurd" consequences.

Challenging the Pathological Tendencies of the Mind

It is not enough to recognize abstractly that the human mind has a predictable pathology. As aspiring critical thinkers, we must take concrete steps to correct it. This requires us to create the habit of identifying these tendencies in action. This is a long-term project that is never complete. To some extent, it is analogous to stripping off onion skins. After we remove one, we find another beneath it. To some extent, we have to strip off the outer layer to be able to recognize the one underneath. Each of the following admonitions, therefore, should not be taken as simple suggestions that any person could immediately, and effectively, put into action, but rather as strategic formulations of long-range goals. We all can perform these corrections, but only over time and only with considerable practice:

Correcting Egocentric Memory.   We can correct our natural tendency to "forget" evidence and information that do not support our thinking and to "remember" evidence and information that do, by overtly seeking evidence and information that do not support our thinking and directing explicit attention to them. If you try and cannot find such evidence, you should probably assume you have not conducted your search properly.

Correcting Egocentric Myopia.   We can correct our natural tendency to think in an absolutistic way within an overly narrow point of view by routinely thinking within points of view that conflict with our own. For example, if we are liberal, we can take the time to read books by insightful conservatives. If we are conservative, we can take the time to read books by insightful liberals. If we are North Americans, we can study a contrasting South American point of view or a European or Far-Eastern or Middle-Eastern or African point of view. If you don't discover significant personal prejudices through this process, you should question whether you are acting in good faith in trying to identify your prejudices.

Correcting Egocentric Righteousness.   We can correct our natural tendency to feel superior in light of our confidence that we possess the truth by regularly reminding ourselves how little we actually know. In this case, we can explicitly state the unanswered questions that surround whatever knowledge we may have. If you don't discover that there is much more that you do not know than you do know, you should question the manner in which you pursued the questions to which you do not have answers.

Correcting Egocentric Hypocrisy.   We can correct our natural tendency to ignore flagrant inconsistencies between what we profess to believe and the actual beliefs our behavior implies, and inconsistencies between the standards to which we hold ourselves and those to which we expect others to adhere. We can do this by regularly comparing the criteria and standards by which we are judging others with those by which we are judging ourselves. If you don't find many flagrant inconsistencies in your own thinking and behavior, you should doubt whether you have dug deeply enough.

Correcting Egocentric Oversimplification.   We can correct our natural tendency to ignore real and important complexities in the world by regularly focusing on those complexities, formulating them explicitly in words, and targeting them. If you don't discover over time that you have oversimplified many important issues, you should question whether you have really confronted the complexities inherent in the issues.

Correcting Egocentric Blindness.   We can correct our natural tendency to ignore facts or evidence that contradicts our favored beliefs or values by explicitly seeking out those facts and evidence. If you don't find yourself experiencing significant discomfort as you pursue these facts, you should question whether you are taking them seriously. If you discover that your traditional beliefs were all correct from the beginning, you probably moved to a new and more sophisticated level of self-deception.

Correcting Egocentric Immediacy.   We can correct our natural tendency to overgeneralize immediate feelings and experiences by getting into the habit of putting positive and negative events into a much larger perspective. You can temper the negative events by reminding yourself of how much you have that many others lack. You can temper the positive events by reminding yourself of how much is yet to be done, of how many problems remain. You know you are keeping an even keel if you find that you have the energy to act effectively in either negative or positive circumstances. You know that you are falling victim to your emotions if and when you are immobilized by them.

Correcting Egocentric Absurdity.   We can correct our natural tendency to ignore thinking that has absurd consequences by making the consequences of our thinking explicit and assessing them for their realism. This requires that we frequently trace the implications of our beliefs and their consequences in our behavior. For example, we should frequently ask ourselves: "If I really believed this, how would I act? Do I really act that way?"

By the way, personal ethics is a fruitful area for disclosing egocentric absurdity. We frequently act in ways that are "absurd"—given what we insist we believe in. If, after what you consider to be a serious search, you find no egocentric absurdity in your life, think again. You are probably just developing your ability to deceive yourself.

The Challenge of Rationality

If the human mind has a natural tendency toward irrationality, in the form of dominating and submissive ego functions, it also has a capacity for rationality, in the form of capacity for self-knowledge. We all have a tendency toward hypocrisy and inconsistency, but we nevertheless can move toward greater and greater integrity and consistency. We can counteract our natural tendency toward intellectual arrogance by developing our capacity for intellectual humility. Put another way, we can learn to continually question what we "know" to ensure that we are not uncritically accepting beliefs that have no foundation in fact.

Moreover, we can counteract our tendency to be trapped in our own point of view by learning how to enter sympathetically into the points of view of others. We can counteract our tendency to jump to conclusions by learning how to test our conclusions for their validity and soundness. We can counteract our tendency to play roles of domination or submission by learning how to recognize when we are doing so. We can begin to see clearly why submission and domination are inherently problematic. We can learn to search out options for avoiding either of these modes of functioning. And we can practice the modes of self-analysis and critique that enable us to learn and grow in directions that render us less and less egocentric. We will focus more extensively on learning to control our egocentrism in Chapter 16, on strategic thinking.

Chapter 11

Monitoring Your Sociocentric Tendencies

L iving a human life entails membership in a variety of human groups. This typically includes groups such as nation, culture, profession, religion, family, and peer group. We find ourselves participating in groups before we are aware of ourselves as living beings. We find ourselves in groups in virtually every setting in which we function as persons. What is more, every group to which we belong has some social definition of itself and some usually unspoken "rules" that guide the behavior of all members. Each group to which we belong imposes some level of conformity on us as a condition of acceptance. This includes a set of beliefs, behaviors, and taboos.

The Nature of Sociocentrism

All of us, to varying degrees, uncritically accept as right and correct whatever ways of acting and believing are fostered in the social groups to which we belong (Figure 11.1). This becomes clear to us if we reflect on what happens when, say, an adolescent joins an urban street gang. With that act, adolescents are expected to identify themselves with:

- A name that defines who and what they are;
- A way of talking;
- A set of friends and enemies;
- Gang rituals in which they must participate;
- Expected behaviors involving fellow gang members;
- Expected behaviors when around the enemies of the gang;

185

- A hierarchy of power within the gang;

- A way of dressing and speaking;

- Social requirements to which every gang member must conform;

- A set of taboos—forbidden acts that every gang member must studiously avoid under threat of severe punishment.

For most people, blind conformity to group restrictions is automatic and unreflective. Most effortlessly conform without recognizing their conformity. They internalize group norms and beliefs, take on the group identity, and act as they are expected to act—without the least sense that what they are doing might reasonably be questioned. Most people function in social groups as unreflective participants in a range of beliefs, attitudes, and behaviors analogous, in the structures to which they conform, to those of urban street gangs.

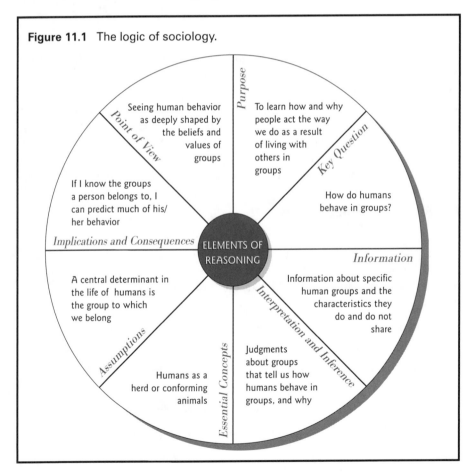

Figure 11.1 The logic of sociology.

This conformity of thought, emotion, and action is not restricted to the masses, or the lowly, or the poor. It is characteristic of people in general, independent of their role in society, independent of status and prestige, independent of years of schooling. It is in all likelihood as true of college professors and their presidents as students and custodians, as true of senators and chief executives as it is of construction and assembly-line workers. Conformity of thought and behavior is the rule in humans, independence the rare exception.

According to the *The Encyclopedia Americana* (1950, vol 7, page 541):

> [There is an] infinity of variations in human behavior, termed good or evil, well or sick, according to the time and place and surrounding mores. The mescalin intoxicated priest carrying out an Indian ritual is adapted and healthy according to the rules of the game. Under other circumstances and in other places his behavior would probably bring him confinement in the police station or in a mental hospital.

To fail to conform to social expectation is to become subject to being cut off from the group: Here is how such a person is characterized in *Tom Brown's School Days* (Hughes, 1882):

> The person whose appearance had so horrified Miss Winter was drawing beer for them from a small barrel. This was an elderly raw-boned woman, with a skin burned as brown as that of any of the mowers. She wore a man's hat and spencer, and had a strong harsh voice, and altogether was not a prepossessing person. She went by the name of Daddy Cowell in the parish, and had been for years a proscribed person. She lived up on the heath, often worked in the fields, took in lodgers, and smoked a short clay pipe. These eccentricities, when added to her half-male clothing, were quite enough to account for the sort of outlawry in which she lived. Miss Winter, and other good people of Englebourn, believed her capable of any crime, and the children were taught to stop talking and playing, and run away when she came near them.

Sociocentric Thinking as Pathology

Sociocentric thinking, as we intend this expression, is egocentric thinking raised to the level of the group. It is as destructive as egocentric thinking, if not more so, as it carries with it the sanction of a social group. In both cases, we find a native and uncritical dogmatism implicit in its principles. And therein lies its pathology. Like egocentric thinking, it is absurd at the level of conscious expression. If sociocentric thinking is made explicit in the mind of the thinker, its unreasonableness will be obvious.

Note the parallels in Table 11.1 for egocentric and sociocentric patterns of thought.

Table 11.1   Egocentric and Sociocentric Patterns of Thought

Egocentric Standard	Related Sociocentric Standard
"It's true because I believe it."	"It's true because we believe it."
"It's true because I want to believe it."	"It's true because we want to believe it."
"It's true because it's in my vested interest to believe it."	"It's true because it's in our vested interest to believe it."
"It's true because I have always believed it."	"It's true because we have always believed it."

Just as individuals deceive themselves through egocentric thinking, groups deceive themselves through sociocentric thinking. Just as egocentric thinking functions to serve one's selfish interest, sociocentric thinking functions to serve the selfish interests of the group. Just as egocentric thinking operates to validate the uncritical thinking of the individual, sociocentric thinking operates to validate the uncritical thinking of the group.

Test the Idea
Thinking About the Groups You Belong To
Make a list of the groups you belong to. Then choose the group you think has influenced you the most in your beliefs, values, and behavior. Complete the following statements:

1. The group that has influenced me the most is probably...
2. This group's main function or agenda is...
3. Comment on as many of the following variables as you can identify with, with respect to the group you have chosen to analyze. To what extent does your membership in this group involve:
   - A name that defines who and what they are;
   - A way of talking;
   - A set of friends and enemies;
   - Group rituals in which you must participate;
   - Expected behaviors involving fellow members;
   - Expected behaviors when around the "enemies" of the group;
   - A hierarchy of power within the group;
   - A way of dressing and speaking;

- Social requirements to which you must conform;
- A set of taboos—forbidden acts, whose violation is punished.
4. One of the key "requirements" of this group is...
5. One of the key "taboos" (what I am forbidden to do) is...
6. A group that my group would look down upon is ... We think of this group as beneath us because...

The idea of sociocentric thinking is not new. Under one label or another, many books have been written on the subject. And it has been the focus of important sociological studies. Almost a hundred years ago, in his seminal book *Folkways*, originally published in 1902, William Graham Sumner wrote extensively about social expectations and taboos. One of the founders of the discipline of sociology, Sumner documented the manner in which group thought penetrates virtually every dimension of human life. He introduced the concept of ethnocentrism in this way:

> Ethnocentrism is the technical name for this view of thinking in which one's own group is the center of everything, and all others are scaled and rated with reference to it.... Each group nourishes its own pride and vanity, boasts itself superior, exacts its own divines, and looks with contempt on outsiders. Each group thinks its own folkways the only right ones, and if it observes that other groups have other folkways, these excite its scorn. (p. 13)

Sumner describes folkways as the socially perceived "right" ways to satisfy all interests according to group norms and standards. He says that in every society:

> There is a right way to catch game, to win a wife, to make one's self appear... to treat comrades or strangers, to behave when a child is born... The "right" way is the way which ancestors used and which has been handed down. The tradition is its own warrant. It is not held subject to verification by experience.... In the folkways, whatever is, is right. (p. 28)

In regard to expectations of group members, Sumner states:

> Every group of any kind whatsoever demands that each of its members shall help defend group interests. The group force is also employed to enforce the obligations of devotion to group interests. It follows that judgments are precluded and criticism silenced.... The patriotic bias is a recognized perversion of thought and judgment against which our education should guard us. (p. 15)

Even young children exhibit sociocentric thinking and behavior. Consider this passage from Piaget's study for UNESCO (Campbell, 1976), which is a dialogue between an interviewer and three children regarding the causes of war:

> Michael M. (9 years, 6 months old): Have you heard of such people as foreigners? Yes, the French, the Americans, the Russians, the English... Quite right. Are there differences

between all these people? Oh, yes, they don't speak the same language. And what else? I don't know. What do you think of the French, for instance? The French are very serious, they don't worry about anything, an' it's dirty there. And what do you think of the Russians? They're bad, they're always wanting to make war. And what's your opinion of the English? I don't know... they're nice... Now look, how did you come to know all you've told me? I don't know... I've heard it... that's what people say.

Maurice D. (8 years, 3 months old): If you didn't have any nationality and you were given a free choice of nationality, which would you choose? Swiss nationality. Why? Because I was born in Switzerland. Now look, do you think the French and Swiss are equally nice, or the one nicer or less nice than the other? The Swiss are nicer. Why? The French are always nasty. Who is more intelligent, the Swiss or the French, or do you think they're just the same? The Swiss are more intelligent. Why? Because they learn French quickly. If I asked a French boy to choose any nationality he liked, what country do you thinking he'd choose? He'd choose France. Why? Because he was born in France. And what would he say about who's the nicer? Would he think the Swiss and French equally nice, or one better than the other? He'd say the French are nicer. Why? Because he was born in France. And who would he think more intelligent? The French. Why? He'd say the French want to learn quicker than the Swiss. Now you and the French boy don't really give the same answer. Who do you think answered best? I did. Why? Because Switzerland is always better.

Marina T. (7 years, 9 months old): If you were born without any nationality and you were given a free choice, what nationality would you choose? Italian. Why? Because it's my country. I like it better than Argentina where my father works, because Argentina isn't my country. Are Italians just the same, or more, or less intelligent than the Argentineans? What do you think? The Italians are more intelligent. Why? I can see people I live with, they're Italians. If I were to give a child from Argentina a free choice of nationality, what do you think he would choose? He'd want to stay an Argentinean. Why? Because that's his country. And if I were to ask him who is more intelligent, the Argentineans or the Italians, what do you think he would answer? He'd say Argentineans. Why? Because there wasn't any war. Now who was really right in the choice he made and what he said, the Argentinean child, you, or both? I was right. Why? Because I chose Italy.

It is clear that these children are thinking sociocentrically. They have been indoctrinated into the belief systems, with accompanying ideologies, of their nation and culture. They cannot articulate why they think their country is better than others, but they have no doubt that it is. Seeing one's group as superior to other groups is both natural to the human mind and propagated by the cultures within which we live.

Social Stratification

Sociocentric systems are used in complex societies to justify differential treatment and injustices within a society, nation, or culture. This feature of complex social systems has been documented by sociologists who have specialized in the phenomenon of social stratification. As virtually all modern societies today are complex, the following characteristics of stratification presumably can be found in all of them. According to Plotnicov and Tuden (1970), Each has social groups that

1. Are ranked hierarchically;

2. Maintain relatively permanent positions in the hierarchy;

3. Have differential control of the sources of power, primarily economic and political;

4. Are separated by cultural and invidious distinctions that also serve to maintain the social distances between the groups; and

5. Are articulated by an overarching ideology that provides a rationale for the established hierarchical arrangements. (pp. 4-5).

Given this phenomenon, we should be able to identify, for any given group in our society, where approximately it stands in the hierarchy of power, what the sources of power and control are, how the distinctions that indicate status are formulated, how social distances are maintained between the groups, and the overarching ideology that provides the rationale for the way things are.

Test the Idea
Identifying Social Stratification

Try to construct a hierarchy of the social groups within the culture with which you are most knowledgeable. First identify the groups with the most power and prestige. What characteristics do these groups have? Then identify the groups with less and less power until you reach the groups with the least amount of power. How do the groups with the most power keep their power? To what extent is it possible for groups with the least power to increase their power? To what extent do they seem to accept their limited power? To the extent that they accept their limited power, why do you think they do?

Sociocentric Thinking Is Unconscious and Potentially Dangerous

Sociocentric thinking, like egocentric thinking, appears in the mind of the person who thinks that way as reasonable and justified. Thus, although groups often distort the meaning of concepts to pursue their vested interests, they almost never see themselves as misusing language. Although groups almost always can find problems in the ideologies of other groups, they rarely are able to find flaws in their belief systems. Although groups usually can identify prejudices that other groups are using against them, they rarely are able to identify prejudices that they are using against other groups. In short, just as egocentric thinking is self-deceptive, so is sociocentric thinking.

Though the patterns of dysfunctional thinking are similar for egocentric and sociocentric thinking, there is at least one important distinction between the two. We pointed out in Chapter 10 that egocentric thinking is potentially dangerous. Through self-deception, individuals can justify the most egregious actions, but individuals operating alone are usually more limited in the amount of harm they can do. Typically, groups engaging in sociocenric thinking can do greater harm to greater numbers of people.

Consider, for example, the Spanish Inquisition, wherein the state, controlled by the Catholic Church, executed thousands of reputed heretics. Or consider the Germans, who tortured and murdered millions of Jews, or the "founders" of the Americas, who enslaved, murdered, or tortured large numbers of Native Americans and Africans.

In short, throughout history and to the present day, sociocentric thinking has led directly to the pain and suffering of millions of innocent persons. This has been possible because groups, in their sociocentric mindset, use their power in a largely unreflective, abusive way. Once they have internalized a self-serving ideology, they are able to act in ways that flagrantly contradict their announced morality without noticing any contradictions or inconsistencies in the process.

Sociocentric Use of Language in Groups

Sociocentric thinking is fostered by the way groups use language. Groups justify unjust acts and ways of thinking through their use of concepts or ideas. For example, as Sumner points out, sociocentrism can be exemplified by the very names groups choose for themselves and the way they differentiate themselves from what they consider lesser groups:

> When Caribs were asked whence they came, they answered, "We alone are people." The meaning of the name Kiowa is "real or principal people." The Lapps call themselves "men." Or "human beings." The Greenland Eskimo think that Europeans have been sent to Greenland to learn virtue and good manners from the Greenlanders.... The Seri of Lower California... observe an attitude of suspicion and hostility to all outsiders, and strictly forbid marriage with outsiders. (p. 14)

In the everyday life of sociocentric thinkers, we can find many self-serving uses of language that obscure unethical behavior. During the time when Europeans first inhabited the Americas, they forced Indians into slavery and tortured and murdered them in the name of progress and civilization. By thinking of the Indians as savages, they could justify their inhumane treatment. At the same time, by thinking of themselves as civilized, they could see themselves as bringing something precious to the savages, namely civilization.

The words progress, savagery, civilization, and true religion, were used as vehicles to exploit the American Indians to gain material wealth and property. The thinking of the Europeans, focused on these ideas, obscures the basic humanity of the peoples exploited as well as their rightful ownership of the land that they had occupied for thousands of years.

Sumner says that the language social groups use is often designed to ensure that they maintain a special, superior place:

> The Jews divided all mankind into themselves and the Gentiles. They were "chosen people." The Greeks called outsiders "barbarians."… The Arabs regarded themselves as the noblest nation and all others as more or less barbarous.… In 1896, the Chinese minister of education and his counselors edited a manual in which this statement occurs: "How grand and glorious is the Empire of China, the middle Kingdom!"… The grandest men in the world have come from the middle empire.… In all the literature of all the states equivalent statements occur.… In Russian books and newspapers the civilizing mission of Russia is talked about, just as, in the books and journals of France, Germany, and the United States, the civilizing mission of those countries is assumed and referred to as well understood. Each state now regards itself as the leader of civilization, the best, the freest and the wisest, and all others as their inferior. (p. 14)

Disclosing Sociocentric Thinking Through Conceptual Analysis

Concepts are one of the eight basic elements of human thinking. We cannot think without them. They form the classifications, and implicitly express the theories, through which we interpret what we see, taste, hear, smell, and touch. Our world is a conceptually constructed world. And sociocentric thinking, as argued above, is driven by the way groups use concepts.

If we had thought using the concepts of medieval European serfs, we would experience the world as they did. If we had thought using the concepts of an Ottoman Turk general, we would think and experience the world that he did.

In a similar way, if we were to bring an electrician, an architect, a carpet salesperson, a lighting specialist, and a plumber into the same building and ask each to describe what he or she sees, we would end up with a range of descriptions that, in all likelihood, reveal the special "bias" of the observer.

Or again, if we were to lead a discussion of world problems between representatives of different nations, cultures, and religions, we would discover a range of perspectives not only on potential solutions to the problems, but sometimes as to what a problem is in the first place.

It is hard to imagine a skilled critical thinker who is not also skilled in the analysis of concepts. Conceptual analysis is important in a variety of contexts:

1. The ability to identify and accurately analyze the range of distinctions available to educated speakers of a language (being able to distinguish between meanings of words, given educated usage).

2. The ability to identify the difference between ideological and nonideological uses of words and concepts (being able to figure out when people are giving special, unjustified meaning to words based on their ideology).

3. The ability to accurately analyze the network of technical meanings of words that define the basic concepts within a discipline or domain of thinking (being able to analyze the meanings of words within disciplines and technical fields).

Many problems in thinking are traceable to a lack of command of words and their implicit concepts. For example, people have problems in their romantic relationships when they are unclear about three distinctions: 1) between egocentric attachment and genuine love; 2) between friendship and love; and (3) between misuse of the word love (as exemplified by many Hollywood movies) and the true meaning of the word love shared by educated speakers of the English language.

Revealing Ideology at Work Through Conceptual Analysis

People often have trouble differentiating ideological and nonideological uses of words. They are then unable to use the following words in a nonloaded way: capitalism, socialism, communism, democracy, oligarchy, plutocracy, patriotism, terrorism. Let's look at this case in greater detail.

When the above words are used ideologically, they are applied inconsistently and one-sidedly. The root meaning of the word is often lost, or highly distorted, while the word is used to put a positive or negative gloss on events, obscuring what is really going on. Hence, in countries in which the reigning ideology extols capitalism, the ideologies of socialism and communism are demonized, democracy is equated with capitalism, and plutocracy is ignored. In countries in which the reigning ideology is communism, the ideology of capitalism is demonized, democracy is equated with communism, and oligarchy is ignored. The groups called "terrorists" by some are called patriots by the others.

If we examine the core meanings of these words and use them in keeping with the core meanings they have in the English language, we can recognize contradictions, inconsistencies, and hypocrisy when any group misuses them to advance its agenda. Let us review the core meanings of these terms as defined by Webster's New World Dictionary:

- *Capitalism*: an economic system in which all or most of the means of production and distribution, as land, factories, railroads, etc, are privately owned and operated for profit, originally under fully competitive conditions; it has generally been characterized by a tendency toward concentration of wealth.

- *Socialism*: any of the various theories or systems of the ownership and operation of the means of production and distribution by society or the community rather than by private individuals, with all members of society or the community sharing in the work and the products.

- *Communism*: any economic theory or system based on the ownership of all property by the community as a whole.

- *Democracy*: government in which the people hold the ruling power either directly or through elected representatives; rule by the ruled.

- *Oligarchy*: a form of government in which the ruling power belongs to a few persons.

- *Plutocracy*: 1) government by the wealthy; 2) a group of wealthy people who control or influence a government.

- *Patriotism*: love and loyal or zealous support of one's own country.

- *Terrorism*: use of force or threats to demoralize, intimidate, and subjugate, especially such use as a political weapon or policy.

To this day, countries in which the reigning ideology is capitalism tend to use the words socialism and communism as if they meant "a system that discourages individual incentive and denies freedom to the mass of people." Countries in which the reigning ideology is socialism or communism, in their turn, tend to use the word capitalism to imply the exploitation of the masses by the wealthy few. Both see the use of force of the other as terrorist in intent. Both see the other as denying its own members fundamental human rights. Both tend to ignore their own inconsistencies and hypocrisy.

The Mass Media Foster Sociocentric Thinking

The mass media and press in a country tend to present events in the world in descriptive terms that presuppose the correctness of the self-serving world view dominant in the country. As critical consumers of the mass media, we must learn to recognize when language is being used ideologically (and so violating the **basic** meanings of the terms themselves). We must learn how to recognize sociocentric bias wherever we find it.

Many examples of sociocentric thinking can be found in the mass media. This is true, in part, because the media are an inherent part of the culture within which they function. Because much of the thinking within any given culture is sociocentric in nature, we can expect the sociocentric thinking of the culture to be furthered through the mass media as vehicles of large-scale social communication.

For example, the mass media routinely validate the view that one's own country is "right" or ethical in its dealings in the world. This cultivates one-sided nationalistic thinking. The basic idea is that all of us egocentrically think of ourselves in largely favorable terms. As sociocentric thinkers, we think of our nation and the groups to which we belong in largely favorable terms. It follows, therefore, that the media will present in largely unfavorable terms those nations and groups that significantly oppose us.

For example, to most citizens of the United States, it seems naturally to be a leader of all that is right and good in the world. The mass media largely foster this view. When we look critically at the mainstream mass media of a country, it is easy to document the bias of its presentations of the important events in the world.

It follows that the mainstream news media are biased toward their country's allies, and prejudiced against its enemies. The media therefore present events that regard the countries of allies in as favorable a light as possible, highlighting positive events while downplaying negative events. As for its enemies, the opposite treatment can be expected. Thus, positive events in the countries of one's enemies are either ignored or given little attention while negative events are highlighted and distorted. The ability of a person to identify this bias in action and mentally rewrite the article or representation more objectively is an important critical thinking skill.

In the United States, for example, because Israel is our ally, our media usually ignore or give minor attention to mistreatment of the Palestinians by the Israelis. On the other hand, because Fidel Castro of Cuba is our enemy, mainstream news writers take advantage of every opportunity to present Castro and Cuba in a negative light, ignoring most achievements of the Cuban government (e.g., in the area of universal education and medical care).

Let's consider some examples from the news to exemplify this pattern of sociocentric bias in the news.

U.S. Releases Files on Abuses in Pinochet Era (from *New York Times*, July 1, 1999, p. A11)

Historical background. In 1973 a group of military officers overthrew the government of the democratically elected president of Chile, Salvador Allende. Their announced justification was that Allende was trying to replace democracy with communism. At the time of the coup the U.S. government repeatedly denied any involvement in the coup and any knowledge of the torture and murder of people considered enemies of the coup leaders and the imposed political structure. Accordingly, the mainstream news media presented the official U.S. position (along with its official explanations) as the truth of the matter. The coup leaders were presented as a positive force against communism. The democratically elected government was presented as a threat to our way of life. The coup, in other words, was presented favorably. Human rights violations were played down.

Contents of article. In this article, written some 27 years after the coup, the mainstream media finally admitted that the United States played a significant role in the Chilean coup. The article states:

The C.I.A. and other government agencies had detailed reports of widespread human rights abuses by the Chilean military, including the killing and torture of leftist dissidents, almost immediately after a 1973 right-wing coup that the United States supported, according to the once-secret documents released today.... The Clinton Administration announced last December that, as a result of the arrest of General Pinochet (who seized power in the coup), it would declassify some of the documents.

Another article in the New York Times, dated November 27, 1999 (article entitled "Judge Is Hoping to See Secret Files in U.S.," p. A14), states, "The Nixon Administration openly favored the coup and helped prepare the climate for the military intervention against the Socialist Government of Salvador Allende Gossens, by backing loans, financing strikes, and supporting the opposition press."

Significance.   This account illustrates how successfully sociocentric renditions of events are rendered by the news media at the time of their occurrence and for many years thereafter. It also points out, in its failure to suggest—even now—that some significant breach of morality originally occurred, or that, even worse, breaches of our announced values are common. There is also no criticism of the media for their failure at the time to discover and publish the truth of the U.S. involvement in the coup.

U.S. Order to Kill Civilians in Korea Illegal, Experts Say: Prosecution Seen as Impossible Now (from *San Francisco Chronicle*, Oct. 2, 1999, p. A12 (taken from the Associated Press)

Historical background.   During the Korean War (1950-1953), the news media represented U.S. involvement in the war as a fight, on our side, for the freedom of the South Korean people against a totalitarian government in North Korea (which we presented as dupes of the Chinese communists). That the government we supported in South Korea did not itself function in a democratic fashion and easily could have been represented as our "dupes" was not mentioned in the news coverage of the time. The coverage implied that we were there for humanitarian reasons: to protect the rights of innocent Koreans to have a democratically elected government and universal human rights. The mainstream media also failed to point out any problems with either our involvement in the war or the methods we used to deal with "the enemy."

Contents of article.   This article, written 25 years after the events in question, focuses on the killing of civilian refugees by American soldiers during the Korean War:

The Associated Press reported Wednesday that a dozen veterans of the 1st Cavalry Division said their unit killed a large number of South Korean refugees at a hamlet 100 miles southeast of the Korean capital.... The survivors say 400 people were killed in the mass shooting and a preceding U.S. air attack.... In the 1st Cavalry Division, the operations chief issued this order: "No refugees to cross the front line. Fire at everyone trying to cross lines."

Such orders are patently illegal, military law experts say today. "I've never heard of orders like this, not outside the orders given by Germans that we heard about during the Nuremberg Trials," said Scott Silliman of Duke University, a retired colonel and Air Force lawyer for 25 years.

Yet, "during the 1950-53 war, there were no prosecutions of anything more than individual murders of civilians by U.S. servicemen," the experts note.

In pondering the question: Why were the orders to kill refugees kept quiet all these years?... a retired Colonel who eventually became chief drafter of the Korean armistice agreement commented, "If it was in their unit, then for the sake of the unit they didn't want to report it." He goes on to state that for much of U.S. history, "we've done very badly in not trying these cases.... What bothers me most is the fact that the American public seems to take the side of the war criminal if he's an American."

Significance.   The significance of this article is that, on the one hand, it again is an example of how successfully the news media render sociocentric events at the time of their occurrence and for many years afterward. What is unusual in this article is the suggestion of a pattern of behavior that goes beyond the events at this particular time ("We've done very badly in not trying these cases.... What bothers me most is the fact that the American public seems to take the side of the war criminal if he's an American"). This suggestion of a pattern of American wrong-doing is exceptional, as it diverges from the usual sociocentric tendency of the news. It should be noted, however, that we find this merely in the quote of one individual. The suggestion is not taken up in any follow-up articles. It is not a newsmaker, as was the story of President Clinton's sexual escapades. In this sense, the sociocentrism of the news media is not significantly breached.

Treatment Is New Salvo Fired by Reformers in War on Drugs: Courts, voters beginning to favor therapy, not prisons, to fight crack (from *San Francisco Chronicle*, June 11, 1999, p. A9, taken from the New York Times)

Historical background.   Sufficient historical background is given in the contents of the article itself.

Contents of article.

A dozen years after the national alarm over crack hastened the decline of drug treatment in favor of punitive laws that helped create the world's largest prison system, anti-drug policy is taking another turn. Treatment is making a comeback.... In the crack years of the 1980s, treatment programs were gutted while the drug-fighting budget quadrupled. New reports said crack was the most addictive substance known to humanity, and prisons started to fill with people who once might have received help instead. The number of Americans locked up on drug offenses grew from 50,000 in 1980 to 400,000 today. Yet even during the height of the prison boom, when some people were sentenced to life behind bars for possessing small amounts of a drug, a number of treatment centers continued to have success. While not all addicts respond to treatment, these programs showed that crack was less addictive than some other street drugs, or even nicotine, and that many of its users responded to conventional therapy.

Significance. This article exemplifies the powerful role of the media in feeding social hysteria and thereby affecting social and legal policy. The view advanced by news reports that crack is the most addictive substance known to humanity was the popular view of the day. Also popular in the 1980s was the view that crack users are best dealt with by imprisonment rather than through treatment of the drug abuse problem. The news media reinforced a simplistic Puritanical tradition that is deep in our culture: that the world divides into the good and the evil. According to this social ideology, the good defeat the bad by the use of physical force and superior strength, and the bad are taught a lesson only by severe punishment.

Test the Idea
Identifying Sociocentric Bias in the News I

Read through the newspaper every day for a week and attempt to locate at least one article revealing sociocentric thinking in the news. One of the best ways to do this is to carefully read any articles about the "friends" or "enemies" of your country's power structure. You should be able to identify a bias toward preserving this nationalistic view. Any negative article about one of your country's friends will play down the negative events and present extenuating excuses for those events. You will rarely find positive articles about your country's enemies, for in nationalistic ideology those who are evil do no good.

Use the format we have been using in writing what you have found, including Historical Background (if possible), Contents of the Article, and Significance. It also will be useful if you think through how the article might have been written if it did not reflect a sociocentric bias.

Sometimes an article in the news does not display our socio-centrism, but implicitly documents the sociocentrism of another group. For example, the *New York Times*, June 20, 1999, included an article entitled "Arab Honor's Price: A Woman's Blood" (p. 1), focusing on the sociocentric thinking of Arab religious groups in Jordan. The facts it covers are the following:

- An Arab woman in Jordan was shot and killed by her 16-year-old brother for running away from home after her husband suspected her of infidelity;

- After her husband divorced her, she had run away and remarried;

- Her family had been searching for her for six years in order to kill her. "We were the most prominent family, with the best reputation," said Um Tayseer, the mother. "Then we were disgraced. Even my brother and his family stopped talking to us. No one would even visit us. They would say only, "You have to kill." "Now we can talk with our heads high," said Amal, her 18-year-old sister.

The article goes on to document the way in which traditional Arab culture places greater emphasis on chastity in women than on any other "virtue." The article states:

- "What is honor? Abeer Alla, a young Egyptian journalist, remembered how it was explained by a high-school biology teacher. He sketched the female reproductive system and pointed out the entrance to the vagina. 'This is where the family honor lies!' the teacher declared;

- More than pride, more than honesty, more than anything a man might do, female chastity is seen in the Arab world as an indelible line, the boundary between respect and shame;

- An unchaste woman, it is sometimes said, is worse than a murderer, affecting not just one victim, but her family and her tribe;

- It is an unforgiving logic, and its product, for centuries and now, has been murder—the killings of girls and women by their relatives, to cleanse honor that has been soiled."

Test the Idea
Identifying Sociocentric Bias in the News II
Locate at least one newspaper article containing evidence of sociocentric thinking on the part of some group. Complete these statements:
1. The article I identified is entitled...
2. A brief summary of the article is as follows...
3. The sociocentric thinking depicted in this article is as follows...
4. If this group had not been thinking sociocentrically, and instead had been thinking rationally, it would have behaved in the following way...

The Mass Media Play Down Information That Puts the Nation in a Negative Light

The media not only represents the news in terms favorable to the nation, it also plays down information that puts the nation in a negative light. The news media of the U.S. is a case in point.

When the UN General Assembly opposes the U.S. virtually unanimously, the U.S. media play that down, either by not reporting the vote at all or burying it in fine print or with an obscure notice. For example, most Americans are unaware of the extent to which the United States has stood alone, or virtually alone, in votes of the general assembly of the United Nations. According to the United Nations (2001), the U.S. was *the only nation in the world* voting against the following resolutions:

* Resolutions seeking to ban testing and development of chemical and biological weapons (1981, 1982, 1983, 1984);

* Resolutions seeking to prohibit the testing and development of nuclear weapons (1982, 1983, 1984);

* Resolutions seeking to prohibit the escalation of the arms race into space (1982, 1983);

* Resolutions condemning and calling for an end to apartheid in South Africa (five in 1981, four in 1982, four in 1983);

* Resolutions calling for education, health care, and nourishment as basic human rights (1981, 1982, 1983);

* Resolutions affirming the right of every nation to self determination of its economic and social systems free of outside intervention (1981, 1983).

In 1981, the U.S. and Israel were *the only nations in the world* voting against 11 otherwise unanimous resolutions condemning Israel for human rights abuses committed against the Palestinians. And on December 7, 1987, the U.S. was the only nation to abstain from supporting a unanimous resolution calling for a convention on the rights of the child (United Nations, 2001).

The view that the U.S. fosters about itself, both at home and abroad, is, of course, that of being the leader of the free world. This view would be largely shattered if it were widely reported in the U.S. that, in fact, no other nation is following its lead.

On the one hand, the U.S. media foster the view that the U.S. is the best place to live in the world. At the same time, "The U.S. now imprisons more people than any other country in the world—perhaps half a million more than Communist China (Atlantic Monthly, December 1998)." One state alone, California, "now has the biggest prison system in the Western industrialized world... The state holds more inmates in its jails and prisons than do France, Great Britain, Germany, Japan, Singapore, and the Netherlands combined" (*Atlantic Monthly*, December 1998).

Freedom from Sociocentric Thought: The Beginnings of Genuine Conscience

The thesis of this chapter is that we are by nature sociocentric as well as egocentric. Without a clear understanding of our sociocentric tendencies, we become victims of the conformist thought dominant in social groups, and we become potential victimizers of others who disagree with our group's ideology. What is important is that we begin to identify sociocentrism in our thinking and our lives. Every group to which we belong is a possible place to begin to identify sociocentrism at work in ourselves and others. Once we see the many patterns of social conformity in our lives, we can begin question those patterns. As we become more rational, we neither conform to conform nor rebel to rebel. We act, rather, from a clear sense of values and beliefs we have rationally thought through, values and beliefs we deem worthy of our free commitment.

The Capacity to Recognize Unethical Acts

Only when we can distinguish sociocentric thinking from ethical thinking can we begin to develop a conscience that is not equivalent to those values into which we have been socially conditioned. Here are some categories of acts that are unethical in-and-of themselves:

- SLAVERY: Enslaving people, whether individually or in groups;

- GENOCIDE: Systematically killing large masses of people;

- TORTURE: Using torture to obtain a "confession";

- DENIAL OF DUE PROCESS: Putting persons in jail without telling them the charges against them or providing them with a reasonable opportunity to defend themselves;

- POLITICALLY MOTIVATED IMPRISONMENT: Putting persons in jail, or otherwise punishing them, solely for their political or religious views;

- SEXISM: Treating people unequally (and harmfully) in virtue of their gender;

- RACISM: Treating people unequally (and harmfully) in virtue of their race or ethnicity;

- MURDER: The pre-meditated killing of people for revenge, pleasure, or to gain advantage for oneself;

- ASSAULT: Attacking an innocent person with intent to cause grievous bodily harm;

- RAPE: Forcing an unwilling person to have intercourse;

- FRAUD: Intentional deception to cause someone to give up property or some right;

- DECEIT: Representing something as true which one knows to be false in order to gain a selfish end harmful to another;

- INTIMIDATION: Forcing a person to act against his interest or deter from acting in his interest by threats or acts of violence.

Conclusion

Inescapably, living a human life entails membership in a variety of human groups. And such membership almost always generates sociocentric thought. This holds independently of whether we are speaking of nation, culture, profession, religion, family, or peer group. We find ourselves participating in groups before we are aware of ourselves as living beings. We find ourselves in groups in virtually every setting in which we function as persons. Sociocentric thought is the natural by-product of uncritically internalizing social concepts and values. To the extent that we remain sociocentric, we cannot become independent thinkers, nor can we develop a genuine conscience. The tools of critical thinking enable us to achieve perspective upon the social and cultural bases of our day-to-day thinking. It enables us to judge those bases with standards and criteria that free us from the intellectual confinement of one-dimensional thought. It enables us to locate concepts, standards, and values that transcend our culture and society. It enables us to develop a genuine conscience. It enables us to think within and beyond the social groups to which we belong.

Chapter 12

Developing as an Ethical Reasoner

O ne of the most significant obstacles to fair-mindedness is the human tendency to reason in a self-serving or self-deluded manner. This tendency is increased by the extent to which people are confused about the nature of ethical concepts and principles. In understanding ethical reasoning, the following foundations are essential:

1. Ethical principles are not a matter of subjective preference.
2. All reasonable people are obligated to respect clear-cut ethical concepts and principles.
3. To reason well through ethical issues, we must know how to apply ethical concepts and principles reasonably to those issues.
4. Ethical concepts and principles should be distinguished from the norms and taboos of society and peer group, religious teachings, political ideologies, and the law.
5. The most significant barriers to sound ethical reasoning are the egocentrism and socio-centrism of human beings.

First we will seek to clarify the problem that ethics poses in human life: what ethics is, what its basis is, what it is commonly confused with, what its pitfalls are, and how it is to be understood.

Following that discussion, we emphasize three essential components in sound ethical reasoning: 1) the principles upon which ethics are grounded; 2) the counterfeits to avoid; and 3) the pathology of the human mind.

Why People are Confused About Ethics

The ultimate basis for ethics is clear: Human behavior has consequences for the welfare of others. We are capable of acting toward others in such a way as to increase or decrease the quality of their lives. We are capable of helping or harming others. What is more, we are capable of understanding—at least in many cases—when we are doing the one and when we are doing the other. This is so because we have the raw capacity to put ourselves imaginatively in the place of others and recognize how we would feel if someone were to act toward us in the manner in which we are acting toward them.

Even young children have some idea of what it is to help or harm others. Children make inferences and judgments on the basis of that ethical awareness, and develop an outlook on life that has ethical significance for good or ill. But children tend to have a much clearer awareness of the harm done to them than they have of the harm they do to others:

- "That's not fair! He got more than me!"

- "She won't let me have any of the toys!"

- "He hit me and I didn't do anything to him. He's mean!"

- "She promised me. Now she won't give me my doll back!"

- "Cheater! Cheater!"

- "It's my turn now. You had your turn. That's not fair."

Through example and encouragement, we can cultivate fair-mindedness in children. Children can learn to respect the rights of others and not simply focus on their own. The main problem is not so much the difficulty of deciding what is helpful and harmful but, instead, our natural propensity to be egocentric. Few humans think at a deep level about the consequences to others of their selfish pursuit of money, power, prestige, and possessions. The result is that, though most people, independent of their society, ethnicity, and religion, give at least lip service to a common core of general ethical principles, few act consistently upon these principles. Few will argue that it is ethically justified to cheat, deceive, exploit, abuse, harm, or steal from others, nor hold that we have no ethical responsibility to respect the rights of others, including their freedom and well being. But few dedicate their lives to helping those most in need of help, to seeking the common good and not merely their own self-interest and egocentric pleasures.

As we pointed out in the last chapter, there are acts that rational persons recognize are in-and-of themselves harmful to people. They include slavery, genocide, torture, denial of due process, politically motivated imprisonment, sexism, racism, murder, assault, rape, fraud, deceit, and intimidation.

The United Nations' Declaration of Human Rights, which all countries have ratified, articulates universal ethical principles. And a core of ideas defines the domain of ethicality and ethics, for reasonable people, in a broad and global way. Many fail to act in accordance with ethical principles, nevertheless. At an abstract level, there is little disagreement. Virtually no one would argue that it is ethically justifiable to cheat, deceive, exploit, abuse, and harm others merely because one wants to or simply because one has the raw power to do so. At the level of action, though, mere verbal agreement on general principles does not produce a world that honors human rights. There are too many ways in which humans can rationalize their rapacious desires and feel justified in taking advantage of those who are weaker or less able to protect themselves. There are too many forces in human life—for example, social groups, religions, and political ideologies—that generate norms of right and wrong that ignore or distort ethical principles. What is more, humans are too skilled in the art of self-deception for mere verbal agreement on abstract ethical principles to translate into the reality of an ethically just world.

To further complicate the picture, the ethical thing to do is not always self-evident—even to those who are not significantly self-deceived. In complex situations, people of seeming good will often disagree as to the application of this or that ethical principle to this or that concrete case. One and the same act often receives ethical praise from some and condemnation from others.

We can put this dimension of the problem another way: However strongly motivated to do what is ethically right, people can do so only if they know what is ethically justified. And this they cannot know if they systematically confuse their sense of what is ethically right with their vested interest, personal desires, political ideology, or social mores, or if they lack the capacity to reason with skill and discipline in the ethical domain.

Because of complexities such as these, skilled ethical reasoning presupposes the art of self-critique and ethical self-examination. We must learn to check our thinking for egocentrism, socio-centrism, and self-deception. This, in turn, requires development of the intellectual dispositions we discussed earlier in the book, including intellectual humility, intellectual integrity, and fair-mindedness. Sound ethical reasoning often requires a thinker to recognize and get beyond the pitfalls of ethical judgment: ethical intolerance, self-deception, and uncritical conformity. Sound ethical reasoning often requires us to recognize when our reasoning is a reflection of our social indoctrination. Sound ethical reasoning often requires us to enter empathically into points of view other than our own, gather facts from alternative perspectives, question our assumptions, and consider alternative ways to put the question at issue.

Few adults, however, acquire the skills or insights to recognize the complexities inherent in many everyday ethical issues. Few identify their own ethical contradictions, or clearly distinguish their vested interest and egocentric desires from what is genuinely ethical. Few have thought about the counterfeits of ethical sentiment and judgment or have thought through a coherent ethical perspective in light of the complexities and pitfalls of ethical reasoning. As a result, everyday ethical judgments are often an unconscious mixture of genuine and counterfeit ethics, of ethical insight, on the one hand, and prejudice and hypocrisy on the other—each in a web of beliefs that seem to the believer to be self-evidently true.

Inadvertently, we pass on to our children and students our own ethical blindness, ethical distortions, and closed-mindedness. As a result, many who trumpet most loudly for ethics to be taught in the schools merely want students to adopt their own beliefs and perspectives, however flawed those beliefs and perspectives might be. They take themselves to have THE TRUTH in their pockets. They take their perspective to be exemplary of all ethical truths. What these same people fear most is someone else's ethical perspective taught as the truth: conservatives are afraid of liberals being in charge, liberals are fearful of conservatives, theists of nontheists, nontheists of theists, and so on.

All of these fears are justified. People—except in the most rare and exceptional cases—have a strong tendency to confuse what they believe with the truth. "It's true

---

Test the Idea
Distinguishing Between Indoctrination and Education

As a person interested in developing your thinking, you must clearly distinguish between indoctrination and education. These two concepts are often confused. Using a good dictionary as your reference, complete the following statements (you may want to look these words up in more than one dictionary for a more comprehensive understanding of the terms):

1. According to the dictionary, the meaning of the word indoctrination that contrasts with the meaning of education is…

2. According to the dictionary, the most fundamental meaning of the word education that contrasts with the meaning of indoctrination is…

3. The main difference between education and indoctrination, therefore, is…

Once you feel reasonably clear about the essential differences between these terms, think about your previous schooling and figure out the extent to which you think you have been indoctrinated (in contrast to having been educated). Complete these statements:

1. As a student, I believe I have been mainly (educated or indoctrinated). My reasons for concluding this are…

2. For example…

because I believe it" is, as we have already emphasized, a deep subconscious mindset in most of us. Our beliefs simply feel like "the Truth." They appear to the mind as the truth. In the "normal" human mind, it is always the others who do evil, are deceived, self-interested, closed-minded—never us. Thus, instead of cultivating genuine ethical principles in students, teachers often unknowingly indoctrinate them, systematically rewarding students for expressing the beliefs and perspectives the teachers themselves hold. To this extent, they indoctrinate rather than educate students

The Fundamentals of Ethical Reasoning

To become skilled in any domain of reasoning, we must understand the principles that define that domain. To be skilled in mathematical reasoning, we must understand fundamental mathematical principles. To be skilled in scientific reasoning, we must understand fundamental scientific principles (principles of physics, of chemistry, of astronomy, and so on). In like manner, to be skilled in ethical reasoning, we must understand fundamental ethical principles. Good-heartedness is not enough. We must be well-grounded in fundamental ethical concepts and principles. Principles are at the heart of ethical reasoning.

People thinking through an ethical issue must be able to identify the ethical principles relevant to the specific ethical situation. They must also muster the intellectual skills required to apply those principles fairly to the relevant case or situation. Ethical principles alone, however, do not settle ethical questions. For example, ethical principles sometimes can be applied differently in cases that are ethically complex.

Consider for instance, the question: Should the United States maintain relations with countries that violate human rights? The most important ethical concepts relevant to this question are justice and integrity, yet matters of practicality and effectiveness clearly must be considered as well. Justice and integrity would seem to require cutting off relations with any country that violates fundamental human rights. But is isolating and confronting these countries the most effective way to achieve these high ethical ends? What is more, history reminds us that nearly all countries violate human rights in one form or another—the United States not excluded. To what extent do we have the right to demand that others live up to standards that we ourselves often fail to meet? These are the kinds of challenging ethical issues often ignored by the naive and the good-hearted on the one hand, and the self-deceived cynical on the other.

Because ethical reasoning is often complex, we must learn strategies to deal with those complexities. The three intellectual tasks we believe to be the most important to ethical reasoning are:

1. Mastering the most basic ethical concepts and the principles inherent in ethical issues.

2. Learning to distinguish between ethics and other domains of thinking with which ethics is commonly confused.

3. Learning to identify when native human egocentrism and socio-centrism are impeding one's ethical judgments (probably the most challenging task of the three).

If any of these three foundations is missing in a person's ethical reasoning, that reasoning will likely be flawed. Let's consider these abilities in turn.

Ethical Concepts and Principles

For every ethical question, some ethical concept or set of concepts directly relevant to the question must be identified. One cannot reason well with regard to ethical issues if one does not clearly understand the force of ethical terms and distinctions. Some of the most basic ethical concepts include honesty, integrity, justice, equality, and respect. In many cases, application of the principles implied by these concepts is simple. In some cases it is difficult.

Consider some simple cases. Lying about, misrepresenting, or distorting the facts to gain a material advantage over others is clearly a violation of the basic principle inherent in the concept of honesty. Expecting others to live up to standards that we ourselves routinely violate is clearly a violation of the basic principle inherent in the concept of integrity. Treating others as if they were worth less than we take ourselves to be worth is a violation of the principles inherent in the concepts of integrity, justice, and equality. Every day human life is filled with clear-cut violations of basic ethical principles. No one would deny that it is ethically repugnant for a person to microwave cats for the fun of it. Nor is it ethically acceptable to kill people to get their money or to torture people because we think they are guilty and ought to confess.

Nevertheless, in addition to the clear-cut cases are also complicated cases, requiring us to enter into an ethical dialogue, considering counter-arguments from different points of view. Consider, for example, the question: Is euthanasia ever ethically justifiable? Certainly there are any number of instances when euthanasia is not justified. To consider the question of whether it is ever justified, however, we must consider the various conditions under which euthanasia seems plausible. For example, what about cases involving people who are suffering unrelenting pain from terminal diseases? Within this group are some who plead with us to end their suffering by helping them end their lives (since, though in torment, they cannot end their lives without the assistance of another person).

Given the fact, then, that a person so circumstanced is experiencing intense terminal suffering, one significant ethical concept relevant to this question is the concept of cruelty. Cruelty is defined by Webster's New World Dictionary as "causing, or of a kind to cause, pain, distress, etc; cruel implies indifference to the suffering of others or a disposition to inflict it on others." Cruelty, in this case, means "of a kind to cause" unnecessary pain. It means allowing an innocent person to experience unnecessary pain and suffering when you have the power to alleviate it—without sacrificing something of equal value.

Once cruelty is identified as a relevant concept, one ethical injunction becomes clear: "Strive to act so as to reduce or end the unnecessary pain and suffering of innocent persons and creatures." With this ethical principle in mind, we can seek to determine in what sense, in any given situation, refusing to assist a suffering person should be considered cruel and in what sense it shouldn't.

Another ethical concept that may be relevant to this issue is, "Life is good in itself." The principle that emerges from this concept is, "Life should be respected." Some would argue that, given this principle, life should not be terminated by humans under any circumstances.

As a person capable of reasoning, you should come to your own conclusions. At the same time, you must be prepared to state your reasoning in detail, explaining what ethical concepts and issues seem to you to be relevant, and why. You must be prepared to demonstrate that you have given serious consideration to alternative perspectives on the issue, that you are not ignoring other reasonable ways to think through the question at issue. You must be ready to present what you take to be the most relevant and important facts in the case. You must be prepared to do what any good thinker would do in attempting to support reasoning on any issue in any domain of thought. The fact that an issue is ethical does not mean that you can abandon your commitment to disciplined, rational thought.

Or consider: Under what conditions, if any, is animal experimentation justifiable? Again, one relevant ethical concept is cruelty, for anyone informed about animal experimentation knows that sometimes animals are subjected to extreme pain, anxiety, and suffering in the name of scientific inquiry. People for the Ethical Treatment of Animals (PETA), a proactive animal rights organization, focuses on the negative implications of animal experimentation. PETA, at its Web site, makes claims such as the following:

- Every year, millions of animals suffer and die in painful tests to determine the "safety" of cosmetics and household products. Substances ranging from eye shadow and soap to furniture polish and oven cleaner are tested on rabbits, rats, guinea pigs, dogs, and other animals, despite the fact that test results do not help prevent or treat human illness or injury. In these tests, a liquid, flake, granule, or powdered substance is dropped into the eyes of a group of albino rabbits. The animals are often immobilized in stocks from which only their heads protrude. They usually receive no anesthesia during the tests.... Reactions to the substances include swollen eyes. The rabbits' eyelids are held open with clips. Many animals break their necks as they struggle to escape.

- Chimpanzees are now popular subjects for AIDS research, although their immune system does not succumb to the virus. Chimpanzees are also used in painful cancer, hepatitis, and psychological tests, as well as for research into artificial insemination and birth control methods, blood diseases, organ transplants, and experimental surgery. Their use in military experiments is suspected, but such information is kept secret and hard to verify.... Chimpanzees are highly active and very socially oriented. When kept isolated in laboratories with no regular physical contact with either humans or chimps, they quickly become psychotic.... Because adult chimpanzees are strong and often unmanageable, and because infected chimpanzees cannot be placed in zoos or existing sanctuaries, many chimpanzees are killed before the age of 10.

- Sleep deprivation is recognized as a form of human torture. For decades, sleep deprivation has been used by repressive governments to extract classified information or false confessions from political prisoners. But some people do it legally. These people aren't called torturers. Because their subjects are animals, they're called "scientists".... For more than a quarter century, Allan Rechtschaffen, an experimenter of the University of Chicago, deprived animals of sleep. He started out keeping rats awake for up to 24 hours and then letting them recover. He moved on to total sleep deprivation—he kept rats awake until their bodies could no longer cope and they died of exhaustion. This took anywhere from 11 to 32 days. To prepare the gentle animals for this long nightmarish journey to death, Rechtschaffen stuck electrodes in the rat's skulls, sewed wires to their hearts, and surgically buried thermometers in their stomachs, so that he could track their temperatures and brain waves. To make blood drawing easier (for him), he snaked catheters through their jugular veins, down their necks and into their hearts.... Clinical studies have already shown that humans deprived of sleep suffer from lack of concentration and hallucinations, and that they recover quickly with even brief periods of sleep. So what did Rechtschaffen hope to discover? In his own words, "We established that rats died after 17 days of total sleep deprivation. Thus, at least, for the rat, sleep is absolutely essential."

Information such as this is relevant to the question of whether, to what extent and under what conditions animal experimentation is ethically justified. Some argue that animal experimentation is justified whenever some potential good for humans may emerge from the experiment. Others argue that animal experimentation is unethical because there are always alternative ways, such as computer simulations, to get the information being sought. At its Web site, PETA claims:

- More than 205,000 new drugs are marketed worldwide every year, most after undergoing the most archaic and unreliable testing methods still in use: animal studies.... Many physicians and researchers publicly speak out against these outdated studies. They point out that unreliable animal tests not only allow dangerous drugs to be marketed to the public, but may also prevent potentially useful ones from being made available. Penicillin would not be in use today if it had been tested on guinea pigs—common laboratory subjects—because penicillin kills guinea pigs. Likewise, aspirin kills cats, while morphine, a depressant to humans, is a stimulant to cats, goats, and horses. Human reactions to drugs cannot be predicted by tests on animals because different species (and even individuals within the same species) react differently to drugs.

- The Physician's Committee for Responsible Medicine reports that sophisticated non-animal research methods are more accurate, less expensive, and less time-consuming than traditional animal-based research methods.

Some argue that, in experiments in which animal suffering cannot be avoided, the suffering is ethically justified because in the long run the knowledge gained from this experimentation reduces the pain and suffering otherwise endured by humans. These proponents of experimentation argue that minimizing human pain and suffering is a superior ethical end to that of minimizing animal pain and suffering.

When reasoning through complex ethical questions, then, skilled ethical reasoners identify the ethical concepts and facts relevant to those questions and apply those concepts to the facts in a well-reasoned manner. In coming to conclusions, they consider as many plausible ways of looking at the issue as they can. As a result of such intellectual work, they develop the capacity to distinguish when ethical questions are clear-cut and when they are not. When ethical issues are not clear-cut, it is important to exercise our best ethical judgment.

The Universal Nature of Ethical Principles

For every ethical issue, there are ethical concepts and principles to be identified and used in thinking through the issue. Included in the principles implied by these concepts are the rights articulated in the Universal Declaration of Human Rights. This set of rights, established on December 10, 1948, by the General Assembly of the United Nations, holds that the:

> ...recognition of inherent dignity and of the equal and inalienable rights of all members of the human family is the foundation of freedom, justice, and peace in the world .... Disregard and contempt for human rights have resulted in barbarous acts which have outraged the conscience of mankind, and the advent of a world in which human beings shall enjoy freedom of speech and belief and freedom from fear and want has been proclaimed as the highest aspiration of the common people.

The Universal Declaration of Humans Rights was conceived as "a common standard of achievement for all peoples and all nations." It is a good example of an explicit statement of important ethical principles. It is significant, we believe, that every nation on earth has signed the declaration.

Here are a few of the principles laid out in the 30 articles of the declaration:

- All humans are born free and equal in dignity and rights.

- Everyone has the right to life, liberty, and security of person.

- No one shall be held in slavery or servitude.

- No one shall be subjected to torture or to cruel, inhuman, or degrading treatment or punishment.

- Everyone has the right to a standard of living adequate for the health and well-being of himself and of his family.

- Everyone has the right to education.

- Everyone has the right to freedom of peaceful assembly and association.

- Everyone is entitled to all the rights and freedoms set forth in this declaration, without distinction of any kinds, such as race, color, sex, language, religion, political or other opinion, national or social origin, property, birth, or status.

- All are equal before the law and are entitled without any discrimination to equal protection of the law.

One ability essential to sound reasoning is the ability to identify ethical principles relevant to the issue at hand. In Test the Idea 12.2, you should think through the identification and application of some of these principles with respect to a specific ethical question.

Test the Idea
Recognizing Violations of Human Rights Based Universal Ethical Principles

In this activity, we will briefly describe an issue as presented in a New York Times article, "Iraq Is a Pediatrician's Hell: No Way to Stop the Dying." We then will ask you to identify any violations of human rights suggested by the manner in which events are characterized.

This article focuses on the medical problems for sick children in Iraq "when the country's medical system is all but paralyzed as a result of economic sanctions imposed by the United Nations eight years ago." The article states that hospitals cannot obtain the medical equipment and supplies they need to handle diseases from the complicated to the "easily curable ailments." This means that virtually all children with leukemia, for example, die in Iraq. The article mentions a three-year-old girl with leukemia, Isra Ahmed, who bleeds profusely from her nose, gums, and rectum. The hospital's chief resident, Dr. Jasim Mazin, says that the hospital lacks the equipment to perform the kind of operation she needs. He states, "We're helpless." He goes on to say, "Iraq used to be the best country in the Arab world in terms of science and medicine. Now we can't even read medical journals because they are covered by the embargo." Dr. Mazin said his worst period came in April 1998 when he lost 75 children to chest infections and gastroenteritis. He believes all of them could have been saved with antibiotics commonly available in neighboring countries. Assume for this exercise that the factual claims in this article are accurate.

Complete the following statements:

1. If the United Nations sanctions are responsible for the conditions discussed in this article, the following human rights have been violated by the United Nations...

2. If you believe one or more violations of human rights exist in this situation, complete the following statements:

   • The universal ethical principle violated was...

   • For this ethical principle to be honored, the following action would have been called for in this situation...

Though the principles outlined in the Universal Declaration of Human Rights are universally accepted in theory, even democratic countries do not necessarily live in accordance with them. For example, on October 5, 1998, the *New York Times* ("Amnesty Finds 'Widespread Pattern' of U.S. Rights Violations," p. A11) reported that Amnesty International was citing the United States for violating fundamental human rights. The Amnesty International report stated that "police forces and criminal and legal systems have a persistent and widespread pattern of human rights violations."

In the report, Amnesty International protested the U.S. failure "to deliver the fundamental promise of rights for all." The report states, "Across the country thousands of people are subjected to sustained and deliberate brutality at the hands of police officers. Cruel, degrading, and sometimes life-threatening methods of constraint continue to be a feature of the U.S. criminal justice system."

Pierre Sane, Secretary General of Amnesty International for six years, said, "We felt it was ironic that the most powerful country in the world uses international human rights laws to criticize others but does not apply the same standards at home."

Every country agrees in theory to the importance of fundamental human rights. In practice, though, they often fail to uphold those rights.

> **Test the Idea**
> **Identifying Violations of Human Rights Based on Universal Ethical Principles**
> Identify a newspaper article that either directly or indirectly implies at least one governmental violation of human rights. Complete the following statements:
>   1. The main substance of this article is…
>   2. The reason this article suggests to me at least one governmental violation of human rights is…
>   3. The universal ethical principle(s) violated is/are…

Distinguishing Ethics from Other Domains of Thinking

In addition to understanding how to identify ethical concepts and principles relevant to ethical issues, skilled ethical reasoners must be able to distinguish between ethics and other domains of thinking such as social conventions, religion, and the law. Too often, ethics is confused with these other modes of thinking. It is not uncommon, for example, for social values and taboos to be treated as if they define ethical principles.

Thus, religious ideologies, social "rules," and laws are often mistakenly taken to be inherently ethical in nature. If we are to accept this amalgamation of domains, by implication every practice within any religious system is necessarily ethical, every social rule is ethically obligatory, and every law is ethically justified. We could not judge, then, any religious practices—such as torturing unbelievers—as unethical.

In the same way, if ethics and social conventions were one and the same, every social practice within any culture would necessarily be ethical—including social conventions in Nazi Germany. We could not, then, ethically condemn any social traditions, norms, mores, and taboos—however ethically bankrupt we think them to be. What's more, if ethics and the law were inextricable, by implication every law within any legal system would be ethical by definition—including laws that blatantly violate human rights.

It is essential, then, to learn to routinely differentiate ethics and other modes of thinking commonly confused with ethics. This will enable us to criticize commonly accepted, yet unethical, social conventions, religious practices, political ideas, and laws. No one lacking in this ability can truly live a life of integrity.

Ethics and Religion

To exemplify some of the problems in confusing ethics with other disciplines, let us return for a moment, to the question: Are there any conditions under which euthanasia is ethically justifiable? Rather than understanding this as an ethical question, some take it to be a religious question. Therefore, they think through the question using religious principles. They see some religious principles, namely, the ones in which they believe, as fundamental to ethics.

They argue, for example, that euthanasia is not ethically justifiable because "the Bible says it is wrong to commit suicide." Because they do not distinguish the theological from the ethical, they are likely to miss the relevance of the concept of cruelty. They are not likely to struggle with the problem. This may mean that they find it difficult to feel any force behind the argument for euthanasia in this case or to appreciate what it is to experience hopeless torment without end.

A commitment to some set of religious beliefs may prevent them from recognizing that ethical concepts take priority over religious beliefs when they conflict, as the former are universal and the latter are inherently controversial. Reasonable persons give priority allegiance to ethical concepts and principles, whether these concepts and principles are or are not explicitly acknowledged by a given religious group. Religious beliefs are, at best, supplementary to ethical principles but cannot overrule them.

Consider this example: If a religious group were to believe that the firstborn male of every family must be killed as a sacrifice and failed to exercise any countervailing ethical judgment, every person in that group would think themselves to be ethically obligated to kill their firstborn male. Their religious beliefs would lead them to unethical behavior and lessen their capacity to appreciate the cruel nature of their behavior.

The genuinely ethical thing to do in a society that propagates the above religious belief would be to rebel and resist what others consider to be obligatory. In short, theological beliefs do not properly override ethical principles, for we must use ethical principles to judge religious practices. We have no other reasonable choice.

Religious Beliefs Are Socially or Culturally Relative

Religious relativity derives from the fact that there are an unlimited number of alternative ways for people to conceive and account for the nature of the "spiritual." The Encyclopedia Americana, for example, lists over 300 different religious belief systems. These traditional ways of believing adopted by social groups or cultures take on the force of habit and custom. They are handed down from one generation to another. To the individuals in a given group, despite the large number of possibilities, their particular beliefs often seem to be the ONLY way, or the only REASONABLE way, to conceive of the "divine." For most people these religious beliefs influence their behavior from cradle to grave. Religions answer questions like this:

- What is the origin of all things? Is there a God? Is there more than one God? If there is a God, what is his/her nature? Are there ordained laws that exist to guide our life and behavior? What are these laws? How are they communicated to us?

How should we treat transgressions of these laws? What must we do to live in keeping with the will of the divine?

Religious beliefs bear upon many aspects of a person's life—with rules, requirements, taboos, and rituals. Many of these regulations are neither right nor wrong, but simply represent social preferences and subjective choices. However, sometimes, without knowing it, social practices, including religious beliefs or practices, violate basic human rights. Then, they must be criticized. For example, if a society accepts among its social practices any form of *slavery, torture, sexism, racism, persecution, murder, assault, rape, fraud, deceit, or intimidation*, it should be ethically criticized. For example, in religious warfare ethical atrocities are often committed. The question, then, ceases to be one of social preference and relativity. No religious belief can legitimately be used to justify violations of basic human rights.

Test the Idea
Distinguishing Between Ethics and Religion

Focus on one religious belief system (as commonly held) to identify possible confusions between theological beliefs and ethical principles. See if you can identify any practices within the religion that might be critiqued as unethical. See also if you can identify any practices that the religion considers unethical that are in fact unrelated to ethics. Select any religion about which you are sufficiently knowledgeable to find possible problems of the sort we are considering. As an example remember the case of those religious believers who think that a woman who commits adultery should be stoned to death.

Ethics and Social Conventions

Let us return to the relationship of ethics and social conventions. For more than a hundred years in the United States, most people considered slavery to be justified and desirable. It was part of social custom. There can be no question that, all along, this practice was unethical. Moreover, throughout history, many groups of people, including people of various nationalities and skin colors, as well as females, children, and individuals with disabilities, have been victims of discrimination as the result of social convention treated as ethical obligation. Yet, all social practices that violate ethical principles deserve to be rejected by ethically sensitive, reasonable persons no matter how many people support those practices.

Unless we learn to soundly critique the social mores and taboos that have been imposed upon us from birth, we will accept those traditions as "right." All of us are deeply socially conditioned. Therefore, we do not naturally develop the ability to effectively critique social norms and taboos.

Practices That Are Socially or Culturally Relative

Cultural relativity derives from the fact that there are an unlimited number of alternative ways for people in social groups to go about satisfying their needs and fulfilling their desires. Those traditional ways of living within a social group or culture take on the force of habit and custom. They are handed down from one generation to another. To the individuals in a given group they seem to be the ONLY way, or the only REASONABLE way, to do things. For most people these practices guide their behavior from cradle to grave. They answer questions like this:

- How should marriage take place? Who should be allowed to marry, under what conditions, and with what ritual or ceremony? Once married what role should the male play? What role should the female play? Are multiple marriage partners possible? Is divorce possible? Under what conditions?

- Who should care for the children? What should they teach the children as to proper and improper ways to act? When children do not act as they are expected to act, how should they be treated?

- When should children be accepted as adults? When should they be considered old enough to be married? Who should they be allowed to marry?

- When children develop sensual and sexual desires, how should they be allowed to act? With whom, if anyone, should they be allowed to engage in sexual exploration and discovery? What sexual acts are considered acceptable and wholesome? What sexual acts are considered perverted or sinful?

- How should men and women dress? To what degree should their body be exposed in public? How is nudity treated? How are those who violate these codes treated?

- How should food be obtained and how should it be prepared? Who is responsible for the obtaining of food? Who for its preparation? How should it be served? How eaten?

- How is the society "stratified" (into levels of power)? How is the society controlled? What belief system is used to justify the distribution of scarce goods and services and the way rituals and practices are carried out?

- If the society develops enemies or is threatened from without, who will defend it? How will they engage in war?

- What sorts of games, sports, or amusements will be practiced in the society? Who is allowed to engage in them?

- What religion is taught to members of the society? Who is allowed to participate in the religious rituals or to interpret divine or spiritual teachings to the group?

- How are grievances settled in the society? Who decides who is right and who wrong? How are violators treated?

Societies regulate virtually every aspect of a person's life—with rules, requirements, taboos, and rituals. Many of these regulations are neither right nor wrong, but simply represent social preferences and subjective choices. However, sometimes, without knowing it, social practices violate basic human rights. Then, they may be criticized. For example, if a society accepts among its social practices any form of *slavery, torture, sexism, racism, persecution, murder, assault, rape, fraud, deceit,* or *intimidation,* it is subject to ethical criticism. The question ceases to be one of social preference and relativity.

Schools and colleges often become apologists for conventional thought; faculty members often inadvertently foster the confusion between convention and ethics because they themselves have internalized the conventions of society. Education, properly so called, should foster the intellectual skills that enable students to distinguish between cultural mores and ethical precepts, between social commandments and ethical truths. In each case, when conflicts with ethical principles exist, the ethical principles should rule.

Test the Idea
Distinguishing Between Ethics and Social Conventions

Prior to and during the civil rights movement in the United States, many whites believed that African Americans were intellectually inferior to them. This belief gave rise to laws that denied African Americans basic human rights. It would be hard to find a clearer case of socially accepted conventions leading to socially defended unethical practices.

Identify one newspaper article that embodies the confusion between social conventions and ethical principles. What we are looking for is an article in which a commonly held social belief results in the denial of some person's or group's basic human right(s):

1. The substance of this article is...
2. The reason this article implies at least one violation of human rights is...
3. The universal ethical principle(s) violated was/were...

Ethics and the Law

As persons interested in developing your ethical reasoning abilities, you should be able to differentiate not only ethics and social conventions but also ethics and the law. What is illegal may be ethically justified. What is ethically obligatory may be illegal. What is unethical may be legal.

Laws often emerge out of social conventions. Whatever is acceptable and expected in social groups becomes the foundation for many laws. But, because we cannot assume that social conventions are ethical, we cannot assume that human laws are ethical.

What is more, laws are ultimately made by politicians whose primary motivation is often power, vested interest, or expediency. One should not be surprised, then, when politicians are not sensitive to ethical principles or confuse ethical principles with social values or taboos.

Ethics and Sexual Taboos

The problem here is that social taboos are often matters of strong emotions. People are often disgusted by someone's violating a taboo. Their disgust signals to them that the behavior is unethical. They forget that what is socially unacceptable may not violate any ethical principle but, instead, be a violation of a social convention of one kind or other.

One obvious area to think through, based on this common confusion, is the area of human sexuality. Social groups often establish strong sanctions for unconventional behavior involving the human body. Some social groups inflict strong punishments on women who do no more than appear in public without being completely veiled, an act socially considered indecent and sexually provocative. The question for us, then, is when is human behavior that is considered illicitly sexual by some society a matter for ethical condemnation, and when is it properly considered a matter of social nonconformity?

Our overall goal—which we hope this chapter will inspire readers to pursue—is to become so proficient in ethical reasoning and so skilled in distinguishing matters of ethical principle from matters of social taboo, legal fact, and theological belief that you will rarely confuse these domains in your experience and, rather, render to each of them their due consideration and weight in specific cases as they might arise in your life. In the Test the Idea activities that follow, you can gain some practice in developing these important skills.

Test the Idea
Ethics, Social Taboos, and Criminal Law

In this exercise, we will briefly describe the substance of two news articles. Both articles depict examples of cases in which a given social group has established a law with a significant punishment attendant on its violation, regarding behavior judged by that group to be highly unethical. Think through how you would analyze and assess the act in question using the distinctions discussed in this chapter.

Here are some questions to think about as you read summaries of these articles:

- Would you conclude that the social group in question has properly or improperly treated the sexual behaviors in each case as matters worthy of ethical condemnation?

- To what extent should these behaviors be considered serious crimes?
- Ethically and rationally speaking, how in your judgment should the two cases be treated?

Read each article summary, and answer the questions above for each one. Explain your reasoning. In each case, you may have to make explicit some of your assumptions about important details of the case that may not be in the article summary. Your judgment might vary depending on what details you suppose.

For example, you might come to a different judgment depending on whether violence or outright bodily harm is involved. As you work through the activities, take into account the probable reasoning that might be advanced against your position (for example, you might say, "Someone might object to my reasoning by saying ... To them my reply would be...").

Article 1 (San Francisco Chronicle, Feb. 6, 1999)

We read, "For the first time in 23 years, the Philippines executed a prisoner yesterday, a house painter convicted of raping his 10-year-old stepdaughter. Leo Echegaray, 38, was put to death by lethal injection after months of legal delays and an emotional nationwide debate over the death penalty." Philippines president Joseph Estrada refused to stop the execution of Leo Echegaray, "despite pleas from the Vatican, the European Union, and human rights groups." Amnesty International "called Echegaray's death 'a huge step in the wrong direction for human rights in the Philippines'." President Estrada said that the execution signifies "proof of the government's determination to maintain law and order."

After reflecting on the questions we asked you to consider for both articles, come to a determination as to whether, in your best judgment, the punishment fit the crime. Then complete these statements:

1. I believe that the law leading to this execution is or is not an ethically justified law, because...

2. If you believe the law itself violated some human right or ethical principle, complete the following statements:

   a. The reason this case contains at least one violation of human rights is...

   b. The universal ethical principle(s) violated is/are...

   c. From a strictly ethical point of view, the following action would have been called for in this situation...

3. If you believe the law was ethically justified, complete the following statements:
   a. The reason why this case does not contain any violations of human rights is...
   b. The relevant ethical principle(s) that justified this action is/are...

Article 2 (New York Times, Oct. 21, 1999)

This article, entitled "Boy, 11, Held on Incest Charge, Protests Ensue," states "the case of an 11-year-old Swiss-American boy charged with aggravated incest has led to an international dispute over the treatment of children in the American Justice System." The boy, "is accused of making inappropriate sexual contact with his 5-year-old sister when the children were in their yard." According to the article, after an arraignment date was set, the boy was released into foster care. "The boy has been living with his mother, stepfather, 13-year-old sister and two half-sisters, ages 5 and 3, in Evergreen, CO...A neighbor, Laura Mehmert, testified at the hearing that in May she saw the boy touching the younger girl's genitals with his face and hands. After speaking with the boy's mother, the neighbor reported the incident to the authorities. On Aug. 30, the boy was arrested and led in handcuffs from his home. Since then he has been held without bail in a county juvenile center." According to Manual Sager, spokesman for the Swiss Embassy in Washington, the circumstances of the boy's arrest "seemed disproportionate to us to the charges." He said the boy was taken into court in handcuffs and foot chains. According to Hanspeter Spuhler, director of the Swiss-American Friendship Society, "It's just a travesty... The reason why it's such a big deal to the Swiss and the Europeans is because this is part of growing up, playing doctor or something. If indeed he touched her inappropriately, then it will be talked over with the parents." The boy's parents fled to Switzerland with their other three children "out of fear that their three daughters would also be taken from them."

After reflecting on the questions we directed you to consider for both articles, come to a determination as to whether, in your best judgment, ethics is being confused with religious ideology, social conventions, or the law in the main issue that is the focus of the article. For your consideration, we have provided a brief analysis of the two fundamentally different perspectives that might be said to be indirectly implied in the article as it is written.

A Traditional View of Children's Sexuality

Children are not naturally sexual beings. If they engage in sexual acts, they are behaving in a mentally unhealthy manner. What is more, if older children behave in a sexual way toward a younger child, the younger child will be permanently damaged, and the older child should be punished as a criminal would be punished. If the parents of children who engage in sexual behavior fail to take harsh action against that behavior, they are contributing to unhealthy mental development of their children, and therefore are not fit to rear those children.

An Opposing View

To engage in sexual behavior is a natural part of human life. It is natural, normal, and healthy for children to experience, explore, and appropriately express sexual desires. Very often, children invent games (such as "playing doctor") as a form of exploring their sexual feelings with other children. Parents who understand the biological make-up of humans and the natural desire of children to explore their sexual desires will not punish children for having, or appropriately acting upon, sexual thoughts and feelings. Rather, they should look upon exploratory forms of sexual behavior as part of most children's lives.

This latter view seems to be implied in the article by Hanspeter Spuhler, director of the Swiss-American Friendship Society, who states, "It's just a travesty. The reason why it's such a big deal to the Swiss and the Europeans is because this is part of growing up, playing doctor or something. If indeed he touched her inappropriately, then it will be talked over with the parents." In this view, if problems seem to be present with the child's behavior respecting sexuality, the parents will be expected to help the child overcome the problem as parents are generally expected to help children develop as responsible persons. The role of authorities, then, is to help the parents develop their abilities to deal with their children as effectively as possible rather than acting as punitive bodies.

Now, given these two differing perspectives, how would you answer the following questions:

1. From an ethical perspective, which of these points of view seems the more reasonable, given what you know from reading the article and from your own thinking?

2. To what extent do you think ethics is confused with social conventions in the minds of the legal authorities in this case?

3. To what extent do you think religious ideology might play a role in the thinking of either of the above perspectives?

4. To what extent do you think the law upholds what is ethical in this case or, conversely, reflects poor ethical reasoning?

5. How do you think this case should have been handled, given what is ethical for the children at issue and their parents? Do you agree with the way it was handled by the authorities, or would you have acted differently had you been in charge of the case? Explain your reasoning.

Test the Idea
Cultural Practice and Ethics

On June 12, 1999, the *New York Times* (p. A4) reported that in Muslim West Beirut, Lebanon, women and men are expected to avoid sunbathing together except when they are engaged or married to one another. At one beach only a handful of women could be seen, and most were fully clothed, and sheltered by tents or beach umbrellas. Those who swam simply strolled into the water, until their baggy dresses began to float along beside them... "I don't bring my fiancée here because if someone said something like "what a beautiful girl," there'd have to be a fight," said Hassam Karaki, who sat with other men on an all-male beach.

Randa Harb, 27, wore a modest pair of shorts and a tank top as she sat under an umbrella with her bare-chested husband and young son. "If you wear a bathing suit, you're going to attract more attention," Mrs. Harb said. "So my husband won't let me, because he doesn't want people to look and talk..."

Lebanon is not alone, of course, as home to a culture averse to women showing too much skin. In Iran, a strict Islamic republic, the insistence on female "modesty" means that women may not even enter hotel pools. In most Arab countries, except among elites, a standard woman's bathing costume is a dress.

Now answer the following questions:

1. To what extent does the cultural practice of denying women the right to wear swimsuits at beaches and swimming pools where men are present seem ethical or unethical to you?

2. On what ethical concepts and principles do you base your reasoning?

Determining Ethical Dimensions of Cultural Practices

On March 6, 1999, the New York Times (p. A15), reported:

In Maine, a refugee from Afghanistan was seen kissing the penis of his baby boy, a traditional expression of love by his father. To his neighbors and the police, it was child abuse, and his son was taken away....

[Some sociologists and anthropologists] argue that American laws and welfare services have often left immigrants terrified of the intrusive power of government. The Afghan father in Maine who lost his son to the social services, backed by a lower court, did not prevail until the matter reached the state Supreme Court, which researched the family's cultural heritage—while making clear that this was an exceptional case.

The same article also focuses on female circumcision, or genital mutilation, as some call it.

"I think we are torn," said Richard A. Shweder, an anthropologist and a leading advocate of the broadest tolerance for cultural differences. "It's a great dilemma right now that's coming up again about how we're going to deal with diversity in the United States and what it means to be an American."

Some, like Mr. Shweder, argue for fundamental changes in American laws, if necessary, to accommodate almost any practice accepted as valid in a radically different society if it can be demonstrated to have some social or cultural good.

The article states that Mr. Shweder and others defend controversial practices including the common African ritual that opponents call female genital mutilation, which usually involves removing the clitoris at minimum ... But going more than halfway to tolerate what look like disturbing cultural practices unsettles some historians, aid experts, economists, and others ... Urban Jonsson, a Swede who directs the United Nations Children's Fund (UNICEF), said that there is "a global ethical minimum" regarding cultural practices. "There is a non-ethno-centric global ethicality," and that "scholars would be better occupied looking for it rather than denying it.... I'm upset by the anthropological interest in mystifying what we have already demystified. All cultures have their bad and good things."

Now answer the following questions:

1. Focusing on each case presented in this article separately, to what extent is there an ethical component to each?

2. To what extent do you think it is true that any culture has "bad" and "good" practices? Or do you think that all practices within a culture are to be honored?

3. To the extent that an ethical case exists for opposing positions described by this article, what ethical concepts and principles would have to be taken into account when determining the most reasonably defensible position for each?

4. The cases inherent in this article focus on culturally accepted practices that other cultures consider unethical. To what extent do you think each case contains a violation of human rights? Explain your reasoning.

It is important that you develop your ability to determine for yourself whether any belief system, practice, rule, or law is inherently ethical. To be skilled at ethical reasoning means to develop a conscience that is not subservient to unethical laws, or to fluctuating social conventions, or to controversial, theological systems of belief.

But consistently sound ethical reasoning, like consistently sound complex reasoning of every type, presupposes practice in thinking through ethical issues. As you face ethical problems in your life, the challenge will be in applying appropriate ethical principles to those problems. The more often you do so, the better you will become at ethical reasoning.

Understanding Our Native Selfishness

In addition to the above, ethical reasoning requires command over our native tendency to see the world from a self-serving perspective. Chapter 10, on human irrational tendencies, focuses on the problem of human self-centeredness at length. Here we apply some of the major points of that chapter to problems in ethical reasoning.

Humans naturally develop a narrow-minded, self-centered point of view. We feel our own pain; we don't feel the pain of others. We think our own thoughts; we do not think the thoughts of others. And as we age, we do not naturally develop the ability to empathize with others, to consider points of view that conflict with our own. For this reason, we are often unable to reason from a genuinely ethical perspective. Empathy with the thinking of others, then, is not natural to humans. Nevertheless, it is possible to learn to critically think through ethical issues. With the right practice, we can acquire the skill of considering situations from opposing ethical perspectives.

As we have argued in previous chapters, the human tendency to judge the world from a narrow, self-serving perspective is powerful. Humans are typically masterful at self-deception and rationalization. We often maintain beliefs that fly in the face of the evidence right before our eyes and engage in acts that blatantly violate ethical principles. What is more, we feel perfectly justified in doing so.

At the root of every unethical act lies some form and degree of self-delusion. And at the root of every self-delusion lies some flaw in thinking. For instance, Hitler confidently believed he was doing the right thing in carrying out egregious acts against the Jews. His actions were a product of the erroneous beliefs that Jews were inferior to the Aryan race, and that they were the cause of Germany's problems. In ridding Germany of the Jews, he believed himself to be doing what was in the best interest of his Germany. He therefore considered his actions to be completely justified. His unethical ethical reasoning resulted in untold human harm and suffering for millions of people.

To become skilled at ethical reasoning, we must understand that ethical reasoning means doing what is right even in the face of powerful selfish desires. To live an ethical life is to develop command over our native egocentric tendencies. It is not enough to espouse the importance of living an ethical life. It is not enough to be able to do the right thing when we ourselves have nothing to lose. We must be willing to fulfill our ethical obligations at the expense of our selfish desires. Thus, having insight into our irrational drives is essential to living an ethical life.

Test the Idea
Identifying Your Unethical Behavior

Each of us engages in unethical behavior, but few of us recognize that we do. To become highly skilled at ethical reasoning, we must become everyday observers of our own thoughts and actions. Over the next week, closely observe your behavior to "catch" yourself doing something unethical (like being selfish, or hurting someone unjustifiably).

Complete the following statements for five "unethical acts":

1. This situation in which I behaved unethically is as follows...

2. The unethical action I engaged in was...

3. The reason(s) why this act was unethical is/are...

4. The basic right(s) I violated is/are...

5. To avoid behaving unethically in future such situations, I should...

To develop as an ethical reasoner, then, we must deeply internalize the fundamental roots of ethics. This means learning to identify and express ethical concepts and principles accurately. It means learning how to apply these principles to relevant ethical situations and learning to differentiate ethics from other modes of thinking that are traditionally confused with ethics. Finally, it means taking command, with intellectual humility, of one's native egocentrism. Without such an organized, well-integrated, critically based approach to ethics, some counterfeit of ethics, but not ethics itself, is the likely result. To date, all across the world, ethics has routinely been confused with other domains of thinking. The use of ethics and its misuse have been nearly one and the same.

Chapter 13

Analyzing and Evaluating Thinking in Corporate and Organizational Life

Introduction

Living a human life, as we have seen, entails a variety of relationships and membership in a variety of human groups. Both the relationships and the groups to which we belong typically have a profound influence on our thinking, our emotions, and our desires. In Chapter 11, we considered the broadest implications of this fact, especially the implications of sociocentrism, a term that highlights group-dominated thinking in human life. In this chapter, we will focus somewhat more narrowly, on the problem of thinking effectively and working for change in corporate and other organizational structures.

To think effectively in corporate and organizational settings, it is helpful to consider the logic of these structures and explicitly face the questions one should ask when operating within them. The more we understand the logic of our circumstances, the more effectively we can act.

Here is our plan. We will deal with the logic of organizational structures in some detail first, approaching their potential transformation from a number of different standpoints, including that of three predictable obstacles: the struggle for power, group definitions of reality, and bureaucracy. We will also look at the problem of "misleading success" as well as the relation between competition, sound thinking, and success. We will spell out some essential questions each of us should ask when working within a corporate or organizational setting. Following that, toward the end of the chapter, we will analyze six hypothetical cases illustrating some of the ways critical thinking might be applied to decision-making in a corporate or organizational setting. We will close the chapter with a list of conditions essential for success in facilitating a culture of critical thinking. The conditions we list suggest ways that an organization or corporation can begin to organize itself for long-range success through the use of critical thinking.

There are a number of factors we must take into account in thinking our way through organizational and corporate structures, factors that interact in different ways in different settings. Often we lack some of the vital facts we need to make sound decisions and must therefore judge in terms of probabilities rather than certainties. Often we cannot answer all the questions we would like to answer. In any case, critical thinking does not guarantee us the truth—rather, it affords us a way to maximize our best chance for it.

Critical Thinking and Incremental Improvement

The success of any organization is largely a function of the quality of the thinking done within it. But success is usually partial rather than complete. Doing one thing well, we may do another thing poorly. Thinking well in one context, we may think poorly in another. We may achieve our goals in the short-run at the expense of achieving them in the long-run. We may succeed simply because we perform at a somewhat higher level than the competition. We rarely have absolute success in human life. The spirit of critical thinking is an organized and disciplined way of achieving continual improvement in thinking and therefore of attaining fuller and more complete success over time. It consists in thinking at progressively higher levels in virtue of a deliberate and practical commitment to quality of thinking.

Test the Idea
Self-Assessment

Name one domain or context (for example, the professional domain) in which you believe that you think reasonably well and compare it to another in which you believe your thinking to be of lower quality (for example, in intimate relationships). Explain the "evidence" you have that convinces you of this.

An Obstacle to Critical Thinking Within Organizations: The Covert Struggle for Power

To what extent are organizations and institutions capable of making a commitment to critical thinking? For one, every organization, every institutional structure, consists not only of a multiplicity of individuals, but a hierarchy of power among those individuals. No matter how noble the ultimate goals of an organization are, there is often a struggle for power beneath the surface. In this struggle, the thinking motivating the behavior of individuals may be highly complex as well as obscure. Personal strategies in use may be tacit, that is, not apparent even to those who are using them. Some strategies in the struggle for power are particularly deceptive.

For example, in a best selling book *The 48 Laws of Power,* Robert Greene (1998) puts into blatant language, 48 strategies that he claims are effectively used by those who seek and gain power. A short sampling of them is revealing:

- "Never outshine the Master."
- "Never put too much trust in Friends; learn how to use enemies."
- "Conceal your intentions."
- "Always say less than necessary."
- "Get others to do the work for you, but always take the credit."
- "Make other people come to you—use bait if necessary."
- "Learn to keep people dependent on you."
- "Use selective honesty and generosity to disarm your victim."
- "When asking for help, appeal to people's self-interest…"
- "Pose as a friend, work as a spy."
- "Crush your enemy totally." (pp. ix–xi)

Greene goes on to argue for a private, though deliberate, commitment to deviousness: "In the world today…it is dangerous to seem too power hungry, to be overt with your power moves. We have to seem fair and decent. So we need to be subtle—congenial yet cunning, democratic yet devious…Everything must appear civilized, decent, democratic, and fair. But if we play by those rules too strictly, if we take them too literally, we are crushed by those around us who are not so foolish." (p. xvii)

He continues: "Power requires the ability to play with appearances. To this end you must learn to wear many masks and keep a bag full of deceptive tricks…Deception is a developed art of civilization and the most potent weapon in the game of power. You cannot succeed at deception unless you take a somewhat distanced approach to yourself—unless you can be many different people, wearing the mask that the day and the moment require…Playing with appearances and mastering arts of deception are among the aesthetic pleasures of life. They are also key components in the acquisition of power." (pp. xx–xxi)

It is our considered view that most of the strategies that Greene recommends are ethically unjustifiable except in rare circumstances and for compelling reasons. We are also dubious as to the extent to which most persons could explicitly adopt those strategies without suffering pangs of conscience. Nevertheless, we recognize that some individuals—those we have called "selfish" or "sophistic" critical thinkers—do act in ways that come close to embodying the kinds of strategies that Greene recommends.

Test the Idea
The Game of Power

To what extent do you agree with Robert Greene's claim "...all of us hunger for power, and almost all of our actions are aimed at it...?" (xix) Think through your view of this idea as well as his view of the implications it has (e.g., that, as a result, it makes sense to engage in this struggle for power aggressively and without pangs of conscience).

We recognize that all humans engage in self-deception and manipulation. There are contradictions and inconsistencies in the behavior of all humans. Therefore, it is wise to develop the ability to detect deviousness and cunning in human behavior. This requires that we learn the art of interpreting intentions not from explicit statements and "public" behavior alone, but from decisions and acts that typically escape notice. We must become students of the human ego and its machinations. We must become keenly aware of the fact that much human motivation is below the level of consciousness. Deciphering the motivations that underlie human behavior and the character of individuals is a challenging activity, yet one in which we must all develop skills if we want to protect ourselves in the real world of manipulation, power struggles, and vested interest.

Within all organizational or institutional structures, the thinking of some is treated as having more force, more authority, than that of others. High position in a hierarchy naturally leads others to yield. What is more, there is an incentive in most stratified groups for those with superior position to hold the view that their thinking is superior to those below them. To some extent this is natural, for if I am superior to you in authority and power and yet admit that your thinking is better than mine, I raise the question as to whether you should have more authority and I less. The more mistakes in thinking I admit to, the less credibility I usually have.

Test the Idea
The Game of Power Once More

Do you see the difference between the view we are expressing about power and that of Greene, or do you think that, when all is said and done, both are more or less the same? (We hold, for example, that you can become effective in protecting yourself in the game of power without adopting unethical strategies in the process. We do not believe that because your opponents are unethical in their attempts to defeat you that you must adopt unethical strategies simply to protect yourself). This, of course, is a dispute very much alive in the real world. For example, it is argued in agencies like the CIA which have used such strategies as assassination and the overthrow of foreign governments (with the plea that these are the lessor evils in the case).

The main point is this: We must learn to take into account the power and position of persons with whom we deal in corporate and other organizational structures. We must be cautious in sharing our private thoughts, especially those that might offend those in power. If our views diverge in any way from the received views, it is prudent to be cautious lest our views be perceived as a personal threat to those in power

Another Obstacle: Group Definitions of Reality

Within all organizations, there is a natural generation of "favorable self-description" or "self-serving representation." This involves an image the organization fosters of itself, both inwardly and outwardly. How explicitly and openly these representations are stated varies from organization to organization, as does the degree of contradiction between presentation and fact. By their very nature groups have a vested interest in presenting the most favorable picture of themselves to those outside. Typically, therefore, a rosier picture than is actually the case is created for external consumption. Even within an organization there are usually some truths that remain unspoken and taboo. Being an "insider" does not mean you can say anything you want to other insiders.

For example, some doctors are aware of more medical malpractice than they are willing to publicly discuss. Lawyers sometimes play down the fact that some lawyers routinely bill clients for more time than they spend on their clients' cases and that judges sometimes decide a case as a result of their personal beliefs and reaction to the appearance and demeanor of the accused, rather than by the relevant facts of the case and the meaning and intent of the law. Sociologists study this phenomenon under the categories of "in-group and out-group" behavior. Social psychologists study it under the category of social self-deception.

Test the Idea
Group Definitions of Reality

When we experience people we do not *first* see the person as a set of independent characteristics and then synthesize the parts into a whole. Rather, we typically see people as "instant" wholes. We interpret the "parts" accordingly. Behind these judgments, that often occur in a fraction of a second, are often an organized set of "definitions" of how things are. Hence, a person in management will often approach a "union" man with as many preconceptions as the union man approaches him. Select some job or professional situation in which you had a role. Review it in your mind and see if you can isolate any of the implicit (biased) "definitions" that guide behavior and perceptions on the job. How were you supposed to behave? How were others supposed to behave? Can you think of any situation in which you "opposed" some definition implicit in the established view of things? Do you remember how that opposition was received?

These realities must be taken into account in seeking to establish a culture of critical thinking within any organization or institution. This does not mean that it is unrealistic to attempt to foster that culture. But it does mean that the advantages of critical thinking may not be apparent to all concerned. In the short run, critical thinking may expose short-comings in the status quo. Those who personally gain from the status quo may be threatened by such an exposure of weaknesses. Individuals may confuse critical thinking with negative thinking or mistakenly assume that critical thinking is equivalent to whatever they personally happen to think. Individuals may also feel personally threatened by discussions that may suggest potential problems associated with them and their work. One must proceed with great caution in these circumstances.

A Third Obstacle: The Problem of Bureaucracy

No matter how successful any organization may be at the present, there is no guarantee of future success. The challenge is to break-through the natural assumption that future success is somehow guaranteed. In companies and organizations transitioning from small to large, for example, one must explicitly face the difficulty of emerging bureaucracy. Bureaucratization is a state in which employees work increasingly by fixed routine rather than through the exercise of intelligent judgment. With bureaucracy, narrowness in thinking emerges. There is a proliferation of hard-and-fast rules and fixed procedures—wrongly thought to contribute to efficiency and quality control. With bureaucracy in place, the original goal of an organization fades into the background. Individuals within the organization begin building small bastions of power and devising ways of warding off any potential threats to their power. Change is usually interpreted as a threat.

The problem of bureaucracy exists in virtually all large organizations—for example, in legal systems that sacrifice justice to power and expediency; in public health systems that poorly serve the health of the citizens; in schools that fail to educate; in governmental structures that serve the vested interests of those in power rather than the public. Large bureaucracies generate a vast network of regulations and tacit "strategies" that define "appropriate" rules of conduct. They stifle creativity and innovation. Important questions are coldly received. Thinking that challenges the status quo is stifled. Innovative thinking is dismissed as irresponsible, absurd, unreasonable, or impractical. Rules and regulations become ends in themselves rather than vehicles for reasonable decisions.

All organizations, even small ones, have a natural tendency toward stagnation. This includes a tendency to lose sight of their original goals, a tendency to begin to serve those who operate it rather than those it purports to serve. But largeness presents special problems. And large organizations that do not have to face any real competition are doubly at risk of becoming bureaucratic. Governmental bureaucracies, for example, are notorious for serving the vested interest of those who operate them, rather than the interests of those they were originally designed to serve. They typically respond only to public scandal or to the few with the external power to put political pressure on them. Rigidity and a lost sense of mission are their normal state.

Test the Idea
Bureaucratic Thinking

Can you think of any situation in which you experienced problems that resulted from "bureaucratic thinking?" Can you identify how, in this situation, attachment to fixed routine prevented someone from exercising intelligent judgment? Do you see a relationship between a "letter-of-the-law mentality" and bureaucratic thinking? In your experience how widespread is the problem of bureaucratic thinking in your culture?

The Problem of Misleading Success

Poor thinking does not necessarily reveal itself immediately as such. The fact is that even thinking of the most absurd kind may prove successful for a time, if it caters to the egocentrism and prejudices of people and fits into an established logic of power. We can see this clearly in a historical context if we examine some of the Facist thinking which, though deeply flawed, was accepted by highly intelligent people, including leaders of German industry, in the 1930's and 40's.

Winston Churchill (1948) summarizes the thinking of Adolf Hitler in *Mein Kampf*:

> Man is a fighting animal; therefore the nation, being a community of fighters, is a fighting unit. Any living organism which ceases to fight for its existence is doomed to extinction. A country or race which ceases to fight is equally doomed. The fighting capacity of a race depends on its purity. Hence the need for ridding it of foreign defilements. The Jewish race, owing to its universality, is of necessity pacifist and internationalist. Pacifism is the deadliest sin; it means the surrender of the race in the fight for existence. The first duty of every country is therefore to nationalize the masses; intelligence in the case of the individual is not of first importance: will and determination are the prime qualities. The individual who is born to command is more valuable than countless thousands of subordinate natures. Only brute force can ensure the survival of the race; hence the necessity for military forms. The race must fight; a race that rests must rust and perish. Had the German race been united in good time, it would have been already master of the globe. The new Reich must gather within its fold all the scattered German elements in Europe. A race which has suffered defeat can be rescued by restoring its self-confidence. Above all things the Army must be taught to believe in its own invincibility. To restore the German nation, the people must be convinced that the recovery of freedom by force of arms is possible. The aristocratic principle is fundamentally sound. Intellectualism is undesirable. The ultimate aim of education is to produce a German who can be converted with a minimum of training into a soldier...(pp. 55–56)

Despite the absurdity of this thinking, the vast majority of Germans came to accept it, including, we should emphasize, the heads of German industry. German industrial leaders were quite willing to work within the confines of (absurd) Nazi ideology—as long as it brought profits. For almost five years, this thinking seemed to produce economic and military success. German industry thrived. German aggression triumphed. Fascist ideology flourished.

History provides us with many examples of successful, but poor, thinking based on the Immediate-Gain-Above-All-Else mentality—i.e., the plantation system based on slavery; the factory system based on child labor; Stalin's system of forced labor; and more recently, the asbestos industry, the tobacco industry, and the nuclear power industry. More pointedly, of special note are the American Oil industry's success in taking advantage of the monopolistic practices of OPEC to achieve windfall profits or the global emphasis on short-term economic gain over environmental health. Short-term thinking that sacrifices the public good may bring immense short-term profits. The long-term costs of their thinking are enormous, and often go far beyond the strictly economic dimensions of life.

For example, historians generally agree that Hitler could not have succeeded without the support of the heads of industry. The cost of their thinking—along with that of their fellow Germans—included upward of 50,000,000 lives lost and untold human suffering. We should never assume that individuals will automatically think critically, not even people of high position or high intelligence.

The problem of short-term vested interest thinking can be found both on a large scale and in everyday "mundane" business practices. In one case, a United States District Court Judge in Norfolk, Virginia found that the nation's largest income-tax preparation company had engaged in false advertisement in using the phrase "rapid refund" and other terms "deliberately intended to disguise expensive loans that Block arranges for people anticipating refunds on their income taxes." The judge found that Block had gone to great lengths "to conceal the reality that, rather than receiving refunds, clients were taking out high interests loans to obtain their money a few days

Test the Idea
Short-Term Thinking
Can you think of any situation in which you experienced problems that resulted from "short-term thinking?" Can you identify how, in this situation, attachment to a short-term goal prevented someone from recognizing significant problems for the future? In your experience how widespread is the problem of short-term thinking? Some might argue that short-term thinking, even thinking such as implied in the quote above by the Block company executives, is good business thinking if significant scandal can be avoided.

sooner." He pointed out that in some loans "the annual percentage rate charged was more than 500 percent." He also roundly condemned the company for "signing consent decrees promising not to engage in false advertising," and then after "they consented to one state's order they have simply taken their advertisements to a new jurisdiction and continued to run similarly offensive advertisements." (*New York Times*, Business Day, February 28, 2001)

A key question is how can organizations, both small and large-scale, avoid defective forms of thought, i.e., rigid thinking, short-range thinking, bureaucratic thinking, ideological thinking, or just plain unethical thinking? That is, how can organizations, in the light of predictable obstacles, cultivate critical thinking as an organizational value? How can we, situated as we are, persuade leadership in the organizations in which we live and work that critical thinking is a key to long-range growth and dynamic change fueling that growth? Our answers to these questions will emerge as we synthesize our thinking at the close of this chapter.

We can advance the discussion now by exploring some of the connections between competition, sound thinking, and success.

Competition, Sound Thinking, and Success

Businesses, in contrast to governmental agencies, have the "advantage" of needing to make a profit to survive. Unlike governmental bureaucracies, which become largely a world unto themselves, businesses must continually pass the muster of competition. Only a few, like large oil companies colluding on a world-wide basis to fix prices, are able to force everyone else to conform to their demands. Most businesses face genuine competition they must meet to survive.

For example, out of new (small) businesses, 3 out of 4 fail in the first year; 9 out of 10 over a ten year period. Failure is much more common in business than success. The market is a stern task master. This forces companies to do some critical thinking, at least enough to survive the competition.

Nevertheless, large-scale success in business, even over 20 or 30 years, is no guarantee of success in the future. When businesses become large they become bureaucratized. When they become bureaucratized, they verge toward organizational stagnation. Their thinking is paralyzed by red tape and policies and procedures that prevent growth and adjustment to changing circumstances and realities.

When bureaucratic thinking rules an organization, it tends to lose market strength and growth potential. It's earnings decline; it becomes less competitive, and rigidity becomes the order of the day. Examples include the American auto industry (from 1960-1980), Woolworth, Motown Records, the Sears catalog division, and Rolls-Royce. All significantly declined despite holding a previously strong place in the market. Each lost the spirit of innovation. Sears began to significantly decline when it failed to successfully participate in the mail-order boom and General Motors when it ignored the small-car revolution until it had lost major market share to Japanese auto makers.

Stagnating Organizations and Industries

In the vast majority of stagnating organizations or industries, thinking is used to justify *not* changing, to defend the status quo, not to transform it. Defective thinking becomes an internal obstruction: justifying a refusal to seriously consider evidence that indicates flaws. Weak earnings, low morale, obsolete product lines, are rationalized. Poor thinking is denied. The evidence that should precipitate a change in thinking is set aside or denied. It is very difficult for a critical thinker to work effectively in an organization trapped in poor thinking. This is one of the many reasons that excellent thinkers tend to gravitate toward organizations which are smaller, less committed to a party line, more open to innovation and new lines of thought.

Poor corporate thinking produces poor policies, rigid bureaucratic procedures, resistance to change, complacency, and internal conflict—though not necessarily all at once, and certainly not all from the beginning. Only when critical thinking is a corporate value will an organization remain dynamic in the long-run. Critical thinking as an organizational value serves as a motivator to routinely "re-think" policies, procedures, and ideas. Change becomes a given, but of course not change for change sake. Rather, change becomes the product of new thinking that has effectively analyzed and assessed more established thinking, retaining what is well-grounded and relevant, replacing what is out of touch or inaccurate. With critical thinking as the instrument, one never jumps off the deep end. One learns to read the relevant evidence from multiple standpoints.

Questioning Organizational Realities

In light of the analysis developed thus far in the chapter, there are a set of fundamental questions we should ask in reflecting on the limiting conditions within which we work:

- To what extent is there a struggle for power underway in the organization?
- To what extent must we deal with "power hungry" individuals?
- What is the hierarchy of power in the organization? To what extent are those at the top easily threatened by thinking that diverges from their own?
- How does the organization present itself both within and without? Are there any important contradictions or inconsistencies between the two? To what extent do inconsistencies exist between how the organization represents itself and how it actually functions?
- To what extent is short-range thinking dominant in the organization?

- To what extent is there a problem of bureaucratic inefficiency within the organization?
- To what extent is there a problematic "ideology" that stands in the way of change?
- To what extent is the organization forced to compete meaningfully with other organizations?
- To what extent is the organization suffering from stagnation?
- To what extent is bad short-term thinking misleading the leadership of the organization?
- To what extent are ethical considerations ignored or denied in favor of vested interest within the organization?

Test the Idea
Dealing with Reality
Think through the questions listed above focusing on the organization for which you work, or on an organization for which you worked in the past.

Now, using the elements of thought, we can refine or follow-up on the background questions we just asked:

- **Purpose.** What is the announced purpose or mission of this organization? To what extent is the announced purpose or mission an accurate characterization of the actual functioning of this organization? What is your personal mission in this organization? How does it relate to the actual functioning of the organization? What is the personal agenda of those immediately above you in the organization? To what extent do those agendas serve the announced purpose of the organization? To what extent is it consistent with your agenda?

- **Problems.** What kinds of problems does the organization have to solve to function effectively? What expertise or special skills do you have with respect to those problems? To what extent can you help the organization solve the problems it has? What are the main problems the organization tends to focus on? To what extent are these problems the most important ones facing the organization?

- **Information.** What kinds of information or factual data does the organization need to function effectively and solve the problems that it exists to solve? What role do you have to play with respect to those information-gathering processes? How skilled are you in analyzing and evaluating information gathered? What information do you need to take into account to understand what is going on in this organization? How much of the information is made explicit? How much of it is buried behind the scenes? What is the announced distribution of power in the organization? To what extent is the announced distribution of power an accurate characterization of the actual functioning of this organization? What power do you have within the organization? How can you gain more power and influence within it? What important information, if any, is being ignored by those in power? What problems are being ignored or under-estimated?

- **Key Concepts**. What are the key concepts or ideas that underlie the mission or day-to-day activities of the organization? To what extent are there conflicting concepts or ideas vying for the allegiance of members of the organization? How do these ideas relate to those who wield the most power in the organization?

- **Conclusions**. Given the way the organization functions day-to-day, what is the thinking that is driving the organization? What "conclusions" or "solutions" are incorporated in organizational practice?

- **Assumptions**. What are some of the key assumptions that underlie the dominant thinking of the organization? What are the key assumptions underlying your thinking in the organization? Which are most questionable?

- **Implications**. What are the long-term implications of the organization continuing in the direction it is now headed? What are some implications for you if you remain with the organization?

- **Point of View**. What is the dominant point of view in the organization? What other possible ways to look at things ought to be considered? Is leadership open to considering alternative ways of thinking? How does your point of view relate to the dominant organizational viewpoint?

Each of these questions, taken seriously, enables us to think more accurately and realistically about the organization and the role we might seek to play. They enable us to form the big picture, to put things into a larger perspective, to adopt goals and strategies that make sense. They make it possible to protect ourselves.

Test the Idea
Dealing with Reality II
Spend some time pondering the questions in the section you just read. The idea is that the more time we spend analyzing the logic of the organizations within which we work, the better we can function within them (assuming our analysis does not imply we should leave).

Assessing Irrational Thinking in Organizational Life

We all participate in life in a multi-dimensional way. We play many roles. We become involved in many groups, organizations, and institutions. For the most part, we act in settings in which critical thinking is not a basic value on the part of others. Often, we are dealing with people who are egocentric or irrational in various dimensions of their lives. Often, we are dealing with people who are striving for more power and are willing to sacrifice basic values to their short-term vested interest. Often, we are dealing with people who are easily threatened by thinking that differs from their own or with bureaucracies enveloped in red tape and disfunctional regulations or with people who are significantly self-deceived. Sometimes we are dealing with people who use critical thinking skills to obscure rather than reveal the truth and are principally focused on their own selfish advantage. Sometimes we may find ourselves working within an industry that has a negative effect on the quality of life in the community—e.g., the tobacco industry.

Nevertheless, it is in our long-term interest to develop as thinkers, to apply our best thinking in our lives, and to become lifelong learners. It is in all our interests that critical thinking becomes part of the culture of the organizational structures in society. The question is: "how can we use our thinking to best advantage in settings that often do not reward the best thinking and may at times punish it?"

There is no simple answer to this question. Becoming skilled in analyzing and assessing our personal circumstances in organizational structures takes insight and practice. We must ask the right questions, but we must also discover the essential facts. In the end, our judgments will still often be no more than probabilities. Let us look at some hypothetical cases and consider some elementary thinking about the logic of the decisions they offer. The thinking we propose is merely illustrative. We do not consider it definitive. A great deal would depend on the precise facts of the situation. We present our analysis as merely plausible and reasonable (as far as it goes). You might disagree with us in one or more case. Your analysis might be better than ours—or at least a plausible alternative.

Case # 1: An American Auto Maker Executive or Manager during the 1970s or '80s

You recognize that your company (and other American companies) is losing market share to Japanese automobile manufacturers. This trend is not denied by the company, but is explained as a product of the "fact" that Japanese workers work harder and more efficiently than American workers (with their union protections). Within the received view of management, the solution to the problem is that Japanese imports should be restricted since the competition is "unfair." It seems to you that emerging data gathered from auto plants operated by Japanese companies in America (using American labor) support the conclusion that the problem is not that of American worker laziness but rather of poor (American) management. You recognize that your view will not be well received by upper management and that your future with the company may be jeopardized by pressing this viewpoint. What are your options?

Analysis of Case # 1: The options in a case like this will vary in accordance with the specific facts in the situation and must be determined in context. Some facts may be hard to obtain. For example, it is often difficult to predict what individuals may do in circumstances in which you have not observed them. What is more, how individuals respond is dependent on how they interpret the situation. How they interpret the situation, in turn, depends in part on how the situation is presented to them and what their interests are. You may not be well positioned to make accurate predictions regarding the probable response of a number of people.

Clearly, your overall choice is to stay or go. If you stay, you must decide whether to try to influence present company policy or simply do your best within it. If you decide to influence company policy you must decide how to present your views in the least challenging way, and to whom and under what circumstances. If you decide to go, you must decide your timing and your transition to another job situation. As part of this thinking, you should make sure you are not simply trading one inflexible environment for another.

In addition, your values and needs are crucial. To what extent is it important to you to feel that you are part of a thriving concern? To what extent will you be frustrated if you suppress your actual views and work in a setting in which views that you consider inaccurate are being used as a basis for company decision-making? To what extent can you derive satisfaction simply by doing your job to the best of your ability within the context of decisions you cannot control? To what extent can you indirectly and behind the scenes encourage the company to move in the direction that you consider is important? What are your long-term hopes and plans? What would you like to be doing in five years? In ten years? What does all of this add-up to in your mind?

Case # 2: A Professor Recognizing the Need for Academic Reform

You are a professor with tenure in an academic department at a State University. You observe a number of problems that are not being addressed by the university. You notice that professors are largely assessed in terms of their ability to get along with the other professors in their department, on the one hand, and by their popularity with students, on the other—rather than by their professional standing and actual teaching ability. You recognize that some professors who are poor teachers and questionable scholars are promoted. You recognize that some professors who are excellent teachers and scholars are released. In addition, you discover that many graduating seniors lack fundamental reading, writing, and thinking skills. You recognize also that it is politically dangerous to suggest to faculty committees that there are serious problems of instruction and learning at the university. You also come to recognize, through informal conversations, that the administration is not likely to adopt any policy that will bring it into serious conflict with the faculty.

Analysis of Case # 2. The options in a case of this kind, like case # 1, varies in accordance with the specific facts in the situation and must be determined in context. As in case # 1, some of those facts may be hard to come by. There is always the problem of predicting what particular individuals may do in circumstances in which you have not yet observed them. In this case, the problem is largely political rather than academic. The political problem is one of gaining sufficient support for reform among those who have the power to facilitate it. Clearly, those most threatened by reform will organize to defend their interests, as soon as they see those interests threatened. The political issue becomes one of determining how to motivate those open-minded enough to see the need for reform—while minimally threatening those likely to oppose it. Of course, like most organizational political problems, much of the work must be done behind the scenes rather than openly. Few will openly oppose the idea of more effective assessment of professors or measures designed to produce more effective instruction. Yet within a large organization there are always many ways for those whose interest is in perpetuating the status quo to undermine reform efforts.

One option is to take the long view and work quietly behind the scenes over a number of years. Another option is to concentrate one's efforts on improving one's own scholarship and instruction, ignoring the problems requiring action on the part of others. A third is to become an agent for change in a larger arena, seeking to document problems in a more global way, while studiously avoiding documenting "local" problems. In this latter case, one might write articles or books on the general problems facing universities. A fourth option is to leave academia for industry.

As always, your personal values, preferences, and needs are very important. In which option are you likely to be doing the sorts of things that motivate and fulfil you? Some people seem to thrive in a political environment, others find it distasteful and unrewarding. Some seem able to work well within a system that has significant problems. Others find it difficult to "ignore" or set aside systemic problems while functioning within a system.

Case # 3: Working in a Setting in which There is Significant Personal Conflict

You are working in a setting in which there is a great deal of personal conflict. You find yourself suffering from stress even though you are not a party to the conflict. Each side in the conflict attempts to draw you in on their side.

Analysis of Case # 3. Here are some of the crucial questions: To what extent is the conflict a matter of conflicting personalities or conflicting styles? To what extent are there important issues at the root of the personal conflict? How would you assess the rationality of the conflicting sides? To what extent does the conflict relate to the structure of power and to questions of power? What are the implications of one or the other side winning the struggle? What are the implications for the individuals?

What are the implications for the organization? To what extent can you change your own thinking—the thinking that is leading you to feel stress? To what extent can you focus inward on your immediate job and escape involvement in the conflict? Ideally, what is the best way to resolve the conflict? What are the chances of the "best way" being achieved? Is there anything you can do to facilitate resolution of the conflict?

Case # 4: Working for an Unreasonable Boss

You are working in a setting in which the main person you must answer to is an irrational person, one given to extreme mood swings and to blaming others for his own deficiencies. Though irrational much of the time, he sees himself as a reasonable person who does not suffer fools gladly.

Analysis of Case # 4. Since the person you are working for is significantly irrational, appeal to his reason will be ineffective. Secondly, since he has significantly more power than you have, you have no choice but to pander to his ego and thereby avoid his wrath or to seek other employment or both. If you make the mistake of attempting to show him that he is being irrational, you will regret it, for he will find a way to conceptualize your behavior in a negative way and seek ways to punish you for "misrepresenting" him.

Case # 5: An Unreasonable Employee (with an underdog ego)

You are supervising an employee with an "underdog" ego. He regularly blames himself for mistakes he makes, but does not make any serious improvement. He is always willing to negate himself, but does not seem to be able to make progress. He continually promises to do better, but does not.

Analysis of Case # 5. Since the person working for you has an inferiority complex and lacks insight into his own make-up, appeals to his reason will be ineffective. The best solution will probably be to release him and try to hire a more rational person in his place. If you decide to work with him, you must set a specific time-line with specific expected improvements. You must follow-through on that timeline and on the consequences you establish in the event he does not improve. It is very unlikely that a person who is used to criticize himself as a substitute for changing himself will escape the pattern by himself (unless, in his more rational moments, he recognizes the pattern and is strongly motivated to change).

Case # 6: An Unreasonable Employee (with a dominating ego)

You are supervising an employee with a "top dog" ego who is also a skilled weak-sense critical thinker. She regularly finds ways to blame others for her deficiencies. She has an explanation for every mistake. The problem almost always turns out—when she does not blame it on others—to be a result of her having too little resources or out of date equipment or other circumstances beyond her control. She is very creative in evading personal responsibility for any problem or mistake.

Analysis of Case # 6 . Since the person working for you has a superiority complex and lacks insight into her own make-up, appeals to reason will be ineffective. The best solution will probably be to release her and try to hire a more rational person in her place. If you decide to work with her, you will have a great deal of difficulty because of her skills of rationalization. Since she already thinks of herself as performing at a high level and this conception is an important part of her self-identity, it will be very difficult to get her to take ownership of his deficiencies.

Case #7: A College President Uses College Funds to Support a Project at His Sister's Request

You are an administrator on a college campus reporting to the president. A local public school submits a request to the college for textbook covers. The school asks that the college produce paper covers with the college's logo and information about what the college offers printed on back. In this way, the college is able to market its programs while also providing the school with the covers it needs. As the Vice President of Community Relations, this request comes to your office. At first glance the request seems reasonable. But as you inquire further into the request you find that the person submitting it is the sister of your college president. When you bring the situation to the president for discussion, he says that he knew his sister would be submitting it. Furthermore he says that, since the college will be able to advertise its programs in a relatively inexpensive way by granting the request, he supports it. You mention your concern that it might seem to others that the real reason why the request was granted is because the president is motivated to help a family member. You also tell the president that should other schools make similar requests you will be hard-pressed not to grant them given the fact that you will be doing it for this one school. You add that the college cannot afford to do this for all schools in the large city within which you live. The president says not to worry, that it is unlikely that any other school will make such a request. He also says that he is not granting the request because his sister made it, rather that he thinks it is a good way of marketing the college's programs. He tells you not to get so worked up about things.

Analysis of Case #7: One option is simply to accept the president's reasoning. Because the book covers are going to provide information about the programs offered by the college, you can justify using money from the marketing budget to fund the project. On the other hand, it seems clear that the real reason behind the plan is to use college funds to help the president's sister. Reasoning further with the president seems futile since it seems clear that he is committed to his position. Moreover you know from your past interactions with him that when he has a vested interest in a project he will become disgruntled if you try to convince him that he should consider alternative ways of looking at the situation.

The question you must answer is whether it is in your best interest and in keeping with your values to proceed with the request. You will need to decide whether you are able, in good conscience, to work within the conditions set by the president and the current power structure. If you leave the college and move to a new college, will you likely find yourself in a similar situation? Since you understand how the "old boy network" operates, could you even get a job at another college or, through his connections, might the president be able to effectively block other opportunities you might have for employment? Do you have other viable career possibilities?

If you decide to tell the president you cannot in clear conscience support the project, what would the likely implications be? Would he find opportunities to "punish" you? Might he, for example, refuse to give you an annual pay increase? Might he see that you do not receive further promotions? Might he find another position for you on campus, one with less responsibility and power so that you cause him fewer problems?

Test the Idea
Analyzing Situations

Generate your own case for analysis. First, describe a problematic situation at work. Then, analyze the situation. What are your options for action?

The Power of Sound Thinking

Any company or industry that makes critical thinking a company-wide or industry-wide value acquires the ability to anticipate and effect constructive change, for only critical thinking can provide the impetus for continual re-thinking and evaluation of all present ideas, policies, and strategies. Without critical thinking built into the culture of an organization, short-range thinking is likely to predominate. Of course, short-range thinking may work for a time. For a time, it may be new. It may represent essential change. But if novel thinking is not eventually subject to critique, to adjustment, to refinement, to transformation, then, sooner or later, it becomes problematic and rigid.

One challenge we face in bringing critical thinking into any organizational structure is that, upon being questioned, most people think they already think critically and therefore that there is nothing significant for them to learn. If you ask all of those present in a room full of people: "Would all those who think uncritically please raise your hand?" you are likely to have no takers. There is a natural illusion fostered by the human mind that leads all of us to think that our own thinking is well-tuned to reality—even when it is not, in fact *especially* when it is not. Only as people begin to develop as thinkers do they commonly recognize that their own thinking is often flawed and in need of transformation.

The result is that any really new corporate leadership must break-through the mundane self-deception characteristic of human thinking itself. It must overcome what might be called "the natural attitude." Hence, corporate leadership based on critical thinking must not only define a purpose and communicate that purpose, but an intrinsic part of that purpose must be commitment to critical thinking on the job at all levels. It is not enough that an organization have and communicate a purpose, it must be a *well-thought-through purpose*. It is not enough to energize workers, there must be a mechanism in place that helps ensure that the energy is intelligently used and effectively applied. Achieving, for example, a balance between control and empowerment is something that must be carefully thought through, for only *quality of thought and analysis* will generate the right balance.

The same holds for the balance between policy and autonomy. The employees and the managers must exercise judgment regarding both. Poor judgment regarding either will not effect a release from paralysis. By the same token, "listening to employees and customers" should be listening to them *critically*. In short, the notion of dynamic change and growth presupposes that the change and the growth are *the right change* and *the right growth*, and those judgments require nothing less than critical thinking. Unfortunately, *critical thinking cannot be presupposed*. It must be systematically fostered. Once a balance is achieved between policy and autonomy, between control and empowerment, and critical thinking is systematically fostered, it releases the collective energy of all parties in an organization.

When rigid thinking becomes pronounced, and the individuals in an organization no longer feel part of a vital purpose, or connected to the company's activities as a whole, a negative atmosphere emerges. Employees become estranged from the company, though part of it. They may or may not verbalize that estrangement. They will perceive their superiors as irresponsive to them and to their needs. Policies will seem to lack sense or be connected to the facts of their workaday world. They may hide their perceptions, believing that their perceptions would be rejected or ridiculed. Their only connection with their work becomes their paycheck, and perhaps a few friends who share their views.

Some Personal Implications

Use the following list of recommendations to assess your internalization of the main points of this chapter and your willingness to put the ideas into action:

1. Establish the personal habit of routinely evaluating your thinking on the job. This includes answering and up-dating your answers to the following questions: What is your central goal in light of the job you have or role you play on the job? What are the obstacles or difficulties you face in accomplishing your job or fulfilling your role? What are you best at? What evidence do you have to support your conclusions? What do you do least well? What evidence do you have to document your conclusions? What strategies are you using to improve your job performance?

2. Determine your level of power. What power do you have in virtue of your position? What additional power do you have, in comparison to others, in virtue of your willingness to think critically and face unpleasant realities?

3. Determine the level and quality of thinking of those with whom you work. How would you assess the strengths and weaknesses of the thinking of your fellow workers? How does their thinking impact you?

4. Determine the "in-house" definitions of reality. What "party-lines" or "propaganda" are generated on the job which you recognize to be both self-serving and, of course, false? To what extent must you verbally honor that propaganda as a condition of being taken seriously?

5. Assess the level of bureaucratic thinking at your company. This will tie into "in-house" definitions of reality and favored "myths." Remember that bureaucracy is a state in which employees work increasingly by fixed routine rather than through the exercise of intelligent judgment. With bureaucratization, narrowness in thinking emerges. There is a proliferation of hard-and-fast rules and fixed procedures that make change difficult (when not impossible).

6. Assess the level of short-term thinking at your company.

7. Assess the level of stagnation in your company (or in your industry).

8. Assess the level of egocentric thinking among those you work with (this ties in with # 3 in this list).

9. Assess your own involvement, as a thinker, in "in-house" definitions of reality, party-lines, propaganda, as well as in bureaucratic, short-term, and egocentric thinking. Reconcile this analysis with your response to question # 1 in this list.

Conclusion

Membership in human groups is a blessing and a curse. The pressure to conform to the dominant thinking in a group is an inescapable problem. It is hard to improve one's thinking when forced to work with others who routinely assume that their unsound thinking is sound. What is more, we should never forget that within corporate and other organizational structures the full range of human emotions, motivations, and interests play themselves out. The flaws of the group and the flaws of the individuals in the group interact in a multitude of ways. In all of this, there is commonly a struggle for power taking place. Both group self-deception and the negative personal characteristics of the individuals (in the group) have an impact on corporate and organizational life.

To think effectively in corporate and organizational settings, we must understand, therefore, not only the general logic of these structures, but also the specific logic of the particular organizations in which we are living and working. In the privacy of our minds we must learn to ask the right questions. We must focus on essential facts. We must decide on our personal priorities. We must take the long view. We must be realistic and practical. We must be comfortable with probabilities, and we must be willing to test our ideas and change them in the light of our critically analyzed experience.

If we can successfully persuade organizational leadership to work toward a culture of critical thinking, both we and the organization can benefit in a lifelong way. Here are some important conditions for success:

1. The leadership must consist in essentially rational persons with an abiding recognition that they, and everyone else in the organization, are capable of thinking and performing at a higher level than they are at present.

2. The leadership must be intellectually humble, and hence, recognize mistakes they have made in the past, the limitations of their own present knowledge, and have a desire to grow and develop as thinkers.

3. The leadership must take a long-term view of building a culture of critical thinking within the organization. Short-term thinking must be used only as a stopgap measure and should not be typical of the thinking of the organization.

4. The leadership must be willing to release those persons who will actively resist making critical thinking an essential element in the organization's mission.

5. All key personnel must, over an extended period of time, become proficient in analyzing and evaluating thinking.

6. All key personnel must strive to be explicit as to the thinking (especially the assumptions) they are using in making key decisions. They must also be willing to fair-mindedly consider the pro's and con's of alternative possible decisions.

7. All key personnel must actively invite alternative points of view and strive to incorporate the strengths and insights of those views.

8. The language of critical thinking must be actively adopted as the language in which policies and decisions will be discussed.

9. Critical thinking will be used in the conduct of meetings on all issues. (What is our purpose? What is the key question here? What data do we need to make this decision? Is there another way to interpret these data? What are we taking for granted here? Do we need to question that? What other points of view do we need to consider?).

10. All key personnel and departments will operate with the assumption that whatever we do, and however high our present level of performance, we can perform at a higher level (tomorrow, next week, by mid year).

11. All policies, rules, regulations, and procedures are open to being questioned and replaced by a better policy, rule, regulation, or procedure. No policy, rule, regulation, or procedure will be maintained simply because it is traditional. All will be kept to a minimum. All must effectively serve a clear-cut purpose.

12. All attempts to build domains of power within the organization that do not clearly support the mission of the organization will be resisted.

13. All communications within the organization will be models of clarity, accuracy, brevity, and relevance.

14. All employees will maintain a portfolio of self-assessment, in which personal strengths and weaknesses are documented, as well as strategies adopted to improve one's performance and effectiveness.

15. In hiring personnel, an emphasis should be placed on candidates who are open-minded, willing to consider constructive criticism, and having a low level of ego-involvement in their work and relationships. During the probation period, special steps should be taken to verify these qualities.

Obviously, excellent planning and well-designed staff development in critical thinking could play a significant part in making these policies a practical reality. It is doubtful that significant changes in the thinking of an organization can take place without excellent planning, long-term commitment, and expertise in such a shift. As Stephen Covey (1992) puts it:

> I have long advocated a natural, gradual, day-by-day, step-by-step, sequential approach to personal development. My feeling is that any product or program—whether it deals with losing weight or mastering skills—that promises "quick, free, instant, and easy" results is probably not based on correct principles. (p. 29)

Peter Senge (1990) puts it this way:

> Recognizing that most new ideas in American management get caught up in the dynamics of the fad cycle leads to some sobering questions. What if the time required to understand, apply, and eventually assimilate the new capabilties suggested by a "new idea" is longer than the fad cycle itself? If organizations have an "attention span" of only one or two years (some might say one or two months), is it impossible to learn things that might require five or ten years? (p. x)

In any case, whether an organization is or is not open to significant change, our first responsibility must be to the integrity of our own lives as persons and thinkers. We serve others best by being true to ourselves. We must play the most positive role we can play in any organization of which we are a part, but when rigidity sets in, the most positive role we can play may be to leave and go our separate way.

Chapter 14

The Power and Limits of Professional Knowledge (And of the Disciplines that Underlie Them)

Professional Fallibility and the Glut of Information

The sheer quantity of information we are exposed to grows exponentially. So immense is it that no one person can acquire anything but a tiny and diminishing percentage of it. To add to our burden, much of the information generated is disseminated *with* a "spin," an agenda, a vested interest defining and interpreting it. Much information comes to us from professionals, persons officially certified as possessors of important knowledge. Yet the quality of what we are offered is very uneven. Our welfare depends upon our ability to do a good job assessing it. Doctors, lawyers, accountants, economists, media pundits, and many, many others tell us what we should and should not do, what is required for, and what will threaten, our welfare.

In this chapter, we suggest some ways to gain critical leverage on the information and advice given to us by professionals and by the disciplines that underlie professional learning and practice. We shall build on the insights of previous chapters. We shall therefore assume that you are now keenly aware that all humans are fallible, in predictable ways:

- *Subject to a tendency to egocentric thinking*—which leads a person to assume that his concerns are more important than those of others;

- *Subject to a tendency to sociocentric thinking*—which leads a person to assume that the groups to which he belongs are superior to others;

- *Subject to a tendency to self-deception*—which leads a person to twist the facts to achieve immediate self-justification (at the expense of an honest owning of mistakes and mis-deeds);

- *Subject to a lack of intellectual "virtues"*—which leads a person to blind himself to the extent of his ignorance, his inconsistencies, his failure to enter sympathetically into views that disagree with his own, his tendency to avoid complexity, and his fear of disagreeing with members of groups whose approval he seeks;

- *Subject to a tendency to violate basic intellectual standards*—which leads a person to think in ways that are often unclear, inaccurate, imprecise, irrelevant, superficial, narrow-minded, illogical, and unfair;

- *Subject to the influence of vested interest*—which leads a person to focus on power, money, and prestige (usually at the expense of the rights or well being of others).

These facts alone should make us wary of the pronouncements of any human being, "professional" or otherwise. Yet we need to be more than wary. We must know where to look for probable weaknesses and how to recognize likely strengths.

All information is not created equal. All professions are not on the same level of credibility. We should distinguish between professionals of different types and learn when it makes the best sense to question them. We should understand the academic disciplines that underlie the professions and the manner in which they are taught and learned. The first half of the chapter will deal with a sample analysis of some of the professions, most notably those of engineering and medicine. The second half of the chapter will deal with the disciplines that underlie the professions and the manner in which they are represented, taught, and learned. We shall then focus on the gap between the manner in which disciplines represent themselves to the public (in order to gain funding in the academic world) and the actual consequences of the manner in which they are taught and learned.

Let us begin with the contrast between the ideal of professional knowledge and the manner in which professional thinking is applied in the real world.

The Ideal of Professional Knowledge

Professional knowledge is, among other things, a form of power. It gives advantages to those who have it and disadvantages to those who lack it. For example, it can be used to minimize or maximize suffering. It can serve selfish human desires or meet basic human needs. It can be used to create conditions for conflict or those that contribute to peace and understanding. It can be used to destroy or preserve the environment and the lifeforms that inhabit it. It can contribute to a less just or a more just world. It can advance irrational or rational ends.

To the extent that we are committed to fair-mindedness, we are committed to professional knowledge being acquired and used to minimize human suffering, to meet basic human needs, to preserve rather than destroy the environment, to contribute to a more just world, and to serve rational rather than irrational ends. In providing justification for the public funding of instruction in the various professions, spokespersons argue that their professions serve ends in the public interest.

Ideally, professionals acquire knowledge not to benefit a selected few but, rather, to distribute benefits in the broadest and most just way. Even those who argue that the pursuit of professional knowledge should be free and untrammeled support that argument with the view that the free-wheeling search for professional knowledge will confer, in the long run, the greatest benefit on the largest number. But to what extent are professions serving these higher ends? To what extent are they fulfilling the promises made on their behalf when they seek funding for public instruction and for research? How can we learn to think about professions, and within our own, in the most powerful and rational way? These are the questions that lie behind the critique of professional *thinking*.

Who Should We Believe?

This chapter presents a plausible argument for suspecting a significant gap between the promised benefits of the various professions and the actual effects of them. It makes no further claim. How large that gap is in any professional field is a matter for systematic study. In the next chapter, this general argument is followed up with a more detailed argument for the field of psychology and mental health. In both cases, we would expect numerous qualifications and corrections to emerge from further inquiry.

In any case, as consumers of professional knowledge and advice, we need to think critically in deciding who to believe and what to do with such advice. Consider the following excerpt from an article in the New York Times (November 21, 2000):

N.A.S.D Accuses Dean Witter of Fraud in Sale of 3 Funds

Legal troubles continued to mount yesterday for Morgan Stanley Dean Witter & Co. when securities regulators accused the investment bank's brokerage unit of misleading thousands of investors into buying mutual funds that resulted in losses of $65 million.

In a rare case of litigation between a major Wall Street firm and the National Association of Securities Dealers, the securities industry's self-regulatory organization, Dean Witter Reynolds is being accused of fraud for the way it sold three bond funds in 1992 and 1993. Dean Witter sold more than $2 Billion of shares in the funds to more than 100,000 investors, many of them beyond retirement age and some of them elderly, the association's regulatory arm said in a complaint filed yesterday.

Dean Witter told its brokers to promote the funds as safe but high-yielding alternatives to certificates of deposit without adequately disclosing how much riskier the funds were, the complaint said.

In this case, some 100,000 investors did not use good thinking in trusting the recommendations of professionals at Dean Witter. As consumers we must develop our ability to evaluate the thinking of the professionals we hire to support our interests. Otherwise we can too easily become victims of those more concerned with serving their interests than ours. We cannot assume, in other words, that professionals necessarily have our best interests in mind. As critical thinkers, we learn to look beyond the rhetoric of professionals to the actions in which they engage. We then analyze that behavior in terms of the thinking behind it.

This chapter and the next are included in the book because, to become a critical consumer of information, it is essential that one gain some sense of how to avoid or deal with the possible problem of bad advice, or worse, malpractice, on the part of professionals. By malpractice we mean any wrongful use of professional knowledge or information that leads to needless waste, unnecessary suffering, gratuitous harm, or injustice.

Of course, the problem is not always confined to the acts of an isolated group of individuals, as in the case of the Dean Witter scandal. Consider the great U.S. Savings and Loan debacle. In this case, a whole industry (through their lobbyists) persuaded the U.S. Congress to remove regulatory restrictions that prevented them from lending money without a specified level of collateral. The slogan of "de-regulation!" substituted for sound thinking. In essence, lobbyists asked the public to guarantee the solvency of Savings and Loan institutions while allowing them to make questionable loans. The result of the collapses that followed was an additional debt burden of approximately $9,000 for every man, woman, and child in the United States.

The asbestos and tobacco industries have engaged in similar self-serving misrepresentations over many years—with significant harm to the public. In these cases, the public was assured by industry spokespersons that there was no danger to them at the same time that numerous official and "professionals" in the industries knew that their product constituted a mortal threat to the consumer. Government officials trusted the integrity of the industry spokespersons, who, it turns out, were more concerned with profit and public relations than the public good.

Or consider the recent report issued by the National Academy of Sciences on medical errors (*New York Times*, Nov. 30, 1999). The report pointed out not only that medical mistakes cause up to 98,000 unnecessary deaths per year, but also that health care providers could reduce the number of errors by 50 percent in the next five years by simply collecting and analyzing data on unsafe practices, as does the aviation industry. If this article is accurate, then present instruction in the health care professions is resulting in an unacceptable level of errors and malpractice. Ideally, learning to think "medically" should have preempted this large-scale problem from arising in the first instance.

Learning to think about a profession in a rational way requires that we understand both the strengths and weaknesses of the profession. Each profession represents a way of thinking that has power and value. But no professional way of thinking is better than the quality of thinking of the individual professional who applies it. For remember, all professional thinking necessarily occurs within the context of the full humanity of the thinker and in a world in which a struggle for power is continual. One problem of which we need to be aware is the problem of false loyalty to a profession on the part of many if not most professionals. Another is the problem of non-disclosure, of obtaining information that takes into account the behind the scene activities of powerful interests that may set aside the public good for the short-term gains of the few.

True and False Loyalty to a Profession

True loyalty to a profession is a product of the commitment to ensure that the profession, both in general and in particular cases, serves the public interest. False loyalty to a profession is formed either by an uncritical acceptance of the "ideology" every group engenders, or arises as a product of a fear of being disapproved or punished by other members of the profession—if one deviates from expected behavior. In being socialized into a profession—and socialization is part of being trained in a profession—one learns how to present oneself to outsiders, how to express one's authority as a professional, and how to protect fellow professionals from criticism—except in group-approved ways.

True loyalty to a profession is born of recognition of the profession's potential power for good in the world. It is not blind commitment to practices in the profession as they stand. It is not given by the intensity with which one defends the profession. The fact is that ethically sensitive persons who are also astute thinkers find themselves, from time to time, in dilemmas in which they are torn between their consciences, on the one hand, and the in-group pressure not to publicly criticize the profession, on the other.

Consider the legal profession. True loyalty to the profession of the law, for example, derives from a commitment to the creation of a society in which just laws are applied justly to individuals and institutions, irrespective of the power, wealth, and social status of those individuals and institutions. Such loyalty recognizes that all the legal professions are to be judged by the degree to which they enhance personal and social justice. Such loyalty begins with a recognition that the law as applied in society is far from the law as it should be applied, and that justice is not always served by the established legal system.

False loyalty to the legal profession takes the form of a defense of those dimensions of the law that fail to serve the end of justice—sometimes out of fear, sometimes out of ignorance, and sometimes out of vested interest. When persons are socialized into a profession so as to become uncritical defenders of the present practices of the profession; both the profession and the potential good of the profession suffer. To put this another way, a person retards the development of a profession by uncritically defending it. This defensiveness engenders a false sense of loyalty. Conversely, when practitioners recognize weaknesses in a profession, they are well on their way to contributing to its strengths. It is a strength, an important strength, to recognize one's weakness. Unfortunately, we have not yet reached the phase of development of human professional knowledge wherein each profession, as taught, routinely discloses publicly its most salient weaknesses and failures.

We should all come to recognize the limitations of those professions, with which we must deal, beginning with the problem of false loyalty.

The Gap Between Fact and Ideal

Two objective phenomena—human fallibility and vested interest—account for why few, if any, professions are close to approximating the ideal of professional knowledge and practice. These two phenomena are at the root of much of the misuse of professional knowledge in the world:

1. **Human fallibility:** All professional knowledge is acquired, analyzed, and put to use in the world by individuals subject to the pitfalls of human weakness, self-deception, and a variety of pathological states of mind (e.g., prejudice, egocentrism, or sociocentrism).

2. **Vested interest:** Human professional knowledge exists in a world of power, status, and wealth. The struggle over all three significantly influences what information is acquired within any profession, how it is interpreted, and how it is used.

It follows that we should be skeptical of any description of a human professional knowledge-constructing enterprise that characterizes itself as an approximation of an ideal. Rather, we should approach human professions as in some state of contradiction between an announced ideal and actual reality. In this way, we can realistically take into account the weaknesses as well as the strengths of the profession and thereby contribute to the higher state of development of the profession.

If we begin with the hypothesis that there is some gap between the ideal of any profession and its actual practice, we are much more likely to identify the misuses of information and professional knowledge on the part of human professions. We will come to see that, to some extent and in some discoverable ways, the phenomena of human fallibility and vested interest are operating. No profession has isolated, or could isolate, itself from the irrational dimensions of the human mind in action in human affairs. And, as always, we deal with irrationality best by raising it to the level of conscious recognition, not by sweeping it under the rug or denying it. All illusions about present practice become blinders rendering us incapable of protecting our interest and impeding full development of the profession. Both those who use information disseminated by professionals and those who generate that information should have a realistic conception of the profession.

So we begin with two premises:

1. Every profession has great potential for contributing to human welfare in the world.
2. Nevertheless, the information and professional knowledge that professions generate are subject to mistakes, distortion, and misuse by fallible, self-interested humans at every stage of collection, construction, and use.

We should not assume, then, that professional associations, schools, or universities— even official ethics committees set up by professions—are exempt from irrational influences. We should not assume that professions are now, or at any previous time in history were, motivated to disclose their weaknesses. We should not assume that any profession is willing to put us on guard against self-deception or vested interest in the profession's present practices. For example, only rarely do professions document weaknesses in the professional preparation of those certified in the profession, and when they do, that documentation is frequently marginalized, discredited, or restricted to insiders.

Accordingly, as critical thinkers, it is helpful to recognize the inevitable difference between theory and practice. With the hypothesis that in all likelihood some gap exists, we are much more likely to discover it. With the recognition that any documentation of a gap is likely to be resisted, we are more likely to be politically astute in its disclosure.

Of course, our hypothesis of inconsistency between the ideal and real should not prevent us from noticing very different degrees and forms of inconsistency. Some professions are undoubtedly much closer to the ideal. Some professions are more vigilant about the pitfalls that attend their practice. We, in turn, should guard against our hypothesis becoming a self-fulfilling prophesy in our minds, for then it itself constitutes evidence of self-deception on our part. Though we should be alert to problems in a profession, we should not see problems where none exist. Let us now look at a couple of sample professions and begin to consider further strategies to use in our thinking.

Assessing A Profession or a Professional Conclusion: Matters of Fact, Matters of Opinion, Matters of Judgment

To effectively assess thinking within a discipline, it is important to become proficient in distinguishing three kinds of questions:

1. Those for which it is possible to achieve a definite, verifiable answer;
2. Those for which all answers are matters of personal preference;
3. Those for which reasoned judgment is essential and wherein proposed, conflicting, and reasonable answers must be evaluated to determine which are stronger and which weaker, as responses to the question.

The first and third kinds of questions—matters of fact and matters of judgment—are most important to distinguish in evaluating professions and the questions they take up.

This being so, it is very important, when assessing professionals, to have some sense of the nature of the "discipline" underlying the profession and the manner in which that discipline is typically used as well as the way is being used in a given case. For example, there are many questions answered by engineers—chemical, electrical, hydraulic, marine, and mechanical—which have definitive answers obtained by inserting objective data into established formulas based on mathematics or physics. For example, if a mechanical engineer needs to figure out the power developed in the cylinder of a reciprocating engine, he simply divides the foot pounds of work performed by the piston in one minute by 33,000. His data include the mean effective pressure (in pounds per square inch), the length of stroke of the piston (in feet), the area of the piston (in square inches), and the number of working strokes per minute. There are literally hundreds of thousands of questions engineers are called upon to answer which have definite answers. These answers can be calculated by established procedures based on physical science and mathematics. The probability of error in such questions is low. There is an established method for verifying the accuracy of the answer.

Of course, we should recognize and remember that not everyone working on an engineering project is an engineer, not every engineer is doing engineering, and not every question raised in engineering is a question with a definite answer. We should be alert to the misuse of the term "engineering" in such expressions as *management* engineering, *sales* engineering, and *business* engineering—where the authoritative sound of the word is used to hide practices lacking the scientific and mathematical basis of 'engineering' in its proper use.

Let us take the example of engineering a little further. Even though engineering is based on science and mathematics, it does not follow that all of its questions have definite answers. There are many engineering questions that for best settlement, require wit, ingenuity, judgment, and practical experience. For example, most engineering projects involve a sequence of planning, design, creation, and economical operation of a process that entails building a structure. This process as a whole commonly involves many questions of judgment, in addition to many questions of fact. The answers to questions become most definite the more specialized and limited they are. So when specifications are set for a particular part required, and those specifications are fulfilled by the production of that part, there is typically a high degree of scientific accuracy and precision delivered by the engineer or engineers in question. This does not mean a mistake cannot happen, but it does mean that a mistake is rare and can be verified as such.

However, engineering projects often involve large public expenditures and/or have significant environmental and economic implications. The public interest may be deeply involved. However, with the injection of politics and vested interest, objectivity often suffers a severe blow. Press releases, public relations campaigns, and other professional "spin doctors" whose skills are those of rhetoric, public relations, and propaganda shape the flow of information to the public. Their services are often for sale to the highest bidder. Such professionals are adept at fostering public impressions and views. They do this not principally by evidence and argumentation, but through understanding the psychology of the public: its impatience with complexity, its susceptibility to fear and suggestiveness, and its general impressibility.

Consider the field of hydraulic engineering. The field itself is based on physical laws governing water and other liquids. But water of sufficient quality and quantity is essential to human well being. There is often, therefore, a great deal of money involved in gaining access to water. The result is that major money interests are often importantly involved. The well being of people is also at stake. How water projects are conceived and carried out becomes a matter that goes far beyond questions of engineering.

Of course, when people with vested interests are involved, they cannot be trusted to represent the facts in a fair and objective manner. Someone must argue for the public interest, and that argument must be given sufficient attention in the media to affect public view. Of course, what the media covers and how they cover it depends on persons whose thinking is often based on "media" considerations in the first place. We cannot assume that media pundits are excellent thinkers or are dispassionate judges of the public interest.

Consider the Panama Canal. As an engineering project, it was a great achievement. However, the political machinations that proceeded and accompanied it, together with the corruption and death that it entailed, were horrendous. In the process, President Teddy Roosevelt, in effect, stole the necessary land from Columbia and conspired in the creation of a new country, Panama. The mass media in the U.S. presented the facts of the case as the government represented those facts. The public was not in a position to know what was going on behind the scenes.

A similar tale of bribery, corruption, and theft of public lands accompanied great engineering projects of the last half of the 19th Century in the U.S.—the building of canals and railroads. For excellent documentation of this history, consult especially Gustavus Myers' excellent book, *History of the Great American Fortunes* (1908).

Engineering, then, is a science and an art. Many of its questions have definite, demonstrable answers. But both the context for the use of engineering, and the consequences for human good and ill, are not simple matters of science or math. They connect with politics, economics, vested interests, and environmental values and concerns. The broad issues generated are often complex matters of judgment. They require special scrutiny on the part of anyone with the ability to think critically. And the position of engineering, as a field, is parallel to those of other scientifically based disciplines.

Medicine, for example, like engineering, is both a science and an art. Many of its questions have definite, demonstrable answers. But very often, internal politics bulks large, often larger than in engineering. We can see this in examining its history. Consider:

> When Edward Jenner hit upon the notion of a smallpox vaccine in 1797, the Royal Society of London scolded him for risking his reputation on something 'so much at variance with established knowledge, and withal so incredible.' When the Hungarian physician Ignaz Semmelweis figured out that physicians' unwashed hands were causing fatal infections among new mothers at the University of Vienna in the 1850s, he lost his own position there. (*Newsweek*, Nov. 27, 2000)

Similarly, in our day, the medical field is highly resistant to the notion that viruses and bacteria play a large part in heart disease, cancer, and other modern plagues—despite growing evidence that they do (Ewald, 2000). According to biologist Ewald, when Barry Marshall first reported his findings on the infectious cause of ulcers in 1983, his peers ignored the discovery until seven years later when it was highlighted in a magazine.

The complexity of modern medicine, including the extent of its ignorance, is just now being recognized by some. Some important medical problems are documented in a book entitled *Clinical Epidemiology: A Basic Science for Clinical Medicine* (Sackett, Haynes, & Tuigwell, 1985), with emphasis on the use of clinical diagnostic strategies, the selection of diagnostic tests, and the interpretation of diagnostic data. Systematic problems are documented. At the University of Arizona College of Medicine, Ann Kerwin, Maryls Witte, and Charles Witte (1995) have founded the Curriculum on Medical Ignorance. This program fosters the idea that it is only through knowledge of our ignorance that we can learn, and that learning itself presupposes ignorance. Through the program students are encouraged to "question, ponder, revise, create, discover, and learn how to learn."

Ivan Illich (1976), in his classic book, *Medical Nemesis*, assembles a mass of evidence from authoritative medical sources to support the thesis that: "The medical establishment has become a major threat to health. The disabling impact of professional control over medicine has reached the proportions of an epidemic."

Research in medicine has principally been controlled by those who deeply believe the orthodox theories of health and disease. Research based on new theories has always faced opposition from the status quo. Resistance to new theories is not typically a product of any principle of science itself, but rather of the power of the personal ego of individuals, the pressure to conform to the group, and vested interest. Science is not the only thing that influences the minds of doctors and other medical practitioners. For example, though much of the progress toward the eradication of disease has emerged as a result of preventative public health measures, only a small portion of research and medical expenditure has gone toward prevention of disease. Doctors are trained with the implicit view that medicine plays its role best by "curing" diseases rather than preventing them. Diagnostics and treatment, not public policy and prevention, are the guiding motifs. What is more, doctors are not usually paid for patients who don't get sick, but rather for those that do.

What, then, are we implying? Not only the obvious, but also the not so obvious. Obviously, we must be on the outlook for egocentrism, socio-centrism, and self-deception inappropriately influencing professions. The following is less obvious:

- that we should carefully distinguish questions of fact from questions of judgment;

- that we should especially scrutinize the influence of politics, economics, and media spin doctors on the presentation of "facts."

- that we should always distinguish public interest from special and vested interests.

The Ideal Compared to the Real

Another way to approach professions is through an analysis of the disciplines underlying them and the manner in which those disciplines are represented and taught. We of course recognize that every profession is a powerful mode of thinking that can make a significant contribution to human welfare. However, we must be cautious not to assume that ideal conceptions of the disciplines are equivalent to their actual practices. Rather, reasonability requires that we hypothesize some gap between expressed ideals and actual practice.

Let us therefore experiment with the process of comparing and contrasting the relationship between the ideals that are implied in the way disciplines represent themselves publicly (at the universities and colleges) with the actual consequences of their instruction.

We shall examine some initial elements of this critique. Our examples are not advanced as flawless examples of critical thinking in action but, rather, as illustrations of how we might begin to put the above insights into action in our mode of thinking. We will begin by looking at a variety of academic disciplines from this perspective, followed by some initial reflections in each case.

In this chapter, we will begin with mathematics and then consider the so-called hard sciences of physics, chemistry, and biology. We will then reflect upon the human sciences, the so-called soft sciences, and finally, literature, the arts, and philosophy.

Each case is guided by two important insights:

1. All professional knowledge in use in the world is based in academic disciplines and is subject to the pitfalls of human fallibility on the part of individuals using it.

2. The teaching of all professions occurs within a culture, and is thus influenced by the pursuit of power and vested interest within the culture.

Professions Based on the Ideal of Mathematics and Abstract Quantification

If there are professions free from human fallibility and vested interest, it is those based in mathematics, for presumably the study of abstract quantification favors no group over any other and, therefore, seems least likely to encourage or engender self-deception in its practitioners. But even a cursory examination of the topic suggests a gap between ideal and reality even here.

Let us briefly review the promise of math instruction itself, a promise used to justify the large sums of money necessary to maintain math instruction at all levels of schooling. That promise can be stated in the following terms:

> We live today in a world in which mathematics proficiency is increasingly important to success in life. Our world is complex and technological, and mathematics is crucial to both understanding its complexity and operating within its technological dimensions. Our investment in mathematics is sensible because, through it, we are providing society with the mathematicians, engineers, and technical experts necessary to meet worldwide competition. What is more, mathematics proficiency is important to everyone. Many problems and issues of daily personal and public life have an important quantitative dimension. Large-scale math instruction provides the citizenry with the quantitative concepts, principles, and tools by means of which they are able to perform successfully in both their personal and public life. Through it, persons learn to transfer logical thinking to other domains of professional knowledge and thought.

To what extent is the ideal realized? How far are we from it? What are some of the hidden consequences deriving from large-scale math instruction that the promise of the ideal does not take into account? What alternatives do we have to our present practice? To what extent are we getting what we are paying for? To what extent is our social investment in mathematics having the promised effect? To what extent are we realistic in our conception of the value and real consequences of large-scale math instruction at every level of schooling?

In our view, there is a large gap between the promised social gain from math instruction and the actual result. The gap is twofold. The first problem is inherent in the negative consequences for persons unable to perform at some minimal level at school—those who fail at school math. The second problem is the failure of citizens who are certified by schools as competent in math who do not use mathematics successfully in dealing with public and social issues. We are alleging, then, that both the persons who fail officially and those who pass officially constitute evidence of a major problem in math instruction.

The Pain and Suffering of Those Who Fail

Let us begin with the manner in which mathematics is taught and the high stakes associated with success or failure in it. Success in mathematics is given high status in the schools. Some level of mathematical proficiency is required to be certified as having successfully completed elementary school, then middle school, high school, and college. Persons who find themselves unable to perform at the level taken to be essential experience a great deal of mental distress and anguish. Some proficiency in math is a college-entrance requirement. What is more, persons who fail in math, except in rare circumstances, are not allowed to graduate from high school or college. Some level of proficiency in math is enforced as a precondition for graduation.

Loss of Self-Esteem and Opportunity to Receive Higher Education

We rarely talk about, or attempt to assess, the damage resulting from loss of self-esteem and loss of opportunity to advance in school on the part of the many persons who perform poorly in mathematics. Isn't it possible that many of those who do not perform well in math might yet perform at high levels in other domains of learning? Aren't we wrongfully denying those who fail in math an opportunity to succeed in other areas, especially because many disciplines involve virtually no math?

If we look at the everyday problems of our professional and personal lives, how many require the levels of proficiency in mathematics that testing and certification require? A case can easily be made for simple arithmetic, no doubt, but what about algebra and geometry? How often does the average person face a problem that requires the use of concepts and principles of algebra and geometry—beyond, perhaps, simple percentages? It is not obvious that mathematical proficiencies beyond that of basic arithmetic should be required of all persons. Might we be better off making math optional beyond elementary arithmetic and the simplest algebra? Might we not be better off merely providing incentives to motivated persons to study and excel at math? What is the point of lifelong penalties for those who do poorly in math?

Low Level of Math Competency of Those Who Pass School Examinations

There is a second gap between ideal and real regarding mathematics instruction. Supposedly a society in which all citizens are taught to think mathematically will be able to use math successfully in dealing with public issues involving a quantitative dimension. For example, assessing the national budget involves comprehending large sums and their significance in a variety of budgetary issues. Assessing the significance of damage to the environment from pollution, assessing the loss of natural resources, assessing public health issues, and many other public issues require people to make judgments involving large figures. But it seems reasonable to question how many citizens are actually able to make these judgments reasonably, even when simple math is involved. And consider the many people who cannot seem to manage a personal budget. Many who have passed the school exams in math are failing the real task of using math successfully in their lives.

Test the Idea
Math and You

Think about your education and answer the following questions:

1. To what extent would you say that, while in school or college, you mastered fundamental concepts in math and, as a result, are able to effectively use that professional knowledge in coming to informed conclusions about public issues with a mathematical dimension? To what extent would you say that you memorized definitions and procedures sufficient to pass tests but insufficient to understand the basic concepts underlying the math you were doing? Now, see if you can give examples of when you last used math in your daily life. What level of math was it?

2. To what extent would you say that the math requirements you had to meet were appropriate measures to require of all persons? What reasoning would you use to justify your conclusions?

3. In your view, should persons be prevented from being accepted by a college on the basis of low math scores alone?

4. How often have you faced a problem in your life that required the use of concepts and principles of algebra and geometry?

The Ideal of Science: Physics, Chemistry, Astronomy, Geology, and Biology

Historically, the idea of science was based on the notion that it was important to ask questions about, and consequently think about, the world in a new way—a way that emphasized a carefully controlled empirical study of the world. The idea of science is based on the notion that, instead of thinking about what the world must be like, given our basic assumptions and preconceptions about it, we should discover, through empirical thinking and inquiry, what it is actually like. We must assume that the fundamental ideas through which we think traditionally about the world may be incorrect or misleading. We must be willing to question our seemingly self-evident beliefs about the world and entertain the assumption that they might be false. The idea of empirical thinking and carefully controlled experimentation was taken to be the key to gaining sound professional knowledge of the world.

This ideal of science emerged as a critical response to previous human inquiry in which the reasoning of important thinkers appeared to be inappropriately influenced by beliefs of a highly egocentric and sociocentric nature. Among those great thinkers were Plato, Aristotle, Augustine, and Aquinas—whose qualities of reflection and reasoning were taken at one time to be self-evident guarantors of professional knowledge. Their views of the physical and natural world were rarely questioned. With the emergence of science, however, such wide-ranging thinkers were increasingly recognized to be biased by questionable assumptions at the root of their thought. Most obviously, it appeared that pre-scientific thinkers often uncritically assumed metaphysical or religious concepts at the foundations of their thought about the world. What is more, the traditional questions asked seemed rarely to focus on testable characteristics in the world.

In the "new" view, which emerged during the Renaissance (1400–1650), one became a scientist when one committed oneself to modes of inquiry based on controlled experimentation. The fields of physical and natural sciences, then, separated themselves from the field of philosophy and became fields of their own. Many of the early scientists set up their own laboratories for this purpose. This commitment, it was assumed, would maximize discovery of the actual laws and principles that operating in the physical and natural worlds and minimize the influence of human preconceptions about the world. There can be no doubt that this notion of science represented a real advance in the pursuit of professional knowledge about the physical and natural worlds.

Physics, chemistry, astronomy, geology, and biology are among the best cases one can choose for professions in which human self-deception and vested interest have been minimized. It does not follow, however, that these factors are not present. So let us now turn briefly to an expression of the promise of instruction in the physical and natural sciences. That ideal is formulated in ways that parallel the justification and argument for social investment in instruction in mathematics:

> We live today in a world in which scientific understanding and proficiency are increasingly important to success in life. Our world is complex, and technological and scientific thinking is crucial to understanding both its physical and natural complexity and its technological dimensions. Our investment in science instruction is well spent because, through it, we are providing society with the scientific and technological experts it requires to be competitive. What is more, scientific understanding and proficiency are important to everyone. Many problems and issues, not only in daily personal life but also in public life, have an important scientific dimension. Large-scale science instruction provides the citizenry with the scientific concepts, principles, and tools by means of which they are able to perform successfully in both personal and public ways.

To what extent is this ideal being fulfilled by science instruction as it exists today? It can be argued that the reality is a long distance from the ideal. Consider the following:

- Though virtually all citizens are given many years of instruction in science, is there not abundant evidence to suggest that most people do not think scientifically about everyday scientific problems and issues? For one, can most high-school graduates distinguish why astronomy is a science and astrology is not? What accounts for many high school graduates believing in astrology?

Isn't there ample evidence to demonstrate that:

- Many, if not most, people cannot explain the difference between theological and scientific questions?

- Many, despite years of science instruction, have not formulated a single scientific hypothesis or designed a single scientific experiment and would not be able to effectively distinguish well-designed from poorly designed scientific experiments?

- Many cannot explain the role of theory in science and cannot, therefore, explain why the theory of evolution in biology cannot be reasonably compared to the interpretation of one reading of the Bible that the world is no more than a few thousand years old?

- Many cannot explain how to distinguish a scientific question from any other kind of questions and, consequently, do not treat scientific questions differently from other kinds of questions?

- Many cannot accurately explain any basic concepts, laws, or principles of science and do not use those concepts, laws, or principles in accounting for the world they experience?

- Most do not read any scientific articles, books, or even magazines (such as Scientific American or Discovery) and would have trouble understanding them if they did?

These questions, and their most plausible answers, suggest a large gap between the promise of science instruction and the actual effect of that instruction on the lives of most people.

What is more, these questions can be contextualized for each of the various physical and natural sciences. Everywhere the word science appears, one could substitute one of the sciences—physics, chemistry, astronomy, geology, or biology. Consider the following reformulation for the field of biology:

- Though virtually all citizens are given instruction in biology, is there not abundant evidence to suggest that most people do not think biologically about everyday biological problems and issues?

- What accounts for the fact that many, if not most, people cannot explain the difference between a theological and a biological question?

- Isn't it true that most persons who are given instruction in biology have not formulated a single biological hypothesis or designed a single biological experiment and would not be able to effectively distinguish well-designed from poorly designed biological experiments?

- Isn't it true that most people cannot explain the role of theory in biology and cannot, therefore, explain why the theory of evolution in biology cannot be reasonably compared to the interpretation of one reading of the Bible that the world is no more than a few thousand years old?

- Isn't it true that most people cannot explain how to distinguish a biological question from any other kind of question and, consequently, do not treat biological questions differently from other kinds of questions?

- Isn't it true that most people cannot accurately explain any basic concepts, laws, or principles of biology and do not use biological concepts, laws, or principles in accounting for the biological features of the world they experience?

Test the Idea
The Physical and Natural Sciences and You
Answer the following questions regarding your education:

❏ Why is astronomy a science and astrology not? Do you believe in astrology? If you do, what do you base that belief on? How do you reconcile that belief with the basic principles of science?

❏ Can you explain the difference between theological and scientific questions?

❏ Have you ever formulated a scientific hypothesis or designed a scientific experiment? If you answer "yes," explain what your hypothesis was and the design of your experiment.

❏ Explain the basic role of theory in science. Then explain why the theory of evolution in biology can, or cannot, be evaluated by citing passages in the Bible.

❏ Select any basic concept, law, or principle of science, state it, then explain it using examples from your experience.

The Ideal of Social Science:
History, Sociology, Anthropology, Economics, and Psychology

In light of the success of the physical and natural sciences, it was predictable that those interested in the study of human life and behavior would look to the paradigm of scientific methodology as a means by which questions about the nature of human behavior could be as definitively settled as those about gravity, chemical reactions, plants, and animal life. Many scholars in the professions focused on humans expected a revolution within their professions as a result of a commitment to the application of controlled experiment. By this rigorous process, it was thought, hypotheses about human life could be confirmed or falsified. Foundational truths about human life and behavior could be discovered and built upon.

There is one major problem with this conception of the study of human behavior. Briefly, it might be expressed as follows: Human behavior is the result of the meaning–creating capacity of the human mind and is much more a product of human thinking than human instinct. Furthermore, a variety of influences have an impact on how humans think (and therefore on how they feel and what they want). Humans are highly complex, multidimensional creatures, which makes the study of human behavior through the scientific method subject to many limiting qualifications at best.

For example, as humans we are born into a culture at some point in time in some place, and reared by parents with particular beliefs. We form a variety of associations with other humans who are equally variously influenced. Our minds are influenced in all of the following dimensions, but not to the same extent or in the same way:

- **sociologically**: our mind is influenced by the social groups to which we belong;
- **philosophically**: our mind is influenced by our personal philosophy;
- **ethically**: our mind is influenced by our character;
- **intellectually**: our mind is influenced by the ideas we hold, by the manner in which we reason and deal with abstractions and abstract systems;
- **anthropologically**: our mind is influenced by cultural practices, mores, and taboos;
- **ideologically and politically**: our mind is influenced by the structure of power and its use by interest groups around us;
- **economically**: our mind is influenced by the economic conditions under which we live;
- **historically**: our mind is influenced by our history and by the way we tell our history;
- **biologically**: our mind is influenced by our biology and neurology;
- **theologically**: our mind is influenced by our religious beliefs and attitudes;
- **psychologically**: our mind is influenced by our personality and personal psychology.

What is more, these influences are not only subject to almost unlimited variation among themselves, but humans are capable of discovering each of these influences, reflecting on them, and then acting to change them in an almost unlimited number of ways. Consider how much more difficult it would be to study the behavior of mice if each mouse were to vary its behavior from every other mouse depending on a unique combination of prior influences within each of the above categories. Moreover, consider what the study of behavior of mice would be like if they could discover that we were studying them and began to react to our study in the light of that professional knowledge. And how could we even proceed to study them if they were to decide at the same time to study us studying them?

The very idea of studying human behavior scientifically faces enormous difficulties by virtue of the diverse nature of human behavior. It faces enormous difficulties by virtue of the diverse simultaneous influences upon humans as we think, feel, and act in the world, and the capacity of humans to notice and modify virtually any aspect of the thoughts, feelings, and desires that drive our behavior. In light of these considerations, let us examine the sort of promissory claims made on behalf of the social sciences.

The ideal of science is based on the fact that it is possible in principle to ask questions about any aspect of the world. Such questions can be asked in a way that enables us to pursue answers by means of carefully controlled empirical study rather than on the basis of abstract reasoning following from human preconception. There is no reason why, in principle, humans should not be studied empirically. In studying humans as well as in studying other animal species in the world, it is essential that carefully controlled experimentation correlated with falsifiable hypotheses are used as the guiding keys to gaining dependable professional knowledge of the human world. What is more, it is essential that humans be taught professional knowledge of themselves so we can make intelligent decisions about our own conditions of life.

Each profession will make specific claims emerging from its potential (viewed ideally) history, sociology, anthropology, economics, and psychology, approximately as follows.

History as an Ideal

If we as humans do not study the mistakes of the past, we are bound to repeat them. History enables us to grasp the nature of our own past, how we have come to be the way we are, the problems we have had to overcome, the forces that have acted, and are acting, upon us. Such study and such an understanding are essential to our well-being. In this way, we can appreciate our heritage, what we have lived and died for, and the evolution of our culture as a people. Without it, we make our decisions in the dark.

Sociology as an Ideal

We humans are social animals. It is in our nature to live and function within groups. To be free creatures, we need to understand the social conditions under which we live and act. All human groups define themselves in predictable ways. These groups create social requirements and social taboos. They devise ways to identify the "in-group" and the "out-group." They create a collective ideology that justifies the way power is divided and the manner in which wealth is distributed. If we understand ourselves as social beings, we can maximize the quality of our lives and the conditions under which we better ourselves. Insight into social reality is an important, if not crucial, need for freedom and social justice to emerge and thrive.

Anthropology as an Ideal

Professional historians trace human history back some 30,000 to 40,000 years. Anthropologists trace human history back one or two million years and link that history seamlessly with the history of other creatures on our planet. Instruction in anthropology provides the perspective and insight into human reality that no other profession can provide. It gives us a much wider breadth of human reality than most other social professions. It helps remind us how variable human culture is and how hard it is to judge one culture from the perspective of another. Many of the world's problems are traceable to an ethnocentrism that the study of anthropology serves to correct.

Economics as an Ideal

Much of human life is concerned with the striving of humans to meet our needs and fulfill our desires. The study of the conditions and systems in which and through which humans seek to satisfy their needs and fulfill their desires is economics. Most social institutions can be understood much more deeply if we understand them in relationship to economic forces. Much of what happens in human life is a product of economic forces. Wars and depressions often result from economic conditions. Starvation and plenty result from economic conditions. Many, if not most, of the large decisions made by human groups are based on their perception of economic realities. Many of the cruelties and atrocities in the world are highly influenced by economic realities. Money, and all of those goods into which money can be transformed, are crucial determinants of human life. If we do not study and understand economic reality, we are likely to suffer as a result.

Psychology as an Ideal

The nature and operations of the human mind are a central determinant in human life. The scientific study of the mind, therefore, can enable us to maximize our control over our own mental health. We can identify the pathologies of the mind in a way parallel to the way we identify the pathologies of the body. We can study causes and consequences of human mental health and disease. We can train practitioners to use the professional knowledge that psychological research collects in counseling and therapy, thereby helping individuals who are in need of mental assistance. With our professional knowledge, we can assist the courts in determining what prisoners are mentally safe to parole, which persons are of sound mind, and which parents are fit or unfit to rear children. We can advise lawmakers on which deviant social practices are mentally healthy and which are not. In general, psychology contributes to the mental health and optimal mental functioning of humans.

Test the Idea
The Social Sciences and You

Choose one of the social professions you have studied (history, sociology, anthropology, economics, or psychology). Read the above description of the promised aim of the profession. Then assess the extent to which your learning approached that ideal. What is your reasoning is based on?

The Social Sciences as Taught and Practiced

Though the social professions have promised much, clearly the promise falls far short of the ideal. What is more, serious questions can be raised as to whether it is even appropriate to use the word "science" to characterize the status of the social professions. Typically, the social professions are highly "multilogical." Many divergent points of view and frames of reference compete within the social professions. Often it is possible to get contradictory judgments from different practitioners in the social fields.

On the instructional level, we are clearly far from delivering the benefits that have been promised by those who argue for that instruction. To put it one way, few persons learn, as a result of instruction in history, to think historically, or, as a result of instruction in the other social fields, to think sociologically, anthropologically, economically, or psychologically. Instruction is often designed so that persons are certified as professionally knowledgeable in the content of a course when they have done no more than successfully cram for a true/false or a multiple-choice exam.

It is not clear that the study of history, sociology, anthropology, economics, and psychology has led to a better world (that is, with less war, cruelty, human suffering, and injustice). Actually, our belief that we have been educated as a result of the instruction we have received may render us more self-deceived than we would be without that instruction. this might lead us to believe that we know more than we do within a discipline.

The social studies could, and should, make a significant contribution to a better world. Insights into historical, anthropological, and economic thinking are relevant to critical thinking. These professions, however, are rarely taught in such a way as to contribute to the development of critical thought. For example, though sociology as taught emphasizes that humans tend to behave in keeping with the mores and taboos of social groups, rarely are persons given assignments in which they must make explicit and critically assess the mores and taboos of any of the groups to which they belong. The result is that the persons usually leave sociology classes with little insight into the nature of their own social indoctrination. They do not seem to gain in autonomy as a result of instruction. The mores and taboos of their social groups and of the broader society rule them as much at the end of their instruction, as far as we can see, as they did at the beginning. Persons begin and end as consummate conformists in language, dress, values, and behavior. They have not, on the whole, begun to think historically, anthropologically, sociologically, or economically.

The Ideal of the Arts and Humanities:
Music, Painting, Sculpture, Architecture, Dance, Literature, and Philosophy

The professions that exist within the arts and humanities typically have a twofold dimension:

1. A dimension of appreciation and cultivation;
2. A dimension of performance.

The first dimension is much more questionable as an area of professional knowledge, and its contribution to the quality of life is a likely domain for debate. The second dimension is much more objective and demonstrable.

The Promise of the Fine Arts and Literature

The ideal of instruction in the fine arts and literature could briefly be put as follows: There are two consequences that follow from the study of the fine arts and literature with regard to appreciation and cultivation: esthetic appreciation and (high) culture. The fine arts and literature introduce the person to the study of what is beautiful in painting, sculpture, architecture, dance, music, drama, and literature. This study elevates the person's taste and provides insight into objects and experiences not available to those who have not come to appreciate fine art. Without this study, few will see beauty in fine painting, sculpture, dance, music, drama, and literature. Without it, many will prefer the superficial, the trivial, the vulgar, and the stereotyped to that which is truly unique and beautiful. Those who fail to achieve an appreciation of fine arts and literature are denied an important dimension of human experience and fulfillment.

The Reality of Instruction in the Fine Arts and Literature

The real results of instruction in literature and the fine arts seem distant from the above ideal. Consider the following:

•   Though virtually all citizens are given years of instruction in some dimensions of at least some of the fine arts and literature (usually literature), is there not abundant evidence to suggest that most people do not think esthetically or artistically as a result? Attempts to elevate the taste of most people seem to be a failure. Most people, even after a college education, seem to prefer the products of the popular media to the products of the artistic community. What is more, it is hard to determine what percentage of those whose supposed preference for the products of the artistic community is in truth a pretense born of self-delusion, enabling them to feel superior to the common herd.

- What accounts for the fact that most of us cannot give an intelligible explanation for our judgments about what we consider beautiful in painting, sculpture, architecture, dance, music, drama, or literature?

- Isn't it true that most people have not thought about the role of beauty and art in our lives and are not interested in doing so?

- Isn't it true that most people cannot explain how to distinguish an artistic question or issue from any other kind of questions and issues and tend to respond to such questions in superficial and uninterested ways?

- Isn't it true that most people cannot accurately explain any basic concepts or principles of any of the fine arts or literature and do not use those concepts or principles in accounting for the world they experience?

- Finally, isn't it true that few people change their reading habits as a result of instruction in literature and, consequently, are just as unlikely to read important literature at the end of instruction as they were at the beginning?

It seems likely that some exception must be granted to the judgments implied above in the domain of trained performance in the fine arts and literature. The most successful form of instruction in the fine arts and literature is in the area of skill development: basic painting, sculpting, dancing, singing, acting, and writing skills, as well as performing on a musical instrument. It is questionable, however, to what degree most of the performances made possible by this training rise to the level of esthetic or artistic excellence. In any case, only a small minority of persons develops a level of excellence in the performing arts.

The Promise of Philosophy

The profession of philosophy makes an interesting case. On the one hand, it makes some of the most sweeping claims for itself and on the other hand seems to deliver so little. Let us look at the traditional case made for the value of instruction in philosophy.

We as humans are capable of living two kinds of lives: an unreflective or a reflective life. When we live unreflectively, we live as a conformist, trapped in the world of our own unanalyzed desires and social conditioning. We do not live as free agents. We do not choose our basic and ultimate values. We do not understand the actual options implicit in a human life. We behave in ways that are contradictory to the values we say we believe. We do not understand the forces at work in our lives, nor do we understand what is valuable and wasteful in them. Often, as unreflective persons, our lives are shot-through with irrationality, prejudice, and self-delusion.

Conversely, when we live reflectively, we become the agents of our own destiny. We begin to act as genuinely independent persons. We see a world beyond the world of our personal egocentrism and social ethnocentrism. We come to terms with our own basic and ultimate values. We make decisions based on the actual options available to us. We begin to understand the forces at work in our lives and act consciously with respect to them. We discover the power of rationality and use that power to minimize our prejudices as well as our involvement in self-delusion. The study of philosophy lays the foundation for living a reflective life.

The Reality of Philosophy

Clearly, the promise of philosophy is rarely fulfilled. The most likely reason for this discrepancy is that living a reflective life is not the usual focus of the coursework offered in philosophy. Instead, the coursework focuses on highly abstract issues (What is being? What is reality? What is time? What is knowledge? What is beauty? What is freedom?) through the reading of arguments and counter-arguments of a highly abstract sort. The arguments themselves are typically the products of professional philosophers who make their way in the profession by addressing themselves successfully to others who are trained in the "moves" considered appropriate by philosophers in their traditions of abstract argumentation. Philosophers write, except for rare occasions, for a specialized audience (of philosophers) already familiar with a specialized terminology, a range of technical distinctions, and a way of talking, thinking, and arguing uncommon in everyday life. If it is reflective, it is reflective in a special, narrow, and technical sense, in the sense of specialists talking to other specialists in an esoteric language.

Philosophical issues are so posed by professional philosophers, typically, that neither an actual case, nor any possible evidence could settle them. The findings of other professions are often ruled out of the discussion by definition:

"You are turning the question into a sociological (psychological, historical, or biological) one. Let us stick to the philosophical one!" The result is that the issues that philosophers argue about are not really subject to being settled by the discovery of any empirical evidence. The various positions are ones that can be argued for and against without end. Positions in the field are not refuted. They are abandoned when they become professionally unfashionable.

As a result, few persons understand the significance to philosophers of any of the positions taken. The predominant response of an outsider is "Who cares?" A small—typically exceedingly small—minority of persons become philosophy majors who, after some years of graduate study, learn how to argue about a range of philosophical questions and philosophical positions (usually the ones treated as significant in their seminar classes) to the satisfaction of some group of professional philosophers.

The result is that few persons develop the skills of argumentation that would qualify them as plausible contributors to the argumentation in which professional philosophers engage. Few persons see any connection between traditional philosophical argumentation and the conditions of their own lives. Few persons are more reflective about their own lives as a result of taking courses in philosophy. Actually, persons often develop a positive dislike of the subject as a result of their classroom experience and carefully avoid taking additional courses in the subject or doing further reading in it.

Finally, the most ironic fact about the field of philosophy is that it is far from clear that professional philosophers are any more reflective about the manner in which they are living their own lives than are members of any other profession. One of the reasons for this is that, rhetoric to the contrary, philosophers themselves have little or no training in, or professional incentive to engage in, self-reflection. Rather, they are limited by their training to the development and submission of abstract argumentation about abstract issues to professional journals (read then by a small number of professional philosophers). Neither students of, nor professors in, philosophy are expected to come to terms with the concepts, values, or principles implicit in their personal life or behavior. Learning how to think reflectively about one's life seems to be an art rarely focused upon and, therefore, rarely mastered.

Test the Idea
The Ideal and the Real

At the beginning of this chapter, we stated that there are two primary reasons why a significant gap exists between the ideal and the real in academic and professional fields. These are human fallibility and vested interest. Choose two of the subjects focused on in this chapter, and for each answer, complete the following:

1. Reread the section in this chapter that focuses on the subject you have chosen. Write your understanding of the ideal as presented by us. State and elaborate the main points. Then write your understanding of the real as presented by us. Again, state and elaborate the main points.

2. Assuming that we are correct in our view that a gap exists between the ideal and the real in this field of study, how do you think human fallibility and vested interest might play a role in creating this gap?

3. How might human fallibility and vested interest be reduced in this profession?

4. If you do not believe there is a gap between the ideal and the real, how would you articulate the field as an ideal?

Conclusion

As critical thinkers, we must be careful not to assume that things are actually the way they are represented in human life. The human mind has a strong predisposition to fallibility and is highly susceptible to vested interest. Human nature and vested interest are to be found at work in all professions and disciplines, and in all domains of human life. To understand a field of knowledge, including professional knowledge, we must understand it realistically. To contribute to it productively, we must view it as an imperfect construction. To use it effectively in our daily life, we must internalize the mode of thinking integral to the profession, and be aware that when we or others think, we do so with fallible human minds operating in a world of power struggles and vested interest.

This is not an argument for cynicism but, rather, for healthy skepticism. This chapter presented one possible set of beginning points from the perspective of which we can begin to appreciate the limitations of human professional knowledge and of the conditions under which human professional knowledge is constructed and applied.

To the extent that we are committed to the development of fair-mindedness, we are committed to professional knowledge being acquired and used to minimize human suffering, to meet basic human needs, to preserve rather than destroy the environment, to contribute to a more just world, and to serve rational rather than irrational ends.

We are historically far from accomplishing the ideal, and far less consideration is being given to narrowing this large gap than is deserved. We need to grant full credit to the powerful modes of thinking implicit in the best practices of professions, but we also must recognize that, for those modes of thinking to flourish, they must develop out of a realistic critique of present practice.

Chapter 15

Strategic Thinking
Part One

T here are two phases to strategic thinking. The first involves the understanding of an important principle of mental functioning. The second involves using that understanding strategically to produce a mental change in ourselves. In this chapter and the next, we move back and forth between important understandings and strategies based on them. Strategic thinking is the regularization of this practice. From understanding to strategy—and from strategy to self-improvement—is the pattern we are looking for. Using critical thinking strategies systematically to improve our lives is characteristic of the "practicing" thinker.

Understanding and Using Strategic Thinking

If I understand that the mind has three functions—thinking, feeling, and wanting— and that these functions are interdependent—by implication, I realize that any change in one of them is going to produce a parallel shift in the other two. It follows, then, that if I change my thinking, there should be some shift at the level of feeling and desire. For example, if I think you are insulting me, I will feel some resentment and a desire to respond to that insult.

By the same token, if I feel some emotion (say, sadness), my thinking will be influenced. It follows, then, that if I experience an irrational negative emotion or an irrational desire, I should, in principle, be able to identify the irrational thinking that is creating that feeling and desire.

Once I discover irrational thinking, I should be able to modify that thinking by more reasonable thinking. Finding the thinking to be irrational, I should be able to construct a more reasonable substitute. I can then work to replace the irrational with the rational thinking. As the new, reasonable thinking takes root, I should experience some shift in my emotions and desires. More reasonable emotions and desires should emerge from more reasonable thinking.

Now to a specific case. Suppose you are in competition for a promotion with a colleague that you do not like. Suppose also that this colleague is given the promotion and he is now supervising you and criticizing your work. Your interpretation of him and the situation will naturally lead to feelings of resentment on your part and a desire to see your colleague fail. Given your thinking and resultant feelings, it will be very hard for you to be "objective" about events. Part of your negative thinking and feelings may be subconscious and, in any case, you will lack the motivation to be fair.

Much human thinking is subconsciously suppressed. Through active work, however, you can bring it to the surface of your conscious mind. You can do this by first recognizing that underlying every irrational feeling is based in an irrational thought process. By figuring out exactly what feeling you are experiencing, you can begin to trace the feeling to the thinking that is leading to it. Hence, as in the case above, you should be able to spell out the probable unconscious thoughts that are fueling your irrational jealousy of, and anger toward, your colleague.

You will usually find that suppressed thoughts are highly egocentric and infantile. These covert thoughts are what often cause negative emotions. If you can determine the irrational thinking that is driving your emotions and behavior, you have a better chance of changing the emotions and behavior by working on the unreasonable thinking that is causing them.

Whenever you feel your irrational jealousy emerging, you deliberately think through the egocentric logic of jealousy. You do it again and again until you find productive, rational feelings and desires emerging. Since many of the most powerful thoughts, feelings, and desires, though, are unconscious and primitive, we should not expect ourselves to be able to completely displace all irrationality. Yet, by making our irrational thoughts explicit, we can better attack them with reason and good sense. We can be better persons with healthier emotions and desires if we learn how to undermine, and thereby diminish, our irrational emotions and desires.

Now let's look at how we proceeded from understanding to strategy and from strategy to improvement in the example above:

The understanding.   The human mind has three interrelated functions: thinking, feeling, and desiring, or wanting. These functions are interrelated and interdependent.

The strategy.   Whenever you find yourself having what may be irrational emotions or desires, figure out the thinking that probably is generating those emotions and desires. Then develop rational thinking with which to replace the irrational thinking you are using in the situation. Finally, whenever you feel the irrational negative emotions, rehearse the rational thinking, using this format:

1. Explicitly state what the feelings and desires are.

2. Figure out the irrational thinking leading to them.

3. Figure out how to transform the irrational thinking into rational thinking— thinking that makes sense in context.

4. Whenever you feel the negative emotion, repeat to yourself the rational thoughts you decided you needed to replace the irrational thoughts, until you feel the rational emotions that accompany reasonable thinking.

In this chapter and the next, we briefly review some key concepts, principles, and theories discussed thus far in the book, followed by examples of strategic thinking based on the examples. The aim is *illustration*, not comprehensiveness.

We hope you will develop ideas of your own for improvement. There are no formulas for a simple and painless life. Like you, we are working on the problem of targeting and removing our defective thinking. Like you, we are working to become more rational and fair-minded persons. We must recognize the challenge that this development represents.

As with all forms of personal development, development of thinking means transforming deeply ingrained habits. It can happen only when we take responsibility for our own growth as rational persons. Learning to think strategically must become a lifelong habit. It must replace the habit most of us have of thinking impulsively, of allowing our thinking to gravitate toward its own, typically unconscious, egocentric agenda.

Are you willing to make self-reflection a lifelong habit? Are you willing to become a strategic thinker? Are you willing to unearth the irrational thoughts, feelings, and desires that lurk in the dark corners of your mind? Are you willing to develop a compassionate mind? If so, you should find these two chapters on strategic thinking useful.

Components of Strategic Thinking

Before proceeding to examples of strategic thinking, please note that strategic thinking has two additional components. You will have these to add to your intellectual repertoire as you seek to implement any of the strategies outlined in this chapter:

1. **An identifying component.** You must be able to figure out when your thinking is irrational or flawed.

2. **An intellectual action component.** You must actively engage and challenge the acts of your own mind.

In the intellectual action component, you must figure out four things:

1. What is actually going on in the situation as it stands.
2. Your options for action.
3. A justifiable rationale for choosing one of the options.
4. Ways of reasoning with yourself when you are being unreasonable, or ways of reducing the power of your irrational state of mind.

Test the Idea
An Introduction to Strategic Thinking

Identify an area of your personal or professional life in which you use thinking that is possibly irrational. If you are having trouble, think of a situation in which you felt a powerful negative emotion and had difficulty dealing with it. Write out the answers to these questions:

1. What is actually going on in the situation as it stands? Elaborate on the details.
2. What are your options for action?
3. Which option seems best? How do you know? Can you view the situation in any other competing ways?
4. Construct the reasoning you need to rehearse when you are again in this situation or a similar situation. If you have trouble doing this activity, read the example in the next section.

The Beginnings of Strategic Thinking

Let us now consider some basic concepts, principles, and theories of critical thinking, providing examples of strategic thought as implied by those principles. In each case, we will start with a key idea. We then will explore strategies for improving thinking based on that idea. We will begin with a more formal approach to the example given at the beginning of this chapter.

Key Idea #1: Thoughts, Feelings, and Desires are Interdependent

As noted already, it is important to recognize that the mind is composed of three functions: thinking, feeling, and desiring (or wanting). Wherever one of these functions is present, the other two are present as well. And these three functions are continually influencing and being influenced by one another. Our thinking influences our feelings and desires. Our feelings influence our thinking and desires. Our desires influence our thinking and feeling. We cannot immediately change our desires or feelings. It is only thinking that we have direct access to. It makes no sense for someone to order you to feel what you do not feel or to desire what you do not desire. We do not change feelings by substituting other feelings, or desires by substituting other desires. But someone can suggest that we consider a new way to think. We can role-play new thoughts, but not new emotions or desires. It is possible to reason within a point of view with which we do not agree. By rethinking our thinking, we may change our thinking. And when our thinking changes, our feelings and desires will shift in accordance with our thinking.

Strategic Idea

With a basic understanding of the interrelation among thoughts, feelings, and desires, we should be able to routinely notice and evaluate our feelings. If, for example, I experience a degree of anger that I sense may be unreasonable, I should be able to determine whether the anger is or is not rational. I should be able to evaluate the rationality of my anger by evaluating the thinking that gave rise to it. Has someone truly wronged me, or am I misreading the situation? Was this wrong intentional or unintentional? Are there ways to view the situation other than the way I am viewing it? Am I giving a fair hearing to these other ways? By pursuing these questions, I can come closer to a rational view of the situation.

Even if my way of viewing the situation is justified, and I do have good reason to feel some anger, it does not follow that I have acted reasonably, given the full facts of the situation. I may have good reason to feel angry, but not to act irrationally as a result of that anger.

This strategy might be roughly outlined as follows:

1. Identify a feeling you have experienced that you suspect might be irrational (a feeling such as irritability, resentment, arrogance, or depression).
2. What thinking would account for the feeling? There may be more than one possibility here. If so, figure out which possibility is most likely.
3. Determine the extent to which the thinking is reasonable. Pay close attention to the reasons you give to justify the thinking. Is it possible that these are not your actual reasons? Can you think of any other motives you might have? Consider alternative interpretations of the situation.
4. If you conclude that the feeling is irrational, express precisely why you think so.
5. Construct thinking that would represent a rational response in the situation. Actively attack the irrational thinking with the thinking that is rational. Actively rehearse the thinking that represents a rational response.

For example, suppose I read an article about a fatal disease and come to the conclusion, from reading the symptoms, that I probably have the disease. I then become depressed. Late at night I think about how I will soon be dead, and I feel more and more depressed as a result. Clearly, the irrational feeling is the depression I am feeling. It is irrational because, until a doctor examines me and confirms a diagnosis, I have no good reason for believing that I actually have the disease in question. My irrational thinking is something like this:

> I have all the symptoms described in the article. So I must have this awful disease. I am going to die soon. My life is now meaningless. Why is this happening to me? Why me?

In the same situation, rational thinking would be something like this:

> Yes, it is possible that I have this disease, given that I seem to have what appear to be symptoms of it, but very often the same symptoms are compatible with many different bodily states. Given this, it is not likely that I have this rare disease, and, in any case, it will do me no good to jump to conclusions. Still, as a matter of prudence and for peace of mind, I should go to the doctor as soon as possible to get a professional diagnosis. Until I get this diagnosis, I should focus my thinking on other, more useful things to think about than an unsubstantiated possibility.

Whenever I find myself feeling depressed about what the article said, I rerun the rational thinking through my mind and give myself a good talking-to as well:

> Hey, don't go off the deep end. Remember, you will see the doctor on Monday. Don't put yourself through unnecessary pain. Remember, there are probably a lot of possibilities to account for your symptoms. Come back down to earth. Remember the Mother Goose rhyme, "For every problem under the sun, there is a solution or there is none. If there be one seek till you find it. If there be none, never mind it." Don't wallow in misery when it doesn't do any good and only diminishes the quality of your life today.

> And now, how about scheduling some tennis for this afternoon, and a good movie for tonight?

Test the Idea
Focusing on the Relationship Between Thoughts, Feelings, and Desires I

Focusing on a negative feeling you sometimes or often experience, go through the five-point strategy outlined in the section you just read, writing out your answers in detail.

A similar approach can be taken to changing irrational behavior grounded in irrational desires or motivations:

1. Identify the questionable behavior (behavior that is getting you in trouble, causing problems for you, or causing problems for someone else).

2. Identify the precise thinking leading to that behavior. What is the thinking that is generating the motivation to act in this manner?

3. Analyze the extent to which the thinking is justified, without leaving out any significant relevant information.

4. If the thinking is irrational, develop thinking that would be reasonable in this situation.

5. Actively attack the unreasonable thinking with reasonable thinking.

We might use many examples here to illustrate our point. But let's choose one that deals with a large segment of irrational human behavior. Here we are thinking of the many times when people abandon a commitment to change a bad habit because they are unwilling to work through the pain or discomfort that accompanies changing habits. Here's how the irrational behavior arises:

1. We notice that we have developed some bad habit that we would like to end. We realize, quite reasonably, that we shall have to make a change in our behavior. This could involve giving up any of the following habits: smoking, drinking too much alcohol, eating foods that are not good for us, not exercising enough, spending too much time watching television, spending too much money, not studying until just before an examination, and so on.

2. We make a resolution to change our bad habit.

3. For a short time, we do change our behavior, but during that time we experience pain or discomfort. These negative emotions discourage us. So we give up.

The irrational feelings are not the sensations of pain or discomfort. These reactions are to be expected. The irrational feeling is discouragement that emerges from the discomfort and causes us to give up our resolution to change. This feeling is a result of irrational thinking (probably subconscious), which can be put into words roughly as:

> I should be able to change my behavior without experiencing any pain or discomfort, even if I have had this habit for years. This pain is too much. I can't stand it. Furthermore, I really don't see how my changed behavior is helping much. I just don't see much progress given all of the sacrificing I am doing. Forget it. It's not worth it.

This thinking makes no sense. Why should we expect to experience no pain or discomfort when changing a habit? Indeed, the reverse is true. Discomfort or pain of some kind is an essential by-product of going through a process of withdrawal from almost any habit. The appropriate rational thinking is something like this:

> Whenever I am trying to change a habit, I must expect to feel discomfort, and even pain. Habits are hard for anyone to break. And the only way I can expect to replace the habit with rational behavior is to endure the necessary suffering that comes with change. If I am not willing to endure the discomfort that goes hand-in-hand with breaking a bad habit, I'm not really committed to change. Rather than expecting no pain, I must welcome it as a sign of real change. Instead of thinking "Why should I have to endure this?" I rehearse this thinking: "Enduring this is the price I must pay for success." I must apply the motto: No pain, no gain.

Test the Idea
Focusing on the Relationship Between Thoughts, Feelings, and Desires 2

Focusing on some questionable behavior you sometimes engage in, go through the five-point strategy as outlined in the section you just read and write out your answers in detail. As soon as you have a chance, experiment with making some change in your behavior that you have wanted to make. See if you can succeed now with new thinking at your disposal. Don't forget the essential ingredient of predicting, and accepting, discomfort or pain as a likely hurdle in the process of change.

A Caveat: Powerful Emotions That Seem Disconnected from Thought

Sometimes we find ourselves struggling with emotions or passions that seem disconnected from thought. At least, we may not know what thinking to trace the emotion to. Whatever the exact thought is, it seems unconscious, primitive, and powerful. For example, suppose a man or woman feels powerful urges to have sex with persons other than their spouse and suppose further that these urges become very intense when alone with a particular person. The urge may be experienced as irresistible at the moment. How do we reconstruct the primitive thinking at the root of such urges? Very possibly the thinking may be different for women and men. The common denominator might be suggested by the primitive desire to prove our sexual attractiveness and therefore reinforce feelings of being "masculine" or "feminine." As Freud demonstrated, the thinking of the unconscious mind may be very hard to plumb. It may take years to uncover and bring to consciousness deeply primitive unconscious thoughts. And even then it may be hard to be sure we are correct in our analysis. In cases like these, we should experiment with a variety of strategies. If the urge results in consequences harmful to another person, then we should harness the thinking of our conscience, making the harm as explicit as we can to ourselves, and keeping that ethical logic before our minds, like a mantra, especially for those times when we actively experience the urge. If obeying the urge does not result in any obvious harmful consequences other than to violate a social convention, then the solution may be to act on the urge, but only in private. In many societies of the past, many dissenters violated social norms and conventions in private.

Key Idea #2: There is a Logic to This, and You Can Figure It Out

As a critical thinker, you approach every dimension of learning as requiring the construction of a system of meanings in your mind that makes sense and enables you to make logical inferences about the subject of your focus. We use the expression "the logic of..." to designate such a system. As a critical thinker, you recognize that there is a logic to academic subjects (a logic to chemistry, physics, mathematics, and sociology). There is also a logic to questions, problems, and issues (a logic to economic questions, social problems, controversial issues, and personal problems). There is a logic to situations. There is a logic to personal behavior. There are explicit and implicit logics, admitted and hidden logics. There is a logic to warfare and a logic to peace, a logic to offense and a logic to defense. There are political logics, social logics, institutional logics, and cultural logics.

There is a logic to the way the human mind works, a logic to power, a logic to domination, to mass persuasion, to propaganda, to manipulation. There is a logic to social conventions and a logic to ethical concepts and principles. There is theo-logic, bio-logic, and psycho-logic. There is even patho-logic (the logic of disease and malfunctioning). Each can be figured out by the disciplined, critical mind.

Using the elements of thought to figure out the basic logic of something is a practice to which we hope you are becoming accustomed. It is a powerful strategy for achieving perspective and gaining leverage or command. In this section, we confine ourselves largely to the logic of personal life.

In every human situation or context, multiple systems of meaning are usually present. As a critical thinker, you engage in a process of figuring out why your associates, friends, clients, children, spouses, and employers relate to you in the way they do. This is true because everyone makes sense of the situations of their own life in some way. To do this, they must, at least implicitly, make use of the eight elements of thought. If you can identify the elements of others' thinking, you can better understand where they are coming from.

You can assume all of the following:

- Everyone you interact with has purposes or objectives they are trying to achieve.
- Everyone has problems that relate to those purposes.
- They are basing their reasoning on some information.
- They come to conclusions based on that information, conclusions that may or may not be logical in the circumstance.
- They take certain things for granted, or make certain assumptions.
- They use certain key ideas or concepts in their thinking.
- They think within a point of view, within a frame of reference that may keep them from seeing things objectively.
- There are consequences that result from their thinking.

By assuming that there is always a logic to what happens not only in the world but also in the mind of those who operate in the world, you are empowered in your pursuit of understanding. You therefore are led to question superficial explanations and seek deeper ones. You are led to question:

- the goals and purposes of those you interact with,

- the way they define their questions and problems,

- the assumptions they are making,

- the information they are using to support their arguments,

- the conclusions (inferences) they come to,

- the concepts that guide their thinking,

- the implications inherent in their thinking, and

- the point of view from which they are looking at situations.

- Just as you question the logic of the thinking of those around you, you also question the logic of your own thinking.

Strategic Idea

When you realize that there is a logic to everything, you can think through the logic of the situations in which you find yourself. You can apply this principle in a number of directions, depending on your precise goals and objectives. Consider the questioning "inner voice" of the activist thinker focused on understanding the logic of his or her own thinking or the logic of others' thinking:

1. **Questioning goals, purposes, and objectives.** What is the central purpose of this person? This group? Myself? I realize that problems in thinking are often the result of a mistake at the level of basic purpose. I realize that I must develop skill in shifting my goals and purposes. I realize that I must be clear about my purposes, about others' purposes, about alternative purposes. I realize that I can always question my purposes, as well as the purposes of others.

2. **Questioning the way in which questions are framed, problems are posed, and issues are expressed.** What issues have to be addressed in this situation? What is the key question I should raise? I realize that if the problem is misconceptualized, it will not be solved. If I have misconceived the question, I will not find the answer. Furthermore, I understand the value of sticking to the question at hand, of not wandering to other issues before effectively dealing with the question at issue. I want to be aware of situations in which others are failing to stick to the question at issue.

3. **Questioning information and sources of information.** What information do I need to gather to figure out what is going on? Where can I get it? How can I test it? What information are others using? Is it accurate? Is it relevant to the issue at hand? I realize that if I lack the information I need to effectively deal with this issue, my reasoning will be impaired. I also understand the problems inherent in using incorrect information in reasoning.

4. **Questioning interpretations or conclusions.** What interpretations, judgments, or conclusions are crucial to this situation? What conclusions am I coming to?

What conclusions are others coming to? I understand that there is often more than one way to interpret situations. I value the ability to consider multiple ways to do so, weighing the pros and cons of each, before coming to a decision. I also want to be able to assess the quality of the conclusions that others are coming to.

5. **Questioning the assumptions being made.** What is being taken for granted? Is this a reasonable assumption? What would be reasonable to assume in this situation? I recognize that, because assumptions usually are unconscious in thinking, it is often difficult to determine what is being taking for granted. I want to be able to identify and correct my faulty assumptions. I also want to be able to accurately assess the assumptions others are using.

6. **Questioning the concepts being used.** What main ideas or concepts are being used? What implications follow from this idea? What main ideas, or concepts, are crucial to making sense of this situation? I understand that whenever we think, we use concepts, and the way we use them both determines and is determined by the way we think in situations. Therefore, I must continually raise my awareness of the way concepts are being used, both by myself and by others.

7. **Questioning the point(s) of view being considered.** What point(s) of view have to be considered? Have I failed to take into account some point(s) of view that are relevant to understanding and thinking-through the issue? I realize that good reasoning often involves considering more than one way of looking at things. I therefore understand the value in being able to consider issues from multiple viewpoints. I recognize when others are unable or unwilling to see things from alternative viewpoints.

8. **Questioning implications.** Given the reasoning I am doing, what are the likely implications, positive and negative? What are the implications if I reason to this conclusion versus that conclusion? I understand that, whenever I reason, implications follow from my reasoning. Thus, I need to think through the potential consequences of decisions I am considering. I also question the implications of others' thinking.

Just as we can seek to understand our own logic, we can seek to understand the logic of others. Perhaps an example will be helpful here. Imagine a person whose everyday life is based on the following thinking:

> The simple pleasures are the key to happiness: sleeping, gardening, walking, nature, telling jokes, listening to music, reading books. Do not seek more power or money than is necessary to get by. Do not seek to change the world in significant ways because no matter what you do, nothing much will change. The people at the top will always be corrupt and they will always have the power to hurt you. The large masses of people are lazy and irresponsible and always will be. Do not get involved in the affairs of others. Avoid gossip. Don't worry about what other people have. Don't worry about injustice; those who do unjust acts will naturally suffer negative consequences. Take things as they come.

> Don't take yourself too seriously. Be ready to laugh at yourself. Avoid conflict. When you
> do a job, do it well. Value your friends and support them. They will help you when you
> need them.

It would be of no use to attempt to persuade this person to become active in any social, political, or moral cause. If you understand the basic logic of her thinking, you recognize that her response will always be the same: "You can't fight city hall. Don't worry about it. Those people will get their just deserts. Stay out of the battle. You can't do any good. And you probably will do yourself some harm."

The logic of this thinking has many implications, some positive, and some negative. On the positive side, this thinking leads this person to enjoy life far beyond that enjoyed by most people, as she is continually seeing ordinary events—which most people treat as unimportant and insignificant—as objects of pleasure and delight. For example, the simple act of looking out the window at a bird on a tree limb engenders inner warmth. On the other hand, she assumes no ethical responsibility for any action that is not directly within her immediate control. The logic of her thinking makes her indifferent to the fate of others not immediately connected to her. Though she is a reader, she reads only fiction and that only for distraction and amusement.

Now let us put our commentary into the logic of this thinking in such a way as to pin down the elements of the logic inherent in it:

1. The main goal or purpose of this person is to enjoy life and to avoid involvement in any painful struggle. The first part of this purpose is fully justifiable because people have a right to enjoy life. The second part is questionable, and there is more than one way to evaluate it. Here is one reasonable way: On the one hand, insofar as this person would expect others to be concerned when injustice was done to her, she is obligated to help others who experience injustice. On the other hand, if she would not expect others to be at all concerned about any injustice she might experience, she is justified in not concerning herself with injustice being done to others.

2. The main issue or question for this person is something like this: How can I arrange the affairs of my life in such a way as to maximally enjoy the simple things of life and avoid involvement in any problems beyond those experienced by my immediate family? In evaluating this question, the same reasoning would apply as that expressed in evaluating the purpose (in number 1 above).

3. The main information this person used in pursuing her goals was information about immediate matters of daily life. Again, the use of this information is partially justified. It is justified in that this particular information enables the thinker to achieve her purpose. However, the thinker fails to use information in her thinking that would enable her to contribute to making the world more just (information about the large number of people who are acting every day to improve conditions in the world, information about the large numbers of people who could be helped through some basic acts of kindness, and so on).

4. The main assumptions this person uses in thinking are: Simple pleasures are always available to everyone and are more important than socially praised possessions; in the world of power, nothing ever really changes; and only immediate family members have any moral claims on us. Again, the first assumption is justifiable for the reason stated in purpose (number 1 above). The second assumption is simply not true. Even though power structures are difficult to change, they certainly can be changed through dedication and hard work. Many examples can be cited to support this point. With respect to the third assumption, this person would most likely expect others, outside her immediate family, to help her if some injustice were being done to her. Therefore, a likely unconscious assumption in her thinking is: "If some injustice is being done to me, I expect others to help me out. After all, I have a right to justice."

5. Some of the main concepts this person uses in thinking are these principles: The best way to live is to enjoy life's simple pleasures; no matter what you do, you can't change city hall; and people who behave in unethical ways will suffer the law of natural consequences. The first concept or principle, concerned with "simple pleasures," is being used justifiably because it helps this person enjoy the small pleasures in life, to appreciate all of the many simple everyday joys. The second principle, "you can't change city hall," is not logical because every day, through diligence and perseverance, people help bring about improvement within institutions. The third principle, involving "natural consequences," is also illogical because many people are behaving unethically each and every day and suffering not at all while they are causing suffering to innocent others. By using this idea in thinking, this person irrationally justifies her unwillingness to help make the world a more humane place.

6. The main conclusion (inference) this person comes to is: I can best enjoy life by keeping to myself and to my immediate family, by surrounding myself with the things I like, by taking time every day to appreciate the small joys that life brings. Given the information this person uses in her thinking, her conclusions logically follow. Because she does not take into account information that would imply an ethical obligation to help reduce injustice, she concludes that she has no ethical obligations outside her immediate family.

7. The points of view of this person are: seeing every day as uncomplicated and filled with simple delights; and seeing her ethical obligations as applying only to her immediate family. This person is concerned only with her own point of view, and those of her family members, but not of others.

8. The main implications of this person's thinking are that she will appreciate the many small pleasures in life, but do nothing to contribute to the well-being of society. This person is concerned only with the implications that come with enjoying life. She is unconcerned about her doing nothing to help make the world a more just and humane place within which to live.

Test the Idea
Focusing on the Logic of Someone's Thinking

Think of someone that you know well—a spouse, parent, a child, an employer, or a friend. Try to figure out the logic of this person's thinking by focusing on the eight elements of his or her thought. Humans in many circumstances and contexts act with a hidden agenda. As a consequence, human behavior is often other than it seems to be. After figuring out the logic of this person's thinking, try to assess the thinking that he or she does within each element. Complete this template:

1. The main purpose of this person is... I think this person is or is not justified in pursuing this purpose because...

2. The main issue for this person, and its related question, is... I think this question is/is not worth pursuing because...

3. The main information this person uses in pursuing his or her goals is... This information should/should not be used in this person's thinking because...

4. The main assumptions this person uses in thinking are... These assumptions are/are not justifiable because...

5. The main concepts this person uses in thinking are... These concepts are/are not being used justifiably because...

6. The main conclusions this person comes to are... These conclusions are/are not logical because...

7. The point of view of this person is... This person is/is not fully considering the relevant viewpoints of others because...

8. The main implications of this person's thinking are... This person is/is not concerned about these implications because...

Key Idea #3: For Thinking to Be of High Quality, We Must Routinely Assess it

Consistently high-quality thinking routinely assesses itself for flaws and then improves itself by replacing low-quality thinking with higher-quality thinking. As rational persons strongly motivated to improve our thinking, we not only think, but we think about our thinking from a critical vantage point. We routinely apply universal intellectual standards to our thought. That is, we continually strive to think in a clear, precise, accurate, relevant, logical, broad, deep, significant, and defensible ways. We learn how to check our thinking regularly using these criteria.

Strategic Idea

As disciplined thinkers, we routinely apply intellectual standards to our thinking so as to assess and improve its quality. Consider the voice of a thinker focused on applying intellectual standards:

- Focusing on clarity in thinking. Am I clear about my thinking? Can I state it precisely? Can I elaborate on it in detail? Can I give an example from my experience? Can I illustrate it with an analogy or a metaphor? What about the thinking being expressed to me? Should I ask for the main point? Do I need an elaboration? Do I need an example? An illustration?

- Focusing on precision in thinking. Am I providing enough details for the other person to fully comprehend my meaning? Do I need more detail and specifics on the thinking of so-and-so?

- Focusing on accuracy in thinking. Am I certain that the information I am using is accurate? If not, how can I check to see whether it is? How can I check on the accuracy of the information in this book?

- Focusing on relevance in thinking. How does my point bear on the issue at hand? Or does it? How does my statement relate to what he just said? How is his question related to the question we are discussing?

- Focusing on logicalness in thinking. Given the information I have gathered, what is the most logical conclusion I can come to in this situation? Or what is one of several logical conclusions? I'm not sure whether what he is saying is logical. What is another feasible conclusion? What is another conclusion that makes more sense? What are the logical consequences that might follow from this decision?

- Focusing on breadth in thinking. I wonder whether I need to consider another viewpoint, or other relevant viewpoints, before coming to a conclusion? In thinking-through the issue at hand, what are the points of view that I am obligated to consider if I am reasoning in a disciplined manner?

- Focusing on depth in thinking. What are the complexities inherent in this issue? Am I inadvertently dealing with a complex issue in a superficial way? How can I dig beneath the surface of the situation and deal with what is most problematic in it?

- Focusing on justification in thinking. Is his purpose justified? Is my purpose justified, given the circumstances, or is it somehow unfair or self-contradictory or self-defeating, given the facts? How is he using these terms? Is he using them in keeping with established usage? Is he stretching the meaning of the key words beyond the limit of their meaningfulness?

Test the Idea
Focusing on Intellectual Standards in Questioning

In order to improve your ability to ask important and relevant questions in everyday life situations, focus on one intellectual standard per week and try to ask as many questions as you can think of on a daily basis relevant to that standard. Focus on each of the categories of questions described above.

The idea is to ask these questions so often in that week that you begin to bring them explicitly into your thinking (so that asking them becomes more intuitive to you). By practicing asking them for a week, you will be more likely to ask them when they are relevant to the context you are in.

If, for example, you are focusing on clarity in thinking, you will ask the following kinds of questions:

Am I clear about my thinking? Can I state it precisely? Can I elaborate on it in detail? Can I give an example from my experience? Can I illustrate it with an analogy or a metaphor? What about the thinking being expressed to me? Should I ask for the main point? Do I need an elaboration? Do I need an example? An illustration?

Chapter 16

Strategic Thinking
Part Two

A s we learned in the previous chapter, strategic thinking is based on a two-part process that involves *understanding a key idea and developing a strategy for action based on that idea.*

This chapter is devoted to egocentrism—the most significant barrier to development of critical thinking. Chapter 15 covered the first three key ideas, so we begin with key idea #4.

Key Idea #4: Our Native Egocentrism Is a Default Mechanism

To understand the human mind, we must recognize its essential duality. On the one hand, the human mind has an instinctive tendency toward irrationality. On the other hand, it has a native capacity for rationality. To effectively take command of our mind, we must develop the ability to (1) monitor the mind's tendency toward egocentric or irrational thinking, and (2) attack it with corrective rational thought.

Our irrational mind is not concerned with the rights or needs of others. It has no ethical dimension to it. Our rational mind, properly developed, is both intellectual and ethical. It has intellectual command of itself and ethical sensitivity as well. Intellectual skill and fair-mindedness are joined into one integrated mode of thinking. When our rational mind is underdeveloped or not engaged, however, our native egocentrism functions as a default mechanism. If we don't control it, it controls us!

Strategic Idea

It is possible for us to use our knowledge of egocentric thought to combat it. The more we know about human egocentrism, the more we can recognize it in ourselves, and thus the more we can attack or overrule it. One of the ways to achieve this end is to develop the habit of analyzing the logic of our own thinking. We model the inner voice of the critical thinker using this strategy and the following questions:

1. **We can analyze our goals and purposes.** What am I really after in this situation? Are my goals reasonable? Am I acting in good faith? Do I have any hidden agenda?

2. **We can question the way we define problems and issues.** Is this a reasonable way to put the question at issue? Am I biasing or loading the question by the way I am putting it? Am I framing the question in a self-serving way? Am I asking a question simply to pursue my selfish interests?

3. **We can assess the information base of our thinking.** What information am I basing my thinking on? Is that a legitimate source of information? Is there another source of information I need to consider? Am I considering all the relevant information, or only the relevant information that supports my view? Am I distorting the weight of the information in a self-serving way, blowing some of the information out of proportion while diminishing the value of other relevant information? Am I egocentrically refusing to check on the accuracy of some information because, if I find out it is not accurate, I will be forced to change my view?

4. **We can rethink our conclusion or interpretation.** Am I coming to an illogical conclusion because it is in my interest to do so? Am I refusing to look at this situation more logically because I simply don't want to, because if I do, I will have to behave differently?

5. **We can analyze the ideas or concepts we are using in our thinking.** How am I using the ideas most basic to my thinking? Am I using words in keeping with educated usage, or am I slanting or misusing some words to serve my vested interest?

6. **We can identify and check our assumptions.** What am I assuming or taking for granted? Are those assumptions reasonable? Are they in any way self-serving or one-sided? Am I making egocentric assumptions in my thinking (such as, "Everyone always dumps on me," or "Life should be without problems," or "There's nothing I can do; I'm trapped")? Are my expectations of others reasonable or am I assuming a double standard?

7. **We can analyze our point of view.** Am I refusing to consider another relevant point of view so I can maintain my own self-serving view? Am I fully taking into account the viewpoint of others, or am I just going through the motions of "hearing" without actually listening to what others are saying? Put another way, am I honestly trying to understand the situation from another perspective, or am I merely trying to win an argument, to score points?

8. **We can follow through on the implications of our thinking.** Am I genuinely thinking through the implications, or possible consequences, of my thoughts and behavior, or would I rather not consider them? Am I avoiding thinking through implications because I don't want to know what they are (because then I will be forced to change my thinking, to think more rationally about the situation)?

Now let's walk through an example that suggests how a person might use reasonable thinking to detect irrational thought. What follows is a snapshot of the thinking of a hypothetical person as he examines a recent situation in his life. The numbered items 1 through 8 correspond to the list above.

The situation is as follows: I was in the video store on Friday night with my wife, and we were choosing a movie to watch that evening. She wanted to watch a romance movie, and I wanted to watch an action movie. I gave her all the reasons I could think of why the movie I wanted to watch was better. But now I realize that I was simply trying to manipulate her into going along with me. As I was giving her all of these good reasons for going along with my movie, all the while I was subconsciously thinking, I should get to watch what I want to. I don't like romantic movies, so I shouldn't have to watch them. In addition, since I'm paying for the movie, I should get to choose it:

1. In this situation, my purpose was to convince my wife that my reasoning for choosing the movie I wanted was better than her reasoning. I realize my purpose was egocentric because, now that I think of it, my reasoning wasn't any better than hers. My true purpose was to get what I wanted, even if I had to manipulate my wife to get it.

2. The key question I was posing was, "What do I need to say to convince (or really manipulate) her into going along with my choice of movies?" I now realize this question was egocentric because it is unethical to act in bad faith toward anyone, especially toward someone you say you love. My question was completely selfish and shows that I really didn't care at all what my wife wanted.

3. The main information I used in my reasoning was the fact that I was paying for the movie, as well as information about how best to manipulate my wife. This would mainly be what I have learned about her through my experience. For example, she usually goes along with me if I push hard enough, because she likes to please me. Also, I have learned that if I tell her that she always ends up liking the movies I choose, that usually convinces her to go along with me. Now that I think about it, I don't know if she really likes those movies or just says she does to please me. I know that I used this information in an egocentric way because I wasn't trying to look at information that would support our choosing her movie, just information to support my position. I wasn't noticing how I was leaving out relevant information that would support her position.

4. The main conclusions I came to were that we should choose the movie I wanted to watch, and that she probably would like it, too. I realize these conclusions were irrational because they were based completely on selfish thinking and just enabled me to feel good about choosing the movie I wanted.

5. The key concepts I was using in my thinking were manipulation, because my main purpose was to manipulate her into going along with me, and the principle, "Whoever is paying for the movie should get to choose what we will watch." I realize I wasn't justified in using these concepts in my thinking, because they were completely self-serving and caused me to act in an unethical way.

6. The main assumptions I was using in my thinking were: "If I can effectively manipulate my wife, I can get what I want. If my wife acts like she likes the movies I choose, she does like them. Whoever pays for the movie should get to choose it." I realize these assumptions were egocentrically formulated because they are not based in sound reasoning. And they were enabling me to justify my unethical behavior.

7. The point of view from which I was reasoning was in seeing my wife as someone to be easily manipulated, and seeing myself as justified in choosing the movie because I was paying for it. I realize these points of view were egocentric because I never can be justified in acting in bad faith toward someone I love.

8. The implications that followed from my thinking were that I was able to manipulate her, but she probably resented having to go along with my movie choice. Also, she was not able to enjoy the movie she wanted because I insisted on having my way. I realize these implications would not have occurred if I had been thinking and behaving rationally. If I had been rational, I would have thought and behaved in a way that demonstrated that I respected the desires of my wife. She would have enjoyed the time we spent together more by getting to watch what she wanted, and knowing that I was willing to do something for her rather than always expecting her to sacrifice for me.

Test the Idea
Focusing on the Logic of Your Egocentric Thinking

Identify a situation you were recently in that, in looking back on the situation, you realize you were probably irrational. Go through each of the elements of your reasoning as described in the strategy above, analyzing the justifiability of your thinking and behavior. Try to be as honest as you possibly can, remembering that our egocentrism is always ready to deceive us into thinking we are honest when we are not. Complete the following statements:

1. The situation was as follows...
2. In this situation, my purpose was...
3. I realize my *purpose* was egocentric because...
4. The key *question* I was posing was...
5. I realize this question was egocentric because...
6. The main *information* I used in my reasoning was...
7. I know that I used this information in an egocentric way because...
8. The main *conclusions* I came to were...
9. I realize these conclusions were irrational because...
10. The key *concepts* I was using in my thinking were...
11. I realize I was not justified in using these concepts in this way, and that I was irrationally distorting them, because...
12. The main *assumptions* I was using in my thinking were...
13. I realize these assumptions were egocentrically formulated because...
14. The *point of view* from which I was reasoning was...
15. I realize this point of view was egocentric because...
16. The *implications* that followed from my thinking were...
17. I realize these implications would not have occurred if I had been thinking and behaving rationally. If I had been rational, I would have thought and behaved in the following way...

Key Idea #5: We Must Become Sensitive to the Egocentrism of Those Around Us

Because human beings are, by nature, egocentric and few are aware of how to exercise control over their egocentric thinking, it is important that we develop the ability to recognize egocentrism in the thinking of those around us. We must recognize, though, that even highly egocentric people sometimes act rationally, so we must be careful not to stereotype. Nevertheless, it is reasonable to expect that everyone will behave irrationally sometimes, so we must learn to evaluate behavior in an open-minded, yet realistic, way. When we understand the logic of egocentrism, when we become adept at identifying its self-serving patterns, we can begin to master it.

We draw a distinction between attacking our own irrationality and attacking that of others. Often with others we must bite our tongue, as it were, and distance ourselves from people who are fundamentally irrational. Or, at least, we must learn to deal with their egocentrism indirectly. Few people will thank us for pointing out egocentrism in their thinking. The more egocentric people are, the more resistant they are to owning it. The more power egocentric people have, the more dangerous they are. As rational persons, then, we learn to better deal with the irrationality of others rather than be controlled or manipulated by it.

When thinking irrationally, people find it difficult to think within the perspective of another. We unconsciously refuse to consider information that contradicts our ego-centered views. We unconsciously pursue purposes and goals that are not justifiable. We use assumptions in our thinking that are based in our own prejudices and biases. Unknowingly, we are systematically engaging in self-deception to avoid recognizing our egocentrism in operation.

Another problem relevant to dealing with the egocentric reactions of others is our own egocentric tendency. When we interact with others who are relating to us egocentrically, our own irrational nature is easily stimulated into action or, to put it more bluntly, "our buttons are easily pushed." When others relate to us in an ego-centered way, violating our rights and or ignoring our legitimate needs, our own native egocentrism will likely assert itself. Ego will meet ego in a struggle for power. When this happens, everyone loses. We therefore must anticipate our own egocentric reactions and come up with the appropriate rational thinking to deal with it.

Strategic Idea

Once we are aware that humans are naturally egocentric, and that most people are unaware of their native egocentrism, we can conclude that, in any given situation, we may well be interacting with the egocentric rather than the rational dimensions of those persons' minds. We therefore can question whether they are presenting rational ideas and pursuing rational purposes, or whether they are operating with irrational motives of which they are unaware. We will not take for granted that others are relating to us in good faith. Rather, we will observe their behavior carefully to determine what their behavior actually implies.

Moreover, because we know that our irrational nature is easily activated by irrationality in others, we can carefully observe and assess our own thinking to ensure that we do not become irrational in dealing with others who are egocentric. We will be on the lookout for our own ego-centered thinking, and when we recognize it, we will take steps to "wrestle it down" and refuse to be drawn into irrational games—whether initiated by others or by our own egocentric tendencies. When we realize we are dealing with an irrational person, we will not let that person's irrationality summon our irrational nature. We will refuse to be controlled by the unreasonable behavior of others.

Strategically, the best thing to do is to avoid contact with highly egocentric people whenever possible. When we find ourselves deeply involved with that sort of person, we should seek a way to disengage ourselves when possible. When disengagement is not possible, we should minimize contact or act in such a way as to minimize stimulating their ego.

We can minimize the stimulation to a person's ego by recognizing the conditions under which most highly egocentric reactions take place—namely, when people feel threatened, humiliated, or shamed, or when their vested interest or self-image is significantly involved. By getting into the habit of reconstructing in our own minds the point of view of others, and therefore of frequently thinking within the perspective of others, it is possible to anticipate many of the egocentric reactions of those around us. We then can choose a course of action that sidesteps many of the land mines of human egocentrism.

Test the Idea
Dealing with the Egocentrism of Others

Think of a recent situation in which you believed someone you were interacting with became irrational in his or her response to you. Complete these statements:

1. The situation was...
2. What I did/said was...
3. The reaction of this person was...
4. I believe this person's thinking was...
5. I think this reaction/thinking was egocentric because...
6. The best response I could have made to this egocentric behavior would have been...
7. I might have been able to avoid stimulating an egocentric response in the first place by...

Recognizing When Another Person's Egocentrism Brings Out Your Egocentrism

Think of a recent situation in which you felt yourself becoming irrational in reaction to someone else's irrationality. Complete these statements:

1. The situation was...
2. I reacted in the situation by...
3. In thinking through the situation, I realize that a more rational way to respond to the other person would have been...

Key Idea #6: The Mind Tends to Generalize Beyond the Original Experience

One of the important truths that Jean Piaget, the noted child psychologist, discovered about children is that they overgeneralize their immediate feelings. If something good happens to them, the whole world looks good to them. If something bad happens to them, the whole world looks bad to them. He called this phenomenon ego-centric immediacy. What Piaget did not emphasize, however, is that the same reaction patterns are found in much adult thinking. It is fair to say that everyone has some difficulty putting the ups and downs of daily life into a long-range perspective. It is not easy to keep things in proper perspective, given the strength of our immediate (emotional) reactions.

Once we begin to interpret situations or events in our life as negative, we also tend to generalize that negativity and even, on occasion, to allow it to cast a gloom over our whole life. A broad-based pessimism or a foolish optimism can come to permeate our thinking when negative or positive events happen to us. We move rapidly from thinking of one or two events in our lives as negative (or positive) to thinking of everything in our lives as negative (or positive). Egocentric negative thinking easily leads to indulgent self-pity. And egocentric positive thinking easily leads to an unrealistic state of complacent comfort.

Even a whole nation can be stampeded into an unrealistic state of complacent comfort by the reporting of one positive event. Hence, in England in 1938, after Neville Chamberlain returned to England from Munich holding an agreement with Hitler in his hand, he declared, "Peace in our times!" Most of the people in England rejoiced triumphantly over the success of having obtained Hitler's agreement, without factoring into their thinking Hitler's consistent record of broken promises. The entire nation was transformed into a state of national euphoria brought on by egocentric immediacy.

Rational voices like that of Winston Churchill, expressing skepticism that Hitler would be satisfied with this concession, were thrust aside as alarmist and without foundation. But Churchill had looked at the events at hand using a long-term, realistic perspective.

Consider an everyday problem for many people who tend to see the world in largely negative terms. They wake up in the morning and have to deal with a few unexpected minor problems. As the day progresses, and as they deal with more "problems," everything in their lives appears negative. The snowball of bad things happening gets bigger and bigger as the day passes. By the end of the day, they are unable to see any positive things in their lives. Their thinking (usually tacit of course) is something like this:

> Everything looks bad. Life isn't fair. Nothing good ever happens to me. I always have to deal with problems. Why does everything bad happen to me?

Controlled by these thoughts, they lack the ability to counteract unbridled negativity with rational thoughts. They can't see the many good things in their lives. Their egocentric mind is shielding them from the full range of facts that would change their way of thinking so they could see things in a more realistic and, in this case, a more positive light.

Strategic Idea

If we intervene with rational thoughts at the point at which egocentric negativity begins, before it completely pervades the mind's functioning, we have a better chance of reducing or overthrowing it. The first step requires that we become intimately familiar with the phenomenon of egocentric immediacy. Then we should begin to identify instances of it in our own life as well as the lives of those around us.

The second step requires that we develop a rich and comprehensive list of the facts of our lives. It is important that we develop this list not when we are in the throes of an egocentric "fit" but, instead, when we are viewing the world from a rational perspective.

We also want to develop a long-range perspective to call upon when necessary to give the proper weight to individual events, whether positive or negative. We must establish in our mind what our most important values are. We must frame in our mind a long-range historical perspective. We must bring those values and this perspective strongly before our mind when lesser values and the distortions of egocentric immediacy begin to dominate our thoughts and feelings. When we have a well-established "big picture" in our mind, what are in effect small events will remain small, not blown out of proportion.

When we perceive that our thinking is tending toward egocentric immediacy, we can actively undermine it through comprehensive rational thinking. This involves reasoning with ourselves, pointing out flaws in our thinking, identifying and

---

Test the Idea
"Big Picture" Thinking

Think of a situation you were recently in where you felt an intense negative emotion that generated a chain reaction of further negative states in your mind, leading to a generalized feeling of depression. At that moment, your life looked bleak and unforgiving. Figure out the "big picture" thinking that was missing from your mind as you fell prey to egocentric immediacy.

Complete these statements:

1. The objective situation was as follows...
2. Irrationally responded to the situation by...
3. I felt these negative emotions...
4. The "big picture" thinking that I needed but did not develop is something like the following...
5. The information I was failing to consider in my thinking was...
6. I can best avoid this situation in the future by...
7. I now realize...

presenting relevant information we are ignoring, pointing out information we are distorting, checking our assumptions, and tracking the implications of our thinking. In short, by developing a deep and comprehensive "big picture" in our mind, by keeping this comprehensive view as much as possible in the foreground of our thinking in daily life, we can minimize our own tendency toward egocentric immediacy. We can become skilled in recognizing what truly is small and large in our life. We can chart our course more effectively, navigating through passing storms and deceptively quiet seas alike.

Key Idea #7: Egocentric Thinking Appears to the Mind as Rational

One of the primary reasons human beings have difficulty recognizing egocentric thinking is that it appears to the mind as perfectly reasonable. No person says to himself or herself, "I shall think irrationally for a while." When we are most under the sway of irrational states (for example, in a state of irrational rage), we typically feel quite indignant and unfairly put-upon. Egocentric thinking blinds us in a variety of ways. We deceive ourselves.

When we are irrational, we feel rational. Our perceptions seem perfectly justified. And, not recognizing any flaws in our thinking, we see no reason to question those thoughts. We see no reason to behave differently. The result is that there is little or no chance of overriding the dysfunctional behavior that is dominating us. This is especially true when our egocentric thinking is working to get us what we want.

Strategic Idea

Once we recognize that egocentric thinking appears in the human mind as rational thinking, and can exemplify this truth with specific examples from our own life, we are potentially in a position to do something. We can learn to anticipate egocentric self-deception. For one thing, we can educate ourselves about the signs of it. We look for signs of shutting down—not really listening to those who disagree with us, stereotyping those who disagree with us, ignoring relevant evidence, reacting in an emotional manner, and rationalizing our irrational behavior (thinking of justifications for our behavior that have little to do with our actual motivation).

Consider the following examples:

Situation 1. You are driving to work. You fail to notice that the off-ramp of your exit is near. You recognize it at the last moment. You cut off someone to get to the off-ramp. He blows his horn at you and shouts. You shout back. You then are cut off by yet another car in a few minutes, and you blow your horn and shout at him.

During these events you feel an inner sense of "rightness." After all, you had to get to work on time. You didn't mean to cut anyone off, but the other guy clearly had no right to cut you off. We often use this kind of simplistic thinking when we deceive ourselves. We ignore evidence against our view. We highlight evidence for our view.

We experience negative emotions accordingly. And we easily feel an acute sense of righteousness about how we think, feel, and act.

Situation 2. You come home after a bad day at work. Your teenage son is playing music loudly and singing in the kitchen. You say, "Could we please have some peace and quiet around here for once!" Your son says, "What's bugging you?" You stomp out of the room, go to your room and slam the door. You stay there for an hour, feeling depressed and angry. You come out and your children and spouse are chatting in the kitchen. They ignore you. You say, "Well, I can see that no one needs me around here!" You walk out, slamming the door.

Sometimes in cases like this we recover from our egocentric immediacy after we cool off. But during the actual events that set us off, we feel righteous in our anger and justified in our depression. We have no trouble thinking of reasons to feed our righteousness or intensify our anger. We can dig up grievances from the past. We can go over them in our mind, blowing them up as much as we care to. We do this with no sense of our own self-deception.

In principle we are capable of learning to catch ourselves in the process of engaging in deception or distortion. We can develop the habit of doing the following:

1. Looking at all events from the point of view of those we disagree with, as well as from our own. If we are in a conversation, we can check ourselves by repeating to the person our understanding of what he or she is saying, and why.

2. Becoming suspicious of our accounts of things whenever we seem completely correct to ourselves while those we disagree with seem completely wrong.

3. Suspending judgment of people and events when we are in the throes of intensive emotions. Reserving judgment for moments when we can quietly question ourselves and review facts with relative objectivity.

Test the Idea
Recognizing and Replacing Irrational Thinking

Think of a situation you were in recently when you thought at the time that you were perfectly rational, which you now realize consisted of self-deception. Complete these statements:

1. The situation was as follows...
2. I behaved in the situation by...
3. At the time, I thought I was rational because...
4. Now I think I may have been irrational because...
5. I rationalized my behavior by telling myself...
6. The real reason I behaved the way I did is...

Key Idea #8: The Egocentric Mind Is Automatic in Nature

Egocentric thinking, unlike rational thought, operates in a highly automatic, unconscious, and impulsive manner. Based in primitive, often "childish," thought patterns, it reacts to situations in programmed and mechanistic ways. We must recognize, therefore, that it often will spring into action before we have a chance to sidestep or prevent it. It fights. It flees. It denies. It represses. It rationalizes. It distorts. It negates. It scapegoats. And it does all of these in the blink of an eye with no conscious awareness of its deceptive tricks.

Strategic Idea

Because we know that the irrational mind operates in predictable, preprogrammed, automated ways, we become interested observers of the egocentric mechanisms of our own mind. We begin to observe the mechanistic moves our mind makes. Rather than allowing thoughts to operate strictly at the unconscious level, we can actively strive to raise them to conscious realization, as Piaget put it. We can work to bring them into full consciousness. This typically will be after the fact—especially in the beginning of our development as critical thinkers. After a time, when we become keenly aware of how our personal ego functions, we can often forestall egocentric reactions by the prior activity of rational thought.

For instance, as presented in key idea #7, we can begin to recognize when our mind rationalizes in patterned ways. We also can become familiar with the kinds of rationalization our mind tends to use. For example, "I don't have time to do this!" may be a favorite rationalization. We could limit its use by remembering the insight, "People always have time for the things most important to them." We then are forced to face the truth about what we are doing: "I don't want to make room in my priorities for this," or "Since I continually say this is important to me, I'm only deceiving myself by saying, 'but I don't have time for it.'"

Over time and with practice, we can begin to notice when we are denying some important truth about ourselves. We can begin to see when we are refusing to face some reality rather than dealing with it openly and directly. We can begin to recognize when we are automatically thinking in a dishonest way, in attempting to avoid working on a solution to a problem.

In principle, then, we can study the tricks and stratagems of our mind to determine its automated patterns. Furthermore, and most important, we can learn to intervene to disengage irrational thought processes—if necessary after they have begun to operate. In short, we can refuse to be controlled by primitive desires and modes of thinking. We can actively work to replace automatic egocentric thinking with reflective rational thinking.

Test the Idea
Focusing on Denial as a Mechanism of Irrationality

Although the egocentric dimension of the mind uses many defense mechanisms to maintain its self-centered view, we will single out just one for this activity: denial. Think of a relationship you are in now in which you have a selfish interest in seeing things a certain way though the facts probably don't support your view. Let's say you want to believe that your spouse really loves you, even though his or her actual behavior toward you indicates that he or she probably is using you (perhaps as a vehicle of his or her self-gratification).

As another example, let's say that you want to believe you are treating your spouse respectfully, though the facts show that you often treat him or her with little respect and consideration. Admitting the truth would be painful to you. Complete these statements:

1. The situation is…

2. What I have denied accepting in this situation is…

3. I have avoided the truth by telling myself the following untruth…

4. I realize I have denied looking at the truth in the situation because…

5. Some implications that have followed from my denial about this situation are…

Key Idea #9: We Often Pursue Power Through Dominating or Submissive Behavior

When thinking irrationally or egocentrically, the human mind often seeks to achieve its goals by either dominating or submissive behavior. Put another way, when under the sway of egocentrism, we try to get our way either by dominating others or by gaining their support through outward submission to them. Bullying (dominating) and groveling (submitting) are often subtle in nature, but they are nonetheless common in human life.

Power is not bad in itself. We all need some power to rationally fulfill our needs. But in human life it is common for power to be sought as an end in itself, or used for unethical purposes. One of the most common ways for egocentric people and sociocentric groups to gain power is by dominating weaker persons or groups. Another way is by playing a subservient role toward a more powerful other to get what they want. Much of human history could be told in terms of the use of these two egocentric functions of individuals and groups. Much individual behavior can be understood by seeing the presence of these two patterns in the behavior of individuals.

Though everyone tends to use one of these behavior patterns more than the other, everyone uses both of them to some extent. Some children, for example, play a role of subservience toward their parents while abusively bullying other children. Of course, when a bigger and tougher bully comes along, the weaker bully often becomes subservient to the stronger one.

When we are egocentrically dominating or submitting, we do not readily recognize we are doing so. For example, people presumably attend rock concerts to enjoy the music. But members of the audience often act in a highly submissive (adoring, idolizing) way toward the musicians. Many people literally throw themselves at the feet of celebrities or take their own definition of significance from distantly attaching themselves to a celebrity, if only in their imagination. In like manner, sports fans often idolize and idealize their heroes, who appear bigger than life to them. If their team or their hero is successful, they vicariously feel successful and more powerful. "We really whipped them!" translates as, "I am important and successful just as my hero is."

Rational people may admire other people, but do not idolize or idealize them. Rational people may form alliances, but not ones in which they are dominated by others. They expect no one to submit to them blindly. They blindly submit to no one. Although none of us fully embodies this rational ideal, critical thinkers continually work toward it in all their relationships.

By the way, traditional male and female sex-role conditioning entails the man dominating the woman and the woman playing a submissive role toward her man. Women were to gain power by attaching themselves to powerful men. Men displayed power in achieving domination over women. These traditional roles are far from dead in present male/female relationships. For example, in many ways the media still portray men and women in traditional gender roles. Because of these and other societal influences, men tend to be more dominating than submissive. Conversely, women tend to be more submissive, especially in intimate relationships.

Strategic Idea

If we realize the prominent role that egocentric domination and submission play in human life, we can begin to observe our own behavior to determine when we are irrationally dominating or submitting to others. When we understand that the mind naturally uses numerous methods for hiding its egocentrism, we recognize that we must scrutinize our own mental functioning carefully to locate dominating and submissive patterns. With practice, we can begin to identify our own patterns of domination and submission. At the same time, we can observe others' behavior, looking for similar patterns. We can look closely at the behavior of our supervisors, our friends, our spouses, our children, our parents, noticing when they tend to irrationally dominate and/or submit to the will of others.

In short, the more we study patterns of domination and submission in human life, the more we are able to detect them in our own life and behavior. And only when we become adept at detecting them can we take steps toward changing them.

Test the Idea
Recognizing Submissive and Dominating Behavior in Ourselves

During the next week, closely observe your behavior patterns to determine whether you tend to behave in a dominating or a submissive manner when you are egocentrically pursuing your desires. Take notes on your behavior during the week. At the end of the week, complete the following statements:

1. I observed myself behaving in a dominating way in the following situations...
2. Some implications of this behavior are...
3. In future similar situations, I will modify my behavior in the following ways...
4. I observed myself behaving in a submissive way in the following situations...
5. The implications of this behavior were...
6. In future similar situations, I will modify my behavior in the following ways...

Key Idea #10: Humans Are Naturally Sociocentric Animals

Not only are humans naturally egocentric but we are also easily drawn into sociocentric thinking and behavior. Groups offer us security to the extent that we internalize and unthinkingly conform to their rules, imperatives, and taboos. Growing up, we learn to conform to many groups. Peer groups especially tend to dominate our life. Our unconscious acceptance of the values of the group leads to the unconscious standard: "It's true if we believe it." There seems to be no belief so absurd but that some group of humans irrationally accepts it as rational.

Not only do we accept the belief systems of the groups to which we belong, but also most important, we act on those belief systems. For example, many groups are anti-intellectual in nature. Groups may expect its members to adhere to any number of dysfunctional behaviors. For example, some youth groups expect members to abuse outsiders verbally and physically (as proof of power or courage). And some groups who share lunch together during the workweek engage in malicious gossip about others in the same work place.

In addition to face-to-face groups we are in, we are influenced indirectly by large-scale social forces that reflect our membership in society at large. For example, in capitalist societies, the dominant thinking is that people should strive to make as much money as possible, though this form of thinking, it might be argued, encourages people to accept a large gap between the haves and have-nots as right and normal.

Or consider this: Within mass societies the nature and solution to most public issues and problems are presented in sensationalized sound-bytes by the news media. As a result, people often come to think about complex problems in terms of simplistic media-fostered solutions. Many people are led to believe that expressions such as "Get tough with criminals!" and "Three strikes and you're out!" represent plausible ways to deal with complex social problems.

What is more, the portrayal of life in Hollywood movies exerts a significant influence on how we conceptualize our problems, our lives, and ourselves. Sociocentric influences are at work at every level of social life in both subtle and blatant ways. There are many socio-centric forces in society.

Strategic Idea

Humans are naturally sociocentric. We must take possession of the idea that, because we are all members of social groups, our behavior reflects the imperatives and taboos of the groups to which we belong. We all, to a greater or lesser degree, uncritically conform to the rules and expectations of the groups of which we are members. When we recognize this, we can begin to analyze and assess that to which we conform. We can actively analyze the rules and taboos of our peer groups and those we are aligned with. We can rationally think through the groups' expectations to determine the extent to which they are reasonable.

When we identify irrational expectations, we can refuse to adhere to those requirements. We can shift our group memberships from those that are flagrantly irrational to those that are more rational. Indeed, we can actively create new groups, groups that emphasize the importance of integrity and fair-mindedness, groups that

---

Test the Idea
Recognizing Problems in Sociocentric Thinking

Identify a group to which you belong. It can be a small group of colleagues at work, friends, a club, a religious group, or a large non-face-to-face cultural group of which you are a part. Complete the following statements:

1. The group I am focused on is...
2. The taboos or behaviors not allowed within the group are...
3. The injunctions or requirements are...
4. In analyzing my behavior in this group, I realize ... about myself.
5. After analyzing this group's taboos and injunctions, I think it is/is not in my interest to be involved in this group, for these reasons...

encourage their members to develop independence of thought and work together in that pursuit.

Or we can minimize the groups we belong to—except for the social groups we cannot escape. With respect to the large-scale socio-centric influences to which we are subjected by the mass media, we can develop an ongoing critical sensitivity that minimizes our falling prey to group influences. In short, by understanding our personal relationship to socio-centric thinking, we can begin to take charge of the influence that groups have over us. We can significantly reduce that influence

Key Idea #11: Developing Rationality Requires Work

Significant development of one's rational capacities takes many years. The "gotta have it now" attitude prevalent in our culture creates a significant barrier to the development of higher-order human capacity. If we want to reap the benefits of a developed mind, there are no easy shortcuts. If we want to become better at reasoning through the complex issues we inevitably will face, we must be committed to that end. Just as baseball players must practice the moves of baseball again and again to be highly skilled at the game, so must committed thinkers.

Strategic Idea

Because we understand that daily practice is crucial to the development of our rational capacity, we can develop the habit of asking ourselves what we are doing today to further our intellectual growth. We realize that we must make it a habit to identify our selfish interests—and correct for their influence over our thinking. When we discover that our selfish nature is often driving the decisions we are making, we can intervene through good-faith empathy with alternative points of view.

We can develop the habit of assessing the extent to which we use the intellectual standards of clarity, accuracy, logical, significance, breadth, depth, and justifiability to assess and improve our thinking. For example, to develop the habit of checking our thoughts for clarity, we can regularly elaborate, and give examples and illustrations when we are presenting our views to others. We also can regularly ask others to elaborate, illustrate, and exemplify their ideas when they are expressing them to us. We can aim to develop similar habits with respect to using the other standards, and periodically assess ourselves to determine whether and to what extent those habits are developing. We can, and should, practice developing an inner voice that leads to routine questioning of others and ourselves.

Test the Idea
Getting in the Habit of Daily Critical Thinking

During the next seven days, document something you do every day that develops your ability to think well. Complete the following statements for each day:

1. Today I engaged in the following thinking/behavior that demonstrates my commitment to becoming a critical thinker...

2. Before I started learning about critical thinking, in similar situations I would have behaved in the following way, rather than in the way described in number 1...

3. My new way of thinking/behaving is better because...

Conclusion

To develop a disciplined mind—a mind that takes responsibility for the quality of its inner workings and continually seeks to upgrade its abilities—presupposes two overlapping yet distinct principles. First, we must develop a deep understanding of how our mind functions. Concepts, principles, and theories serving this end are the focus of this book. It is not enough to read about these concepts, principles, and theories, though. We must internalize them to the point that we can use them routinely to develop unique strategies for targeting and improving the quality of our thinking. When we haven't internalized them well enough to effectively improve our thinking, they are of little or no use to us.

Authentic strategic thinking is thinking that takes a principle or an idea from the theoretical plane and, following its implications on the practical plane, develops a course of action designed to improve what we think, feel, and act. As you think through your behavior, and the patterns of thought that now rule your life, the important question is: How are you going to take important ideas and work them into your thinking so your behavior and emotional life changes for the better? How will you move from abstract understanding to concrete improvements? Only when you are doing strategic thinking regularly—the strategic thinking outlined in this chapter—can you begin to significantly improve as a thinker.

Glossary:
A Guide to Critical Thinking
Terms and Concepts

accurate: Free from errors, mistakes, or distortion. Correct connotes little more than absence of error; accurate implies a positive exercise of one to obtain conformity with fact or truth; exact stresses perfect conformity to fact, truth, or some standard; precise suggests minute accuracy of detail. Accuracy is an important goal in critical thinking, though it is almost always a matter of degree. It is also important to recognize that making mistakes is an essential part of learning. *See perfections of thought.*

ambiguous: A sentence, concept, or thought having two or more possible meanings. Sensitivity to ambiguity and vagueness in writing and speech is essential to good thinking. A continual effort to be clear and precise in language usage is fundamental to skilled thinking. Ambiguity is a problem more of sentences than of individual words. Many sentences are clearly intended one way; any other construal is obviously absurd and not meant. For example, the phrase "make me a sandwich" is never seriously intended to request metamorphic change. For an example of a problematic ambiguity, consider the statement, "Welfare is corrupt." Among the possible meanings of this sentence are the following: 1) Those who administer welfare programs take bribes to administer welfare policy unfairly; 2) welfare policies are written in such a way that much of the money goes to people who don't deserve it rather than to those who do; 3) a government that gives money to people who haven't earned it corrupts both the giver and the recipient. If two people are arguing about whether or not welfare is corrupt, but interpret the claim differently, they can make little or no progress; they aren't arguing about the same point. Evidence and considerations relevant to one interpretation may be irrelevant to others. Therefore, before taking a position on an issue or arguing a point, it is essential to be clear about the issue at hand. *See clarify.*

analyze: To break up a whole into its parts, to examine in detail so as to determine the nature of, to look more deeply into, an issue or situation. All learning presupposes some analysis of what we are learning, if only by categorizing or labeling things in one way rather than another. *See elements of thought.*

argue: There are two meanings of this word that need to be distinguished: 1) to engage in a quarrel, bicker; and 2) to persuade by giving reasons. As developing critical thinkers, we strive to move from the first sense of the word to the second; that is, we try to focus on giving reasons to support our views without becoming egocentrically involved in the discussion. This is a fundamental problem in human life. To argue in the critical thinking sense is to use logic and reason, and to bring forth facts to support or refute a point. It is done in a spirit of cooperation and good will.

argument: A reason or reasons offered for or against something, the offering of such reasons. This term refers to a discussion in which there is disagreement and suggests the use of logic and bringing forth of facts to support or refute a point. *See argue.*

to assume: To take for granted or to presuppose. Critical thinkers can and do make their assumptions explicit, assess them, and correct them. Assumptions can vary from the mundane to the problematic: I heard a scratch at the door. I got up to let the cat in. I assumed that only the cat makes that noise, and that he makes it only when he wants to be let in. Someone speaks gruffly to me. I feel guilty and hurt. I assume he is angry at me, that he is only angry at me when I do something bad, and that if he's angry at me, he dislikes me. Notice that people often equate making assumptions with making false assumptions. When people say, "Don't assume," this is what they mean. In fact, we cannot avoid making assumptions and some are justifiable. (For instance, we have assumed that people who buy this book can read English.) Rather than saying "Never assume," we say, "Be aware of and careful about the assumptions you make, and be ready to examine and critique them." *See assumption, elements of thought.*

assumption: A statement accepted or supposed as true without proof or demonstration; an unstated premise or belief. All human thought and experience is based on assumptions. Our thought must begin with something we take to be true in a particular context. We are typically unaware of what we assume and therefore rarely question our assumptions. In other words, most of our assumptions are unconscious. They operate in our thinking without our knowing it. Much of what is wrong with human thought can be found in the uncritical or unexamined assumptions that underlie it. All of our prejudices, biases, and preconceived generalizations lie in the form of assumptions. We often experience the world in such a way as to assume that we are observing things just as they are, as though we were seeing the world without the filter of a point of view. People we disagree with, of course, we recognize as having a point of view. One of the key dispositions of critical thinking is the on-going sense that as humans we always think within a perspective, that we virtually never experience things totally and absolutistically. There is a connection, therefore, between thinking so as to be aware of our assumptions and being intellectually humble.

By "reasoning based on assumptions" we mean "whatever we take for granted as true" in order to figure something else out. Thus, if you infer that since a candidate is a Republican, he or she will support a balanced budget, you assume that all Republicans support a balanced budget. If you infer that foreign leaders presented in the news as "enemies" or "friends" are in fact enemies or friends, you assume that the news is always accurate in its presentation of the character of foreign leaders. If you infer that someone who invites you to their apartment after a party "to continue this interested conversation" is really interested in you romantically or sexually, you assume that the only reason for going to someone's apartment late at night after a party is to pursue a romantic or sexual relationship. All reasoning has some basis in assumptions we make (but usually do not express openly).

authority: 1) The power or supposed right to give commands, enforce obedience, take action, or make final decisions. 2) A person with much knowledge and expertise in a field, and therefore reliable. Critical thinkers recognize that ultimate authority rests with reason and evidence, since it is only on the assumption that purported experts have the backing of reason and evidence that they rightfully gain authority. Much instruction in school and many social and business practices discourage critical thinking by encouraging persons to believe that whatever the "authority" says is true. As a result, most peole do not learn how to assess authority. *See knowledge.*

bias: 1) A mental leaning or inclination. 2) Partiality, prejudice. We must clearly distinguish two different senses of the word "bias." One is neutral, the other negative. In the neutral sense, we are referring simply to the fact that, because of one's point of view, one notices some things rather than others, emphasizes some points rather than others, and thinks in one direction rather than others. This is not in itself a criticism, because thinking within a point of view is unavoidable. In the negative sense, we are implying blindness or irrational resistance to weaknesses within one's own point of view or to the strength or insight within a point of view one opposes. Fair-minded critical thinkers try to be aware of their bias (in sense one) and try hard to avoid bias (in sense two). Many people confuse these two senses. Many confuse bias with emotion or with evaluation, perceiving any expression of emotion or any use of evaluative words to be biased (sense two). Evaluative words that can be justified by reason and evidence are not biased in the negative sense.

clarify: To make easier to understand, to free from confusion or ambiguity, to remove obscurities. Clarity is a fundamental perfection of thought and clarification a fundamental aim in critical thinking. The key to clarification is the ability to state, elaborate, illustrate, and exemplify the ideas we express.

concept: An idea or thought, especially a generalized idea of a thing or of a class of things. Humans think within concepts or ideas. We can never achieve command over our thoughts unless we learn how to achieve command over our concepts or ideas. Thus, we must learn how to identify the concepts or ideas we are using, contrast them with alternative concepts or ideas, and clarify what we include and exclude by means of them. In this book, the concepts of "critical thinking" and "uncritical thinking" are very important ideas. Everything written can be classified as an attempt to explain one or the other of these two ideas. Of course, each of these ideas is explained, in turn, by means of other ideas. Thus, the concept of "thinking critically" is explained by reference to yet other concepts like "intellectual standards for thought." Each discipline develops its own set of concepts or technical vocabulary to facilitate its thinking. All sports develop a vocabulary of concepts that enable persons to make sense of it if they are trying to understand or master the game. One cannot understand ethics without a clear concept of justice, kindness, cruelty, rights, and obligations.

People are often unclear about the concepts they are using. For example, most people say they believe strongly in democracy, but few can clarify with examples what that word does and does not imply. Most people confuse the meaning of words with cultural associations, with the result that "democracy" means to people whatever we do in running our government—any country that is different from ours is undemocratic. We must distinguish the concepts implicit in the English language from the psychological associations surrounding that concept in a given social group or culture. The failure to develop this ability is a major cause of uncritical thought and selfish critical thought.

conclude/conclusion: To decide by reasoning, to infer, to deduce; the last step in a reasoning process; a judgment, decision, or belief formed after investigation or reasoning. All beliefs, decisions, or actions are based on human thought, but seldom as the result of conscious reasoning or deliberation. All that we believe is, one way or another, based on conclusions that we have come to during our lifetime. Thus, by "coming to conclusions" we mean taking something that we believe we know and figuring out something else on the basis of it. When we do this, we make inferences. For example, if you walk right by me without saying hello, I might come to the conclusion (make the inference) that you were angry with me. If the water kettle on the stove began to whistle, I would come to the conclusion (make the inference) that the water in it had started to boil. In everyday life, we are continually making inferences (coming to conclusions) about the people, things, places, and events of our lives. Yet, we rarely monitor our thought processes, we don't critically assess the conclusions we come to, to determine whether we have sufficient grounds or reasons for accepting them. People seldom recognize when they have come to a conclusion. They confuse their conclusions with evidence, and so cannot assess the reasoning that took them from evidence to conclusion. Recognizing that human life is inferential, that we continually come to conclusions about ourselves and the things and persons around us, is essential to thinking critically and reflectively.

consistency: To think, act, or speak in agreement with what has already been thought, done, or expressed; to have intellectual or moral integrity. Human life and thought is filled with inconsistency, hypocrisy, and contradiction. We often say one thing and do another, judge ourselves and our friends by one standard and our antagonists by another, lean over backward to justify what we want or negate what does not serve our interests. Similarly, we often confuse desires with needs, treating our desires as equivalent to needs, putting what we want above the basic needs of others. Logical and moral consistency are fundamental values of fair-minded critical thinking. Social conditioning and native egocentrism often obscure social contradictions, inconsistency, and hypocrisy.

contradict/contradiction: To assert the opposite of; to be contrary to, go against; a statement in opposition to another; a condition in which things tend to be contrary to each other; inconsistency; discrepancy; a person or thing containing or composed of contradictory elements.

criterion (criteria, pl): A standard, rule, or test by which something can be judged or measured. Human life, thought, and action are based on human values. The standards by which we determine whether those values are achieved in any situation represent criteria. Critical thinking depends upon making explicit the standards or criteria for rational or justifiable thinking and behavior. *See evaluation.*

critical listening: A mode of monitoring how we are listening so as to maximize our accurate understanding of what another person is saying. By understanding the logic of human communication—that everything spoken expresses point of view, uses some ideas and not others, has implications, etc.—critical thinkers can listen so as to enter sympathetically and analytically into the perspective of others. *See critical speaking, critical reading, critical writing, elements of thought, and intellectual empathy.*

critical person: One who has mastered a range of intellectual skills and abilities. If that person generally uses those skills to advance his or her own selfish interests, that person is a critical thinker only in a weak or qualified sense. If that person generally uses those skills fair-mindedly, entering empathically into the points of view of others, he or she is a critical thinker in the strong or fullest sense. *See critical thinking.*

critical reading: Critical reading is an active, intellectually engaged process in which the reader participates in an inner dialogue with the writer. Most people read uncritically and so miss some part of what is expressed while distorting other parts. A critical reader realizes the way in which reading, by its very nature, means entering into a point of view other than our own, the point of view of the writer. A critical reader actively looks for assumptions, key concepts and ideas, reasons and justifications, supporting examples, parallel experiences, implications and consequences, and any other structural features of the written text, to interpret and assess it accurately and fairly. A critical reader does not evaluate a written piece until s/he accurately understands the viewpoint of the author. *See elements of thought.*

critical society: A society that rewards adherence to the values of critical thinking and hence does not use indoctrination and inculcation as basic modes of learning. Instead, it rewards reflective questioning, intellectual independence, and reasoned dissent. Socrates is not the only thinker to imagine a society in which independent critical thought became embodied in the concrete day-to-day lives of individuals; William Graham Sumner, North America's distinguished anthropologist, explicitly formulated the ideal:

> The critical habit of thought, if usual in a society, will pervade all its mores, because it is a way of taking up the problems of life. Men educated in it cannot be stampeded by stump orators and are never deceived by dithyrambic oratory. They are slow to believe. They can hold things as possible or probable in all degrees, without certainty and without pain. They can wait for evidence and weigh evidence, uninfluenced by the emphasis or confidence with which assertions are made on one side or the other. They can resist appeals to their dearest prejudices and all kinds of cajolery. Education in the critical faculty is the only education of which it can be truly said that it makes good citizens (Folkways, 1906).

Until critical habits of thought pervade our society, however, there will be a tendency for schools as social institutions to transmit the prevailing world view more or less uncritically, to transmit it as reality, not as a picture of reality. Education for critical thinking, then, requires that the school or classroom become a microcosm of a critical society.

critical thinking: 1) Disciplined, self-directed thinking that exemplifies the perfections of thinking appropriate to a particular mode or domain of thinking. 2) Thinking that displays mastery of intellectual skills and abilities. 3) The art of thinking about your thinking while you are thinking in order to make your thinking better: more clear, more accurate, or more defensible. 4) Thinking that is fully aware of and continually guards against the natural human tendency to self-deceive and rationalize in order to selfishly get what it wants. Critical thinking can be distinguished into two forms: "selfish" or "sophistic," on the one hand, and "fair-minded," on the other. In thinking critically, we use our command of the elements of thinking and the universal intellectual standards to adjust our thinking successfully to the logical demands of a type or mode of thinking.

critical writing: To express ourselves in language requires that we arrange our ideas in some relationships to each other. When accuracy and truth are at issue, then we must understand what our thesis is, how we can support it, how we can elaborate it to make it intelligible to others, what objections can be raised to it from other points of view, what the limitations are to our point of view, and so forth. Disciplined writing requires disciplined thinking; disciplined thinking is achieved through disciplined writing.

critique: An objective judging, analysis, or evaluation of something. The purpose of critique is the same as the purpose of critical thinking: to appreciate strengths as well as weaknesses, virtues as well as failings. Critical thinkers critique in order to redesign, remodel, and make better.

cultural association: Undisciplined thinking often reflects associations, personal and cultural, absorbed or uncritically formed. If a person who treated me cruelly as a child had a particular tone of voice, I may find myself disliking a person with the same tone of voice. Media advertising juxtaposes and joins logically unrelated things to influence our buying habits. Raised in a particular country or within a particular group within it, we form any number of mental links that, if they remain unexamined, unduly influence our thinking.

cultural assumption: Un-assessed (often implicit) belief adopted by virtue of upbringing in a society. Raised in a society, we unconsciously take on its point of view, values, beliefs, and practices. At the root of each of these are many kinds of assumptions. Not knowing that we perceive, conceive, think, and experience within assumptions we have taken in, we take ourselves to be perceiving "things as they are," not "things as they appear from a cultural vantage point." Becoming aware of our cultural assumptions so that we might critically examine them is a crucial dimension of critical thinking. It is, however, a dimension almost totally absent from schooling. Lip service to this ideal is common enough; a realistic emphasis is virtually unheard of. *See ethnocentricity, prejudice, and social contradiction.*

data: Facts, figures, or information from which conclusions can be inferred, or upon which interpretations or theories can be based. As critical thinkers, we must make certain to distinguish hard data from the inferences or conclusions we draw from them.

dialectical thinking: Dialogical thinking (thinking within more than one perspective) conducted to test the strengths and weaknesses of opposing points of view. (Court trials and debates are, in a sense, dialectical.) When thinking dialectically, reasoners pit two or more opposing points of view in competition with each other, developing each by providing support, raising objections, countering those objections, raising further objections, and so on. Dialectical thinking or discussion can be conducted so as to "win" by defeating the positions one disagrees with—using critical insight to support one's own view and point out flaws in other views (associated with critical thinking in the restricted or weak sense), or fair-mindedly, by conceding points that don't stand up to critique, trying to integrate or incorporate strong points found in other views, and using critical insight to develop a fuller and more accurate view (associated with critical thinking in the fuller or strong sense). *See multilogical problems.*

domains of thought: Thinking can be oriented or structured with different issues or purposes in view. Thinking varies in accordance with purpose and issue. Critical thinkers learn to discipline their thinking to take into account the nature of the issue or domain. We see this most clearly when we consider the difference between issues and thinking within different academic disciplines or subject areas. Hence, mathematical thinking is quite different from, say, historical thinking. Mathematics and history, we can say then, represent different domains of thought. *See the logic of questions.*

dominating ego: The irrational tendency of the mind to seek what it wants through the irrational use of direct control or power over people. Dominating tendencies are an inherent part of one form of egocentric thinking. This form of thinking seeks to gain advantage by irrationally wielding power over another. It is contrasted with *submissive* egocentric thinking in which one irrationally seeks to gain some end by submitting to a person with power. Domination may be overt or covert. On the one hand, dominating egocentrism can involve harsh, dictatorial, tyrannical, or bullying behavior (e.g., a physically abusive husband). On the other hand, it might involve subtle messages and behavior that imply the use of control or force if "necessary" (e.g., a supervisor reminding a subordinate, by quiet innuendo, that his employment is contingent upon unquestioning loyalty to the organization). Human irrational behavior is always some combination of dominating and submissive acts. No one's irrational acts are exclusively one or the other. In the "ideal" of a Fascist society, for example, everyone, but the dictator, is submissive to everyone above him and dominating to everyone below him. *See submissive ego.*

egocentricity: A tendency to view everything in relationship to oneself; to confuse immediate perception (how things seem) with reality; the tendency to be self-centered, or to consider only oneself and one's own interests; selfishness. One's desires, values, and beliefs (seeming to be self-evidently correct or superior to those of others) are often uncritically used as the norm of all judgment and experience. Egocentricity is one of the fundamental impediments to critical thinking. As one learns to think critically in a strong sense, one learns to become more rational, and less egocentric. *See human nature, strong sense critical thinker, ethnocentrism, sociocentrism, and personal contradiction.*

elements of thought: All thought has a universal set of elements, each of which can be monitored for possible problems. They are: purpose, question, point of view, assumptions, inferences, implications, concepts, and information. When we understand the elements of thought, we have a powerful set of tools for analyzing our thinking. We can ask questions such as: Are we clear about our purpose or goal? about the problem or question at issue? about our point of view or frame of reference? about our assumptions? about the claims we are making? about the reasons or evidence upon which we are basing our claims? about our inferences and line of reasoning? about the implications and consequences that follow from our reasoning? Critical thinkers develop skills of identifying and assessing these elements in their thinking and in the thinking of others.

emotion: A feeling aroused to the point of awareness, often a strong feeling or state of excitement. It is important to understand that our emotions are integrally related to our thoughts and desires. These three mental structures—thoughts, feelings, and desires—are continually influencing one another in reciprocal ways. We experiences negative *feelings* for example, when we *think* things are not going well for us. Moreover, at any given moment, our thoughts, feelings and desires are under the influence either of our rational faculties or our native irrational tendencies. When our *thinking* is irrational, or egocentric, irrational *feeling* states emerge. When this happens, we are excited by (what is at base) infantile anger, fear, jealousy, etc., and our objectivity and fair-mindedness decrease. Critical thinkers strive to recognize when dysfunctional thinking is leading to inappropriate or unproductive feeling states. They use their rational passions (which includes, for example, the passion to be fair) to reason themselves into feelings appropriate to the situation as it really is, rather than egocentrically reacting to distorted views of reality. Thus, emotions and feelings are not in themselves irrational; they are irrational only when they arise from egocentric thoughts. Strong sense critical thinkers are committed to living a life in which rational emotions predominate and egocentric feelings reduced to a minimum. *See rational passions and intellectual virtues.*

empirical: Relying or based on experiment, observation, or experience rather than on theory or meaning. It is important to continually distinguish considerations based on experiment, observation, or experience from those based on the meaning of a word or concept or the implications of a theory. Uncritical thinkers often distort facts or experience in order to preserve a preconceived meaning or theory. For example, an uncritical conservative may distort the facts that support a liberal perspective to prevent empirical evidence from counting against a theory of the world that he or she holds rigidly. Uncritical liberals, of course, return the favor by a parallel distortion of facts that support a conservative perspective. Indeed, within all perspectives and belief systems many will distort the facts rather than admit to a weakness in their favorite theory or belief. *See data, fact, and evidence.*

empirical implication: That which follows from a situation or fact, not due to the logic of language, but from experience or scientific law. The redness of the coil on the stove empirically implies a dangerous level of heat.

ethical reasoning: Thinking through ethical problems and issues. Despite popular beliefs to the contrary, ethical reasoning is to be analyzed and assessed in the same way than any other domain of reasoning is. Ethical reasoning involves the same elements and is to be assessed by the same standards of clarity, accuracy, precision, relevance, depth, breadth, logic, and significance. Ethical thinking, when reasonable, is ultimately driven by ethical concepts (for example, *fairness*) and principles (for example, "*Like ethical cases must be treated in a like manner*") as well as sound principles of critical thought. Understanding ethical principles is as important to sound ethical reasoning as understanding principles of math and biology are to mathematical and biological reasoning. Ethical principles are guides for human conduct and imply what contributes to good or harm and/or what one is either obligated to do or obligated not to do. They enable us to determine the ethical value of a behavior even when that behavior is not strictly speaking, an obligation. Ethical questions, like questions in any domain of thought, can either be questions with a clear-cut answer, or questions with competing reasonable answers, matters about which we must strive to exercise our best judgment. They are *never* matters of personal preference. It makes no sense to say, "Oh, you prefer to be fair. Well, I prefer to be unfair!"

ethnocentricity: A tendency to view one's own race or culture as privileged, based on the deep-seated belief that one's own group is superior to all others. Ethnocentrism is a form of egocentrism extended from the self to the group. Much uncritical or selfish critical thinking is either egocentric or ethnocentric in nature. ('Ethnocentrism' and 'socio-centrism' are used synonymously, for the most part, though 'socio-centricity' is broader, relating to any social group, including, for example, socio-centricity regarding one's profession.) The "cure" for ethnocentrism or socio-centrism is empathic thought (thinking within the perspective of opposing groups and cultures). Such empathic thought is rarely cultivated. Instead, many give mere lip service to tolerance, but always privileging the beliefs, norms, and practices of their own culture. Critical thinkers are aware of the sociocentric nature of virtually all human groups, and resist the pressure of "group think" that emerges from "in-group" thinking. They realize that universal ethical standards supercede group expectations and demands where questions of an ethical nature are at issue. They do not assume that the groups to which they belong to be inherently superior to other groups. Instead, they attempt to accurately critique every group, seeking to determine its strengths and weaknesses. Their loyalty to a country is critically based on the principles and ideals of the country and is not based on uncritical loyalty to person, party, or national traditions.

evaluation: To judge or determine the worth or quality of. Evaluation has a logic and should be carefully distinguished from mere subjective preference. The elements of its logic may be put in the form of questions that may be asked whenever an evaluation is to be carried out: 1) Do we clearly understand what we are evaluating? 2) Are we clear about our purpose? Is our purpose legitimate? 3) Given our purpose, what are the relevant criteria or standards for evaluation? 4) Do we have sufficient information about that which we are evaluating? Is that information relevant to the purpose? 5) Have we applied our criteria accurately and fairly to the facts as we know them? Uncritical thinkers often treat evaluation as mere preference or treat their evaluative judgments as direct observations not admitting of error.

evidence: The data on which a judgment or conclusion might be based or by which proof or probability might be established. Critical thinkers distinguish the evidence or raw data upon which they base their interpretations or conclusions from the inferences and assumptions that connect data to conclusions. Uncritical thinkers treat their conclusions as something given to them in experience, as something they directly observe in the world. As a result, they find it difficult to see why anyone might disagree with their conclusions. After all, the truth of their views is, they believe, right there for everyone to see! Such people find it difficult or even impossible to describe the evidence or experience without confusing that description with their interpretation.

explicit: Stated openly and directly; distinctly expressed; definite. The term "explicit" is applied to that which is so clearly stated or distinctly set forth that there is no doubt as to its meaning. What is explicit is often exact and precise, suggesting that which is made unmistakably clear. Critical thinkers strive to make what is implicit in their thinking explicit when that practice enables us to assess the thinking. They realize that problems in thinking often occur when thinking is unclear, vague, or ambiguous.

fact: What actually happened, what is true; verifiable by empirical means; distinguished from interpretation, inference, judgment, or conclusion; the raw data. There is a range of distinct senses of the word "factual." For example, sometimes it means simply "true" as opposed to "claimed to be true"; or "empirical" as opposed to conceptual or evaluative. Sometimes it means "that which can be verified or disproved by observation or empirical study." People often confuse these two senses, even to the point of accepting as true, statements which merely "seem factual," for example, the scientific sounding claim "29.23% of Americans suffer from depression." Purported facts should be assessed for their accuracy, completeness, and relevance to the issue. Sources of purported facts should be assessed for their qualifications, track record, and impartiality. *See intellectual humility and knowledge.*

fair: Treating both or all sides alike without reference to one's own feelings or interests; just implies adherence to a standard of rightness or lawfulness without reference to one's own inclinations; impartial and unbiased both imply freedom from prejudice for or against any side; dispassionate implies the absence of passion or strong emotion, hence, connotes disinterested judgment; objective implies a viewing of persons or things without reference to oneself, one's interests, etc.

fair-mindedness: A cultivated disposition of mind that enables the thinker to treat all perspectives relevant to an issue in an objective manner. It implies having a consciousness of the need to treat all viewpoints alike, without reference to one's own feelings or selfish interests, or the feelings or selfish interests of one's friend's, community, or nation. It implies adherence to intellectual standards without reference to one's own advantage or the advantage of one's group.

faith: 1) Blind belief that does not require proof or evidence. 2) Complete confidence, trust, or reliance. A critical thinker does not accept faith in the first sense, "blind" faith, for every belief is reached on the basis of some thinking, which may therefore be assessed. Critical thinkers have faith or confidence in reason, but this confidence is not "blind." In other words, they recognize that "reason" and "reasonability" have proved their worth in the acquisition of knowledge. Ask yourself, what would it be not to have faith in "evidence," not to have faith in "accuracy," or "relevance?"

fallacy/fallacious: An error in reasoning; flaw or defect in argument; an argument that doesn't conform to rules of good reasoning (especially one that appears to be sound); containing or based on a fallacy; deceptive in appearance or meaning; misleading; delusive.

human nature: The common qualities of all human beings. People have both a primary and a secondary nature. Our primary nature is spontaneous, egocentric, and strongly prone to irrational belief formation. It is the basis for our instinctual thought. People need no training to believe what they want to believe: what serves their immediate interests, what preserves their sense of personal comfort and righteousness, what minimizes their sense of inconsistency, and what presupposes their own correctness. People need no special training to believe what those around them believe: what their parents and friends believe, what is taught to them by religious and school authorities, what is repeated often by the media, and what is commonly believed in the nation in which they are raised. People need no training to think that those who disagree with them are wrong and probably prejudiced. People need no training to assume that their own most fundamental beliefs are self-evidently true or easily justified by evidence. People naturally and spontaneously identify with their own beliefs. They experience most disagreements as personal attacks. The resulting defensiveness interferes with their capacity to empathize with or enter into other points of view.

On the other hand, people need extensive and systematic practice to develop their secondary nature, their implicit capacity to function as rational persons. They need extensive and systematic practice to recognize the tendencies they have to form irrational beliefs. They need extensive practice to develop a dislike of inconsistency, a love of clarity, a passion to seek reasons and evidence and to be fair to points of view other than their own. People need extensive practice to recognize that they indeed have a point of view, that they live inferentially, that they do not have a direct pipeline to reality, that it is perfectly possible to have an overwhelming inner sense of the correctness of one's views and still be wrong. *See intellectual virtues.*

idea (concept, category): Anything existing in the mind as an object of knowledge or thought; concept refers to generalized idea of a class of objects, based on knowledge of particular instances of the class. Critical thinkers are aware of the ideas (or concepts) they are using in their thinking. They recognize that all disciplines are driven by key concepts. They recognize that all thinking presupposes concepts in use. They seek to identify irrational ideas. They seek to use words (expressive of ideas) in keeping with educated usage. *See clarify, concept, logic, and logic of language.*

imply/implication: A claim or truth that follows from other claims or truths. By the "implications of reasoning," we mean "that which follows" from our thinking. It means *that to which our thinking is leading us.* If you say to someone that you "love" them, you *imply* that you are concerned with their welfare. If you make a promise, you *imply* that you intend to keep it. If you call a country a "democracy," you imply that the political power is in the hands of the people at large (as against in the hands of a powerful minority). If you call yourself a "feminist," you imply that you are in favor of the political, social, and economic equality of the sexes. We often test the credibility of a person by seeing if they are true to the implications of their own words. "Say what you mean and mean what you say" is a basic principle of critical thinking (and of personal integrity as well, for that matter).

One of the most important skills of critical thinking is the ability to distinguish between what is actually implied by a statement or situation from what may be carelessly inferred by people. Critical thinkers try to monitor their inferences to keep them in line with what is actually implied by what they know. When speaking, critical thinkers try to use words that imply only what they can legitimately justify. They recognize that there are established word usages which generate established implications. *See clarify, precision, logic of language, critical listening, critical reading, and elements of thought.*

infer/inference: An inference is a step of the mind, an intellectual act by which one concludes that something is so in light of something else's being so, or seeming to be so. If you come at me with a knife in your hand, I would probably infer that you mean to cause me harm. Inferences can be accurate or inaccurate, logical or illogical, justified or unjustified. Inferences are based upon assumptions. *See imply/implication.*

information: Statements, statistics, data, facts, diagrams, etc. that are gathered in any way, as by reading, observation, hearsay, etc. Information itself does not imply validity or accuracy. By "using information in our reasoning," we mean using some set of "facts, data, or experiences" to support our conclusions. In other words, whenever someone is reasoning, it makes sense to ask, "What facts or information are you basing your reasoning on?" The "informational" basis for reasoning is always important and often crucial. For example, in deciding whether to support capital punishment it would be important to know whether or not it deters those who contemplate murder. Each of the following statements represent "information" that one might present to support the position that capital punishment is unjustified:

> "Since the death penalty was reinstated by the Supreme court in 1976, for every 7 prisoners who were executed, one prisoner awaiting execution was found to be innocent and released."

> "At least 381 homicide convictions have been overturned since 1963 because prosecutors concealed evidence of innocence or presented evidence they knew to be false."

> "A study by the U.S. General Accounting Office found racial prejudice in death sentencing…: killers of whites were proportionally more likely to be executed than were killers of blacks."

> "Since 1984, 34 mentally retarded people have been executed."[1]

It is, of course, a separate question as to whether the information presented here is accurate, and we should recognize that the "other" side would present information as well.

insight: The ability to see clearly and deeply understand the inner nature of things. Instruction for critical thinking fosters insight rather than mere performance; it cultivates the achievement of deeper knowledge and understanding through insight. Thinking one's way into and through a subject leads to insights as one synthesizes what one is learning, relating one subject to other subjects and all subjects to personal experience.

intellectual autonomy: Having rational control of ones beliefs, values, and inferences. The ideal of critical thinking is to learn to think for oneself, to gain command over one's thought processes. Intellectual autonomy does not entail willfulness, stubbornness, or rebellion. It entails a commitment to analyzing and evaluating beliefs on the basis of reason and evidence, to question when it is rational to question, to believe when it is rational to believe, and to conform when it is rational to conform. *See know and knowledge.*

intellectual civility: A commitment to take others seriously as thinkers, to treat them as intellectual equals, to grant respect and full attention to their views—a commitment to persuade rather than browbeat. It is distinguished from intellectual rudeness: verbally attacking others, dismissing them, or stereotyping their views. Intellectual civility is not a matter of mere courtesy, but arises from a sense that communication itself requires honoring others' views and their capacity to reason.

(intellectual) confidence or faith in reason: Confidence that in the long run one's own higher interests and those of humankind at large will best be served by giving the freest play to reason—by encouraging people to come to their own conclusions through a process of developing their own rational faculties; faith that (with proper encouragement and cultivation) people can learn to think for themselves, form rational viewpoints, draw reasonable conclusions, think coherently and logically, persuade each other by reason, and become reasonable, despite the deep-seated obstacles in the native character of the human mind and in society. Confidence in reason is developed through experiences in which one reasons one's way to insight, solves problems through reason, uses reason to persuade, and is persuaded by reason. Confidence in reason is undermined when one is expected to perform tasks without understanding why, to repeat statements without having verified or justified them, or to accept beliefs on the sole basis of authority or social pressure.

---

1. *Moratorium Now,* New York Times, November 22, 1999

intellectual courage: The willingness to face and fairly assess ideas, beliefs, or viewpoints to which we have not given a serious hearing, regardless of our strong negative reactions to them. This courage arises from the recognition that ideas considered dangerous or absurd are sometimes rationally justified (in whole or in part), and that conclusions or beliefs espoused by those around us or inculcated in us are sometimes false or misleading. To determine for ourselves which is which, we must not passively and uncritically "accept" what we have "learned." Intellectual courage comes into play here, because inevitably we will come to see some truth in some ideas considered dangerous and absurd and some distortion or falsity in some ideas strongly held in our social group. It takes courage to be true to our own thinking in such circumstances. Examining cherished beliefs is difficult, and the penalties for non-conformity are often severe.

intellectual curiosity: A strong desire to deeply understand, to figure things out, to propose and assess useful and plausible hypotheses and explanations, to learn, to find out. People do not learn well, do not gain knowledge, unless they want knowledge— deep, accurate, complete understanding. When people lack passion for figuring things out (suffer from intellectual apathy), they tend to settle for an incomplete, incoherent, sketchy "sense" of things incompatible with a critically developed, richer, fuller conception. This trait can flourish only when it is allowed and encouraged, when people are allowed to pose and pursue questions of interest to them and when their intellectual curiosity pays off in increasing understanding.

intellectual empathy: Understanding the need to imaginatively put oneself in the place of others to genuinely understand them. We must recognize our egocentric tendency to identify truth with our immediate perceptions or longstanding beliefs. Intellectual empathy correlates with the ability to accurately reconstruct the viewpoints and reasoning of others and to reason from premises, assumptions, and ideas other than our own. This trait also requires that we remember occasions when we were wrong, despite an intense conviction that we were right, and consider that we might be similarly deceived in a case at hand.

intellectual humility: Awareness of the limits of one's knowledge, including sensitivity to circumstances in which one's native egocentrism is likely to function self-deceptively; sensitivity to bias and prejudice in, and limitations of one's viewpoint. Intellectual humility is based on the recognition that no one should claim more than he or she actually knows. It does not imply spinelessness or submissiveness. It implies the lack of intellectual pretentiousness, boastfulness, or conceit, combined with insight into the strengths or weaknesses of the logical foundations of one's beliefs.

intellectual integrity: Recognition of the need to be true to one's own thinking, to be consistent in the intellectual standards one applies, to hold oneself to the same rigorous standards of evidence and proof to which one holds one's antagonists, to practice what one advocates for others, and to honestly admit discrepancies and inconsistencies in one's own thought and action. This trait develops best in a supportive atmosphere in which people feel secure and free enough to honestly acknowledge their inconsistencies, and can develop and share realistic ways of ameliorating them. It requires honest acknowledgment of the difficulties of achieving greater consistency.

intellectually disciplined: The trait of thinking in accordance with intellectual standards, intellectual rigor, carefulness, order, and conscious control. The undisciplined thinker cannot recognize when he or she comes to unwarranted conclusions, confuses ideas, fails to consider pertinent evidence, and so on. Thus, intellectual discipline is at the very heart of becoming a critical person. It takes discipline of mind to keep oneself focused on the intellectual task at hand, to locate and carefully assess needed evidence, to systematically analyze and address questions and problems, to hold one's thinking to intellectual standards such as clarity, precision, completeness, consistency, etc. Such discipline is achieved slowly, bit by bit, and only through deep commitment.

intellectual perseverance: Willingness and consciousness of the need to pursue intellectual insights and truths despite difficulties, obstacles, and frustrations; firm adherence to rational principles despite irrational opposition of others; a sense of the need to struggle with confusion and unsettled questions over an extended period of time in order to achieve deeper understanding or insight.

intellectual responsibility: The responsible person keenly feels the obligation to fulfill his or her duties; intellectual responsibility is the application of this trait to intellectual matters. Hence, the intellectually responsible person feels strongly obliged to achieve a high degree of precision and accuracy in his or her reasoning, is deeply committed to gathering complete, relevant, adequate evidence, etc. This sense of obligation arises when people recognize the need for meeting the intellectual standards required by rational, fairminded thought.

intellectual sense of justice: Willingness and consciousness of the need to entertain all viewpoints sympathetically and to assess them with the same intellectual standards, without reference to one's own feelings or vested interests, or the feelings or vested interests of one's friends, community, or nation; implies adherence to intellectual standards without reference to one's own advantage or the advantage of one's group.

intellectual standards: The term "standard" applies to some measure, principle, model, etc. with which things of the same class are compared in order to determine their quality or value. Intellectual standards are concepts and principles by which reasoning should be judged in order to determine its quality or value. Because their contextualized application generates the specific criteria by which reasoning is assessed, intellectual standards are fundamental to critical thinking. Critical thinkers are able to take their thinking apart (focusing on the elements of reasoning) and assess the parts of thinking based on intellectual standards. The most important intellectual standards for thinking include clarity, accuracy, relevance, precision, breadth, depth, logic, significance, consistency, fairness, completeness, plausibility, probability, and reliability.

intellectual virtues: The traits of mind and intellectual character traits necessary for right action and thinking; the traits essential for fair-mindedness. They distinguish the narrow-minded, self-serving critical thinker from the open-minded, truth-seeking critical thinker. Intellectual traits are interdependent. Each develops simultaneously in conjunction with the others. They cannot be imposed from without; they must be developed from within. The intellectual virtues include: intellectual sense of justice, intellectual perseverance, intellectual integrity, intellectual humility, intellectual empathy, intellectual courage, (intellectual) confidence in reason, and intellectual autonomy.

interpret/interpretation: To give one's own conception of, to place in the context of one's own experience, perspective, point of view, or philosophy. Interpretations should be distinguished from the facts, the evidence, and the situation. (I may interpret someone's silence as an expression of hostility toward me. Such an interpretation may or may not be correct. I may have projected my patterns of motivation and behavior onto that person, or I may have accurately noticed this pattern in the other.) The best interpretations take the most evidence into account. Critical thinkers recognize their interpretations, distinguish them from evidence, consider alternative interpretations, and reconsider their interpretations in the light of new evidence. All learning involves personal interpretation, since whatever we learn we must integrate into our own thinking and action. What we learn must be given a meaning by us, must be meaningful to us, and hence involves interpretive acts on our part. Didactic instruction, in attempting to directly implant knowledge in students' minds, typically ignores the role of personal interpretation in learning.

intuition: The direct knowing or learning of something without the conscious use of reasoning. We sometimes seem to know or learn things without recognizing how we came to that knowledge. When this occurs, we experience an inner sense that what we believe is true. The problem is that sometimes we are correct (and have genuinely experienced an intuition) and sometimes we are incorrect (having fallen victim to one of our prejudices). A critical thinker does not blindly accept what he or she thinks or believes but cannot prove as true. A critical thinker realizes how easily we confuse intuitions and prejudices. Critical thinkers may follow their inner sense that something is so, but only with a healthy sense of intellectual humility.

There is a second sense of "intuition" that is important for critical thinking, and that is the meaning suggested in the following sentence: "To develop your critical thinking abilities, it is important to develop your critical thinking intuitions." This sense of the word is connected to the fact that we can learn concepts at various levels of depth. If we learn nothing more than an abstract definition for a word and do not learn how to apply it effectively in a wide variety of situations, one might say that we end up with no intuitive basis for applying it. We lack the insight into how, when, and why it applies. We develop critical thinking intuitions when we gain the practical insights necessary for a ready and swift application of concepts to cases in a large array of circumstances. We want critical thinking to be "intuitive" to us, ready and available for immediate translation into their everyday thought and experience.

irrational/irrationality: 1) Lacking the power to reason. 2) Contrary to reason or logic. 3) Senseless, absurd. Uncritical thinkers are those who have failed to develop the ability or power to reason well. Their beliefs and practices, then, are often contrary to what is reasonable, sensible, and logical, and are sometimes blatantly absurd. The terms can be applied to persons, acts, emotions, policies, laws, social practices, belief systems, even whole societies… to virtually any human construct. *See reason, rationality and logic.*

irrational learning: All rational learning presupposes rational assent. And, though we sometimes forget it, not all learning is automatically or even commonly rational. Much that we learn in everyday life is quite distinctively irrational. It is quite possible—and indeed the bulk of human learning is unfortunately of this character—to come to believe any number of things without knowing how or why. It is quite possible, in other words, to believe for irrational reasons: because those around us believe, because we are rewarded for believing, because we are afraid to disbelieve, because our vested interest is served by belief, because we are more comfortable with belief, or because we have ego identified ourselves, our image, or our personal being with belief. In all of these cases, our beliefs are without rational grounding, without good reason and evidence, without the foundation a rational person demands. We become rational, on the other hand, to the extent that our beliefs and actions are grounded in good reasons and evidence; to the extent that we recognize and critique our own irrationality; to the extent that we are not moved by bad reasons and a multiplicity of irrational motives, fears, and desires; to the extent that we have cultivated a passion for clarity, accuracy, and fair-mindedness. These global skills, passions, and dispositions, integrated into behavior and thought, characterize the rational, the educated, and the critical person. *See higher and lower order learning, knowledge, and didactic instruction.*

judgment: 1) The act of judging or deciding. 2) Understanding and good sense. A person has good judgment when he or she typically judges and decides on the basis of understanding and good sense. Whenever we form a belief or opinion, make a decision, or act, we do so on the basis of implicit or explicit judgments. All thought presupposes making judgments concerning what is so and what is not so, what is true and what is not. To cultivate people's ability to think critically is to foster their judgment, to help them develop the habit of judging on the basis of reason, evidence, logic, and good sense. Good judgment is developed, not by merely learning about principles of good judgment, but by frequent practice judging and assessing judgments.

justify/justification: The act of showing a belief, opinion, action, or policy to be in accord with reason and evidence, to be ethically acceptable, or both. Education should foster reasonability in students. This requires that both teachers and students develop the disposition to ask for and give justifications for beliefs, opinions, actions, and policies. Asking for a justification should not, then, be viewed as an insult or attack, but rather as a normal act of a rational person.

know: To have a clear perception or understanding of, to be sure of, to have a firm mental grasp of; information applies to data that are gathered in any way, as by reading, observation, hearsay, etc. and does not necessarily connote validity; knowledge applies to any body of facts gathered by study, observation, etc. and to the ideas inferred from these facts, and connotes an understanding of what is known. Critical thinkers need to distinguish knowledge from opinion and belief. *See knowledge.*

knowledge: The act of having a clear and justifiable grasp of what is so or of how to do something. Knowledge is based on understanding or skill, which in turn are based on thought, study, and experience. "Thoughtless knowledge" is a contradiction. "Blind knowledge" is a contradiction. "Unjustifiable knowledge" is a contradiction. Knowledge implies justifiable belief or skilled action. Hence, when students blindly memorize and are tested for recall, they are not being tested for knowledge. Knowledge is continually confused with recall in present-day schooling. This confusion is a deep-seated impediment to the integration of critical thinking into schooling. Genuine knowledge is inseparable from thinking minds. We often wrongly talk of knowledge as though it could be divorced from thinking, as though it could be gathered up by one person and given to another in the form of a collection of sentences to remember. When we talk in this way, we forget that knowledge, by its very nature, depends on thought. Knowledge is produced by thought, analyzed by thought, comprehended by thought, organized, evaluated, maintained, and transformed by thought. Knowledge can be acquired only through thought. Knowledge exists, properly speaking, only in minds that have comprehended and justified it through thought. Knowledge is not to be confused with belief nor with the symbolic representation of belief. Humans easily and frequently believe things that are false or believe things to be true without knowing them to be so. A book contains knowledge only in a derivative sense, only because minds can thoughtfully read it and through that process gain knowledge.

logic: 1) Correct reasoning or the study of correct reasoning and its foundations. 2) The relationships between propositions (supports, assumes, implies, contradicts, counts against, is relevant to…). 3) The system of principles, concepts, and assumptions that underlie any discipline, activity, or practice. 4) The set of rational considerations that bear upon the truth or justification of any belief or set of beliefs. 5) The set of rational considerations that bear upon the settlement of any question or set of questions. The word "logic" covers a range of related concerns all bearing upon the question of rational justification and explanation. All human thought and behavior is to some extent based on logic rather than instinct. Humans try to figure things out using ideas, meanings, and thought. Such intellectual behavior inevitably involves "logic" or considerations of a logical sort: some sense of what is relevant and irrelevant, of what supports and what counts against a belief, of what we should and should not assume, of what we should and should not claim, of what we do and do not know, of what is and is not implied, of what does and does not contradict, of what we should or should not do or believe. Concepts have a logic in that we can investigate the conditions under which they do and do not apply, of what is relevant or irrelevant to them, of what they do or don't imply, etc. Questions have a logic in that we can investigate the conditions under which they can be settled. Disciplines have a logic in that they have purposes and a set of logical structures that bear upon those purposes: assumptions, concepts, issues, data, theories, claims, implications, consequences, etc. The concept of logic is a seminal notion in critical thinking. Unfortunately, it takes a considerable length of time before most people become comfortable with its multiple uses. In part, this is owing to people's failure to monitor their own thinking in keeping with the standards of reason and logic. This is not to deny, of course, that logic is involved in all human thinking. It is rather to say that the logic we use is often implicit, unexpressed, and sometimes contradictory. *See knowledge, higher- and lower-order learning, the logic of a discipline, the logic of language, and the logic of questions.*

the logic of a discipline: The notion that every technical term has logical relationships with other technical terms, that some terms are logically more basic than others, and that every discipline relies on concepts, assumptions, and theories, makes claims, gives reasons and evidence, avoids contradictions and inconsistencies, has implications and consequences, etc. Though all students study disciplines, most are ignorant of the logic of the disciplines they study. This severely limits their ability to grasp the discipline as a whole, to think independently within it, to compare and contrast it with other disciplines, and to apply it outside the context of academic assignments. Typically now, students do not look for seminal terms as they study an area. They do not strive to translate technical terms into analogies and ordinary words they understand or distinguish technical from ordinary uses of terms. They do not look for the basic assumptions of the disciplines they study. Indeed, on the whole, they do not know what assumptions are nor why it is important to examine them. What they have in their heads exists like so many BB's in a bag. Whether one thought supports or follows from another, whether one thought elaborates another, exemplifies, presupposes, or contradicts another, are matters students have not learned to think about. They have not learned to use thought to understand thought, which is another way of saying that they have not learned how to use thought to gain knowledge. Instruction for critical thinking cultivates the students' ability to make explicit the logic of what they study. This emphasis gives depth and breath to study and learning. It lies at the heart of the differences between lower-order and higher-order learning. *See knowledge.*

the logic of language: For a language to exist and be learnable by persons from a variety of cultures, it is necessary that words have definite uses and defined concepts that transcend particular cultures. The English language, for example, is learned by many peoples of the world unfamiliar with English or North American cultures. Critical thinkers must learn to use their native language with precision, in keeping with educated usage. Unfortunately, many do not understand the significant relationship between precision in language usage and precision in thought. Consider, for example, how most students relate to their native language. If one questions them about the meanings of words, their account is typically incoherent. They often say that people have their own meanings for all the words they use, not noticing that, were this true, we could not understand each other. People speak and write in vague sentences because they have no rational criteria for choosing words—they simply write whatever words pop into their heads. They do not realize that every language has a highly refined logic one must learn in order to express oneself precisely. They do not realize that even words similar in meaning typically have different implications. Consider, for example, the words explain, expound, explicate, elucidate, interpret, and construe. Explain implies the process of making clear and intelligible something not understood or known. Expound implies a systematic and thorough explanation, often by an expert. Explicate implies a scholarly analysis developed in detail. Elucidate implies a shedding of light upon by clear and specific illustration or explanation. Interpret implies the bringing out of meanings not immediately apparent. Construe implies a particular interpretation of something whose meaning is ambiguous. *See clarify and concept.*

the logic of questions: The range of rational considerations that bear upon the settlement of a given question or group of questions. A critical thinker is adept at analyzing questions to determine what, precisely, a question asks and how to go about rationally settling it. A critical thinker recognizes that different kinds of questions often call for different modes of thinking, different kinds of considerations, and different procedures and techniques. Uncritical thinkers often confuse distinct questions and use considerations irrelevant to an issue while ignoring relevant ones.

lower-order learning: Learning by rote memorization, association, and drill. There are a variety of forms of lower-order learning in schools that we can identify by understanding the relative lack of logic informing them. Paradigmatically, lower-order learning is learning by sheer association or rote. Hence, students come to think of history class, for example, as a place where you hear names, dates, places, events, and outcomes; where you try to remember them and state them on tests. Math comes to be thought of as numbers, symbols, and formulas—mysterious things you mechanically manipulate as the teacher told you in order to get the right answer.

Literature is often thought of as uninteresting stories to remember along with what the teacher said is important about them. Consequently, students leave with a jumble of undigested fragments, scraps left over after they have forgotten most of what they stored in their short-term memories for tests. Virtually never do they grasp the logic of what they learn. Rarely do they relate what they learn to their own experience or critique each by means of the other. Rarely do they try to test what they learn in everyday life. Rarely do they ask "Why is this so? How does this relate to what I already know? How does this relate to what I am learning in other classes?" To put the point in a nutshell, very few students think of what they are learning as worthy of being arranged logically in their minds or have the slightest idea of how to do so.

monological (one-dimensional) problems: Problems that can be solved by reasoning exclusively within one point of view or frame of reference. For example, consider the following problems: 1) Ten full crates of walnuts weigh 410 pounds, whereas an empty crate weighs 10 pounds. How much do the walnuts alone weigh? and 2) In how many days of the week does the third letter of the day's name immediately follow the first letter of the day's name in the alphabet? We call these problems and the means by which they are solved "monological." They are settled within one frame of reference with a definite set of logical moves. When the right set of moves is performed, the problem is settled. The answer or solution proposed can be shown by standards implicit in the frame of reference to be the "right" answer or solution. Most important human problems are multilogical rather than monological, non-atomic problems inextricably joined to other problems, with some conceptual messiness to them and very often with important values lurking in the background. When the problems have an empirical dimension, that dimension tends to have a controversial scope. In multilogical problems, it is often arguable how some facts should be considered and interpreted, and how their significance should be determined. When they have a conceptual dimension, there tend to be arguably different ways to pin the concepts down. Though life presents us with predominantly multilogical problems, schooling today over-emphasizes monological problems. Worse, and more frequently, present instructional practices treat multilogical problems as though they were monological. The posing of multilogical problems, and their consideration from multiple points of view, play an important role in the cultivation of critical thinking and higher-order learning.

monological (one-dimensional) thinking: Thinking that is conducted exclusively within one point of view or frame of reference: figuring out how much this $67.49 pair of shoes with a 25% discount will cost me; learning what signing this contract obliges me to do; finding out when Kennedy was elected President. A person can think monologically whether or not the question is genuinely monological. (For example, if one considers the question, "Who caused the Civil War?" only from a Northerner's perspective, one is thinking monologically about a multilogical question.) The strong sense critical thinker avoids monological thinking when the question is multilogical. Moreover, higher-order learning requires multilogical thought, even when the problem is monological (for example, learning a concept in chemistry), since students must explore and assess their original beliefs to develop insight into new ideas.

multilogical (multi-dimensional) problems: Problems that can be analyzed and approached from more than one, often from conflicting, points of view or frames of reference. For example, many ecological problems have a variety of dimensions to them: historical, social, economic, biological, chemical, moral, political, etc. A person comfortable thinking through multilogical problems is comfortable thinking within multiple perspectives, in engaging in dialogical and dialectical thinking, in practicing intellectual empathy, in thinking across disciplines and domains. *See monological problems, the logic of questions, the logic of disciplines, and intellectual empathy.*

multilogical thinking: Thinking that sympathetically enters, considers, and reasons within multiple points of view. *See multilogical problems, dialectical thinking, and dialogical instruction.*

national bias: Prejudice in favor of one's country, it's beliefs, traditions, practices, image, and world view; a form of sociocentrism or ethnocentrism. It is natural, if not inevitable, for people to be favorably disposed toward the beliefs, traditions, practices, and world view within which they were raised. Unfortunately, this favorable inclination commonly becomes a form of prejudice: a more or less rigid, irrational ego-identification that significantly distorts one's view of one's own nation and the world at large. It is manifested in a tendency to mindlessly take the side of one's own government, to uncritically accept governmental accounts of the nature of disputes with other nations, to uncritically exaggerate the virtues of one's own nation while playing down the virtues of "enemy" nations. National bias is reflected in the press and media coverage of every nation of the world. Events are included or excluded according to what appears significant within the dominant world view of the nation, and are shaped into stories to validate that view. Though constructed to fit into a particular view of the world, the stories in the news are presented as neutral, objective accounts, and uncritically accepted as such because people tend to uncritically assume that their own view of things is the way things really are. To become responsible critically thinking citizens and fair-minded people, students must practice identifying national bias in the news and in their texts, and to broaden their perspective beyond that of uncritical nationalism. *See ethnocentrism, sociocentrism, bias, prejudice, world view, intellectual empathy, critical society, dialogical instruction, and knowledge.*

opinion: A belief, typically one open to dispute. Sheer unreasoned subjective opinion or preference should be distinguished from reasoned judgment—beliefs formed on the basis of careful reasoning. *See evaluation, judgment, justify, know, knowledge, and reasoned judgment.*

perfections of thought: Thinking, viewed as an attempt to understand or make sense of the world, has a natural excellence or fitness to it. This excellence is manifest in its clarity, precision, specificity, accuracy, relevance, consistency, logicalness, depth, completeness, significance, fairness, and adequacy. These perfections are general achievements of thought. Their absence represent legitimate concerns irrespective of the discipline or domain of thought. To develop one's mind and discipline one's thinking with respect to these standards requires regular practice and long-term cultivation. Of course, achieving these standards is a relative matter and varies to some degree among domains of thought. Being precise while doing mathematics is not the same as being precise while writing a poem, describing an experience, or explaining a historical event. What is more, skilled propaganda, skilled political debate, skilled defense of a group's interests, skilled deception of one's enemy may require the violation or selective application of the above standards. Perfecting one's thought as an instrument for success in a world based on power and advantage differs from perfecting one's thought for the apprehension and defense of fair-minded, balanced truthfulness. To develop one's critical thinking skills merely to the level of adequacy for social success is to sacrifice the higher perfections of thought for pragmatic gain and generally involves more than a little self-deception.

personal contradiction: An inconsistency in one's personal life, wherein one says one thing and does another, or uses a double standard, judging oneself and one's friends by an easier standard than that used for people one doesn't like; typically a form of hypocrisy accompanied by self-deception. Most personal contradictions remain unconscious. People too often ignore the difficulty of becoming intellectually and morally consistent, preferring instead to merely admonish others. Personal contradictions are more likely to be discovered, analyzed, and reduced in an atmosphere in which they can be openly admitted and realistically considered without excessive penalty. *See egocentricity and intellectual integrity.*

point of view (perspective): Human thought is relational and selective. It is impossible to understand any person, event, or phenomenon from every vantage point simultaneously. Our purposes often control how we see things. Critical thinking requires that this fact be taken into account when analyzing and assessing thinking. This is not to say that human thought is incapable of truth and objectivity, but only that human truth, objectivity, and insight is virtually always limited and partial, virtually never total and absolute. By "reasoning within a point of view," then, we mean that there is inevitably some comprehensive focus or orientation to our thinking. Our thinking is focused *on* something *from* some angle. We can change either what we are focused on or the angle of our focus. We often give names to the "angle" from which we are thinking about something. For example, we could look at something politically or scientifically, poetically or philosophically. We might look at something conservatively or liberally, religiously or secularly. We might look at something from a cultural or a financial perspective, or both. Once we understand how someone is approaching a question or topic (that is, what their comprehensive perspective is), we are usually much better able to understand the logic of their thinking as an organized whole.

precision: The quality of being accurate, definite, and exact. The standards and modes of precision vary according to subject and context. *See the logic of language and elements of thought.*

prejudice: A judgment, belief, opinion, point of view—favorable or unfavorable— formed before the relevant facts are known, resistant to evidence and reason, or in disregard of facts that contradict it. Self-announced prejudice is rare. Prejudice almost always exists in obscured, rationalized, socially validated, or functional forms. It enables people to sleep peacefully at night even while flagrantly abusing the rights of others. It enables people to get more of what they want, or to get it more easily. It is often sanctioned with a superabundance of pomp and self-righteousness. Unless we recognize these powerful tendencies toward selfish thought in our social institutions, even in what appear to be lofty actions and moralistic rhetoric, we will not face squarely the problem of prejudice in human thought and action. Uncritical and selfishly critical thought are often prejudiced. Most instruction in schools today, because students do not think their way to what they accept as true, tends to give students prejudices rather than knowledge. For example, partly as a result of schooling, people often accept as authorities those who liberally sprinkle their statements with numbers and intellectual-sounding language, however irrational or unjust their positions. This prejudice toward pseudo-authority impedes rational assessment. *See insight and knowledge.*

premise: A proposition upon which an argument is based or from which a conclusion is drawn. A starting point of reasoning. For example, one might say, in commenting on someone's reasoning, "You seem to be reasoning from the premise that everyone is selfish in everything they do. Do you hold this belief?"

principle: A fundamental truth, law, doctrine, value, or commitment, upon which others are based. Rules, which are more specific, and often superficial and arbitrary, are based on principles. Rules are more algorithmic; they needn't be understood to be followed. Principles must be understood to be appropriately applied or followed. One important set of principles are ethical principles, which are guides for human conduct. Critical thinking is dependent on principles, not rules and procedures. Critical thinking is principled, not procedural, thinking. Principles must be practiced and applied to be internalized. *See higher order learning, lower order learning, and judgment.*

problem: A question, matter, situation, or person that is perplexing or difficult to figure out, handle, or resolve. Problems, like questions, can be divided into many types. Each has a (particular) logic. *See logic of questions, monological problems, and multilogical problems.*

problem-solving: Whenever a problem cannot be solved formulaically or robotically, critical thinking is required: first, to determine the nature and dimensions of the problem, and then, in the light of the first, to determine the considerations, points of view, concepts, theories, data, and reasoning relevant to its solution. Extensive practice in independent problem-solving is essential to developing critical thought. Problem-solving is rarely best approached procedurally or as a series of rigidly followed steps. For example, problem-solving schemas typically begin, "State the problem." Rarely can problems be precisely and fairly stated prior to analysis, gathering of evidence, and dialogical or dialectical thought wherein several provisional descriptions of the problem are proposed, assessed, and revised.

proof (prove): Evidence or reasoning so strong or certain as to demonstrate the truth or acceptability of a conclusion beyond a reasonable doubt. How strong evidence or reasoning have to be to demonstrate what they purport to prove varies from context to context, depending on the significance of the conclusion or the seriousness of the implications following from it. *See domain of thought.*

purpose: Something one intends to get or do, object, aim, goal, end in view. By reasoning having a purpose, we mean that when humans think about the world we do not do so randomly, but rather in line with our goals, desires, needs, and values. Our thinking is an integral part of a patterned way of acting in the world, and we act, even in simple matters, with some set of ends in view. To understand someone's thinking—including our own—we must understand the functions it serves, what it is about, the direction it is moving, the ends that make sense of it. Of course, most of what we are after in our thinking is not obvious to us. Raising human goals and desires to the level of conscious realization is an important part of critical thinking.

question: A problem or matter open to discussion or inquiry, something that is asked as in seeking to learn or gain knowledge. By reasoning upon some *question, issue,* or *problem* we mean that when we think about the world in line with our goals, desires, needs, and values, we often come up against questions we need to answer, problems we need to solve, issues we need to resolve. Therefore, when we find ourselves faced with a difficulty, it always makes sense to say, "What is the question we need to answer?" or "What is the problem we need to solve?" or "What is the issue we need to resolve?" To improve our ability to think well it is important to learn how to put the questions, problems, and issues we need to deal with in a clear and distinct way. Change the question, you change the criteria you have to meet to settle it. Modify the problem, you need to modify how you are going to solve the problem. Shift the issues and new considerations become relevant to its resolution.

rational/rationality: That which conforms to principles of good reasoning, is sensible, shows good judgment, is consistent, logical, complete, and relevant. When we refer to something or someone as "rational," we always have in mind the quality of being based on or informed by sound reasoning and/or justified evidence. Rationality is a summary term like "virtue" or "goodness." It is manifested in an unlimited number of ways and depends on a host of principles. There is some ambiguity in it, depending on whether one considers only the consistency and effectiveness by which one pursues one's ends, or whether it includes the assessment of ends themselves. There is also ambiguity in whether one considers selfish ends to be rational, even when they conflict with what is just. Does a rational person have to be just or only skilled in pursuing his or her interests? Is it rational to be rational in an irrational world? *See perfections of thought, irrational/irrationality, logic, intellectual virtues, weak sense critical thinking, and strong sense critical thinking.*

rational emotions/passions: R. S. Peters (1973) has explained the significance of the affective side of reason and critical thought in his defense of the necessity of "rational passions":

> There is, for instance, the hatred of contradictions and inconsistencies, together with the love of clarity and hatred of confusion without which words could not be held to relatively constant meanings and testable rules and generalizations stated. A reasonable man cannot, without some special explanation, slap his sides with delight or express indifference if he is told that what he says is confused, incoherent, and perhaps riddled with contradictions.
>
> Reason is the antithesis of arbitrariness. In its operation it is supported by the appropriate passions which are mainly negative in character—the hatred of irrelevance, special pleading, and arbitrary fiat. The more developed emotion of indignation is aroused when some excess of arbitrariness is perpetuated in a situation where people's interests and claims are at stake. The positive side of this is the passion for fairness and impartial consideration of claims.
>
> A man who is prepared to reason must feel strongly that he must follow the arguments and decide things in terms of where they lead. He must have a sense of the giveness of the impersonality of such considerations. In so far as thoughts about persons enter his head they should be tinged with the respect which is due to another who, like himself, may have a point of view which is worth considering, who may have a glimmering of the truth which has so far eluded himself. A person who proceeds in this way, who is influenced by such passions, is what we call a reasonable man.

rationalize: To devise socially plausible explanations or excuses for one's actions, desires, beliefs, etc. when these are not one's actual motives. In other words, to rationalize is to give reasons that "sound good," but are not honest and accurate. Rationalization is often used in situations where one is pursuing one's vested interests while trying to maintain the appearance of high moral purpose. Politicians are continually rationalizing their actions implying that they are acting from high motives when, usually, they are acting as they are because they have received large donations from vested interest groups who profit from the action taken. Those who held slaves often rationalized that slavery was justified because the slaves were like children and had to be taken care of. Rationalization is a defense mechanism used by the egocentric mind to enable people to get what they want without having to face the fact that their motives are selfish or their behavior unconscionable. Rationalizations enable us to keep our actual motives beneath the level of consciousness. We can then sleep peacefully at night while we behave unethically by day.

rational self: Our character and nature to the extent that we seek to base our beliefs and actions on good reasoning and evidence. Who we are, what our true character is, or our predominant qualities are, is always somewhat or even greatly different from who we think we are. Human egocentrism and accompanying self-deception often stand in the way of our gaining more insight into ourselves. We can develop a rational self, become a person who gains significant insight into what our true character is, only by reducing our egocentrism and self-deception. Critical thinking is essential to this process.

rational society: *See critical society.*

reasoned judgment: Any belief or conclusion reached on the basis of careful thought and reflection, distinguished from mere or unreasoned opinion on the one hand, and from sheer fact on the other. Few people have a clear sense of which of their beliefs are based on reasoned judgment and which on mere opinion. Moral or ethical questions, for example, are questions usually requiring reasoned judgment. One way of conceiving of subject-matter education is as developing students' ability to engage in reasoned judgment in accordance with the standards of each subject.

reasoning: The mental processes of those who reason; especially the drawing of conclusions or inferences from observations, facts, or hypotheses; the evidence or arguments used in this procedure. In other words, by "reasoning," we mean "making sense of something by giving it some meaning in your mind." Virtually all thinking is part of our "sense-making" activities. We hear scratching at the door and think, "It's the dog." We see dark clouds in the sky and think, "It looks like rain." Some of this activity operates at a subconscious level (for example, all of the sights and sounds about me have meaning for me without my explicitly noticing that they do). Most of our "reasoning" is quite unspectacular. Our reasoning tends to become explicit to us only when it is challenged by someone and we have to defend it. ("Why do you say that Jack is obnoxious? I thought he was quite pleasant.") A critical thinker tries to develop the capacity to transform thought into reasoning at will, or rather, the ability to make his or her inferences explicit, along with the assumptions or premises upon which those inferences are based. Reasoning is a form of explicit inferring, usually involving multiple steps.

reciprocity: The act of entering empathically into the point of view or line of reasoning of others; learning to think as others do and by that means sympathetically assessing that thinking. (Reciprocity requires creative imagination as well as intellectual skill and a commitment to fair-mindedness.)

relevant: Bearing upon or relating to the matter at hand; relevant implies close logical relationship with, and importance to, the matter under consideration; germane implies such close natural connection as to be highly appropriate or fit;

pertinent implies an immediate and direct bearing on the matter at hand (a pertinent suggestion); applicable refers to that which can be brought to bear upon a particular matter or problem. Many people have problems sticking to an issue and distinguishing information that bears upon a problem from information that does not. Merely reminding them to limit themselves to relevant considerations fails to solve this problem. Sensitivity to (ability to judge) relevance can only be developed with continual practice—practice distinguishing relevant from irrelevant data, evaluating or judging relevance, arguing for and against the relevance of facts and considerations.

self-deception: Deceiving one's self about one's true motivations, character, identity, etc. One possible definition of the human species is "The Self-Deceiving Animal." Self-deception is a fundamental problem in human life and the cause of much human suffering. Overcoming self-deception through self-critical thinking is a fundamental goal of strong sense critical thinking. *See egocentric, rational self, personal contradiction, social contradiction, and intellectual virtues.*

selfish interest: Pursuing what is perceived as in one's interest without regard for the rights and needs of others. To be selfish is to seek what one desires without due consideration for others. Being interested in one's welfare is one thing; trampling on the rights of others while one pursues desires unrelated to fundamental human needs is another. As fundamentally egocentric creatures, humans are naturally given to pursue their selfish interest, using rationalization and other forms of self-deception to disguise their true motives and the true character of what they are doing. To develop as fair-minded critical thinkers is to actively work to diminish the power of one's native selfishness, without sacrificing any of one's legitimate concern for one's welfare and long-term good. *See self-deception, rationalization, egocentricity, and fair-mindedness.*

social contradiction: An inconsistency between what a society preaches and what it practices. In every society there is some degree of inconsistency between its image of itself and its actual character. Social contradiction typically correlates with human self-deception on the social or cultural level. Critical thinking is essential for the recognition of inconsistencies, and recognition is essential for reform and eventual integrity.

sociocentricity: The assumption that one's own social group is inherently and self-evidently superior to all others. When a group or society sees itself as superior, and so considers its views as correct or as the only reasonable or justifiable views, and all its actions as justified, there is a tendency to presuppose this superiority in all of its thinking and thus, to think closed-mindedly. All dissent and doubt are considered disloyal and rejected without consideration. Few people recognize the socio-centric nature of much of their thought. *See ethnocentricity.*

Socratic questioning: A mode of questioning that deeply probes the meaning, justification, or logical strength of a claim, position, or line of reasoning. Socratic questioning can be carried out in a variety of ways and adapted to many levels of ability and understanding. *See elements of thought, dialogical instruction, and knowledge.*

specify/specific: To mention, describe, or define in detail; limiting or limited; specifying or specified; precise; definite. Most people's thinking, speech, and writing tend to be vague, abstract, and ambiguous rather than specific, concrete, and clear. Learning how to state one's views specifically is essential to learning how to think clearly, precisely, and accurately. *See perfections of thought.*

strong sense critical thinker: One who is predominantly characterized by the following traits: 1) an ability to question deeply one's own framework of thought; 2) an ability to reconstruct sympathetically and imaginatively the strongest versions of points of view and frameworks of thought opposed to one's own; and 3) an ability to reason dialectically (multilogically) in such a way as to determine when one's own point of view is at its weakest and when an opposing point of view is at its strongest. Strong sense critical thinkers are not routinely blinded by their own viewpoints. They know they have points of view and therefore recognize on what framework of assumptions and ideas their own thinking is based. They realize the necessity of putting their own assumptions and ideas to the test of the strongest objections that can be leveled against them. Learning critical thinking in the strong sense is learning to explicate, understand, and critique our own deepest prejudices, biases, and misconceptions, thereby discovering and contesting our egocentric and sociocentric tendencies. Only if we contest our inevitable egocentric and sociocentric habits of thought, can we hope to think in a genuinely rational fashion. Only dialogical thinking about basic issues that genuinely matter to the individual provides the kind of practice and skill essential to strong sense critical thinking.

We need to develop critical thinking skills in dialogical settings to achieve genuine fairmindedness. If critical thinking is learned simply as atomic skills separate from the empathic practice of entering into points of view that we are fearful of or hostile toward, we will simply find additional means of rationalizing our prejudices. *See fairmindedness.*

submissive ego: Humans are naturally concerned with their interests and are motivated to satisfy their desires. In a world of psychological power and influence, there are two basic ways to succeed: to psychologically "conquer" or "intimidate" (subtly or openly) those who stand in your way, or, alternatively, to psychologically join and serve more powerful others who then: 1) give you a sense of personal importance, 2) protect you, and 3) share with you some of the benefits of their success. The irrational person uses both techniques, though not to the same degree. Those who seem to be more successful submitting to more powerful others have what might be called a "submissive" ego. Those who seem to be more successful using overt force and control have what might be called a "dominating" ego. This behavior can be seen publicly in the relationship of "Rock stars" or "sport stars" to their admiring "followers." Most social groups have an internal "pecking" order, with some playing roles of "leader" and most playing roles of "followers." A fair-minded rational person seeks neither to dominate nor to blindly serve someone else who dominates. *See dominating ego.*

theory: A systematic statement of principles involved in a subject; a formulation of apparent relationships or underlying principles of certain observed phenomena which has been verified to some degree. Often without realizing it, we form theories that help us make sense of the people, events, and problems in our lives. Critical thinkers put their theories to the test of experience and give due consideration to the theories of others. Critical thinkers do not confuse theories with facts.

think: The general word meaning to exercise the mental faculties so as to form ideas, arrive at conclusions, etc.; reason implies a logical sequence of thought, starting with what is known or assumed and advancing to a definite conclusion through the inferences drawn; reflect implies a turning of one's thoughts back on a subject and connotes deep or quiet continued thought; speculate implies a reasoning on the basis of incomplete or uncertain evidence and therefore stresses the conjectural character of the opinions formed; deliberate implies careful and thorough consideration of a matter in order to arrive at a conclusion. Though everyone thinks, few people think critically. We don't need instruction to think; we think spontaneously. We need instruction to learn how to discipline and direct our thinking on the basis of sound intellectual standards. *See elements of thought and perfections of thought.*

truth: Conformity to knowledge, fact, actuality, or logic: a statement proven to be or accepted as true, not false or erroneous. Most people uncritically assume their views to be correct and true. Most people, in other words, assume themselves to possess the truth. Critical thinking is essential to avoid this, if for no other reason.

uncritical person: One who has not developed intellectual skills. In other words, one who is naive, conforming, easily manipulated, dogmatic, easily confused, unclear, closed-minded, narrow-minded, careless in word choice, inconsistent, or unable to distinguish evidence from interpretation. Uncriticalness is a fundamental problem in human life, for when we are uncritical we nevertheless think of ourselves as critical. The first step in becoming a critical thinker consists in recognizing that we are uncritical.

vague: Not clearly, precisely, or definitely expressed or stated; not sharp, certain, or precise in thought, feeling, or expression. Vagueness of thought and expression is a major obstacle to the development of critical thinking. We cannot begin to test our beliefs until we recognize clearly what they are. We cannot disagree with what someone says until we are clear about what they mean. We need much practice in transforming our vague thoughts into clear ones. *See ambiguous, clarify, concept, logic, logic of questions, and logic of language.*

verbal implication: That which follows, according to the logic of the language. If I say, for example, that someone used flattery on me, I imply that the compliments were insincere and given only to make me feel positively toward that person, to manipulate me against my reason or interest for some end. *See imply, infer, empirical implication, and elements of thought.*

vested interest: 1) Involvement in promoting personal advantage, usually at the expense of others. 2) People functioning as a group to pursue collective selfish goals and exerting influences that enables them to profit at the expense of others. Many groups that lobby Congress do so to gain money, power, and advantage for themselves by provisions in law that specially favor them. The term "vested interest" classically contrasts with the term "public interest." A group that lobbies congress in the public interest is not seeking to gain special advantage for a comparative few, but protection for virtually all or the large majority. Preserving the quality of the air is a *public* interest. Building cheaper cars by including fewer safety features is a *vested* interest—It makes more money for car manufacturers. *See selfish interest.*

weak sense critical thinkers: 1) Those who do not hold themselves or those with whom they ego-identify to the same intellectual standards to which they hold "opponents." 2) Those who have not learned how to reason empathically within points of view or frames of reference with which they disagree. 3) Those who tend to think monologically (within one narrow perspective). 4) Those who do not genuinely accept, though they may verbally espouse, the values of critical thinking. 5) Those who use the intellectual skills of critical thinking selectively and self-deceptively to foster and serve their selfish interests (at the expense of truth). 6) Those who use critical thinking skills to identify flaws in the reasoning of others and sophisticated arguments to refute other's arguments before giving those arguments due consideration. Those who are able to justify their irrational thinking with highly skilled rationalizations. *See monological thinking, rationalization, and irrational.*

world view: All human action takes place within a way of looking at and interpreting the world. As human life now stands, very little is done to help people grasp how they are viewing the world and how those views determine the character of their experience, their interpretations, their conclusions about events and persons, etc. In learning critical thinking in a strong sense, we discover our own world view and appreciate the insights of the world views of others. *See bias and interpret.*

References

Atlanta Monthly (1998, Dec.). *The Prison Industrial Complex.*

Campbell, S. (Ed.). (1976). *Piaget Sampler: An Introduction to Jean Piaget through His Own Words.* New York, NY: John Wiley & Sons.

Churchill, W. (1948). *The Gathering Storm.* Boston, MA: Houghton Mifflin Company.

Covey, S. (1992). *Principle-Based Leadership.* New York, NY: Simon and Schuster.

Encyclopedia Americana (Vol. 7). (1950). New York, NY: Americana Corporation, p. 541.

Ewald, P. (2000). *Plague Time.* The Free Press.

Green, R. (1998). *The 48 Laws of Power.* New York, NY: Penguin Books.

Guralnik, D. B. (Ed.). (1986). *Webster's New World Dictionary.* New York, NY: Prentice-Hall.

Hughes, T. (1882). *Tom Brown's School Days.* Philadelphia, PA: Porter & Coates.

Illich, I. (1976). *Medical Nemesis.* New York, NY: Random House.

Kerwin, A., Witte, M., and Witte, C. (1995). *Don't Vanquish Ignorance...Use It Well.* Presentation delivered at the Fifteenth Annual International Conference on Critical Thinking and Education Reform sponsored by the Center for Critical Thinking and Moral Critique, Dillon Beach, CA. (The program is through the University of Arizona School of Medicine in Tucson, AZ).

Myers, G. (1908). *History of the Great American Fortunes* (Vol 2). Chicago, IL: Charles H. Kerr & Co.

Newsweek (2000, Nov. 27). *The Real 'Hot Zone.'*

New York Times (1998, Oct. 5). Amnesty finds 'widespread pattern' of U.S. rights violations.

New York Times (1998, Dec. 28). Iraq is a pediatrician's hell: no way to stop the dying.

New York Times (1999, March 6). Testing the limits of tolerance as cultures mix: does freedom mean accepting rituals that repel the west?

New York Times (1999, June 12). Beautiful beaches and bronzed men, but no bathing belles.

New York Times (1999, June 20). Arab honor's price: a woman's blood.

New York Times (1999, July 1). U.S. releases files on abuses in Pinochet era.

New York Times (1999, Oct. 21). Boy, 11, held on incest charge, and protests ensue.

New York Times (1999, Nov. 22). Moratorium now.

New York Times (1999, Nov. 27). Spanish judge is hoping to see secret files in U. S.

New York Times (1999, Nov. 29). Advertisement by the Turning Point Project entitled: *Invisible Government.*

New York Times (1999 Nov. 30). Group asking U.S. for vigilance in patient safety: wants a federal agency: academy of sciences asserts that rate of medical errors is 'stunningly high.'

New York Times (2001, Feb. 28). Federal Court Ruling on H & R Block.

New York Times (2000, Nov. 21). N.A.S.D. Accuses Dean Witter of Fraud in Sale of 3 Funds.

Oxford English Dictionary, Compact Edition. (1971). Oxford, London: Oxford University Press.

Paul, R. (1995). *What Every Student Needs to Survive in a Rapidly Changing World.* Dillon Beach: CA: The Foundation for Critical Thinking. www.criticalthinking.org.

PETA, 501 Front St., Norfolk, VA 23510, *www.peta.com*, 1999

Peters, R. S. (1973). *Reason and Compassion.* London: Routledge & Kegan Paul.

Plotnicov L, and Tuden, A. (Eds.). (1970). *Essays in Comparative Social Stratification.* Pittsburgh, PA: University of Pittsburgh Press.

Sackett, Haynes, and Tugwell. (1985). *Clinical Epidemiology: A Basic Science for Clinical Medicine.* Boston, MA: Little, Brown, and Company.

San Francisco Chronicle (1999, Feb. 6). First Philippine execution in 23 years: lethal injection for man who raped his stepdaughter, 10.

San Francisco Chronicle (1999, June 11). Treatment is new salvo fired by reformers in war on drugs: courts, voters beginning to favor therapy, not prisons, to fight crack. (Article taken from the *New York Times*).

San Francisco Chronicle (1999, Oct. 2). U.S. order to kill civilians in Korea illegal, experts say: prosecution seen as impossible now (article taken from the *Associated Press*).

Senge, P. (1990). *The Fifth Discipline: The Art and Practice of the Learning Organization*. New York, NY: Currency Doubleday.

Statewatch (2001, Nov. 21). www.statewatch.org/news.

Stebbing, S. (1952). *Thinking to Some Purpose*. London: Penguin Books Ltd.

Sumner, W. G. (1906). *Folkways: A Study of the Sociological Importance of Usages, Manners, Customs, Mores, and Morals*. New York, NY: Ginn and Company.

United Nations. (www.unorg/overview/rights/html). Resolutions 36/96B, 37/98A, 38/18A, 39/65B, 37/73, 37/78A, 38/183M, 39/148N, 38/182, 39/62, 36/12, 36/13, 36/172c, 36/172O, 37/47, 37/69E, 37/69G, 37/69H, 38/19, 38/39E, 38/39I, 36/133, 37/199, 38/124, 36/19, 38/25, 36/15, 36/73,36/120A, 36/120E, 36/146A, 36/146C, 36/147F, 36/173, 36/226B, 42/101.

Index

A

Accelerating change and complexity, 1–2

Accuracy, 51, 53, 59, 65, 84, 97, 100–102, 250, 316, 319, 321, 327, 328, 334
  assessing the accuracy of "factual claims," 101–2
  inaccurate statements, recognizing, 101

Activated ignorance, 82–83

Activated knowledge, 83–84

Active learning, 129–30

Adolescent decisions, 153–54

Advanced thinkers, 47

AIDS, 3–4

Ambiguity, 311–12, 331, 337, 340, 341

Analysis, 12, 35, 48, 59, 61–63, 81, 96, 103, 109, 115, 117, 132–33, 162, 241, 312
  conceptual, 193–95

Analyzed experiences, 132–34

Anthropological influences on thinking, 54, 268

Anthropology, 270

Argument, 18, 19, 32, 274–75, 312, 332, 335, 338, 339

Arrogance, intellectual, 22–23

Arts and humanities:
  ideal of, 272
  philosophy, promise of, 273–74
  philosophy, reality of, 274–75
  promise of the fine arts and literature, 272
  reality of instruction in the fine arts and literature, 272–73

Assault, as unethical act, 202

Assumptions, 26, 75, 115–16, 118–19, 125, 240, 312–13, 323, 325, 330, 340
  cultural, 317
  defined, 86
  distinguishing between inferences and, 85–91
  justification of, questioning, 90–91
  questioning, 287
  and reasoning, 115–16
  reasoning based on, 72

economics, 270
history, 269
ideal of, 267–72
psychology, 270–71
sociology, 269–70
as taught and practiced, 271–72
Sociocentrism, 185–203, 339
disclosing through conceptual analysis, 193–94
freedom from, 201–2
genuine conscience, development of, 201–2
innate, 158
and language in groups, 192–93
logic of, 186
and mass media, 195–201
nature of, 185–87
as pathology, 187–90
revealing ideology through conceptual analysis, 194–95
social stratification, 190–91
unconscious state of, 191–92
unethical acts, capacity to recognize, 202
Sociological influences on thinking, 54, 268
Sociology, 269–70
Socrates, 137
Socratic thinking, 339–40
Solid waste management, 3
Sophistry, 17–18, 231
Sound thinking, power of, 246–47
Sources of information, questioning, 286
Speed thinking, and decision making, 148–49
Spencer, 139
Stages of development of critical thinking, 47–63
beginning thinkers, 47, 52–55
challenged thinkers, 47, 50–52
practicing thinkers, 56–63
unreflective thinkers, 47, 48–50
Stagnation, in organizations/industries, 238

Standards for thinking, 97–127
Stebbing, Susan, 76
Strategic thinking, 277–310
beginnings of, 280
components of, 279–80
dominant/submissive behavior, and power, 305–7
egocentric mind, automatic nature of, 304–5
egocentrism, 293–97
egocentrism, rationality of, 302–3
generalizations, 299–302
high-quality thinking, 290–92
humans as sociocentric animals, 307–9
logic, 284–90
others' egocentrism, 297–99
rationality, development of, 309–10
thoughts, feelings, and desires, 280–84
understanding and using, 277–79
Strong-sense critical thinking, 17–21, 340
component traits of, 20–21
Subconscious thought, bring to level of conscious realization, 68, 87
Submissive egocentrism, 172, 176–81, 340–41
and artifice/self-delusion, 178
barriers to development, creation on, 180
defined, 176
dominating egocentrics, relationships with, 179
examples of, 176–77
and failure, 178–79
logic of, 177
and social groups, 177–78
and success, 178
unconscious beliefs of, 179–80
and work-related contexts, 178
"Successful" egocentrism, 163–64
Sumner, William Graham, 18, 137, 139–40, 316
Superficial approaches, recognizing, 104

The *Financial Times* delivers a world of business news.

Use the Risk-Free Trial Voucher below!

To stay ahead in today's business world you need to be well-informed on a daily basis. And not just on the national level. You need a news source that closely monitors the entire world of business, and then delivers it in a concise, quick-read format.

With the *Financial Times* you get the major stories from every region of the world. Reports found nowhere else. You get business, management, politics, economics, technology and more.

Now you can try the *Financial Times* for 4 weeks, absolutely risk free. And better yet, if you wish to continue receiving the *Financial Times* you'll get great savings off the regular subscription rate. Just use the voucher below.

8 reasons why you should read the Financial Times for 4 weeks RISK-FREE!

To help you stay current with significant
developments in the world economy ...
and to assist you to make informed business
decisions — the Financial Times brings you:

❶ Fast, meaningful overviews of international affairs ... plus daily briefings on major world news.

❷ Perceptive coverage of economic, business, financial and political developments with special focus on emerging markets.

❸ More international business news than any other publication.

❹ Sophisticated financial analysis and commentary on world market activity plus stock quotes from over 30 countries.

❺ Reports on international companies and a section on global investing.

❻ Specialized pages on management, marketing, advertising and technological innovations from all parts of the world.

❼ Highly valued single-topic special reports (over 200 annually) on countries, industries, investment opportunities, technology and more.

❽ The Saturday Weekend FT section — a globetrotter's guide to leisure-time activities around the world: the arts, fine dining, travel, sports and more.

For Special Offer See Over

FT FINANCIAL TIMES
World business newspaper

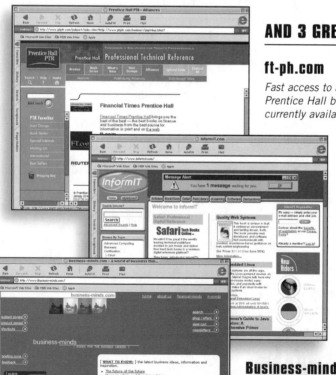